THE
CHRISTIAN
CHURCH

THE CHRISTIAN CHURCH

BIBLICAL
ORIGIN,
HISTORICAL
TRANSFORMATION,
AND
POTENTIAL
FOR THE
FUTURE

Hans Schwarz

AUGSBURG Publishing House • Minneapolis

THE CHRISTIAN CHURCH

Copyright © 1982 Augsburg Publishing House

Library of Congress Catalog Card No. 81-052286

International Standard Book No. 0-8066-1918-X

Scripture quotations unless otherwise noted are from the Revised Standard Version of the Bible, copyright 1946, 1952, and 1971 by the Division of Christian Education of the National Council of Churches.

MANUFACTURED IN THE UNITED STATES OF AMERICA

CONTENTS

PREFACE

I_T PROVED MORE DIFFICULT THAN INITIALLY ENVISIONED_ to complete this volume. I am convinced that it is not possible to assess correctly the church's potential for the future without extensive reference to the church's origin and its major transformations during its journey through the centuries. Yet an understanding of the church cannot be gained by simply narrating its history. Thus a historical, systematic approach to the church's mission and potential must necessarily accentuate certain points and leave many others nearly unmentioned. The responsibility before the tribunal of history, however, requires that the emphases and omissions not be the result of undue bias or ignorance. Thus the present volume is put forth with fear and trembling, but in the hope that the accents concur with the church's origin, call, and mission.

I have taught for a dozen years in a church seminary and have been active in a local congregation, and in the church at large. Many times I have seen the church's shortcomings but I have also seen its viability and promise. May this volume inspire others to love that in the church which carries the promise of its Lord and to amend that which detracts from it.

Again, I want to express my gratitude to the various publishers for their generous concern in allowing quotation of the passages included. The material contained in this book has been presented many times in lectures and discussions with colleagues, students, pastors, and laity. I owe much to the questions, criticisms, and suggestions I have encountered. My special thanks to my colleague, Jim Schaaf, and to Tom Skrenes who undertook the arduous task of improving my style. Phyllis Schaaf must be thanked for typing the final draft of the manuscript with both speed and accuracy, and Patricia Campbell, Joy Hacker, and Carol Hester for helping with earlier drafts. Tom Skrenes and Jon Temme deserve thanks for checking out the numerous references. Jon Temme deserves special merit for compiling an extensive introductory bibliography. Ron Grissom did an excellent job with proofreading and compiling the indexes. Finally, I must mention my patient wife, May, and our growing children Hans and Krista, who displayed amazing patience while the book went through its final stages. But I would like to dedicate this book to my colleagues at Trinity Lutheran Seminary in Columbus, Ohio, and my former students there. In their midst I worked, taught, and learned for nearly fourteen years. They showed me how theology and church can come together to become the lifeblood of the Christian community.

Regensburg, West Germany

Hans Schwarz

ABBREVIATIONS

ACW   *Ancient Christian Writers*. Westminster, MD: Newman, 1946-.

ANFa   *The Ante-Nicene Fathers. Translations of the Writings of the Fathers down to A.D. 325.* American Edition. 10 vols. Grand Rapids, MI: 1950/1.

BC   *The Book of Concord. The Confessional Writings of the Evangelical Lutheran Church.* Translated and edited by Theodore G. Tappert. Philadelphia: Fortress, 1959.

Conc(USA)   *Concilium. Theology in the Age of Renewal.* New York: Paulist, 1965-.

CR   *Corpus Reformation.* Berlin, 1834-.

CSL   *Corpus Christianorum. Series Latina.* Turnholt, 1953-.

DS   Denzinger, Heinrich, and Schönmetzer, Adolf, eds. *Enchiridion Symbolorum.* 34th ed. Freiburg: Herder, 1967.

DS(E)   Denzinger, Heinrich, ed. *The Sources of Catholic Dogma.* Translated by R. J. Deferrari. St. Louis: Herder, 1957.

DVC   Abbott, Walter M., gen. ed. *The Documents of Vatican II.* With Notes and Comments by Catholic, Protestant and Orthodox Authorities. New York: Guild, 1966.

FaCh   *The Fathers of the Church.* A New Translation. Washington, DC, 1947-.

LW   *Luther's Works.* American Edition. 56 vols. Edited by Jaroslav Pelikan. St. Louis, 1955-.

NPNF (FS)   *A Select Library of the Nicene and Post-Nicene Fathers of the Christian Church.* 14 vols. First Series. Grand Rapids, 1956.

NPNF (SS)   ———. 14 vols. Second Series. Grand Rapids, 1952/56.

PG   Migne, Jacques-Paul, ed. *Patrologiae Cursus Completus. Series Graeca.* 169 vols. Paris, 1857-1936.

PL   ———. *Patrologiae Cursus Completus. Series Latina.* 221 vols. Paris, 1841/64.

PRE   *Paulys Real-Encyclopädie der classischen Alterthumswissenschaft.* New ed. begun by Georg Wissowa. Stuttgart, 1894-.

RGG³   *Die Religion in Geschichte und Gegenwart.* 7 vols. 3rd ed. Tübingen, 1956/65.

SM(E)   *Sacramentum Mundi. An Encyclopedia of Theology.* 6 vols. New York, 1968/70.

TDNT   *Theological Dictionary of the New Testament.* 10 vols. Edited by Gerhard Kittel. Translated by G. W. Bromiley. Grand Rapids, MI: Eerdmans, 1964-1976.

WA   *D. Martin Luthers Werke. Kritische Gesamtausgabe.* Weimar, 1883-.

WA.B   ———. *Briefwechsel.* Weimar, 1930-.

WA.TR   ———. *Tischreden.* Weimar, 1912-.

INTRODUCTION:

A CRISIS IN ECCLESIOLOGY

In his Smalcald Articles of 1536 Martin Luther makes a surprising statement: "Thank God, a seven-year-old child knows what the church is, namely, holy believers and sheep who hear the voice of their Shepherd."[1] For us such naive optimism has disappeared in our understanding of the church. The Swiss theologian, Martin Werner, for instance, reminds us that at the center of Jesus' proclamation was the kingdom of God and the imminent parousia. Yet the parousia was indefinitely delayed and the world continued to run its course. So the Messianic community of the first Christians was gradually transformed into the empirical church of stately proportions.[2] In other words, what was expected was the parousia of the Lord. What actually occurred was the coming of the church of permanent duration. Thus we are confronted with the alternative: Is the church an institution founded to overcome the embarrassment of the first Christians over the delay or even total absence of the expected parousia? Or is the church actually something that without twists and turns consequently ensued from the Judeo-Christian tradition?

If we are not yet bothered by the question whether the roots justify the structure, we cannot but wonder about the proper function of the church. At first glance there seems to be no common denominator in its purpose. Of course, one could echo Luther and say that the purpose of the church is to gather the believers and to proclaim and administer the sacraments. But the huge state and people's churches in Europe are so all-inclusive that they have hardly a criterion by which to distinguish between proper and improper proclamation. In most European countries the churches still include the vast majority of the people. But as soon as the churches voice an opinion, the people, whom they supposedly represent, question by whose authority the churches say what they do say. But the churches' clergy are often not much more supportive. Though most of them have to subscribe to certain confessional documents to be admitted to the clergy roster, once they have signed the documents, it is next to impossible for the Protestant churches to insure that the pastors' proclamation is consistent with the church's confessions. It is also widely known that these churches no longer accomplish the task, if they ever did, of gathering the believers. Church attendance is well below 5% of the constituency and even for election of church councils or similar governing structures few participate.

We might also wonder to what extent these churches still have a message of their own. It is well known how the churches in Eastern Europe struggle to preserve some independence from the impingements of their Communist governments. Yet the churches in Western Europe are not in a much better situation. The Church of England, for instance, finds it almost impossible to change its liturgy to contemporary English since it is the government that finally has to approve such revisions. And, through government pressure, the Church of Sweden was forced to ordain women before it was ready to do so. State officials also frequently remind the churches to stay out of controversial issues. Still it would be unfair to say that as a result the churches have become mouthpieces of the state. But they are usually so overwhelmed with the mere ceremonial care for their huge memberships and with providing adequate maintenance of their magnificent medieval edifices that their missionary fervor has largely dissipated.

Yet there is no reason in the United States to congratulate ourselves. Our emphasis on the local congregation has turned many churches into self-serving units that exist for their own sake. They reach out to attract more members primarily in order to balance their own local budgets and to staff their own clientele-centered programs. Even when churches reach out they are overwhelmed by the social and economic problems they encounter and are reduced to near ineffectiveness by the scarcity of funds available. When some denominations have advanced worthy but controversial causes, there usually is coupled with their advocacy a reduction in revenues. Again the question must be asked how the church can stand for what it believes without being reduced to an even smaller minority status than it presently occupies. Though supposedly more than 60% of our nation's population belongs to one denomination or another, only one-fourth of the constituency supports three-fourths of the church's budgets. This means that only approximately 15% of the nation's population makes a considerable financial contribution to the work of the church.

Small wonder then that this situation leaves many pastors and priests in a constant dilemma. Should they become voices crying in the wilderness, and thereby alienate themselves from their congregations and jeopardize their positions, or should they betray the message and proclaim a gospel of goodness that does not offend anybody? Or should they carefully steer a middle course and compromise their call a thousand times? It is exactly this tension between mapping out the way for the church and not offending any of its members that leads to many crises among pastors and priests. What is their actual role in relation to their parishioners? Here the emphasis on the priesthood of all believers has often shown very undesired results. In many cases the pastor has become a mere enabler with the result that no one does anything significant. Yet the other option for the pastor of being the self-appointed leader who does the people's ministry is not preferable. It leads to even greater passivity among the parishioners. Of course, pastors could also take the escape route of being absorbed into a host of administrative and denominational duties and in this manner neglect their call altogether.

Many pastors and priests are becoming increasingly uncertain of their role in relation to the members of the congregations they serve. Apart from Sunday morning they have no regular working hours like most people in other professions and they also do not seem to have clearly defined occupational tasks as do medical doctors or fire fighters. So more and more pastors and priests are resigning to do something "worthwhile." In a situation like this it is more urgent than ever to rediscover the origin and purpose of the church and the reason of existence for the ministerial office.

NOTES

1. Martin Luther, The Smalcald Articles (12), BC, p. 315.
2. Martin Werner, *The Formation of the Christian Dogma. An Historical Study of Its Problem,* trans. with an intr. S. G. F. Brandon (New York: Harper, 1957), esp. pp. 271f.

PART I:

The Formative Era

Though the origin of the church lies within the period covered by the New Testament documents, its formation was not concluded at the end of that period. Only the conquest of the Hellenistic mind allowed the church to become more than an ethnic minority religion. The development of the church's structure and dogma, as we witness it in the apostolic and postapostolic writings, is intrinsic to the formation of the church as we encounter it today and as it was initially envisioned in the great commission (Matt. 28:18f.). The emergence of what is known as early Catholicism is not necessarily an aberration, as Protestant theologians have often claimed. It was part of the consequent development of the church and contained, at least potentially, beneficial aspects for the church's mission. When we now briefly survey the formation of the church, we must pursue the church's course until it extended itself literally to the ends of the then known world and had become the dominant religion in the Roman Empire.

1

The Origin of the Church

IN OUR ATTEMPT TO DISCOVER THE ORIGIN OF THE CHURCH, we are tempted to look immediately at the first Pentecost, the obvious starting point of the Christian church. But such inclination would totally neglect that the Christian church was not a unique occurrence. It has analogous parallels in the Buddhist *sangha* and it certainly finds its historical continuity in the Old Testament covenant community. Thus the origin of the church must be pursued in two ways, in tracing it from its historic development from the Old Testament and by comparing it to other church-like configurations.

1. Origin and meaning of the name "church"

With the term church we denote a structure (the church on the corner of Main and High), the local community assembling in this structure (our church is very active), and a certain denomination (The American Lutheran Church), as well as the community of all Christians (the church universal). The term church is related to the Swedish *Kyrka* and the German *Kirche* and derives itself from the popular Greek term *kyriake (oika)*, meaning the house of the Lord. This usage is in contrast to the Romance language that used derivatives of the Greek term *ekklesia* (such as in Spanish *iglesia*, Italian *chiesa*, and French *eglise*). This term *ekklesia* was commonly used by the earliest Christian community to refer to the church and it is still used in this meaning in Eastern Christianity. The Greek word *ekklesia* is not used strictly to mean church; it can also be used in a secular way to denote an assembly of people.

The New Testament usually uses the term *ekklesia* to talk about the total community of believers or about a particular community of Christians, perhaps in Jerusalem or in Philippi, or even an assembly of Christians in a certain home. Whether the particular use presupposes the universal one and is derived from it, or whether the church and the churches are mentioned in an uncorrelated way will be investigated later. If it were true, however, as some argue, that the particular community is not conceived of as part of the total community, but that the total community is made up of particular communities, then the plurality of churches would be established right in the New Testament. Yet, if a particular community can only be conceived of as part of the larger community, then the notion of unity would be presupposed, a particular community being only a special expression of the whole Christian community.

In our search for the origin of the term church we dare not stop with the New Testament. We could say that *ekklesia* is derived from *ekkalein* (to call forth) or from *ekkletos* (called forth). But the Septuagint uses these two terms very rarely (cf. Gen. 19:5 and Sir. 42:11). Much more frequently, however, we find the word *ekklesia* in the Septuagint. Approximately 100 times this word is used, and almost exclusively, to render the Hebrew term *kahal* into Greek. We should also note that though *ekklesia* in the Septuagint is almost always a translation of the Hebrew *kahal*, this latter word is not in each instance translated with the former. *Kahal* can also be rendered with the Greek word *synagoge* (synagogue).[1] The interchangeability of these terms *ekklesia* and *synagoge* (cf. Prov. 5:14 *en meso ekklesias kai synagoge*) and the meaning expressed with them, namely assembly (of people) seems to indicate that we do not yet encounter in them a technical term. This is even more evident when *kahal* is translated as group or multitude (*ochlos:* Jer. 31:8 and *systasis:* Gen. 49:6). Thus the context of its usage is decisive. Here the qualification *kahal adonai* or *kahal Israel,* whether explicitly mentioned or implicitly assumed makes the difference between a grouping of people and the assembly that worships the Lord or that stands for Israel. The term church in its original sense, and, we may venture to say, even in its present-day usage, does not disclose the purpose it stands for unless it is qualified by appropriate explanations such as in the church universal or the Church of the Latter-Day Saints. To determine the appropriate meaning of the term church we must always inquire what is meant by the term if someone uses it.

It is not sufficient, however, to trace the origin of the term "church" to the Hebrew *kahal.* There is a much closer affinity between the Christian community and the Old Testament covenant community which comes to expression in such terms as Old Testament and New Testament, or Jesus being called the Son of David and the Messiah. Especially in the Gospel of Matthew we notice that Jesus is portrayed as standing in true continuity with the Old Testament. According to this Gospel the historical nation of Israel has neglected and lost its commission to be the light of the nations. Thus the church replaces it and steps into continuity with the Israel of promise. Such assumption of a covenant continuity and replacement is of extreme significance if we want to understand that which came to be the church of Jesus Christ. It would go beyond the scope of our presentation to delineate a history of Israel resulting in the emergence of the church. Yet to understand appropriately Jesus Christ after whom the church is named, we must at least outline the religious situation of the Israel in which Jesus lived and which he addressed.

2. The Jewish community

Postexilic Judaism was not just a repristination of the situation prior to the exile. Though the temple was rebuilt and many Jews returned to Jerusalem under great sacrifice, the temple did not regain its former splendor and the Jewish community in Jerusalem was supplemented by many other communities, from the Samaritans who did not go into exile to those who never returned to Palestine yet continued to adhere to their Jewish religion in an alien land. Since the unifying bonds of the pre-exilic monarchy and the covenant community could not be reestablished, we need not wonder that at the time of Jesus even Palestinian Judaism was far from forming a uniform whole. We hear, for instance, of Sadducees and Pharisees, of Zealots and Essenes. Yet there are some important criteria that made the Jews essentially "Jews," criteria that were adhered to by all of them.

a. The people

The Jewish people had been welded together by remembering a common history. This history was even more important now, since for many the commonly occupied land was no longer the unifying factor. Yet not everyone who was associated with Judaism was actually a Jew. There were proselytes who became circumcised and were baptized with a proselyte baptism and who participated in the Jewish sacrifice. One did not easily become a proselyte, however. We learn from the Talmud: "If at the present time a man desires to become a proselyte, he is to be addressed as follows: 'What reason have you for desiring to become a proselyte; do you not know that Israel at the present time are persecuted and oppressed, harassed and overcome with afflictions?'"[2] After one answers appropriately one was informed of the punishment for the transgressions of the commandments and of the reward for their fulfillment. If one still desired to become a proselyte one was circumcised. Then one was baptized and "when he comes up after his ablution he is deemed to be an Israelite in all respects." [3] One had become part of Israel and shared in the common history. Also one was allowed to be buried among the Jews while other followers of Judaism were still buried among the Gentiles.[4] Though participating in the history of Israel, proselytes were still unable to talk about the patriarchs as their own fathers. This was only possible for their descendants.

There were many people who participated in the synagogue worship and who observed many of the Old Testament commandments, but never became part of the Jewish people. These people, usually called God-fearers (cf. Acts 13:16), were not regarded as Jews.[5] The Jewish historian Josephus mentions that there is not one city in which one does not find people following certain Jewish customs. Many also "attempt to imitate our unanimity, our liberal charities, our devoted labor in the crafts, our endurance under persecution on behalf of our laws." [6] The cohesion among the Jewish people that Josephus mentioned amazed other people too, such as Cicero and Tacitus.[7]

It was important for the Jewish people to remain faithful. Only to the Israelites, they believed, the Old Testament promises would apply. But only the priests, Levites, and the Israelites of pure descent were regarded as true Israelites. If an Israelite woman wanted to marry a priest she had to trace her ancestry through five generations to assure that she was clearly of Israelite descent.[8] People running for public office had to prove their "Jewishness" too. In the postexilic time one also started to use the names of the twelve tribes as proper names to show to which tribe one belonged. We hear that even after Jesus' time the Roman emperors Vespasian, Domitian, and Trajan persecuted those from the tribe of David, perhaps to quench the Messianic hopes still connected with this tribe. From time to time this Jewish exclusiveness aroused the suspicion and the animosity of other nations.

The Jewish separation from the Gentiles and their customs was a necessity for religious and ethnic survival. This relatively small nation could easily have been swallowed up by its neighbors. For instance, the frequent biblical admonitions against marrying a Gentile showed that such marriages did indeed occur and threatened the integrity of the nation. But these admonitions also illustrate the emphasis on keeping to one's own.

As the emphasis on one's ancestry indicates, the Jewish family served as the most important entity for the survival of the Jewish nation. It was especially there that the tradition and cultivation of the Jewish law was furthered.

b. The law

Josephus mentions with understandable pride: "Should anyone of our nation be questioned about the laws, he would repeat them all more readily than his own name. The result, then, of our thorough grounding in the laws from the first dawn of intelligence is that we have them, as it were, engraven on our souls." [9] And then he adds: "To this cause above all we owe our admirable harmony." [10] In other words, the foundation for their peculiar cohesion was laid in the instruction and training received in the parental home. The rabbis taught that the children should obey the laws as soon as it could be individually expected of them and at the approximate age of 13 a boy was then to know and keep all the commandments. [11]

The great emphasis on the law soon led to a codification of the law (Torah) which was identical with the Pentateuch. The prophetic writings were also included in the canon around 200 B.C. [12] Since the law of God was given to regulate the affairs of the Jewish people, the question soon arose how the law could be applied to each concrete situation and also regulate the temple cult. In the preexilic period the priests embodied the living tradition that allowed for precise application of the law. When the law, however, became codified, it was deemed necessary that all the possibilities that were not explicitly covered by it should also be somehow regulated. This led to the emergence of the scribes who studied and explained the Scriptures as they applied to the affairs of the day. Gradually these applications, and, one could even say, additions to the law, attained a status almost equal to the law. It was eventually understood that God had not only given the written law (the Torah), but also the additional applications which had been handed on by the scribes. This oral tradition, the Mishnah (repetition), was not written down until well after the time of Jesus.

Christians might wonder whether the law and its detailed precepts were not felt as an undue restriction on life. Yet this was not the case. The law was understood as God's gift to Israel. Through the law God disclosed himself to Israel and therefore Israel occupied a privileged place among the nations. The Torah was given to Israel as a sign of God's love. Thus

Rabbi Akiba said: "Beloved are Israel in that there was given to them the precious instrument . . . whereby the world was created."[13] The law is not something accidental and arbitrary, but an eternal law and a precious instrument through which the world was created. Underlying this eleva-tion of the law is the equation of law and wisdom. In Proverbs 3:19, for instance, we read: "The Lord by wisdom founded the earth." In the book of Sirach we even have an explicit equation of wisdom and Torah (24:8, 23). Since wisdom is the expression of God's ordering activity in the world, the law is the expression of the God-given cosmic, social, and cultic order which guides everyone in right conduct.

The law is not experienced as oppressive, but "blessed is the man . . . [whose] delight is in the law of the Lord and on his law he meditates day and night" (Ps. 1:1f.). One of the leading scribes in Jerusalem at the time of Jesus, Hillel, consequently could affirm: "More Torah more life; more assiduity more wisdom; more counsel more understanding. . . . He who has acquired words of Torah has acquired for himself the life of the world to come."[14] The Torah is God's life-giving word and its adherence promises temporal and eternal rewards. The study and adherence to the Torah is therefore a holy task; it is not a burden but a joy.

The Torah becomes the sum total of all traditions. It establishes the identity of the Jewish people according to origin, conduct of life, and out-look on eternal issues; and it sets the Jewish people apart from all other groups and nations. The remark in the Book of Esther is certainly correct when it says: "There is a certain people scattered abroad and dispersed among the peoples . . . their laws are different from those of every other people" (3:8). As we see from the sect at Qumran, some also concluded that strict observance of the Torah should lead to a life that avoids all contact with foreigners. Mostly, however, it led to a feeling of superiority, although others could join them too if they were willing to observe the same laws, or at least most of them. Thus the nationalistic and particular-istic tendencies did not lead to an exclusivism that barred others from the rule of God.[15]

c. Temple and synagogue

When we ask where the acquaintance with the law took place, we are first of all referred to the Jewish family. As we have heard, the family proved essential to the survival of the Jewish tradition and community. But the family cannot be seen in isolation from the synagogue service and the visit to the temple, places that reinforced the acquaintance with the law.

The origin of the synagogue is uncertain. Its function as a religious and social meeting place allows us to assume that it originated in the Jewish diaspora. In the third century B.C. we hear about synagogues in Egypt and later also in Palestine.[16] Some even attempt to trace it as far back as the time of Moses, yet without much historical backing.[17] It is much more likely that the birthplace of the synagogue was in the Babylonian exile. While the references to meetings of the elders at the feet of Ezekiel (8:1; 14:1; 20:1) may not actually remind us of a synagogue, the situation is somewhat different when we hear in Ezekiel 11:16: "Thus says the Lord God: Though I removed them far off among the nations, and though I scattered them among the countries, yet I have been a sanctuary to them in a small measure in the countries where they have gone." But it may be wishful thinking to assume that in the Babylonian exile there already existed a full-fledged synagogue similar to the ones we know about at the time of Jesus. Though Ezekiel 11:16 certainly reflects the situation of actual religious services in a distant land,[18] it was not until the time of Jesus that we encounter the synagogue as a fully grown and firmly established institution. During the period of the second temple, services in the synagogue augmented those in the temple, while after the destruction of the temple the synagogue remained without a rival as the focus and center of Jewish religious life. Many of the customs and rituals were then transferred to the synagogue whereas others, such as sacrifice, were so integral to temple worship that they ceased with the temple's destruction.

The second temple was erected in the same place and with the same dimensions as the original structure. It was a fairly modest edifice until Herod the Great (37-4 B.C.) constructed a new and elaborate temple in unprecedented splendor. Finally completed in A.D. 64, it served only a few years until it was thoroughly destroyed except for part of the temple wall, now known as the Wailing Wall. The temple in Jerusalem is the spiritual center of Judaism. In his *History of the Jewish War* Josephus gives a detailed description of the temple, its different divisions, the priests officiating there, and the artwork located in the temple. When Jerusalem was besieged by the Romans, the Jewish people attempted to maintain the sacrifices in the temple, until in the fall of A.D. 70 the sacrifices had to cease when Titus conquered the city and burned the temple.[19] Again in 132-135 the place of the temple was occupied by the Jews and defended with utter tenacity. These historical incidents show us the immense importance of the temple for the Jewish community.

The temple was the place at which the cult and the sacrifices prescribed by the law took place. Each year thousands of pilgrims came to the great temple festivals. The Day of Atonement observed shortly after the Jewish New Year, and soon afterwards the Feast of Tabernacles, a kind of thanksgiving festival at the conclusion of the harvest, and above all the Passover were all celebrated at the temple. The essential part of the Passover celebration was the killing and eating of the Passover lamb. Passover lambs were slaughtered in the court of the priests and the blood poured out at the base of the altar. Then the lamb was brought to a home, prepared, and eaten the same evening within the city walls by a family and their friends, a group usually of 10 to 20 people. Since the Passover lamb was to be slaughtered in the temple, the custom of eating the Passover ceased with the destruction of the temple. Also ending was the morning and evening sacrifice, or the continual offering which was supplemented by other offerings on the Sabbath and other festivals.

Especially at the Passover, when one remembered the exodus from Egypt and looked forward to the day of salvation, Messianic expectations were quite high. The hope for the coming Messiah and the resurrection of the dead was again connected with Jerusalem and its temple.[20] The Israelites remembered that at night they were once freed from the bondage of Egypt and they hoped that at night (of one of the Passover feasts) they would again find fulfillment of redemption when the Messianic time commenced.[21] On occasions the Messianic expectations became so intense that riots and revolts erupted as possible initiation points of the desired fulfillment. Even Josephus tells us that "it is on these festive occasions that sedition is most apt to break out."[22] Up to our own days the hope has not ceased that one day all Jewish people would be redeemed from the yoke of the Gentiles, that the Messiah would bring about this revolution, gather the scattered nation, and lead them back to Jerusalem where they would enjoy a life in peace and freedom.

The temple did not only serve as the focal point of eschatological hopes. The place of the people of God was also the place of prayer. Similar to the synagogue the Torah was read there, the Shema Israel was recited, the 18 benedictions were prayed, and the Psalms, the decalogue, and various responsories were recited. Since the synagogue was in many ways analogous to the temple, it began using many of these prayers. This was especially so after the destruction of the temple when the synagogue services had to replace those of the temple. But already in Sirach (2nd cent. B.C.) we hear that through keeping the law, being kind, and giving alms, the sacrifices could be replaced which were normally taking place at the temple. Sirach says: "He who keeps the law makes many offerings; he who heeds the commandments sacrifices a peace offering. He who returns a kindness offers fine flour, and he who gives alms sacrifices a thank offering" (Sir. 35:1f.). This means we encounter here a spiritualization of the sacrifices, perhaps a necessity for those who because of location or social status could not make the pilgrimage to Jerusalem.

The cult is only one part of the Jewish religious life. Another and perhaps the most comprehensive facet is the wholehearted devotion to the study of the ancient traditions. Frequently a schoolroom was attached to the synagogue in which instruction in the law took place. The famous Jewish scholar Philo even preferred to call the synagogue a house of teaching.[23] When school and synagogue were separate buildings, the school was the more sacred place since it was exclusively used for teaching. The instruction comprised the Halacha (ethos), an interpretation of the Pentateuch which regulates the cult and the life of the people, and the Haggada (exposition) containing everything apart from the Halacha. Within the Haggada are the various aspects of Jewish doctrine, such as history, eschatology, anthropology, etc.

In the synagogue there was a worship service on the Sabbath and two other services during the week. The service included confession of faith, prayer, scripture reading from the Torah (Pentateuch) and the Prophets, a brief sermon, and the blessing. Anybody appointed by the presider of the synagogue could read the Scriptures and address the congregation. Similar to the congregation assembled in the temple, the people in the synagogue were both a listening and a praying community. Therefore the synagogue can also be called a place of prayer (Acts 16:13). Strack and Billerbeck say very appropriately: "It is one of the advantages of Israel over against all pagan nations that it is allowed to pray to the God who listens to prayers and responds to them."[24]

In all their diversity the Jewish people at the time of Jesus were concerned with piety. In joyful obedience to the law of their Lord and to the implications their religious leaders drew from it, they lived their lives and waited eagerly, reluctantly, but never skeptically for the fulfillment of the promises of God. Jesus of Nazareth, the founder and the foundation of the Christian church, was born into this obedient and hoping community.

3. Jesus Christ—founder and foundation of the Christian church

Since Samuel Reimarus, liberal theologians time and again have claimed that Jesus never intended to found the Christian church. They are correct historically, since Jesus was a member of the Jewish community, firmly imbedded in the Jewish faith. Yet they are in error theologically, since without Jesus and his message there would have been no Christian church.

a. Jesus as a member of the Jewish community

The childhood narratives convincingly demonstrate that Jesus was brought up to be a faithful Jew. He was circumcised and instructed in the law, and was obedient to his parents. He also must have taken his actions very seriously since he insisted that John baptize him and prepare him for the imminent advent of the eschaton.[25] Jesus must have heard about John and sought him out to hear his message. In all likelihood he also talked with him and his disciples before he was baptized. Since Jesus' public ministry then started without any reported preparations, we may assume that his baptism had a catalytic impact, similar to the Old Testament call experiences.[26] Though Jesus may have been conscious of his unique relation to God, it was not until after his baptism that he assumed a public ministry. For some time the public ministries of Jesus and John the Baptist ran parallel to each other.[27] Then John was imprisoned and beheaded. His disciples buried him "and they went and told Jesus" (Matt. 14:12), a fact that shows that they felt close enough to Jesus to share with him their sad news. From that moment Jesus' ministry begins its unique path.

Since Jesus began in close proximity to John the Baptist, we may wonder whether Jesus' ministry bore much originality. Indeed, Jesus and John the Baptist agreed at many points. They were both dissatisfied with the current trends in Jewish thought and practice (Matt. 3:7 and 12:34), they shared fervent eschatological expectations (Matt. 3:10 and 7:19), and they were convinced of the necessity of an immediate decision to repent and to dedicate oneself wholly to the service of God (Matt. 3:8 and Mark 1:15). There were also decisive differences between John and Jesus. While John was an ascetic, Jesus was not. Unlike John, he did not stay in the desert, but traveled through the country and even entered the house of notorious sinners (Luke 19:7). Jesus' message did not carry exclusively the somber tone of the impending judgment. For him the time of salvation had already come (Luke 11:20), while for John it was still impending. John was pointing to a mightier one who would come after him and who would baptize with the Holy Spirit (Matt. 3:11). The proof for the changed tone in Jesus' message was reinforced by his actions which he interpreted in the light of the Old Testament imagery of the time of salvation (Matt. 11:4f.; Isa. 35:5f.). But Jesus had great praise for John when he said: "Truly, I say to you, among those born of women there has risen none greater than John the Baptist"; but he put John in the right perspective when he added: "Yet he who is least in the kingdom of heaven is greater than he. . . . For all the prophets . . . prophesied until John" (Matt. 11:11, 13). While John signified the conclusion of the Old Testament, with Jesus and his coming something novel had happened. But what was so new about Jesus?

Until his death Jesus attempted to be a faithful member of the Jewish community. He did not start a new religion as did Mohammed or Buddha. To many he appeared to be a Jewish scribe or a teacher. So we hear at the beginning of his ministry that "on the sabbath he entered the synagogue and taught" (Mark 1:21). More than once Jesus is called teacher (Mark 5:35; 12:19) and his more immediate followers are consequently "students" (*mathetai*) or somewhat incorrectly translated as "disciples" (Mark 3:7). He teaches his disciples (Mark 8:31) who in turn instruct others (Mark 6:30). It is significant that the original New Testament term for the gospel tradition was not *euangelion* (evangel), but *logos* (word) or *logos theou* (word of God), terms which correspond with the Jewish terms for "Holy Scripture." [28]

Jesus indeed may be seen in close connection with the rabbinic tradition, which may also account for the fact that in the New Testament the term *logos* denotes the gospel which tells us of Jesus and his sayings. Consequently, we should not assume that Jesus taught indiscriminately or continually. As the Swedish New Testament scholar Harald Riesenfeld pointed out: "He imposed certain limitations on his preaching as he did in the case of his miracles. And what was essential to his message he taught his disciples, that is, he made them learn it by heart." [29] But Jesus taught not like other rabbis. He also accompanied his teachings with miracles (cf. Mark 2:9), which rabbis usually did not do. Therefore the people remarked that "he taught them as one who had authority and not as the scribes" (Mark 1:22) and assumed that he was a prophet (Mark 8:28). [30] His enemies, however, told the Roman authorities that he was a zealotic rebel and Pilate later convicted him as such.

When we look at the ethnic and geographic boundaries of Jesus' activity, the impression is reinforced that he was a faithful Jew. If the sparse notices in the synoptics are geographically reliable, Jesus stayed within Jewish territory unless he had to flee from his enemies (Mark 8:27). His activity was confined to the Jewish people and when he helped non-Jewish people, he clearly marked this as an exception (cf. Mark 7:24-30). Since the later church was very interested in missionary activity among non-Jewish people, we may be sure they would have emphasized Jesus' outreach among these people if there would have been a historical basis for it. Yet even the rabbis at the time of Jesus did not seem to show the same inhibitions as did Jesus. They "traversed sea and land to make a single proselyte" (Matt. 23:15). Jesus, however, felt himself sent only to Israel.

It was not a narrow sectarian approach that led Jesus primarily to the Jewish people. Jesus' main partners in dialogue and the ones who finally caused his death, were the Pharisees, the leading religious group at his time.[31] Their prime concern was to fulfill the demands of the Torah as interpreted by the tradition. Of course, Jesus had no intention of revolting against the law. "Whoever then relaxes one of the least of these commandments and teaches men so, shall be called least in the kingdom of heaven; but he who does them and teaches them shall be called great in the kingdom of heaven," we hear Jesus say according to Matthew 5:19. With such an attitude he should have had nothing to fear from the Pharisees, the scribes, and the rabbis who largely followed the rabbinic emphasis on the law. All of these groups should have felt comfortable with Jesus.

The situation is somewhat different when Jesus claimed: "I have not come to abolish them [the law and the prophets] but to fulfill them" (Matt. 5:17); and: "For I tell you, unless your righteousness exceeds that of the scribes and the Pharisees, you will never enter the kingdom of heaven" (Matt. 5:20). To complete this emphasis we even hear Jesus say: "The law and the prophets were until John; since then the good news of the kingdom of God is preached" (Luke 16:16). Again, such radicalism was not unknown in Judaism. Thus the scribes and the Pharisees could have heard similar statements from John the Baptist who also did not allow for any kind of religious security and called everybody to repentance. In fact, much of the radical interpretation of the law as we encounter it in the Sermon on the Mount could have been preached by John. Thus calling all Israel to repentance, while painful to the pious Pharisees and scribes, since they attempted to meet the demands of the law to the letter, could not have caused grave problems for Jesus.[32]

But we notice from the above-mentioned passages that Jesus did not only radicalize the law and its demands, he also claimed that with him the time of salvation had come and the law had been fulfilled! And this claim to be the one who ushers in the kingdom, who brings about the fulfillment of the promissory history of Israel, this was the point that caused the controversy with the Jewish leaders. Even at Jesus' trial the high priest inquired: "Are you the Christ, the Son of the Blessed?" (Mark 14:61). But if Jesus had clearly shown Messianic qualities in word and deed, his claims should not have caused his ultimate rejection. In the Jewish creation calendar the year 5000 had awakened Messianic hopes in many people, since the Messiah was supposed to usher in the sixth millenium, the age of the kingdom of God.[33] Thus in the second quarter of the first century A.D. Messianic expectations were especially fervent. For instance, there was the prophet Theudas, who was put to death by the Roman procurator in A.D. 44. There was an Egyptian prophet who arose a few years later and who together with his followers attempted to take over Jerusalem. Again the Roman authorities defeated the coup d'etat. Josephus also mentions that a band of other "deceivers and imposters, under the pretense of divine inspiration fostering revolutionary changes, they persuaded the multitude [in Jerusalem] to act like madmen, and led them out into the desert under the belief that God would there give them tokens of deliverance." [34]

The Messianic hopes usually implied the overthrow of the Roman power in Palestine. It was commonly expected that the Messiah would redeem Israel from exile and servitude and even the whole world from oppression, suffering, war, and above all from heathenism.[35] Along with the redemption from the evil in humanity, the Messiah was expected to save humanity from the evil in nature. The Messianic Age will also bring about great material prosperity. The earth will bring forth an abundance of grain and fruit, which humanity will be able to enjoy without excessive toil.

When we review these expectations, we must agree with Rudolf Bultmann that Jesus' life and activity were certainly not Messianic when measured by traditional standards.[36] Yet to conclude with Bultmann that Jesus did not portray any Messianic claim is also overstating the case. Jesus did not conform to the usual political overtones of Messianic expectations. Some of his followers may have thought differently when he came to Jerusalem to celebrate the Last Supper there, but Jesus did not take over the city and assume a public messiahship (cf. Luke 24:21). He probably refused the title Messiah whenever it was conferred on him.[37] Jesus showed no interest in the political and nationalistic aspirations which were connected with the coming of the Messiah and he did not want to be taken for a political liberator. We hear no word that he conspired against the Roman occupation army or that he wanted to revolt against it. Though the charges against him were finally of political nature, he clearly denied them. If his existence was not Messianic in the usual sense, how should we then describe his life and destiny?

Perhaps we gain an understanding of his person when we remember that in Jesus' trial the High Priest concluded from Jesus' answer to the question: "Are you the Christ, the Son of the Blessed?" (Mark 14:61) that he had committed blasphemy. Why should Jesus' answer lead to such a devastating conclusion? Jesus seemed to have recited only Jewish common eschatological expectations when he said: "I am; and you will see the Son of Man seated at the right hand of Power, and coming with the clouds of heaven" (Mark 14:62). The issue becomes clear when we consider the Old Testament use of the phrase *ego eimi* (I am).

In the Septuagint we find the phrase *ego eimi* several times, especially prominently in Deutero-Isaiah, where it renders into Greek the Hebrew *ani hu* (meaning I [am] he).[38] In Deutero-Isaiah the phrase *ani hu* is used as a solemn statement or assertion that is always attributed to Yahweh (cf. Isa. 41:4; 43:10; 46:4). The phrase asserts polemically that Yahweh is the Lord of history counteracting similar claims made by other gods. It also seems to be a concise abbreviation of the longer form of divine self-predication, especially of "I am Yahweh." While the *ani hu* formula as divine self-predication of Yahweh occurs outside Deutero-Isaiah only in Deut. 32:39, the self-predication "I am Yahweh" is rather widespread in the Old Testament. As Ethelbert Stauffer has pointed out, there is also some evidence that the *ani hu* was used liturgically in the worship of the Jerusalem temple, since the Levites presumably sang the Song of Moses, containing Deut. 32:39 on the Sabbath day of the Feast of the Tabernacles.[39] The use of *ani hu* lived on in the worship service of the temple and the synagogues and was even known to the Qumran community.[40]

At a few decisive places in the gospels Jesus uses the term *ego eimi* in a way analogous to the Old Testament theophany formula. Jesus says, for instance, in Mark 13:6: "Many will come in my name, saying, 'I am he!' and they will lead many astray." [41] In Matthew this theophanic self-predication is expanded into an explicitly eschatological formulation to read: "and saying I am the Christ" (Matt. 24:5). When we now return to the answer that Jesus gave the high priest in Mark 14:62, it is by no means self-evident that we encounter here the use of *ego eimi* in the absolute sense (i.e., with no object following), in analogy to the Old Testament revelational formula *ani hu* or one of its variations. If we just look at Jesus' answer we might assume with equal justification that it was simply a solemn way of saying "yes" as, for instance, Matthew interprets it (Matt. 26:64).[42] The matter becomes clearer, however, if we look at the usage of *ego eimi* in other Markan passages.[43]

The phrase *ego eimi* appears first in Mark 6:50 at the conclusion of the miracle of the walking on water, where Jesus tells his disciples: "Take heart, it is I; have no fear." Here the phrase functions almost in a titular sense and as a revelational formula. In Mark 13:6 Jesus warns his disciples: "Many will come in my name, saying, 'I am he!' and they will lead many away." Again the phrase is used as a formula of revelation or identification, since its misappropriation leads the believer astray. Considering this context we may also conclude that Jesus' use of the *ego eimi* in Mark 14:62 is more than a simple affirmation. It is indeed a revelational formula with which Jesus discloses himself and identifies himself with God. As the words following the *ego eimi* show, the secret is lifted and Jesus unashamedly admits to his Messianic sonship. "In Mark 14:62 therefore Jesus is making an explicit Messianic claim, the Messianic Secret is being formally disclosed." [44]

Since the Messianic secret was carefully preserved in Mark until that point, we may wonder whether Jesus' response does not reflect more the theology of the evangelist than it renders Jesus' own words. Indeed it would be overestimating the historical value of this passage if we would not assume that this passage has been carefully edited to reflect the eschatological hopes of the nascent church.[45] Yet there is also an indirect way of determining the historical veracity of Jesus' response.

Ernst Fuchs had pointed out that in his proclamation Jesus emphasized the will of God in such a way as only someone could do who stood in God's place.[46] For instance, in his parables Jesus does not simply tell us how God acts, but he tells us that God acts the way Jesus acts. Let us illustrate this with the parable of the lost sheep (Luke 15:3-7): When the Pharisees and scribes wondered: "This man receives sinners and eats with them" (Luke 15:2), Jesus told them parables about the care for the lost and sinful, implying that God acts like Jesus. Jesus' response at his trial would then indicate that at the end of his earthly life Jesus did not just act as if he stood in God's place, but he evidently affirmed his identity with God by using the revelational formula "I am." We conclude that most likely the *ego eimi* was Jesus' own response to the high priest. While Jesus did not conform to prevalent Messianic expectations, this reply was at once understood as a Messianic claim. Since this claim could not be reconciled with what they thought the Messiah to be, the high priest and many other people concluded that Jesus had committed blasphemy. But if we concede Jesus' singular role as God's self-disclosure, we must ask whether there is a connection between this role and the emergence of the church. Is there a continuity between Jesus and the church that calls itself after him? We naturally tend to think here of Peter and the promise given to him.

b. Peter—rock and stumbling block

Next to Paul, Simon Peter is certainly the most colorful apostle of the New Testament. Simon was also given a second name (Peter) by Jesus. The gospels, however, are not unanimous when he obtained this name or title. Did he receive it when he first encountered Jesus (John 1:42), when he was called to be Jesus' disciple (Mark 3:16), or when he confessed Jesus to be the Christ (Matt. 16:18)? Since the name Peter is the Greek translation of the Aramaic word *cephas,* meaning rock or stone (John 1:42), we may assume that it functions as a title rather than a proper name. As we can see with names of immigrants, proper names are usually not translated but only adapted to the language of the new country. With titles, however, that function as specific terms, we may more easily assume a translation. We may then conclude that, in analogy to a custom we encounter in the Old Testament (Gen. 17:5) Peter received a special title to denote the function he was to fulfill.

During the earthly life of Jesus, Peter assumed a unique role among the disciples.[47] Together with the sons of Zebedee and his brother Andrew, Peter belongs to the intimate circle of Jesus' followers. But there too he stood in the foreground. He played the chief role in the story of the miraculous catch of fish (Luke 5:1-11); in the transfiguration story he suggested to Jesus the erection of tents (Mark 9:5); and only he dared to imitate Jesus' walking on the water (Matt. 14:29). According to Luke 22:8 he and John were also asked by Jesus to prepare the Last Supper. He also played a prominent role in the events in the Garden of Gethsemane, and, of course, he was the one who betrayed Jesus three times. Almost like their designated speaker he turned to Jesus and questioned him about things the disciples wanted to have clarified (cf. Matt. 18:21; Luke 12:41; and Mark 10:28). In turn Jesus talked to Peter when he addressed all the disciples (Mark 8:29-33). Even in the Gospel of John, where we are introduced to John as the disciple whom Jesus loved (13:23), the special role of Peter remained unchallenged. Immediately we are told about his special name (1:42), and Peter again appears as the speaker of the twelve (6:68). But Peter is not always painted in glorious colors. More than once he was rebuked for his daring behavior, his lack of faith, and his misunderstanding of Jesus' special mission.

Upon this energetic and sometimes hot-tempered human being, Jesus conferred an amazing task when he said, "You are Peter, and on this rock I will build my church, and the powers of death shall not prevail against it. I will give you the keys of the kingdom of heaven and whatever you bind on earth shall be bound in heaven, and whatever you loose on earth shall be loosed in heaven" (Matt. 16:18f.). Of course, the question must be raised as to the authenticity and meaning of this promise. Even if we would doubt that this saying goes back to Jesus, there can be no doubt that it is of ancient character. This is attested in part by the wordplay "You are Peter [Aramaic: *cephas*] and upon this rock [Aramaic: *cepha*] I will build my church." In Greek the wordplay is much weaker with *petros* (Peter) and *petra* (rock) respectively.[48] For instance, Rudolf Bultmann clearly denies that this saying goes back to Jesus, but he still dates it back to the Palestinian church.

It seems strange that Jesus who emphatically proclaimed the nearness, nay even the presence, of the kingdom of God would have established the church. Moreover, the term church *(ekklesia)* occurs only two other times in the gospels, namely twice in Matthew 18:17, a passage that very likely reflects later church practice and that also seems to speak of church in a more local setting. Even considering the function of the twelve that Jesus called and the larger following that he enjoyed, we are unable to solve the issue why Jesus should have founded the church. Jesus was not the only teacher or prophet who had disciples. As we know from prophetic teachers such as John the Baptist, others had disciples too.

Perhaps we could gain a clearer understanding of the relationship between Jesus and the church if we consider once more the famous Matthean passage. When we read the passage, Matthew 16:13-20, we notice that it actually contains two different stories. In the first one Jesus asks his disciples who they think he is and Peter answers with the famous Messianic confession: "You are the Christ, the Son of the living God" (Matt. 16:15). Jesus neither confirms nor denies the validity of the answer. Instead we hear in the second story that Peter will be the rock upon which Jesus will build his church. This commission to Peter would only make sense if Jesus knew himself to be the Messiah, a notion that the evangelist seems to share (Matt. 16:20). If Jesus was the Messiah, then the circle of the disciples was not just a group of people who followed a leader. They actually formed the core of the eschatological community that corresponded to the presence of the Messiah.[49] This eschatological community was not a splinter group or a holy remnant, but the community of the new people of God. That these people prefigure the new Israel is attested by the fact that Jesus' activity was directed to the whole of Israel, and not, as with the Qumran community in a seclusive and separatist way only to a select few.[50] Since Peter was the spokesman for the disciples, the task and promise given to him would publicly acknowledge his position as one who is recognized and affirmed by Jesus. As we have seen, however, the gospels do not present an inherent reason that Peter should have risen to that position.[51] As far as we know, his selection is founded solely on Jesus' will.

It would be wrong, however, if we would identify the church with the kingdom of God. The early Christian community recognized this also, when it preserved Jesus' proclamation of the kingdom of God in which he had pronounced the kingdom both as a present reality and as an eschatological goal. Though the kingdom of God will only be fully realized in the eschaton, the present time is already determined by the foreshadowing of the eschaton. Therefore the church is an eschatological phenomenon, waiting for the full realization of the kingdom but living from its proleptic anticipation.[52] Unlike Matthew, Mark and Luke do not present Peter's commission. But significantly, they too place Jesus' first announcement of his impending passion immediately after Peter confessed Jesus to be the Messiah (Matt. 16:21; Mark 8:31; Luke 9:22). While this announcement is less motivated by the confession of Peter, it is especially fitting in the Matthean context: Jesus is recognized as the Messiah; he designates Peter as the leader of the people of God; and the reason for his move is that he announces his impending passion. Similarly to someone ordering one's household realizing that one's end is near, Jesus entrusts his followers to Peter. Yet it is not an action of concern about the survival of the movement he has initiated. For once, the promise that the powers of death will not prevail against the church makes clear that survival will never be at stake. The church's survival and even victory is assured. Secondly, the promise that Jesus will give to Peter the keys of the kingdom indicates that Jesus does not simply talk about an earthly organization, but about the new people of God. Their ultimate destiny is the entrance into the kingdom of God.

When we now turn briefly to Peter after Easter, Paul introduces him as the first eyewitness to Christ's resurrection (1 Cor. 15:5). Moreover, the two disciples who walked to the village of Emmaus on Easter morning were greeted by the other disciples with the good news: "The Lord has risen indeed and has appeared to Simon!" (Luke 24:34). Actually others had recognized the resurrected one also. Evidently they wanted to give Peter the priority as eyewitness. Then we hear in the moving passage of John 21:15-19 how Peter is again entrusted by the resurrected one with the supervision of Jesus' followers. It is not surprising, therefore, that we see Peter in the Acts of the Apostles as the leader of the emerging Christian community. He is instrumental in having another apostle elected (Acts 1:15ff.); he explains the miracle of Pentecost (2:14ff.); he heals the paralytic by the temple gate (3:6ff.); defends the gospel against its challengers (4:8ff.); he exercises church discipline (5:3ff.); and together with John he also supervises missionary activities (8:14ff.).

When Paul returned to Jerusalem, he naturally went there "to visit Cephas" (Gal. 1:18). When we come to the council of the apostles in Jerusalem Peter was again the one who spoke first (Acts 15:6). But it was James who had the last word and who finally decided whether Mosaic law and circumcision should be imposed on the members of the Gentile world who would join the Christian community. When Paul spoke of the same council meeting, he referred to James, Cephas, and John as respected pillars of the Christian community, with James and not Peter mentioned in first place (Gal. 2:9). He also mentioned that Peter was now to be a missionary among the Jewish people, similar to Paul among the non-Jewish people (Gal. 2:8). We may even be amazed that Paul reported that Peter was afraid of the people coming from James and therefore changed his conduct (Gal. 2:12). Peter seemed to be no longer in a clear leadership position. But the people from Jerusalem did not cause any difficulty for Paul. In his mission among Gentiles, Paul seemed to have enjoyed more freedom than Peter who was active among the Jewish people. Also the remark by Peter upon his release from prison: "Tell this to James and to the brethren" (Acts 12:17), seems to indicate who had become the real leader in Jerusalem.[53]

In Acts 21:18 finally only James and all the elders are mentioned. There need not necessarily have been a power struggle between James and Peter that resulted in James, the brother of Jesus, assuming the supreme authority in Jerusalem.[54] It may have been only natural that James as the brother of Jesus took over while Peter was absent from Jerusalem, at first temporarily and then permanently. Even the men who came from James and whom Peter feared according to Gal. 2:11f. may have been the same Jewish Christians whom we encounter in Acts 15:5 and who perhaps tried to push Peter into steering a more Jewish course without having the explicit approval of James.[55] Yet whether we follow the Book of Acts literally or whether we read it critically, we discern a twofold movement. The first is from the twelve under the leadership of Peter (Acts 2:37) to the apostles and the elders (Acts 15 and 16:4), and to James and all the elders (21:18). The other movement is the shift from Jerusalem and Peter (Acts 1–15) to the Gentile churches and Paul (16–28).[56] So we observe an enlarging of the community from the disciples of Jesus to the church of Jesus Christ which is paralleled with a shift in authority from Peter and the disciples to James and the elders.

c. From the disciples of Jesus to the church of Christ

During the few years that are spanned by the New Testament documents, we encounter an amazing growth of the church. At the beginning Jesus appointed twelve apostles in analogy to the twelve tribes of Israel, and sent them out to be his messengers (Mark 3:14). Barely 40 years later there existed Christian congregations in Rome, Athens, Corinth, and in many places of Asia Minor and Palestine.

The mission of the twelve had been clearly confined to Israel (Matt. 10:5). We are not suprised about this, since Jesus himself usually did not go beyond the Israelite boundaries. The twelve only did what was common among the Jewish people of their time, heeding that "he who is sent by a man is as he who sent him."[57] Similar to their master, Jesus' disciples also had power over unclean spirits on their journeys. We hear too that they addressed their audience with an eschatological message of the impending coming of the kingdom and pronounced judgment over those who rejected them and their message (cf. Luke 10:1ff.; and Matt. 10:5ff.; cf. also Mark 6:6-13). When the Son of man will sit on his glorious throne the twelve "will sit on twelve thrones, judging the twelve tribes of Israel" (Matt. 19:28). They will participate in the Messianic wedding feast (Mark 2:19). James even taught his disciples how to pray with a special prayer. The disciples did not only enjoy the blessings of the commencing eschatological reign. Like Jesus their life should be characterized by an attitude of servanthood (Mark 10:41-45) and they will be persecuted and put to death (Mark 13:9-13 and 10:38). Being the Messiah, Jesus instructed his disciples, giving them the new law (Sermon on the Mount) as the rule for the conduct of life in the Messianic community.[58]

When he saw his earthly life coming to a close, Jesus assembled the twelve to celebrate with them the Last Supper. Whether we accept the synoptic tradition that Jesus' Last Supper was a Passover meal, celebrated at the day of the Passover feast (cf. Mark 14:14 par.), or whether we follow the Gospel of John that this meal was celebrated a day earlier (cf. John 18:28), at that point this farewell meal did not seem to make an overwhelming impression on the disciples. With the exception of Peter, who at least followed Jesus to denounce any connections with him, the rest of the disciples were remarkably absent during the trial and crucifixion. As the appearance of the resurrected one in Galilee indicates (Mark 14:28; 16:7; Matt. 28-16), the disciples may even have fled from Jerusalem fearing that they were next in line to be executed. Perhaps only some women who had been followers of Jesus stayed in Jerusalem (Mark 16:1 par.; John 20:1). As the amazement with which the women encountered the resurrected Christ indicates, not even they expected anything significant to happen after Jesus' death. We may conclude that it was not so much a sacred tradition that was the center of their discipleship, but the personal and intimate bond with their leader. Otherwise the reaction of the two disciples going to Emmaus (Luke 24:19ff.) would be unexplainable. It betrays the deep sorrow and despair that surrounded the disciples once their leader was no longer present.

In this context it is especially interesting that in Luke's Gospel the term disciples (*mathetes*) is no longer used after Jesus' prayer at the Mount of Olives (Luke 22:45). Other terms are used from thereon to refer to Jesus' disciples (Luke 23:49; 22:49). This terminological change seems to indicate a much deeper change. The trust in Jesus that he had once called for was collapsing and Jesus suffered and died abandoned by his disciples Matt. 26:55f.). Perhaps not without reason, the New Testament Epistles avoid the term disciples, and Luke-Acts, where we again find the term, uses it primarily with reference to Christians, the exceptions being Acts 9:25 and 19:1. The term disciple does now no longer refer to those who had been close followers of Jesus though it may still include them.[59] As Acts 6:7 paradigmatically indicates ("the number of the disciples multiplied greatly in Jerusalem, and a great many of the priests were obedient to the faith"), disciples in the Christian sense are not just followers of Jesus, but those who have received faith in Jesus as the Christ. Beyond the portions of the Acts in which Christians are called disciples, even they are no longer referred to by this term.

The big change from the disciples of Jesus to the followers of Jesus Christ seems to have occurred through the Easter events. During the life of Jesus of Nazareth we can already distinguish three groups among his followers. The first one is the group of the disciples *(mathetes)*, from that comes a more select group, the twelve disciples or the twelve apostles (Matt. 10:1-2), and finally there is a larger group of non-itinerant followers (Luke 10:38-42). The circle of the twelve was initially maintained once the disciples gathered after Easter. When Judas Iscariot had vacated his place, Matthias was chosen to replace him in the group. He fulfilled their criteria, having been a disciple who had accompanied Jesus of Nazareth and who had witnessed his resurrection (cf. Acts 1:21-26). The twelve provided the continuity with the earthly Jesus and they also encountered the resurrected Christ (1 Cor. 15:5). They were the leaders of the new people of God and proclaimed the message of the resurrected (Matt. 28:16ff.). Standing for the twelve tribes of Israel they symbolized the claim of Jesus and the later Christian community on the whole Jewish nation (cf. Matt. 19:28).[60]

As the Christian community grew more beyond the confines of Israel, it was no longer considered mandatory to maintain a circle of the twelve. When James, the son of Zebedee was killed, we do not hear that his vacant place among the twelve was filled. Now another group had gained in importance, the apostles whose origin again can be traced to Jesus of Nazareth. Of course, the apostles were originally virtually identical with the twelve. While the usage of the term disciples is primarily confined to the gospels and Luke-Acts, the term apostles is predominantly used in the Pauline letters and in Luke-Acts. Presuppositions for being an apostle is that one is called and sent by Jesus.[61] The apostles were the bearers of the New Testament proclamation and the first Christian missionaries. When we consider the passage of the first sending out of the twelve (Mark 6:7; Matt. 10:1-5 uses the terms disciples, the twelve, and apostles synonomously) we notice that the apostles were sent out in the authority of the one who sent them. In other words, they were Jesus' collaborators.

We remember that Jesus' discipleship collapsed with his imprisonment and death. Since the apostles were originally recruited from within Jesus' discipleship, we cannot claim for them either an uninterrupted continuity, i.e., a continuity from the apostles that Jesus called and sent, to the apostles who became the bearers of the Christian kerygma and the foundation of the Christian church. Since Peter must be seen as an apostle too, this would also apply to his apostolate. Here Karl Heinrich Rengstorf is right when he asserts: "The Gospels and Acts make it quite clear that it was exclusively the act of the risen Lord that this scattered group became a community full of hope and ready for action. The act of the risen Lord, however, was the renewal of the commission of the disciples in their definite institution as *apostoloi* [apostles]." [62] This means that in its Christian form the apostolate does not stand in unbroken continuity with the apostles that Jesus of Nazareth called and sent. The decisive turning point is the resurrection, since it enabled the proclamation of the resurrected one and the gathering of the community of the resurrected Christ.

The apostles were witnesses to the resurrection though not all who saw the resurrected Christ became apostles. The resurrection experiences are not the same as call experiences. As we see especially well in the concluding chapter of the Gospel of John, what is constitutive for the ministry of Peter is not his encounter with the resurrected Christ but his commissioning by the resurrected one. Similarly, when Paul introduced himself to the Christian community in Rome, he emphasized that he had been called to be an apostle (Rom. 1:1).

There are two facets of the apostolic office that are noteworthy. (1) An apostle has an authoritative position within the Christian community. In harmony with the fellow apostles he represents the risen Lord. This leads to the second characteristic, (2) the missionary character of an apostle. An apostle has the task to proclaim the one in whose authority he is sent. This task is not a temporary one after which he turns to other business, but it is valid for the whole interim period between Christ's resurrection and his parousia (cf. Acts 1:6ff.). Being an apostle is therefore a lifelong task. Since his Lord is truly present through him, an apostle is also empowered by the Holy Spirit. Thus the beginning of missionary activity and the actual starting point of the church was Pentecost, the point at which the Spirit was made manifest among the apostles.

The Spirit did not transform the disciples into superhuman beings, but he used them as tools (cf. Acts 10:26). They did not become ecstatic tools void of their own will and responsibility, but they were empowered to carry out the will of their Lord without restraint and fear (cf. Acts 4:19f.). It is a matter of conjecture how many people had the title apostle in the first Christian community. Presumably they included the twelve plus a few others, such as James and Paul. In other words, they were recruited mostly, though not exclusively, from among the disciples of Jesus of Nazareth.

The change in terminology from disciples to apostles does not only indicate the transition from the followers of Jesus to the followers of and believers in Jesus Christ, it also signifies the shift from the exclusive mission to the people of Israel to the universal mission that includes people of all nations. Though this shift is already pronounced by the resurrected Christ when he commanded his disciples to go to all nations (Matt. 28:19; Acts 1:8), there was an immense struggle among the apostles until they fully realized the implications of this change. First the disciples and apostles knew that they should be missionaries only within the confines of Judaism. From Pentecost onward the apostles then addressed people "from every nation" (Acts 2:5). But as Luke tells us, all these people were devout Jews.

When Peter addressed his listeners at Pentecost, it is evident that they were clearly associated with Judaism. He called them to repentance, because they had not followed the Messiah and in their indifference even contributed to the crucifixion of the Messiah. Since this Messiah is now enthroned in power at the right hand of God, it is only proper to recognize him as such (and become Christian). Similar to Matthew in his Gospel, Luke wants to demonstrate here with Peter's remarks that the Christians are not a separatist community. They felt they stood in true continuity to the Messianic expectations (fulfillment) of the Jewish faith. The people who followed the call of the apostles devoted themselves to the apostles' teaching and fellowship, the celebration of the Lord's Supper, and to prayers (Acts 2:42).[63] Unlike the community in Qumran, the first Christian community did not conceive of itself as a remnant.[64] They did not seem to isolate themselves from the Jewish people and they did not demand a special initiation ritual. Even the Christian baptism can be seen in analogy to the Jewish baptism of repentance. Yet it was significant that these people confessed Jesus as Lord (Rom. 10:9). Christ's resurrection and the pouring out of the Holy Spirit gave the disciples the assurance that Jesus was the Messiah and that they were the Messianic community.[65] The whole history of Jesus could now be appropriated as a history of the fulfillment of the Old Testament promises (cf. the Gospel according to Matthew).

Contrary to a first impression, the frequent references to the Christians as the saints (Acts 9:13; Rom. 1:7), does not indicate that the nascent Christian community felt itself superior to the Jewish people. In analogy to the Old Testament community (Exod. 19:6) they realized that they were "a chosen race, a royal priesthood, a holy nation" (1 Peter 2:9). But it would be oversimplified to see them just as a continuation of the Old Testament community. They are holy, because of Jesus Christ (1 Cor. 1:2). Therefore it is important for them to confront Israel with the message of Jesus as the Messiah (Acts 2:36). In a sense they continue Jesus' ministry to the lost sheep of Israel (Matt. 15:24). Even Paul, for whom the mission to the Gentiles had become crucial, was not unconcerned about his own Jewish people (Rom. 11:1). He argued that the mission to the Gentiles was only a means by which later all Israel would be saved (Rom. 11:14-26).

Similar to Jesus, the first Christian community, though it recruited only from among the Jews, did not exclude the Gentiles from salvation. At the council of the apostles, James declared with explicit reference to the Old Testament that Gentiles too are eligible to be incorporated into the Christian community (Acts 15:13ff.). Thus the extension of the mission as described in Luke-Acts, first to the Samaritans, then to those who were pious sympathizers with Judaism (Cornelius), and finally to non-Jewish people, need not be conceived of a radical change within the Christian community.[66] Of course, the rejection and outright persecution of the nascent Christian community by the pious Jews may have speeded up the process of extending the limits of missionary endeavors beyond Judaism.

It is a constitutive moment of the time of Messianic fulfillment that "many nations shall join themselves to the Lord in that day, and shall be my people; and I will dwell in the midst of you" (Zech. 2:11). Since the Christian community had now fully understood Jesus as the Messiah, it was natural that, according to Luke-Acts, James quoted Old Testament passages that described the time of Messianic fulfillment in order to justify and even advocate the legitimacy of mission among the Gentiles. But strangely, the Christian community in Jerusalem under the leadership of the apostles confined itself mainly to the Jewish nation.

A problem, however, arose when especially under the leadership of Paul the missionaries among the Gentiles questioned whether one needed to become a Jew first (be circumcised) before one could become a Christian. After much discussion it was decided that those who were missionaries among the Gentiles needed not make them Jews first, before they could become Christians.[67] Needless to say the Jewish Christians were much more conservative on this issue than those who were working on the Gentile mission fields. But when it became evident that Israel as a whole would not accept Jesus as the Messiah and when in A.D. 70 Jerusalem, as the rallying point of Jewish Messianic hopes was destroyed, the way was open for an all-encompassing catholic church on a predominantly Hellenistic basis. Luke, writing from this perspective, divided God's history of salvation into three epochs. There is first the history of Israel which includes John the Baptist (Luke 16:16).[68] Then comes the history of Jesus' activity on earth (Luke 4:16-19). Finally there is the epoch of the church and its exalted Lord.

In the beginning of Luke-Acts the church is introduced as having a mission to the end of the earth (Acts 1:8). The empowering with the Holy Spirit, constitutive for the Christian community, is seen in antithesis to the confusion of humanity at Babel when it attempted to reach God by building a mighty tower (Gen. 11:1-9).[69] Now conditions have changed and God has reached down and poured out his Spirit as foretold in Joel 2:28f. Thus the church exists in a Messianic and at the same moment eschatological time. Still there are tribulations and persecutions for the church and its members. Yet the Christians know that these tribulations will not continue forever (Acts 14:22). Christians do not withdraw from the world or are pessimistic concerning its affairs. They know that they are to be a light for the Gentiles and to bring salvation to the uttermost parts of the world (Acts 13:47). While the church is the tool of the exalted Lord in this world, it is an interim arrangement, and it is not here to stay. Jesus has already fulfilled the first of his promises, and most certainly his second advent will come too.

NOTES

1. Cf. for the following Karl Ludwig Schmidt, *ekklesia*, F: "The Old Testament and Judaism," in TDNT, 3:527ff.
2. *The Babylonian Talmud. Seder Nashim. Yebamoth,* trans. and intr. with notes, glossary and indices I. W. Slotki (London: Soncino, 1936), 1:310.
3. Ibid., 311.
4. Peter Dalbert, "Proselyt," *Biblisch-Historisches Handwörterbuch,* ed. Bo Reicke and Leonhard Rost, 3:1515.
5. Cf. Hermann L. Strack and Paul Billerbeck, *Kommentar zum Neuen Testament aus Talmud und Midrasch* (Munich: C. H. Beck, 1924), 2:715f., who distinguish in their comments on Acts 13:16 between the full proselytes and the God-fearers or half proselytes.
6. Flavius Josephus, *Against Apion* 2.283, ed. with an English trans. H. St. J. Thackeray (London: Heinemann, 1956), 1:407.
7. Nils Dahl, *Das Volk Gottes. Eine Untersuchung zum Kirchenbewusstsein des Urchristentums,* 2nd ed. (Darmstadt: Wissenschaftliche Buchgesellschaft, 1963) 59.
8. Cf. for the following Joachim Jeremias, *Jerusalem in the Time of Jesus. An Investigation into Economic and Social Conditions During the New Testament Period,* trans. F. H. and C. H. Cave (Philadelphia: Fortress, 1969) 276.
9. Flavius Josephus, *Against Apion* 2:178, 1:365.
10. Ibid., 2.179, 365.
11. So Werner Foerster, *From the Exile to Christ. A Historical Introduction to Palestinian Judaism,* trans. G. E. Harris (Philadelphia: Fortress, 1964) 143.

12. Cf. for the following Helmer Ringgren, *Israelite Religion*, trans. D. E. Green (Philadelphia: Fortress, 1966) 302f.

13. *Pirke Aboth. The Ethics of the Talmud. Sayings of the Fathers* 3.18, ed. with intr., trans., and commentary R. Travers Herford (New York: Schocken, 1962) 87.

14. Ibid., 2.8, 48.

15. Ringgren, 306, seems to shift the balance unduly when he says: "On the whole, the nationalistic and particularistic tendency carried the day, although there were always proselytes, i.e., Gentiles who conformed to Judaism." There are sufficient universalistic moments contained in the Old Testament that the particularistic notion could never dominate exclusively (cf. Isa. 42:6f.; 2:2f.).

16. So Heinz Kremers, "Synagoge," *Biblisch-Historisches Handwörterbuch* 3:1906.

17. For the following cf. the perceptive comments in *Encyclopedia Judaica*, 1971 ed., S.V. "Synagogue: Origins and History," by Louis Isaac Rabinowitz.

18. Cf. Walther Zimmerli, *Ezekiel 1. A Commentary on the Book of the Prophet Ezekiel, Chapters 1-24*, trans. R. E. Clements (Philadelphia: Fortress, 1979) 262, in his exegesis of Ezek. 11:16.

19. Cf. for the following Flavius Josephus, *Jewish War* 5.184-237 and 6.94ff., ed. with an English trans. H. St. J. Thackeray (London: Heinemann, 1956), 3:255-275 and 403ff.

20. Dahl, 65.

21. Strack and Billerbeck, 1:85, adduce references to this hope from rabbinic sources.

22. Josephus, *Jewish War* 1.88, 2:45.

23. Cf. for the following Dahl, 71.

24. Strack and Billerbeck, 1:450.

25. Cf. for the following Charles H. H. Scobie, *John the Baptist* (Philadelphia: Fortress, 1964) 146.

26. Cf. Leonhard Goppelt, *Theologie des Neuen Testaments*. Vol. 1: *Jesu Wirken in seiner theologischen Bedeutung*, ed. Jürgen Roloff (Göttingen: Vandenhoeck & Ruprecht, 1975) 93.

27. Cf. for the following Scobie, 156.

28. So Harald Riesenfeld, *The Gospel Tradition*, trans. by E. M. Rowley and R. A. Kraft (Philadelphia: Fortress, 1970) 20.

29. Ibid., 24. Cf. also the excellent book by Asher Finkel, *The Pharisees and the Teacher of Nazareth. A Study of Their Background, Their Halachic and Midrashic Teachings, the Similarities and Differences* (Leiden: Brill, 1964) 130ff., who shows how closely Jesus followed the rabbinic tradition. He also indicates that in his interpretation of the law Jesus followed more the rabbinic school of Hillel than that of Shammai, since the former displayed more leniency in its decisions, while the Shammites were for strict adherence to the law (135f.).

30. Cf. for the following also Goppelt, 1:75.

31. Cf. for the following ibid., 1:77f.

32. Goppelt, 1:81, incorrectly assumes that this was the main point of controversy.

33. Cf. for the following Abba Hillel Silver, *A History of the Messianic Speculation in Israel from the First Through the Seventeenth Centuries* (Boston: Beacon, 1959 [1927]) 6f.

34. Josephus, *Jewish War* 2.259, 2:425.

35. Cf. for this and the following the helpful summary in Joseph Klausner, *The Messianic Idea in Israel from Its Beginning to the Completion of the Mishnah*, trans. from the 3rd ed. W. F. Stinespring (New York: Macmillan, 1955) 521f.

36. Rudolf Bultmann, *Theology of the New Testament*, trans. K. Grobel (New York: Scribner's, 1951), 1:27.

46   The Formative Era

37. Cf. for a more extensive discussion Hans Schwarz, *On the Way to the Future*, rev. ed. (Minneapolis: Augsburg, 1979) 56ff.

38. Cf. for the following then valuable comments by Philip B. Harner, *The "I Am" of the Fourth Gospel: A Study in Johannine Usage and Thought* (Philadelphia: Fortress Facet Books, Biblical Series, No. 26, 1970), esp. 6-26. See also Schwarz, 58.

39. Ethelbert Stauffer, *Jesus and His Story*, trans. R. and C. Winston (New York: Knopf, 1960) 179.

40. Harner, 23.

41. Ernst Lohmeyer, *Das Evangelium des Markus* (Göttingen: Vandenhoeck & Ruprecht, 1954) 270f.; and W. Manson, "Ego eimi of the Messianic Presence in the New Testament," in *Journal of Theological Studies*, 48:137ff. Cf. also Vincent Taylor, *The Gospel According to St. Mark* (London: Macmillan, 1953) 503f., who is hesitant to see a theophanic formula contained in this passage.

42. It is interesting that Harner, 33f., who gives a very careful analysis of the *ego eimi* formula arrives at the notion that "it is not likely that we can understand the *ego eimi* of Mark 14:62 and Luke 22:70 in an absolute sense." This conclusion is especially surprising since the evidence seems to lead in the opposite direction, namely that the *ego eimi* in Mark 14:62 is indeed used in an absolute sense as divine self-predication.

43. Cf. for the following the careful study by John R. Donahue, *Are You the Christ? The Trial Narrative in the Gospel of Mark*. SBL Dissertation Series, No. 10 (Missoula, MT: Society of Biblical Literature, 1973) 91ff.

44. So rightly Norman Perrin, "The High Priests's Question and Jesus' Answer (Mark 14:61-62)," in *The Passion in Mark; Studies on Mark 14-16*, ed. Werner H. Kelber (Philadelphia: Fortress, 1976) 82.

45. Ernst Haenchen, *Der Weg Jesus: Eine Erklärung des Markus-Evangeliums und der kanonischen Parallellen* (Berlin: Alfred Töpelmann, 1966), 511f., in his discussion with Stauffer rejects the thesis that this passage dates back to Jesus. It simply reflects the expectation of the first Christian community. Since this expectation (the return of Christ before the death of the members of the Sanhedrin) was not fulfilled, the passage was changed in Matthew and Luke. Taylor, 568f., who also admits that this passage reflects the apocalyptic hopes of the church, comes to the conclusion that it is in every way probable that it is actually the reply of Jesus to the challenge of the high priest. Its emphasis lies on the enthronement, and on the enthronement as the symbol of triumph.

46. Ernst Fuchs, "The Quest of the Historical Jesus," in *Studies of the Historical Jesus*, trans. A. Scobie (Naperville, IL: Allenson, 1964) 20f. Cf. also Joachim Jeremias, *New Testament Theology*. Vol. 1: *The Proclamation of Jesus*, trans. J. Bowden (New York: Scribner's, 1971) 253f., who makes the connection between the emphatic use of the word *ego* and Jesus' own conduct.

47. For Peter cf. the excellent book, Oscar Cullmann, *Peter, Disciple, Apostle, Martyr*, trans. F. V. Filson (2nd rev. ed.; Philadelphia: Westminster, 1962), and Oscar Cullmann, *Petros, Cephas*, in TDNT, 6:100-12.

48. Cf. Cullmann, *Peter*, 184ff.

49. So Riesenfeld, 27.

50. Cf. to this issue very perceptively Ferdinand Hahn, "Pre-Easter Discipleship," in *The Beginnings of the Church in the New Testament*. Essays by Ferdinand Hahn, August Strobel, and Eduard Schweizer, trans. I. and U. Nicol (Minneapolis: Augsburg, 1970) 30f. Hahn dismisses very summarily the idea that Jesus could have founded the church. Similarly, Dahl, 167, claims: "The church is a creation of the resurrected one!"

51. So Schmidt, *ekklesia*, in TDNT, 3:523, rightly says: "The special position of Peter is a riddle that must be accepted as such."

52. Cf. Karl Ludwig Schmidt, *basileia*, in TDNT, 1:586f., and *ekklesia*, in TDNT, 3:522.

53. Cf. also R. Newton Flew, *Jesus and His Church. A Study of the Idea of the Ecclesia in the New Testament* (London: Epworth, 1960 [1938]) 133.

54. This is the solution to the issue that Oscar Cullmann prefers.

55. So Otto Karrer, *Peter and the Church. An Examination of Cullmann's Thesis*, trans. R. Walls (London: Nelson, 1963) 42f., whose stringent defense of a lifelong Petrine office is not too convincing.

56. Cf. the interesting book, *Peter in the New Testament. A Collaborative Assessment by Protestant and Roman Catholic Scholars*, ed. Raymond E. Brown, Karl P. Donfried, and John Reumann (Minneapolis: Augsburg, 1973) 55.

57. According to Flew, 79, who refers here to Berakhoth, vol. 5 (Danby, *Mishnah*, 6 et al.).

58. Cf. Riesenfeld, 27ff.

59. Cf. for the following Karl Heinrich Rengstorf, *mathetes*, in TDNT, 4:457f.

60. Cf. for the following Rengstorf, *dodeka*, in TDNT, 2:326f.

61. Cf. for the following Rengstorf, *apostolos*, in TDNT, 1:422.

62. Ibid., 1:430.

63. Cf. Ernst Haenchen, *The Acts of the Apostles. A Commentary*, trans. B. Noble and G. Shinn with H. Anderson and R. Mcl. Wilson (Philadelphia: Westminster, 1971) 190.

64. Cf. for the following Rudolf Schnackenburg, *The Church in the New Testament*, trans. W. J. O'Hara (New York: Herder, 1966) 60.

65. Dahl, 180.

66. So rightly Schnackenburg, 62.

67. Cf. Haenchen, 464f., on how to interpret the seemingly conflicting reports of the apostles' council.

68. Cf. for the following the excellent description in Hans Conzelmann, *The Theology of St. Luke*, trans. G. Buswell (London: Faber, 1960) 16f.

69. To see in the reference to Genesis 11 only pious exegesis, as assumed by Haenchen, 174, seems to miss the point. Certainly there are other motives interspersed, but to exclude the Babel motive is arbitrary, even if the proclamation at this point does not yet reach out beyond the Jewish confines.

2

The Structure of
the New Testament Church

THE CHURCH THAT IS REFLECTED IN THE NEW TESTAMENT could not exist
without appropriate structure. This is true for any organization. The
organizational aspect of the church is reflected in the administration of the
church, in its worship forms, and in the interrelatedness of the different
congregations. Before we deal with these various facets of the church,
we must especially emphasize one point: The new people of God did not
understand themselves as a human creation and under human leadership.
The church was not conceived by the apostles as their own organization
to promote the ideas once preached by their venerated leader. The church
with all its members felt itself solely responsible to its risen and exalted
Lord and it carried on its work in his name and power (cf. Acts 4:19f.).
The important decisions were made under the guidance of the Holy
Spirit (Acts 15:28). Thus we can rightly speak of a theocracy or a *pneuma-
tocracy*.[1] God in his Son and through his Spirit is the empowering, guiding, and sustaining force of the new Christian community.

1. The administration of the church

When we now deal specifically with the administration of the church,
we must first of all delineate that which needs administration, the church
as the new people of God.

a. The church as the new people of God

Paul and Luke-Acts call the new people of God the church (*ekklesia*)
(Gal. 1:13; Acts 5:11). This signifies the continuity between the Old
Testament *kahal* and the new Christian community.[2] The Old Testament
kahal was not the community assembled in the synagogue, but the assembly of the people (of God) and of the temple community.[3] The church
becomes the new eschatological temple community of whom God said: "I

will live in them and move among them, and I will be their God, and they shall be my people" (2 Cor. 6:16). The Christian community should not be understood as a special synagogue or community in analogy to the Qumran or the Essene community. It was the community of the new (cleansed) temple and of the new Jerusalem. Newly established congregations outside Jerusalem are viewed like daughters in relation to their mother, or synagogues in relation to the temple community. Inspections of the newly organized communities by the authorities from Jerusalem and frequent reports to and counsels from them seem to underline this relationship (Gal. 2:12). As the new congregations are representations of the one church, Paul can proudly write to the congregation in Thessalonica: "For you, brethren, became imitators of the churches of God in Christ Jesus which are in Judea" (1 Thess. 2:14).

Another significant term to denote the new people of God is the word *laos* (people). The term occurs approximately 2,000 times in the Septuagint, mainly standing for an ethnic group. Though it is not used exclusively to signify Israel, the frequent use of *laos theou* (people of God) shows that people usually denotes the Israelites as people of God, while other people are referred to as *ethnoi*. The indiscriminate use of the Old Testament Hebrew terms *am* and *goi* to speak about peoples gradually gives way to a more discriminate ethnic and religious use, so that *am* stands for the people of Israel, while *goi* refers to other nations. The indiscriminate use can be seen by comparing Deuteronomy 4:6 with 12:30. In the first passage *goi* is used for Israel and *am* for other nations, while in the second *goi* stands for other nations.

In the New Testament the term *laos* is used frequently; half of the occurrences are in Luke-Acts. Yet this frequent usage, mostly in signifying people, or a group of people (cf. Luke 1:21), is not as significant as the rather deliberate use that we find in Paul and the Pauline literature. There the Septuagint use of denoting with *laos* an ethnic community is now broadened to denote the Christian community. For instance, in Romans 9:25 Paul quotes from Hosea God's promise: "Those who are not my people I will call 'my people,' and he who was not beloved I will call 'my beloved'" (Hos. 2:23). Similarly, Luke tells us that James stated at the apostles' council: "Symeon has related how God first visited the Gentiles, to take out of them a people for his name" (Acts 15:14). In other words, the exclusive either-or, either a member of the *laos* or of the *ethnoi* has been overcome.[4] The ethnic and historical boundaries of the *laos* are no longer binding. *Laos* is now the people of God whom God has called and who confess his Son as Lord. In a vision the Lord even encourages Paul to continue his work in Corinth by saying: "I am with you, and no man shall attack you to harm you; for I have many people [*laoi*] in this city" (Acts 18:10). That the term *laos* can denote the Christian community means nothing less than that those standing in continuity with the Old Testament community are no longer restricted by ethnic and historical boundaries. It is a new community composed of both *laoi* (Jewish people) and *ethnoi* (non-Jewish people).

Yet the ethnic, national, or class boundaries do not suddenly disappear or become irrelevant. Paul admonishes the people in metropolitan Corinth: "Every one should remain in the state in which he was called" (1 Cor. 7:20). In their historical context the differences are still recognized as such. But within the Christian community they are no longer divisive so that they would disturb the new and overarching unity of the people of God *(laos theou)*. The Christians are called "the Israel of God" in Galatians 6:16. Again we should be careful to note that the succession in promise and the inception of the new Jerusalem does not exclude the members of the Israel of old. Its once exclusive boundaries, however, are no longer exclusive. Christ the Lord has transcended them and has bridged the chasm between Jew and Gentile.

Once it was recognized that the Christian community was included in the whole people of God, the use of the term *laos* for members within the Christian community gained increasing popularity. For instance, in the writings of Luke, the term predominantly denotes a group of people, usually the group of people assembled in worship. This group was then referred to as *ho laos* (the laity) in contradistinction from those charged with leadership functions. Justin Martyr can then mention that at the conclusion of the prayers "the people express their approval by saying 'Amen.'"[5] Seeing in *laos* (laity) the proper term for the worshiping people, in distinction from those with a leadership function, we should not forget the other equally important use, namely to refer to the whole people of God who include laity *and* leaders, Jews *and* Gentiles.

An important aspect of the people of God in New Testament times should at least be mentioned parenthetically—the so-called "Jerusalem communists." We hear that

> now the company of those who believed were of one heart and soul and no one said that any of the things which he possessed was his own, but they had everything in common. And with great power the apostles gave their testimony to the resurrection of the Lord Jesus, and great grace was

upon them all. There was not a needy person among them, for as many
as were possessors of land or houses sold them, and brought the proceeds
of what was sold and laid it at the apostles' feet; and distribution was
made to each as any had need. Thus Joseph who was surnamed by the
apostles Barnabas (which means, son of encouragement), a Levite, a
native of Cyprus sold a field which belonged to him, and brought the
money and laid it at the apostles' feet. (Acts 4:32-37)

We might question whether the abolition of private property as portrayed
in our text was actually feasible. Certainly, the Christian community
needed places where they could gather, and it was impossible for the community to support a large number of families and individuals for any
length of time without an adequate subsistence base.[6] Only if they would
have lived together in a monastic or semi-monastic community, such as
the people in Qumran, could we expect that such policies worked.

The neo-Marxist, Ernst Bloch, characterized the situation of the early
Christian community very well when he stated: "No one said that any of
the things he possessed was just his own, but they had everything in common (Acts 4:32), and the goods are collected from gifts, sufficient for the
short span which Jesus still leaves for the old earth."[7] This means that to
some extent the attitude of the Christian community toward property
was shaped by Jesus' own claim that the nearness of the kingdom rendered
all material securities obsolete. While Jesus pointed to himself and his
action as the beginning of the kingdom, in its enthusiasm the Christian
community now expected the completion of the kingdom and the coming
of the parousia. The attitude of the Christian community in Jerusalem
was then quite different from that of the monastic community in Qumran
or from the ideal Old Testament covenant community of which we hear
in Deuteronomy: "But there will be no poor among you . . . and if there
is among you a poor man, one of your brethren . . . you shall not harden
your heart or shut your hand against your poor brother" (Deut. 15:4-7).

In their enthusiastic expectation of the imminent eschaton the Christian community gathered daily for prayer services and common meals,
while their concern about the future moved to the background.[8] They
were solely concerned about spreading the gospel among the Jewish people including the Jews of Greek tongue who lived in Jerusalem. It would
be wrong, however, to see in their attitude towards property and material
possessions a preference for the poor or an aversion toward the rich.
There were still "rich" people left among them who offered their houses
as meeting places (cf. Acts 12:12). Yet if one wanted to withhold prop-

erty for selfish purposes, the consequences were devastating for those individuals (cf. Acts 5:1-11). Yet soon the apocalyptic enthusiasm, oblivious to the provision for the future, ran into difficulties. For instance, we hear that the Hellenists murmured against the Hebrews because their widows were neglected in the daily distributions (Acts 6:1). The situation was worsened by the famine under the Emperor Claudius (cf. Acts 11:28) and the continued unrest in Palestine.[9] Small wonder that Paul was asked at the council of the apostles to "remember the poor" (Gal. 2:10 and Rom. 15:26) in his missionary journeys. The term "poor" here seems to be more a self-identification of the Christian community in Jerusalem rather than to denote individual poor people among them.[10] It may not so much characterize their economic state, though that too left much to be desired, but their fervent hope that the present state of lowliness may soon be rewarded and superseded by the heavenly bliss of the parousia (cf. Matt. 5:3). Christians outside Jerusalem, however, never imitated the Jerusalem example. They were more realistic about the necessity to provide for the needs of the future, especially as they became also more aware of the length of the interim between Christ's resurrection and his parousia.

b. The charismata and diakonia

The episode of the Jerusalem communism shows us that even the Christian community cannot live in pure spontaneity. This became also noticeable when a certain group was neglected in Jerusalem in the daily food distributions. It then became necessary to appoint people "to serve tables" (Acts 6:2f.). This action allowed the apostles to devote themselves "to the ministry of the word" (Acts 6:4). Since the words "to serve" and "ministry" are verb and noun of the same term *diakonia,* denoting "service," they indicate distinctions only in the "offices," i.e., to promote order and justice, but all are joined under the common aspect of service or *diakonia.* The church remembered the words of its Lord that "the Son also came not to be served but to serve" (Mark 10:45) and who "would be first, he must be last of all and servant of all" (Mark 9:35). Similarly, Paul distinguishes between prophecy, service, and teaching (Rom. 12:6f.). But he talks about "the ministry *(diakonia)* of reconciliation" that is given to us through Christ (2 Cor. 5:18) and even about the ministry *(diakonia)* of his apostolate (Rom. 11:13). Thus *diakonia* or service characterizes the attitude in which different functions are carried out.

The term *diakonos* can also be used to single out a certain office. For instance, Paul greets all the saints in Philippi together with the bishops and deacons *(diakonoi)* (Phil. 1:1). We notice two items here: (1) When Paul wrote his letter there were at least two offices in the congregation in Philippi, the one of bishop and the one of deacon. (2) The office of the deacon is mentioned immediately after the office of the bishop, indicating at least an intimate connection.[11] The intimate connection of both offices is also attested to in 1 Timothy 3:1-13 where in the first part of the passage the criteria for a bishop are spelled out, while in the second part the qualities of a deacon are listed. Similarly to a bishop, a deacon must be above reproach, husband of one wife, a good example in his household, and he must "hold the mystery of faith with a clear conscience" (3:9). As it is proper for someone entrusted with earthly goods, a deacon should not be greedy for gain or double-tongued. Unlike a bishop, it is not required for a deacon to be "an apt teacher" (3:2). But we are left unclear in this passage as to the proper function of a deacon.

We may assume that the main duty of a deacon was to serve the congregation and the bishop. One is also tempted to look to Luke's story of the appointment of the "seven deacons" (Acts 6:1-6) for a further description of what the office of the deacon entails. Yet as we noted before, the office of the seven and of the twelve is described as a *diakonia,* a service function. It might be that the passage in Acts 6 does not provide a job description for deacons, but it introduces a community of Hellenistic Christians under the headship of the seven in distinction from a community of Hebrew Christians under the direction of the twelve.[12] Only indirectly do we hear of a serving office that might give us clues to the proper function of a deacon. The meaning of the word deacon, server, and the close (subordinate) association with a bishop seems to substantiate the assumption too that the office of deacon was seen primarily in a serving role. It should also be noted that though in the Jewish synagogue we do not encounter an equivalent to the bishop/deacon offices, we notice a differentiation between those in leadership and those in a more subservient position or who administer the alms.[13]

Once we distinguish between the leadership and a more subservient role, the question emerges whether a leadership function or office does not presuppose a certain charisma or, gift. Especially Adolf von Harnack made an interesting distinction between religious or charismatic ministries relating to the church-at-large and administrative offices relating to the local church.[14] Indeed such thoughts might arise when we read of the multitude of offices as mentioned, for example in 1 Corinthians 12:27ff., where we hear that "God has appointed in the church first apostles, second prophets, third teachers, then workers of miracles, then healers, helpers, administrators, speakers in various kinds of tongues." Paul clearly distinguishes the first three offices from the others. It is, however, legitimate, as it has been done occasionally in the early church to distinguish charismatic offices (i.e., the apostolic, prophetic, and teaching offices), for the right exercise of which a certain God-given charisma is necessary, and the offices that emerge from the sociological necessities of the individual congregations (i.e., the offices of bishops, presbyters, and deacons)? [15] It is certainly true that some offices were designed more to aid a local situation while others were more directed to regional needs. Yet looking at the list in 1 Corinthians 12:27f., we notice that first mentioned are the "charismatic" offices of the apostles, prophets, and teachers, then the "noncharismatic" offices, and at the end Paul mentions "speakers in various kinds of tongues." Glossolalia, being mentioned last, certainly must have something to do with a special charisma and the same must be said for the "workers of miracles." Already at the beginning of the chapter Paul talks about the variety of charismata (1 Cor. 12:4) and he attempts to illustrate this by pointing to the different functions of the members of our body. In Romans 12:6 he also reminds us that the charismata differ according to the grace given to us. Here even prophecy, *diakonia,* and teaching is mentioned in one breath, in addition to a variety of non-institutionalized gifts, such as contributing, giving aid, and doing acts of mercy. We are reminded here of the observation of Eduard Schweizer that "the assertion that the gift of grace is bestowed on *every* church member, and that therefore *every* member is called to service, is constant in the New Testament." [16]

Ultimately every office is a charismatic office, since it is the expression of the measure of grace that has been given to us. The gifts of grace naturally differ in the direction in which they are exercised, but not in their basic service character. This basic similarity is not diminished by the fact that certain services (ministries) were regulated by means of appointment, while others were carried out more spontaneously. The notion that certain offices have no charismatic quality is untrue to the picture of the first Christian community that we gain through the New Testament. It would also introduce a dangerous distinction between first and second class Christians, those who enjoy charisma and those who do not. This would lead to an implicitly boasting attitude of "super-Christians," a trait which is vehemently rejected by Paul.

c. Apostles, presbyters, and bishops

We have noticed there is no essential difference between charismatic and noncharismatic offices; all of them have a basic service character. Since each one's ministry is exercised according to the grace or charisma that God has bestowed upon that person, the various offices conform to the different ministries that the people perform. There is also no clearly perceptible difference between office and ministry. There is a multitude of gifts leading to the exercise of different ministry functions. Thus the church order that we perceive in the first Christian communities varies with locality and time. Offices and ministries are in a state of flux concerning their number, titles, and exact content.[17] For instance, the presbyteral office is modeled in part after Jewish examples, while the episcopate bears Hellenistic analogies.

There seem to be three titles or ministries that merit closer scrutiny. There is first the apostle that, after short prominence, recedes into oblivion and then regains historic strength through the concept of apostolic succession. Then there is the presbyter that at first stands in close connection with the apostle and later is relegated to a secondary administrative position. Finally, we have the term bishop, used only five times in the New Testament, but gaining increasing significance in post-apostolic times.

Apostles: We remember that Jesus never called the people who followed him his disciples. Only when the mission was carried beyond the Jewish confines, the twelve, as they had been commonly called, were named apostles. Then also James, the brother of Jesus, and Paul too were called apostles. But even at that time it was not clear who could be called apostle. For instance, with few exceptions (Acts 14:4-14) Luke reserves the term for the twelve apostles, since they are the witnesses of the early ministry of Jesus (Acts 1:21f.) and therefore they safeguard the tradition. But the apostles do not just guarantee the historical veracity of the Jesus tradition. They were also witnesses to Christ's resurrection and are empowered with the Holy Spirit and therefore guide and direct the Christian community. According to Acts 15 and 16:4 we may even assume that in analogy to the Jewish Sanhedrin the apostles together with the presbyters function as the supreme ruling body and the ultimate teaching authority for the whole church whose decisions are binding for everybody, even for the apostle Paul.[18] When James the son of Zebedee is killed by Herod (Acts 12:2), we do not hear that the circle of the twelve is brought back to its original size by electing a new member. Evidently it was felt that the apostles had a singular function of organizing the church and safeguarding its message, a function which was later assumed by the church as a whole.

When we listen to Paul, we get a different picture of the function of an apostle. Paul did not belong to the disciples of Jesus nor was he one of the first Christians who encountered the resurrected Christ prior to his ascension. But Paul emphasized that he was at least equal to the other apostles and that he worked harder than any of them (1 Cor. 15:11). The unique feature in Paul's position was his encounter with the resurrected Christ. This encounter did not just commission him as we notice with the other apostles (Matt. 28:18f.), but it meant a complete change in his direction from the persecutor of the Christians to a fervent missionary of the Christian gospel. He knows now that he is "called to be an apostle, set apart for the gospel of God" (Rom. 1:1) and even set apart before he was born (Gal. 1:15). Small wonder that this results in a missionary consciousness unparalleled by what we know from the New Testament about the other apostles.

Paul is far from being an enthusiast. Though visions and revelations of the Lord were not unknown to him (2 Cor. 12:1), he boasts of his weakness to demonstrate that God's grace does not despise such a weak tool (2 Cor. 12:9). This means he does not emphasize his own person but the grace of God active in him.[19] He claims to be sent "not to baptize but to preach the gospel" (1 Cor. 1:17), though he is willing to baptize occasionally, while others who were sent out to proclaim the gospel did this on a more frequent basis (cf. Acts 8:38).

If somebody questions Paul's authority he is quick to point out that he is "an apostle—not from man nor through men, but through Jesus Christ and God the Father" (Gal. 1:1). Since he is "a servant of Christ" (Gal. 1:10), he is not trying to please people or seek favors from them. In other words, he is not dependent on people though as an ambassador of Christ and entrusted with the message of reconciliation (2 Cor. 5:19f.), he is directed to all of them, whether Jews or Gentiles. Though Paul's apostolic authority may have been challenged in other areas, he was never questioned about his qualification for the apostolate by the apostles in Jerusalem. For instance, the first time he went to Jerusalem, after his conversion, he had a brief visit with Peter and James the brother of Jesus (Gal. 1:18f.). But Paul's report does not imply that he visited them to be instructed in the Christian message or to have his apostolic authority verified. When he visited again Jerusalem years later, it was not because the authorities in Jerusalem wanted to question him. On the contrary, Paul tells us that the trip was done on his initiative and on account of divine revelation: "I went up by revelation; and I laid before them the gospel which I preach among the Gentiles, lest somehow I should be running or had run in vain" (Gal. 2:2).

It is noteworthy that Paul was afraid that his mission and his endeavor to build up the church might have been in vain. This shows that Paul doubted whether a strictly immediate knowledge of the gospel that he represented was a trustworthy enough basis for proclamation. It is more than curiosity that led him to Jerusalem and inquire to what extent his message conformed with the Christian tradition. Though Paul's apostolate was of unique nature he knew that the church was built up not by a diversity of gospels and apostolates, but only through the one gospel under the guidance of the one apostolate.[20] Yet Paul's fears proved wrong. Nothing needed to be added or changed in the way he presented the gospel and he was received into fellowship (Gal. 2:9).

At the decisive points of the Christian proclamation Paul perceives himself as part of the common tradition.[21] Yet it is not simply a human tradition that he represents. For instance, the tradition of the Lord's Supper has its origin in the Lord who was not only the initiator of the Christian message but, as the one who is present, its immediate verification. When Paul refers to the resurrection again he recites tradition. While he does not say that he received it from the Lord, he invites a test of the validity of the tradition by mentioning that most of the eyewitnesses are still alive (1 Cor. 15:6).

It has become clear that the apostles do not guarantee the tradition, but the Lord himself to whom they witness and who, as the present Lord, verifies their witness. It is therefore understandable why it was not necessary to maintain an institution of the apostolate on a permanent basis. The apostles were the historic starting point who helped to shape the Christian community and its message. Once the community and its message were established, the apostles could recede, since they were not part of the message. When later Gnostic ideas threatened the church and its message, the church rediscovered its apostolic heritage and felt it was necessary to emphasize that nothing should be accepted as gospel if it was not in line with apostolic teaching. Thus the apostolate as a criterion for distinguishing true from false teaching gained new importance.[22] We will pursue this line further when we consider the development of the canon.

Presbyters: At a few places the office of the presbyters is intimately connected with that of the apostles, depicting them as the decisive teaching authority of the whole church (Acts 15 and 16:4). The Jerusalem apostles and presbyters have an authoritative and a representative voice in the teaching of the church. They should be seen in analogy to the Jewish Sanhedrin.[23] Yet the emergence of presbyters is relatively late. Acts 11:30 which mentions the Jerusalem presbyters who receive relief from Paul and Barnabas seems to have been inserted accidentally prior to the council of the apostles.[24] This seems to go hand in hand with the de-emphasis on the apostles, the disappearance of Peter from Jerusalem, and the assumption of leadership in Jerusalem by James (cf. Acts 21:18). It is also interesting that Paul does not mention anything about presbyters in those letters of which his authorship is unquestioned. Paul rather emphasizes the function of the multitude of offices within the community, such as those who teach, exhort, and give aid (Rom. 12:7f., and 1 Cor. 12:28). The authority for Paul, therefore, does not come so much from a certain office but from the work that has been performed.

Soon there emerges a need for a more structured concept of the office. For instance, Luke tells us that when Paul and Barnabas left the congregations they had established, they "appointed elders [presbyters] for them in every church, with prayer and fasting, they committed them to the Lord in whom they believed" (Acts 14:23). Again Luke tells us that from Miletus Paul calls together the elders of the church at Ephesus (Acts 20:17). Paul admonishes them to "take heed to yourselves and to call the flock, in which the Holy Spirit has made you guardians [bishops], to feed the church of God" (Acts 20:28). The context of this verse makes clear that the presbyters should function as the leaders of the congregation and preserve the apostolic tradition against false teachings. In their leadership role, the presbyters are equated here with the bishops. In 1 Peter 5:1-5 we notice a more extensive description of the presbyteral office. Again they appear in leadership function to tend God's flock that is in their charge. They are admonished against misuse of their office and are reminded that Christ is the chief shepherd. In other words, they guard the apostolic tradition against wrong teaching. Since Christ is their chief example they do not function independently in their office. Unlike Luke, 1 Peter does not assign to the presbyters, but only to Christ, the title "guardian" or bishop (1 Peter 2:25).

We also notice that in 1 Peter, as in some other places in the New Testament, the term presbyter or elder is defined by contrasting it with the phrase "you that are younger" (1 Peter 5:5; cf. 1 Tim. 5:1). This may indicate that only older and experienced people qualified as presbyters. As 2 John 1 and 3 John 1 show, the title presbyter could also refer to someone who was an esteemed teacher or prophet. Yet usually there was a college of presbyters who acted together in their leadership function. This collegial function seems to distinguish them from a bishop who acted more independently in his decisions.

Bishops: Of the five times that we find the term bishop used in the New Testament, once it refers to Jesus Christ himself (1 Pet. 2:25 RSV Guardian). In the other places people are addressed as bishops and in each instance they are leaders of congregations. In one instance we notice that the term bishop is used interchangeably with presbyter (Acts 20:17-28) and at another place we see that the deacons are closely associated with the bishops (Phil. 1:1). Then in the letter to Titus we are told that Titus was to appoint elders (presbyters) in every town (Titus 1:5) and suddenly, after a brief description of what a presbyter should be, we are confronted with an extensive profile of a bishop (Titus 1:7). This close association leads us to conclude that the functions of a bishop and a presbyter must have been very close to each other, if not identical.

In 1 Tim. 3:1 we are told that one can aspire to the office of a bishop, implying that it has clearly defined characteristics. But again we are not told what the office entails. We only hear that there are five demands made on someone seeking this office: (1) While no ascetic holiness is expected, a bishop must be morally reliable and an ethical example. (2) While celibacy is not required, a bishop must prove his leadership qualities by being a good leader of his own household. (3) A bishop must be a good teacher and preacher. (4) Since he is in charge of a congregation, a bishop must be an experienced Christian and not a newly converted person. (5) To fulfill his leadership role, a bishop must also have a good reputation among non-Christians. There is no doubt that in 1 Timothy the office of a bishop is already institutionalized. It is also noteworthy that a bishop is referred to in the singular, showing perhaps a trend towards only one bishop in each congregation.

We can now summarize the three offices that have been mentioned. The presbyters have their background in the synagogue leadership and tend to be collegial in the exercise of their leadership. The bishop and deacons belong closely together, with the deacons supporting the bishop by looking after the material needs of the members in the congregation.

Their origin seems to be in the Hellenistic world and the leadership function of the bishop tends to be monarchic. Yet when we think of Peter, James, and Paul, there was sufficient natural leadership in apostolic Christianity that neither pattern (presbyters or bishop and deacons) clearly developed. Once Judaistic Christianity, however, went its own unfortunate way into isolation, avenues opened for the church governance under the leadership of the bishops.

2. The worshiping community

While leadership patterns could be developed from existing Jewish or Hellenistic examples, the problem was not so easily solved once we turned to the worship forms of the Christian community. Worship is the lifeblood of a religious organization and its forms and contents are constitutive for the community's self-understanding. Since the Christians emerged in a Jewish environment it was imperative to clarify their relationship to the Jewish community both in terms of the sources and forms of worship. Christians had to decide what status they would attribute to the Jewish Scriptures (the Old Testament) and they also had to address the question whether they should develop a worship life of their own.

a. The church and the Old Testament

With respect to the issue of continuity and discontinuity with Judaism, Jesus served in many ways as the example for the emerging church. Yet Jesus' relationship to the Jewish faith was not as simple as we might initially assume. Jesus' radical claim for total love toward God and neighbor relativized all other claims that the tradition made. Jesus did not accept the tradition uncritically but scrutinized its intention and effect. Where it expressed the unqualified concern for God and neighbor and therefore benefited humanity, it was accepted. If these criteria were not met, the tradition was reinterpreted to conform to them. Since Jesus himself was a faithful Jew he fulfilled the law and also participated in the Jewish festivals (Passover!). At the outset of his ministry, the synoptics tell us that he went to the synagogue and taught there (Mark 1:21; Matt. 4:23; Luke 4:16). We also get the impression that he was well versed in the law and the prophets, the main corpus of the Jewish Scriptures, and that he quoted them freely. His disciples attempted to imitate his attitude towards the Jewish law, and adhered to many Jewish customs. For instance, they still observed the Sabbath (cf. Matt. 24:20).

Even Easter, the turning point from the pre-Christian to the explicitly Christian community, does not mark a categorical break with the tradition. There is the continuity between Yahweh and the father of Jesus Christ, between the Jewish Scriptures and the first Christian Bible (the Old Testament), and between a group of Jewish people and the first Christians. The Jewish Scriptures became the Christian Old Testament, a document which was diligently read and exegeted by the Christians. Passages such as Isaiah 53 and Psalm 22 became crucial in explaining the significance of the suffering and death of Jesus. It seems that the whole Gospel according to Matthew was written in the deliberate attempt to demonstrate that the Old Testament messianic promises had found their fulfillment in Jesus.

The Jewish Scriptures had not become superfluous. The Old Testament soon became juxtaposed to the specifically Christian Scriptures, the New Testament. For instance, Paul mentions that the (Old Testament) law was our custodian until Christ came (Gal. 3:24). He also allegorizes the Old Testament story of Hagar and Sarah (Gen. 16:15; 21:2), applying it to the Old Testament covenant and the new covenant under which the Christian community lives (Gal. 4:21-31). But Paul does not want to reject his Jewish heritage. He calls Abraham our father who serves us as an example of faith (Rom. 4:12) and he is convinced that God has not rejected his people Israel (Rom. 11:1).

We may conclude that the mere progression from the Old Testament covenant to the new one, and from the promise to Israel and its fulfillment, did not imply an abolition of the Israel of old. The Christian community in Jerusalem did not intend to become a separatistic community similar to Qumran or even a holy remnant.[25] In Luke-Acts, we hear that Peter addressed his Jewish citizens as "brethren" (Acts 2:29) and we are told that the first Christians frequented the temple (Acts 2:46). Peter and the twelve saw their mission initially in converting the people of Israel for the Messiah (Gal. 2:7f.; Acts 2:39) and at first they did not consider a mission to the Gentiles. Through the return of the disciples from Galilee to Jerusalem this holy city became the center of Christianity. When Paul referred to the Christian community there as the church of God (Gal. 1:13) and its members as the saints (Rom. 15:25), he perhaps did so to indicate its influential status. Soon, however, he also addressed other congregations as the church of God, who represented the whole church in a specific area (1 Cor. 1:2) and he called their members saints.

The high hopes remained unfulfilled that the whole house of Israel would soon accept the resurrected Lord as their savior. When Luke-Acts tells us that the Jerusalem Christians had favor with all the people (Acts 2:47; 4:21), then this perhaps exaggerated assessment must be balanced with Luke's reports of imprisonment, warning, and punishment of the apostles and later even of the whole congregation (cf. Acts 4:1-22 and 8:1-3).[26] These unpleasant and unfavorable conditions in Jerusalem may have reminded the first Christians that Jesus did not intend to exclude the pagans from salvation, though he considered himself to be sent "only to the lost sheep of the house of Israel" (Matt. 15:24). When Paul asked the other apostles at the council in Jerusalem about the legitimacy of the mission to the Gentiles, James affirmed that the time must be ripe for God "to take of them a people for his name" (Acts 15:14). The idea no longer prevailed that the pagans would be allowed to join once Israel is converted. With reference to the Old Testament the conclusion was reached that the pagans did not have to wait until they could join the saints. Yet the twelve, and especially Peter, did not seem to engage in active mission among the Gentiles. This was the perogative of Paul (Gal. 2:8f.).

The twelve and the church in Jerusalem evidently felt a stronger salvation historic allegiance to the Jews in Israel than to those in the diaspora who usually were more influenced by Hellenism. At the same time it was agreed that the Gentiles need not accept the law and be circumcised to become Christians. This was a major breakthrough, since at first the Christians accepted the cultic law without reservations. The so-called decree still contained four moral obligations, binding for all Christians, (1) to refrain from eating anything that was sacrificed to the idols, (2) from eating blood, (3) from consuming what had been strangled, and also (4) from unchastity, i.e., from marrying close relatives (Acts 15:29).[27] These obligations, however, could be justified without referring to the cultic law by simply appealing to common Christian moral precepts. Even Paul advised the Christians in Corinth not to eat meat that had been offered in sacrifice (1 Cor. 10:28). He prefaced his advice, however, with a comment that "all things are lawful, but not all things are helpful" (1 Cor. 10:23), admitting that while Christians are not bound to refrain from anything, the concern for others may indeed make them forfeit certain "rights." So Justin tells us at the beginning of the second century that Gnostic Christians eat meat which has been offered for sacrifice; while others rather sacrifice their life than eat this meat.[28] It is noteworthy that Paul addresses Gnostic libertinism in 1 Corinthians. Still in the second half of the second century we hear that Christians do not use the blood even of edible animals in their food.[29] That Hellenistic Christianity would adhere to these precepts for so long underscores our assumption that we are not confronted here just with Jewish cultic prescriptions.

The Jews in Jerusalem who believed in Jesus as the Messiah did not follow the Jewish cult completely. We hear that they attended the temple together. But we do not notice that they also attended the synagogue unless we interpret the remark, "they will put you out of the synagogues" (John 16:2; cf. also 12:42), to suggest that they first attended the synagogue and then were thrown out of it against their will. They may also have had their own places to assemble from the very beginning, where they broke bread together (Acts 2:46). But in either case, their conduct would have been similar to that of the Jewish parties, such as the Zealots, the Qumran community, or even the Pharisees, who participated in the common worship and also had private gathering places. Even their claim of being the true Israel was not unrivaled by other groups. The only fundamental difference lies in their recognition of Jesus as the Messiah. This difference had profound implications for the Christian worship.

b. The church and its worship

At first the Christian community in Jerusalem participated in the Jewish cult, as we conclude from the remark that "day by day, attending the temple together and breaking bread in their homes, they partook of food with glad and generous hearts" (Acts 2:46). This notice, which presumably depicts a very early stage, also shows that the Christians assembled in private homes for common meals that were consumed with joyous manner and with generosity for the poorer members. Initially these common meals may have been part of the Eucharistic fellowship. Very likely we have a description of such a worship in Acts 2:42 where Luke writes: "And they devoted themselves to the apostles' teaching and fellowship, to the breaking of bread and the prayers."

The service opened with instructions (cf. Acts 20:7) for which, when possible, the letters of the apostles were read. It is noteworthy that four of Paul's letters (1 Thess. 5:26; 1 Cor. 16:20; 2 Cor. 13:12; and Rom. 16:16) as well as 1 Peter conclude with the command to kiss each other with a holy kiss or the kiss of love (1 Peter 5:14). This mutual kiss which is only mentioned in these places in the New Testament is the sign and the seal of the forgiveness extended to the members of the community and the forgiveness in turn received by them.[30] Thus forgiveness is the proper preparation for the celebration of the meal. This is also shown in 1 Cor. 16:22 where the formula: "If any one has no love for the Lord, let him be accursed," points to the need of forgiveness. The sequence "Our Lord, come!" then introduces the eschatological expectation anticipated and celebrated in the Eucharist. We have seen from Acts 2:46 that the meal concluded with the singing of psalms and with prayers.[31] The custom of extending forgiveness is also attested to by the Eucharistic liturgy of the early church in Rome, Egypt, and Africa.

The instruction through apostles is followed by the fellowship or the common meal or love feast *(agape)* which in turn is followed by the breaking of bread or the Eucharist. The breaking of bread was not a complete meal but consisted only of the opening and closing rites of the (Passover) meal. While in Acts 2:42 a distinction is made between the common meal (fellowship) and the Eucharist, we notice in Acts 20:7f. that the Eucharist is celebrated after midnight, evidently separated from the common meal. One of the reasons for separating the *agape* feast from the Eucharist becomes apparent from Paul's discussion with the Christians in Corinth (1 Cor. 11:17-22). The common meal was no longer a time for sharing but became an orgy of self-indulgence (cf. also Jude 12). Paul even suggests that the meal should be eaten at home as not to offend others and violate the sacramental character of the Eucharist. The narration of the Lord's Supper according to Mark seems to indicate also that the Eucharist was usually preceded by a meal when it says: "And as they were eating, he took bread, and blessed, and broke it, and gave it to them" (Mark 14:22). The common meals were, however, too popular to die out.

Separated from the Eucharist the common meals became semicultic *agape* feasts at which one came to enjoy table fellowship with other Christians. They were followed by biblical readings, singing of psalms, and discussions.[32] In Rome the *agape* feasts could also consist of feeding the poor in one of the more affluent houses or simply by giving the poor food packages which they could take home and eat there. While the common meals are largely fellowship meals and attempt to express the concerns for each other's physical well-being, the Eucharist bears clearly cultic features.

To some degree the Eucharist goes back to the Last Supper that Jesus celebrated with his disciples. We have the text of the so-called Last Supper in four versions: [33]

(1) The oldest document in which words of the Lord's Supper are recorded is Paul's first letter to the Corinthians, most likely dating back to the spring of A.D. 54 (1 Cor. 11:23-25).

(2) The second oldest literary source is Mark 14:22-25 which we find again with minor modifications in Matthew 26:26-29.

(3) A very peculiar tradition is preserved in Luke 22:15-20, since there also exists a shorter version of the same text which stops abruptly after "And he took bread, and when he had given thanks he broke it and gave it to them saying, 'This is my body' " (Luke 22:19). The longer version is analogous to the version in Mark, Matthew, and Paul. It is impossible to assume that with this shorter version Luke would advocate the communion with bread only, since two verses earlier Luke mentions of Jesus that "He took a cup, and when he had given thanks he said, 'Take this and divide it among yourselves' " (Luke 22:17). This explicitly states communion with wine. Most likely the longer text is the older one, since also more of the older manuscripts witness to its existence. The shorter text may owe its existence to the attempt to recite only the beginning words of the institution of the Lord's Supper and therefore leave the uninitiated in the dark concerning its exact meaning.

(4) Though the Gospel of John does not mention the words of institution explicitly, it mentions the words concerning the bread in the context of one of Jesus' discourses (cf. John 6:51c).

The fact that the Lord's Supper is mentioned in all the major New Testament sources indicates the importance of this tradition. Yet how far can we trace back this tradition? While Matthew seems to present a variation of Mark, Luke seems to be more original than Paul. But the many Semitisms in Mark indicate that it is still older than Luke. Yet even Mark seems to be an emendation of an earlier version. Therefore it may be safe to assume that we have at least two (Mark and Paul) or perhaps even three (John) distinct strands of the tradition concerning the Lord's Supper, all going back to originally Hebrew and Aramaic sources that coincide in their basic content. This leaves open the possibility that we have a common tradition that has reliably preserved some of what Jesus actually said during his last meal.[34]

What makes this Last Supper so special that it decidedly shaped Christian worship? First we dare not isolate the Last Supper from the meals that Jesus shared daily with his disciples and from those he shared with sinners and other people of dubious reputation (cf. Luke 15:2). Very likely the meals that the first Christians celebrated were a continuation of the daily meals that the disciples had with their master. But they were no sentimental relics. Since they culminated in the Eucharist, they are only understandable from the first Eucharist, the Last Supper. Since the

Last Supper was a Passover meal, in analogy to the Jewish Passover at Jesus' time, it had a twofold aspect.[35] (1) It commemorated the gracious preservation of the houses that were marked with the blood of the Passover lambs (Exod. 12) and redemption from the bondage in Egypt. (2) It looked forward to the coming redemption. "In this night they were redeemed and in the same night they once will be redeemed," says Rabbi Jehoshua ben Chananja in his comments to Exodus 12:42.[36] The Passover night is the night of the coming of the Messiah and the Passover month is the month of the first and the last redemption.[37] Jesus did not just celebrate the Passover with his disciples but, as Luke 22:14-20 tells us, he explicitly announced that he would drink no more from the wine (and eat from the bread) until God had publicly erected his kingdom. This fasting coupled with the eschatological emphasis must have been firmly imprinted in the memory of the disciples. But there are other surprise moments contained in Jesus' Last Supper.

As head of the house Jesus presided over the Passover and presumably was the homilist, explaining the meaning of the unleavened bread, the bitter herbs, the fruit sauce, and the lamb. Usually this was done by referring to them as symbols of the redemption from Egypt and signs of future redemption. After this homily the table prayer was said over the bread, the lamb was eaten, and a thanksgiving prayer over the cup followed. Surprisingly Jesus added to the first prayer: "This is my body which is given for you. Do this in remembrance of me" (Luke 22:19). And then added to the second: "This cup which is poured out for you is the new covenant in my blood" (Luke 22:20). To the surprise of his disciples, Jesus talked about himself as a sacrifice. He anticipated his death and interpreted it as the eschatological Passover sacrifice. He died in a substitutionary way and therefore made the final salvation possible through a new covenant.

In the eating and drinking the disciples participated in the salvific activity of his death. But he also commanded them to continue this practice "in remembrance of me." This does not mean that one should merely remember Jesus' death, though this is certainly not excluded. The celebration of the Lord's Supper included the plea to God that Christ's sacrifice was not in vain. God was reminded what has happened on the cross so that he would bring his salvation to completion. Thus the celebration of the Eucharist is a continuous reminder for God and his people of the salvation yet to be completed. In this hoping anticipation the daily Eucharist resumed and identified the hope, connected with the Passover.

Most likely, the first Christians also celebrated their own Christian

Passover. Traces of this custom can be found in the Passover meals of the Quartodecimanians, a group in Asia Minor and Syria that celebrated the Passover parallel to the Jews on the evening of the fourteenth of Nisan and the night of the fifteenth. In their observance they fasted for the Jews and read and explained the Passover narrative in Exodus.[38] The fasting was centered on the Messiah who was expected to return during a Passover night.[39] At the first cockcrow the fasting ended and the *agape* meal and then the Eucharist commenced in which the Lord was united with his followers. While the commemoration of Sunday as the day of the resurrection was not unknown in New Testament times, in these circles one felt still close enough to the origin and date of the original supper that one celebrated the Last Supper on the fourteenth of Nisan and the resurrection on the sixteenth regardless of the day of the week on which it fell.

Gradually the notion evolved of celebrating the Christian Passover on Easter Sunday, i.e., the Sunday following the 14/15 of Nisan. In 155 Bishop Polycarp of Smyrna visited Bishop Anicetus of Rome and we hear that they disagreed on the date of Easter. Polycarp represented the Quartodecimanian solution of celebrating Easter on the 16th of Nisan and Anicetus insisted on observing it the Sunday following the 16th of Nisan.[40] While they could not reach an agreement they tolerated their differences. Barely 50 years later the sentiment had changed when Bishop Victor of Rome demanded that the congregations in Asia Minor follow the Roman example. When these congregations resisted under Polycrates of Ephesus, Victor excommunicated them in 192. Though this action did not have much affect in the East, the situation was different when the Council of Nicea took official action in 325 and condemned the Quartodecimanians as Judaistic heretics. It is doubtful whether this move was done with persuasive theological reasoning. More likely it was an action that strengthened the power of the bishop in Rome and therefore paved the way for the introduction of the papacy.

While the reference to the first day of the week (Matt. 28:1) at which Mary Magdalene and Mary discovered the empty tomb might still be understood in line with the Jewish custom considering Sunday as the first day of creation, the situation is different when we hear in Rev. 1:10 of the Lord's day (Sunday). Already in the New Testament times the Sunday must have had preferred status, since Paul designated the first day of the week as the day in which the alms should be collected. It is also a day on which the Eucharist is celebrated (Acts 20:7). We do not get the impression, however, that it is some kind of Christian Sabbath on which certain work should not be performed. It was not until Emperor Constantine elevated the Sunday in 321 to a public holiday that the idea emerged that one should desist on that day from certain activities. While the church enjoyed the public sanctioning of the Sunday, it never considered it a legally binding Sabbath. Thomas Aquinas perceived this correctly when he said that the church maintains a seven day week with one day of rest "not by virtue of the precept [i.e., the Decalogue], but by the institution of the Church and the custom of Christian people." [41] We remember that Jesus and his disciples kept the Sabbath. But his protest against a work-righteous attitude towards the Sabbath (Mark 2:27f.), as well as Paul's emphasis on the Christian freedom from observing certain days, months, and seasons (Gal. 4:9f.), did not allow for the development of a Christian Sabbath. This is especially emphasized by the fact that both in the East and the West Sunday has been celebrated as the day of creation, also in terms of the new creation, but not as the (Jewish) day of rest. Yet commemorating Christ's resurrection, the Sunday always enjoyed special status.

Our consideration of the New Testament church and its worship would be incomplete if we would not at least touch briefly upon baptism, the rite that initiates one into the Christian community. There is no doubt that the first Christian community demanded a baptism "in the name of Jesus Christ" (Acts 2:38) for the forgiveness of sins.[42] Yet what significance did the Christian baptism have? In analogy to the baptism of John the Baptist, it must have been a baptism of repentance. But unlike other baptismal rites, such as the baptism by John the Baptist or the baptismal ritual in the Mandaean community, the Christian baptism was a singular act which was not repeated once uncleanliness or sin intruded again.

The New Testament impresses on us the significance of baptism. According to the synoptics, Jesus himself was baptized (Mark 1:9-11 par.) and the Gospel of John mentions that Jesus himself occasionally baptized (John 3:22; 4:1). But unlike the Lord's Supper, Christian baptism at best can be traced back to the resurrected Christ. For instance, in a later addition to Mark we hear the resurrected one say: "He who believes and is baptized will be saved" (Mark 16:16). Here baptism is viewed as a necessary precondition for salvation. The same is implied when, according to John, Jesus says to Nicodemus: "Unless one is born of water and the spirit, he cannot enter the kingdom of God" (John 3:5). When we come to the well-known command: "Go therefore and make disciples of all nations, baptizing them in the name of the Father and of the Son and of the Holy Spirit" (Matt. 28:19), again we are confronted with a word attributed to the resurrected Christ.

Why did the first Christian community put such emphasis on baptism if it was not directly commanded by Jesus of Nazareth? Perhaps Paul can help us a step further when he writes: "We were buried therefore with him by baptism into death, so that as Christ was raised from the dead by the glory of the Father, we too might walk in newness of life" (Rom. 6:4). This means that the Christian baptism is the appropriation of Jesus' death and resurrection. As such it could not date back to Jesus of Nazareth. Yet if his death and resurrection can be appropriated to the individual Christian, we need not be surprised that the Christian community saw a special significance in this rite. With his understanding of baptism Paul also gave the saying of Jesus new meaning when he said: "If any man would come after me, let him deny himself and take up his cross and follow me" (Mark 8:34). When the one baptized is sealed with the sign of the cross, he/she receives the salvational benefits of the cross of Christ and at the same time becomes Christ's property.

The Christian baptism is not just a baptism of repentance. According to the evangelist this was already predicted by John the Baptist when he said: "I baptize you with water for repentance, but he who is coming after me . . . will baptize you with the Holy Spirit and with fire" (Matt. 3:11). Since the fire is used here metaphorically to allude to the last judgment, this would mean that Christ's baptism will lead beyond the final judgment to life eternal. It is also a baptism that will endow its recipients with the gift of the Holy Spirit. For instance, when Paul comes to Ephesus he finds a group of people there who were baptized by John the Baptist (Acts 19:1-7). As soon as they were baptized again in the name of Jesus Christ and Paul had laid his hands upon them, they received the gift of the Spirit. Occasionally there seems to be a distinction between the actual baptism (for repentance) and the laying on of hands (imparting of the Spirit) (Acts 8:12-14ff.; Acts 10:44-48).[43] The impartation of the Holy Spirit and baptism are, however, closely connected, as shown by the fact that once the Spirit was poured out at Pentecost, the apostles started to baptize. From then on, baptism was a regular consequence of the missionary activity of the Christian community. Even Paul, who was encountered by the Lord on his way to Damascus, still had to be baptized to receive the Spirit (Acts 9:17f.).

Though Paul admits that he was not the first to baptize (Rom. 6:3), he gives final shape to the biblical understanding of baptism. In Romans 6 he used terminology borrowed from mystery cults to describe baptism. In the mystery cults of imperial Rome the idea of death and rebirth of the one dedicated to the godhead played an important role.[44] The destiny of the godhead, death, and resurrection, was often understood as being transferable to the believer. Paul uses this terminology to show that our baptism enables us to participate in Christ's death and resurrection. But he does not talk about our initiation and consecration as would be expected in mystery religions. Contrary to an understanding of death and rebirth of the godhead in terms of cyclical repetition, Paul also tells us that we are made part of the singular and unique historical event of the death and resurrection of Christ. This incorporation enables us to be certain of our new life which we enjoy already and of our coming resurrection. If we are in Christ, Paul says, we should show forth this new creation in our daily life (Rom. 6:4). The indicative of our new existence of freedom from sin therefore leads Paul to the ethical imperative of living this new existence.

In talking about baptism, Paul is not tied to one particular kind of imagery or terminology. To explain its significance he can also use ontological terminology saying, "for as many of you as were baptized into Christ have put on Christ" (Gal. 3:27). Or, "therefore if any one is in Christ, he is a new creation" (2 Cor. 5:17). Paul even uses baptismal images without explicitly mentioning baptism when he says that when God established us in Christ, he put his seal upon us (so that we are his property), and gave us his Spirit in our hearts as a guarantee (2 Cor. 1:21f.). For Paul, baptism has no magic dimension that it would automatically guarantee our salvation. It is always possible for us to break away from the covenant that God establishes with us in baptism (cf. 1 Cor. 10:1-5).

Baptism was never conceived of in the New Testament as an individualistic act occurring only between Christ and us. Through our incorporation into Christ we are all one (Gal. 3:28), "for by one Spirit we were all baptized into one body" (1 Cor. 12:12). Baptism therefore establishes the unity between the Christians and makes us part of the body of Christ, i.e., the church visible and celestial. Baptism is incorporation into the visible body of Christ. To understand the full implications of this incorporation, we must briefly consider the Jewish baptism of proselytes according to which the Christian baptism is patterned at this point.[45] When pagans converted to Judaism their children were baptized too. But if children were born after the parents had converted, they did not need to be baptized, because they had become members of the Jewish community through their parents. Concerning baptism into the Christian faith, we find a very peculiar situation in the New Testament. While the time span covered there would have allowed for second generation baptisms, we have no reports in the New Testament of the baptism of descendants, whether infants or adults, of those who had already been Christians. Would this mean that, in analogy to Jewish proselyte baptism, Christian baptism is only applicable to those who enter the Christian community from outside, but not to those who have been born within it?

Paul tells the Christians at Corinth that "the unbelieving husband is consecrated through his wife, and the unbelieving wife is consecrated through her husband. Otherwise, your children would be unclean, but as it is they are holy" (1 Cor. 7:14). We might want to conclude from this statement that a child being sanctified through its parents, need not be baptized. Yet Paul does not address here the issue of baptism. He simply states that non-Christian members of Christian families are already within the Christian sphere of influence and not under the influence of foreign and demonic powers.[46] We might infer then that with infants, who are already within the Christian sphere of influence, this implicit relationship to the Christian faith would be formalized and officially sanctioned as soon as possible. This means that unlike adults, infants should be baptized without waiting until a formal desire for conversion would be expressed. The same, of course, holds for infants of adults who are converting to the Christian faith.

That infants of those who converted to Christianity were baptized is indirectly attested with the formula that adults were baptized "with all their family" (cf. Acts 16:15-33). As the Pauline imperative following the baptismal indicative implies, faith is a necessary result of baptism. But this does not mean that adults were baptized indiscriminately. The formula *ti kolyei* (what prevents me) that occurs frequently in connection with the conversion baptisms (cf. Acts 8:36; 11:17) presupposes some kind of examination about possible hindrances to baptism. An insert in part of the Western textual tradition in the story of the baptism of the minister of Candace points in the same direction. After the minister asks: "What prevents me?", the text continues: "If you believe with all your heart you may [be baptized]" and the response is: "I believe that Jesus Christ is the Son of God" (Acts 8:37). A creedal confession in Jesus as the Lord (cf. Rom. 10:9) seems to be a necessary part of an adult baptism. This does not mean that such a confession was not made when an infant was baptized. It then had to be spoken by adults (members of the believing community) on behalf of the infant.

3. Unity and diversity

While the worshiping community finds its unity in Christ, even a casual reading of the New Testament will show us that already the first Christian community was subject to clashes of opinions and outright disagreements. The question we want to pursue now is whether there is some kind of unity in this diversity or whether the diversity itself is a constitutive ingredient of the Christian proclamation.

The German New Testament scholar Ernst Käsemann claimed that "the tensions between Jewish Christian and Gentile Christian churches, between Paul and the Corinthian enthusiasts, between John and early catholicism are as great as those of our own day."[47] But Käsemann does not want to imply that the early Christian community was governed by chaos. All changes, tensions, and contradictions notwithstanding, he asserts early Christianity proclaimed one church, but not in the sense of a monolithic organization. Rather, the unity of the church was conceived of as an eschatological phenomenon in which the early church participated through the reality and truth of the Holy Spirit.

Our question is not whether Käsemann overstates his case by pointing out the analogy between our contemporary ecclesiastical pluralism and that of early Christianity, but rather whether he did not underestimate the difficulties and divergencies in nascent Christendom. After all, only a very select corpus of Scripture is represented in the New Testament, namely those writings that were accepted as normative. For the currents represented in the New Testament Käsemann's statement is certainly correct. In the light of the tensions between "Hebrews" and "Hellenists" (Acts 6:1), between Paul and Gnostic enthusiasts (1 Cor. 4:8-14), and between the weak and the strong (Rom. 15:1), we must considerably tone down Luke's attempt to portray the first Christian community as a homogeneous unity (cf. Acts 2:43-47).

The first Christian community had to develop its own communal structure, its own governance, its own belief system, and its own sacred writings. As we have seen,

> the Apostolic Age is full of embodiments of purposes and principles of the most instructive kind: but the responsibility of choosing the means was left for ever to the Ecclesia itself, and to each Ecclesia guided by

ancient precedent on the one hand and adaptation to present and future needs on the other. The lesson-book of the Ecclesia, and of every Ecclesia, is not a law but a history.[48]

The church realizes that it is part of the history of God's people, culminating in the history of Jesus of Nazareth, and being continued in the presence of the resurrected Lord. God in Christ is the focal point and unifying force within all diversity. This becomes especially clear when Paul appeals for unity to various groups and congregations.[49] "There are varieties of gifts, but the *same Spirit;* and there are varieties of service, but the *same Lord;* and there are varieties of working, but . . . the *same God"* (1 Cor. 12:4f.), argues Paul. We were all baptized into *one body* of Christ, the church, and we participate in *one Spirit* (1 Cor. 12:13). The God who gives steadfastness and encouragement enables the Christians to live together in harmony in accordance with the words of their Lord Jesus Christ (cf. Rom. 15:5). There is *"one* Lord, *one* faith, *one* baptism, *one* God and Father of us all" (Eph. 4:5f.), Paul also reiterates to the Christians in Ephesus.

This unity in Christ that Paul expresses was experienced by the Christian community and it transcended all other differences. It is therefore difficult to see in the New Testament a justifiable basis for American denominationalism. All its serious tensions notwithstanding, the church of the New Testament time felt tied together through a bond of unity. For instance, Paul does not hesitate to collect gifts from the congregations he supervises "for the poor among the saints in Jerusalem" (Rom. 15:26). In turn Paul tells the congregations that the saints "under the test of this service they will glorify God by your obedience in acknowledging the gospel of Christ, and by the generosity of your contribution for them and for all others" (2 Cor. 9:13). Similarly, the mutual support among the members of the community (cf. Acts 4:36f.) and the caring for the widows among the members of the Christians in Jerusalem (Acts 6:1) indicate that there was a bond among the Christians that endured all tensions.

The unity of the Christian community is also expressed through the use of the term *ekklesia* (church). In the Book of Acts singular and plural use of the word *church* are intermingled.[50] For instance, Luke writes that the churches were strengthened in faith (Acts 16:5); he reports about the church at Antioch (Acts 13:1), and he tells us that Paul appointed elders "in every church" (Acts 14:23). The usage of the term church does not indicate that the one church is divided into churches or that an aggregate of churches results in *the* church. It is rather that in different places *the* church is manifested in local congregations. Whether it is the Hellenistic congregation in Antioch or the Jewish congregation in Jerusalem, they are all covered under the same term. Paul uses the terms church and churches as promiscuously as does Luke. For instance, he tells the congregation in Corinth that speaking in tongues should occur in such a manner that the church is edified (1 Cor. 14:4), he tells them that he teaches everywhere in every church (1 Cor. 4:17), and he introduces his principles "in all the churches" (1 Cor. 7:17).

It is also significant that he writes "to the church of God which is at Corinth" (1 Cor. 1:2), meaning the church as it is manifested in the Christian community in Corinth.[51] The church is always manifested in local congregations, bearing local flavor and adjusting to local situations. Diversity therefore is a necessary ingredient to make the church truly local. The individual congregation appropriates that which constitutes unity, God in Christ Jesus, and allows him to speak to its local needs (cf. 1 Thess. 2:14 which is a striking illustration of this principle). However, when the unifying principle, God in Christ Jesus, no longer comes to expression clearly, a separation from those who obscure the name and power of Christ is necessary (cf. 1 John 2:19). As 2 John suggests, heretics who deny God in Christ Jesus should not be accepted in anyone's house and even greetings should not be exchanged with them (2 John 10f.). Such separation was especially necessary in the case of the Judaistic Christians.

At the apostles' council in Jerusalem, Judaistic Christians attempted to enforce circumcision and the keeping of the law of Moses for all Christians (Acts 15:5).[52] Perhaps the false brethren that Paul encounters (Gal. 2:4) are also Judaistic Christians, and certainly they are those who are "zealous for the law" in Jerusalem and who want to accuse Paul of teaching apostasy.[53] Judaistic Christians therefore believe in Jesus as the Messiah. Yet they assert that admission to the true Israel is only possible through circumcision and obedience to the law. Though James, the brother of Jesus and head of the Christian community in Jerusalem, became the patron saint of the Judaistic Christians, he hardly agreed with them. As we see from the negotiations at the apostles' council in Jerusalem, he leaned much more toward Paul, perhaps pursuing a mediating position. Yet after he was stoned by the Jewish authorities in A.D. 62-63,[54] and the dissension of Judaistic Christians with both Jews and non-Judaistic Christians became more evident, they emigrated to Pella in Eastern Jordan in A.D. 66 or 67. This move was also partly an attempt to avoid the emerging war with the Romans that led to the destruction of Jerusalem in A.D. 70.

Of course, not all Jewish Christians were Judaistic Christians. In the middle of the second century Justin Martyr still tells of two kinds of Jewish Christians: those who stay in the church and emphasize the Jewish elements in Christian teachings and customs, and those who do not associate with non-Jewish Christians unless they accept the Jewish law.[55] This latter branch were the actual Judaistic Christians. They also preferred to be called Ebionites or the poor, mindful of the blessings that Jesus pronounced upon the poor (cf. Matt. 5:3), and were perhaps the poor in the first Christian community. Their opponents, however, explained their name in a more derogatory way and considered them as the poor in mind or those with a poor faith in Christ. Occasionally they were also called Nazoreans, derived from the Hebrew *nasar* meaning to observe, which indicates that they observed secret traditions.

In various parts of the East, such as Cyprus and Syria, Judaistic Christians survived well into the fourth century A.D., often portraying decidedly Gnostic features as the polemics of the early Christian writers indicate. Yet the Judaistic Christians had not much of a future. The Jews soon disagreed with them because of their faith in Jesus as the Messiah and in his resurrection, and because of their sacraments. But the non-Judaistic Christians also disagreed with them because of their observance of the Jewish law. Above all their views were offensive to non-Judaistic Christians who believed that Jesus was adopted as Son of God in his baptism because it seemed to indicate that his death and resurrection had no salvific significance. Judaistic Christians believed that Jesus was simply a saint since he fulfilled the law, and if anyone else would have done the same, he could also have become a Christ.[56] Nevertheless, Judaistic Christianity seems to have survived outside Christianity and decidedly influenced the Islamic faith.[57] For instance, Judaistic Christian influence can be seen in the Muslim food laws, in the emphasis on purification, in Mohammed's idea of bringing the true law, in his evaluation of Jesus as prophet and as God's word *(logos)* and in his vehement denial of Jesus' divinity. Since the unifying power, namely God in Christ Jesus, was no longer present to a significant degree in Judaistic Christianity, it excluded itself from the Christian unity and went its own way.

NOTES

1. So rightly Nils Dahl, *Des Volk Gottes*, 183.
2. Jürgen Moltmann, *The Church in the Power of the Spirit. A Contribution to Messianic Ecclesiology*, trans. M. Kohl (New York: Harper, 1977) 148, claims that "the church is not the organization that succeeds Israel in salvation history. It does not take Israel's place." Some might perhaps disagree with Moltmann on this point. But when he continues that the church "cannot have any desire to push Israel out," he is certainly correct.
3. Cf. for the following Dahl, 182.
4. Cf. for the following Hermann Strathmann, *laos*, in TDNT, 4:54.
5. Justin Martyr, *The First Apology* 1.67, FaCh 1:107.
6. Cf. Ernst Haenchen, *The Acts of the Apostles*, 233f., who argues against the abolition of private property among the Jerusalem Christians.
7. Ernst Bloch, *Das Prinzip Hoffnung* (Frankfurt: Suhrkamp, 1969) 3:1488.
8. Cf. for the following the excellent book by Martin Hengel, *Property and Riches in the Early Church. Aspects of a Social History of Early Christianity*, trans. J. Bowden (Philadelphia: Fortress, 1974) 39ff.
9. Cf. Joachim Jeremias, *Jerusalem in the Time of Jesus*, 140ff., for details of the famine and its exact dating.
10. Cf. Otto Michel, *Der Brief an die Römer*, 11th ed. (Göttingen: Vandenhoeck & Ruprecht, 1957) 333, who concedes this possibility in his exegesis of Rom. 15:26.
11. So Hermann W. Beyer, *diakonos*, in TDNT, 2:89f.
12. Cf. Haenchen, 267, to this passage, who arrives at the same conclusion.
13. Cf. Beyer, *diakonos*, 2:90f.
14. Cf. Adolf von Harnack, *The Expansion of Christianity in the First Three Centuries*, trans. and ed. J. Moffatt (Freeport, NY: Books for Libraries, 1972 [1904/5]), 1:427-35.
15. Cf. Hans Lietzmann, *The Beginnings of the Christian Church*, trans. B. L. Woolf (New York: Scribner's, 1937) 190, who answers this question in the affirmative.
16. Eduard Schweizer, *Church Order in the New Testament*, trans. F. Clarke (London: SCM, 1961) 186.
17. Cf. for the following the excellent comments by Rudolf Schnackenburg, *The Church in the New Testament*, 26ff.
18. Cf. the insightful comments by Günther Bornkamm, *presbyteros*, in TDNT, 6:663.
19. Karl Heinrich Rengstorf, *apostolos*, in TDNT, 1:439f., rightly mentions the similarity of the mission consciousness of Paul and Jeremiah. Yet we should also note that Paul is not just a prophet sent by God. He is also a bearer of tradition and one who acts in harmony and consultation with the other apostles.
20. So rightly Heinrich Schlier, *Der Brief an die Galater*, 11 ed. (Göttingen: Vandenhoeck & Ruprecht, 1951) 35ff., in his comments on Gal. 2:2.
21. Cf. for the following Hans Conzelmann, *1 Corinthians*, trans. J. W. Leitch (Philadelphia: Fortress, 1975) 195, in his exegesis of 1 Cor. 11:23a.
22. Yet Walter Schmithals, *The Office of Apostle in the Early Church*, trans. J. E. Steely (Nashville: Abingdon, 1969) 262ff., in his attempt at explaining the origin of the apostolate of the twelve primarily as a result of Hellenistic Christianity in its struggle with the Gnosis, diminishes unduly the historical roots of the apostolate and overemphasizes its later anti-Gnostic resurgence.
23. So Günther Bornkamm, *presbyteros*, in TDNT, 6:663.
24. Cf. ibid.
25. So Schnackenburg, 59f.
26. Cf. Dahl, 177, who points out the exaggeration in Acts 4 and mentions that the picture is quite different in the synoptic tradition.

27. For a good interpretation of this so-called decree, cf. the comments by Haenchen, 468ff.
28. Justin Martyr, *Dialoge with Trypho* 34f., FaCh 1:200f.
29. Minucius Felix, *The Octavius* 30, ANFa 4:192.
30. For the following cf. the perceptive comments by Gustav Stählin, *phileo,* in TDNT, 9:136 and 139f.
31. Cf. for a good description of the early Christian worship Joachim Jeremias, *The Eucharistic Words of Jesus,* trans. N. Perrin (Philadelphia: Fortress, 1977) 117ff.
32. Cf. for the following Hans Lietzmann, *The Founding of the Church Universal. A History of the Early Church,* trans. B. L. Woolf (New York: Scribner's, 1950), 2:125; and Tertullian, *Apology* 39.16f. FaCh 10:101, who tells us about the *agape* feasts among the Christians in Rome.
33. Cf. for the following the exhaustive treatment by Jeremias, *Eucharistic Words,* 138-203.
34. So ibid., 203, attempts to trace back to Jesus himself the core of the Eucharistic words.
35. Cf. ibid., 206f.
36. As quoted in Hermann L. Strack and Paul Billerbeck, *Das Evangelium nach Matthäus erläutert aus Talmud und Midrasch* (Munich: C. H. Beck, 1922) 85, in their comments on Matt. 2:15.
37. August Strobel, *"Die Passa-Erwartung als urchristliches Problem in Lc 17:20f.,"* *Zeitschrift für die neutestamentliche Wissenschaft* 49 (1958): 157-96, has developed very convincingly the connection between the redemption from Egypt and the redemption through the coming Messiah, a feature which was continued in the understanding of the Eucharist.
38. Bernhard Lohse, "Quartadezimaner," in RGG³, 5:733.
39. Cf. *Epistula Apostolorum* 15-26, trans. H. Duensing, in E. Hennecke and W. Schneemelcher, *New Testament Apocrypha,* trans. R. McL. Wilson (London: Lutterworth, 1963), 1:199-209.
40. Eusebius, *The History of the Church from Christ to Constantine* 5.24, trans. G. A. Williamson (Minneapolis: Augsburg, 1975) 231f., adduces many details to this conflict.
41. Thomas Aquinas, *The Summa Theologica²* q 122 a 4 r 4, trans. the Fathers of the English Dominican Province (London: Burns Oates & Washbourne, 1935), 12:188.
42. So Schnackenburg, 45f.
43. Cf. Oscar Cullmann, *Baptism in the New Testament,* trans. J. K. S. Reid (Naperville, IL: Allenson, 1950) 11f.; and cf. also Haenchen, 304, who comments on Acts 8:17 that for the Lukan congregations baptism and laying on of hands formed a unity. Yet Luke distinguishes here for other reasons the baptism through Philip from the laying on of hands through the apostles Peter and John.
44. Cf. for the following the excellent comments in Michel, 139f.
45. Cf. for the following Cullmann, *Baptism,* 24ff.
46. Cf. Conzelmann, *1 Corinthians,* 122, in his exegesis of 1 Cor. 7:14. For a different, but less convincing, exegesis of this passage cf. Cullmann, *Baptism,* 45.
47. For this and the following see Ernst Käsemann, "Unity and Multiplicity in the New Testament Doctrine of the Church," in *New Testament Questions of Today,* trans. W. J. Montague (Philadelphia: Fortress, 1969) 256f.
48. So very perceptively already Fenton J. A. Hort, *The Christian Ecclesia. A Course of Lectures on the Early History and Early Conceptions of the Ecclesia and Four Sermons* (London: Macmillan, 1898), pp. 232f.; and cf. the instructive book by W. D. Davies, *Christian Origins and Judaism* (London: Darton, Longman & Todd, 1962), who brings the above quote on p. 229.
49. Cf. for the following the excellent comments by Schnackenburg, 129f., who states that the common confession of their Lord and Messiah binds the Christians together.
50. Cf. for the following the illuminating comments in Schmidt, *ekklesia,* in TDNT, 3:505.

51. Cf. to this passage ibid., 3:507.
52. Cf. for the following the excellent description in Hans Joachim Schoeps, *Jewish Christianity. Factual Disputes in the Early Church,* trans. D. R. A. Hare (Philadelphia: Fortress, 1969) 18f.
53. Cf. also Haenchen, 608f., in his exegesis of Acts 21:20f., who does not identify them directly as Judaistic Christians.
54. Cf. Flavius Josephus, *Jewish Antiquities* 20.9.1, trans. L. H. Feldman, in *Flavius Josephus,* 9 vols. (London: Heinemann, 1969), 9:497, who provides us with details to this incident.
55. Justin Martyr, *Dialogue with Trypho* 47, FaCh 1:218.
56. So Hippolytus, *Philosophumena or the Refutation of All Heresies* 7.34, trans. F. Legge (New York: Macmillan, 1921), 2:93.
57. Schoeps, 138ff., provides detailed information.

3

One Holy, Catholic, and Apostolic Church

THE PERIOD IN WHICH THE NEW TESTAMENT WRITINGS ORIGINATED was formative for the church. We have seen that the church emerged as an entity independent of Judaism but nevertheless deeply rooted in it. Once the church had loosened its ties to Judaism, the next big step was to acquire a thought structure commensurate with its predominantly non-Jewish mission. It was becoming evident that the church was evolving into a global structure extending from one part of the Roman Empire to the other.

The adaptation to different thought patterns was a mixed blessing. While it provided the opportunity for contextualizing the Christian faith, it also opened the danger of compromising Christian beliefs with popular religious and philosophical ideas. Therefore the notion has been introduced that the acute Hellenization, i.e., the movement of Christianity into the Hellenistic civilization, undermined the Hebrew understanding of God and Christ. For instance, the German theologian Adolf von Harnack judged that this process turned Christianity into a monotheistic religion for the Greco-Roman world.[1] There is truth in this statement. However, we must also consider that without opening itself to the Hellenistic and Roman world and its thought forms, the Christian church would have remained a religion of an ethnic minority. Yet entering this foreign world brought with it the threat that the Christian faith would become absorbed into it, thereby losing its missionary fervor.

In the 19th century Edwin Hatch had ventured a remarkable justification for this Hellenization process, though slightly different from ours, when he claimed: "It is an argument of the divine life of Christianity that it has been able to assimilate so much that was at first alien to it. It is an argument for the truth of much of that which has been assimilated, that it has been strong enough to oust many of the earlier elements."[2] As Hatch noticed, this kind of reasoning may not prove the perennial necessity of the elements assimilated, but it strongly points to the propriety of this process at that time.

Yet another danger loomed on the horizon. A freshly emerging institution that grew as rapidly as the Christian church, was prone to become an aggregate of various local churches. In the long run they might pursue their own line of development to such an extent that a unifying principle would hardly be recognizable. To combat these threats, and at the same time to grasp the opportunities that had opened, the church (1) looked for a commonly accepted canon of sacred writings that served as a basis for preaching and teaching; it (2) clarified its own understanding of its unifying power, God in Christ Jesus; and it (3) developed a centralized teaching hierarchy that stood in continuity with its apostolic roots. Canon, dogma or creed, and apostolic office became the guardians and growing edges of the one, holy, catholic, and apostolic church.

1. The formation of the canon

The term canon is derived from the Hebrew *kaneh* meaning cane. In Greek it usually stands for rule, norm, or guideline. This is the meaning that Paul attributes to the word when he says: "Peace and mercy be upon all who walk by this rule" (Gal. 6:16). In the third century, canon still meant normative. Finally, in the fourth century we hear of the canon as the books of the Old and New Testaments.[3]

The formation of the canon was provoked primarily by two reasons—the death of the first-generation eyewitnesses, and attempts of suspicious-looking movements to introduce their own sacred writings or collections into Christian life. For instance, in the second century, Marcion presented a canon that consisted of the Gospel of Luke, "purified" from all Old Testament references, and thirteen similarly amended letters of Paul. Yet being able to produce his own canon did not help him. Marcion was excommunicated in A.D. 144 by his congregation in Rome. Similarly, the claim by individuals or groups that a certain apocalypse or gospel had been written by an apostle, such as Peter, did not assure its acceptance into the canon. Besides the historical claim that a scripture was written at least by a disciple of an apostle, it had to meet the theological criterion of being within the lines of the rule of faith. Yet most of all, to be considered trustworthy it had to be accepted as scripture by Christian congregations in a certain geographical region, such as Asia Minor, or in the whole church. There are actually three stages that we can discern in the formalization of the canon: (1) the rise of certain Christian writings to the status of scripture, (2) the forming of scripture into closed subcollections, such as the gospels or the Old Testament prophets, and (3) the final formation and standardization of the canonical lists.

The Bible that Jesus and his contemporaries were familiar with was the Law and the Prophets. Around 275 B.C. the Pentateuch had been translated into Greek and in the next two centuries most of the other books were also translated into the Greek vernacular. Some books originally written in Greek also gained prominence in Judaism such as the Books of Maccabees and the Wisdom of Solomon. While the Sadducees preferred to accept only the Torah, it was not until the Synod of Jamnia (around A.D. 100) that the Pharisees finally decided on the exact number of books in the Hebrew Scriptures. As we have seen in the Dead Sea Scrolls there were books in circulation that were not accepted into the Hebrew canon. Secondly, from the quotations of Hebrew Scriptures at Qumran we realize that the Greek translation of the Septuagint is certainly not inferior to the Masoretic Hebrew Old Testament text.[4] It is significant that the church accepted the Septuagint canon, including the Old Testament apocrypha. This acceptance reveals that the Old Testament references used in the New Testament did not need to be translated but were already available in Greek.

The earliest New Testament writings are the letters of Paul. The first mention of the Gospels is in a remark by Justin Martyr, who died around 165 in Rome and who called them memories written by apostles and those who followed them, containing the sayings of Christ.[5] He also tells us that they were called Gospels and read together with the Prophets on Sunday.[6] When Justin Martyr cites from non-canonical materials, he shows his acquaintance with a wider gospel tradition than that of the four Gospels. Yet the church did not want to include more than four Gospels. Perhaps this was done to indicate an analogy to the four prophetic books of the Old Testament, Isaiah, Jeremiah, Ezekiel, and the twelve minor prophets. The Book of Daniel was not counted as a prophetic book in the Old Testament. To accept a fifth gospel would have borne too much analogy to the five books of the Pentateuch. It would have opened the possibility to see the Gospels and therefore the message of Jesus as the new law.[7]

While the main body of the New Testament canon was agreed upon relatively soon, its periphery remained undecided for several centuries. In the Greek church, for instance, the Letter to the Hebrews and the Letter of James were not accepted. In the Syrian East, the book of Revelation, the Letter of Jude, and the shorter catholic letters were treated with distrust. On the other hand, some Greek congregations liked the Shepherd of Hermas, the Letter of Barnabas, and 1 Clement. In Syria, both letters of Clement were held in high esteem. Even the Didache was accepted by some.[8] Paul, too, quoted non-canonical material when he wrote: "As it is written, 'What no eye has seen, nor ear heard, nor the heart of man conceived, what God has prepared for those who love him'" (1 Cor. 2:9). Though Origen claims that Paul used here a quote from the Apocalypse of Elijah, the quote cannot be verified in any known canonical or extra-canonical Old Testament literature.[9] We are better off with the Letter of Jude in which we find quotations from Enoch (14f.) and the Assumption of Moses (9). Both are early Gnostic writings contained in the Old Testament epigrapha. These few examples illustrate that there was considerable freedom among the New Testament writers to quote a variety of authorities as long as they conveyed the Christian message.

As far as the number of New Testament writings was concerned, the 39th Easter letter of Athanasius of Alexandria, written in 367, provided, as far as we know, the earliest list of the same Old and New Testament writings that we have today in our Bible. According to him the New Testament contains four Gospels, the Luke-Acts, fourteen letters of Paul, including Hebrews, seven catholic letters, and Revelation.[10] This list soon became normative for the Greek church. In the West too, the Synod of Rome in 382 decided under Pope Damasus to follow the list of Athanasius, though variations in the succession of the individual writings persisted. Jerome had been one of the driving forces in the West to accept the example of the East. The North African Synods of Hippo Regius in 393 and Carthage in 397 followed the example of Rome, though after extensive debate and while preserving some independence in arranging the sequence of the writings. Augustine, first as a presbyter and later as bishop, was influential in persuading the North African churches to follow the example of Rome.

The canonical list of books was not slavishly followed. For instance, up to the 5th century the Syrian church had a much shorter canon than the main church and it also used the Diatessaron for reading the gospels in worship. This Diatessaron was a synopsis of the four Gospels and had been compiled by the Syrian church father Tatian around A.D. 170. Conversely, we see from Canon Muratori, named after its discoverer, a librarian from Milan, Italy, that by the end of the second century the church in Rome affirmed a canon of scriptures which in essence contains the same writings that make up our modern New Testament canon. Of some of the others that are included the writer concedes that there is resistance to having them read at worship.[11] Our brief review seems to indicate two things: (1) The basic collections of the New Testament documents were established fairly early in the history of the church. (2) One of the prime criteria for including something into the canon was whether the writing had sufficient theological substance to be used in a worship service.

Since the canon was sacred scripture and had become the source of theological reflection, we must now ask whether it could fulfill its purpose to further and safeguard the unity of the church. Ernst Käsemann in a provocative essay, "The Canon of the New Testament and the Unity of the Church" (1951), vehemently denies that it could ever function in that capacity. The very fact, he claims, that we have four Gospels instead of one, each with its own special sources and emphasis indicates a diversity rather than a unity. There is the Letter of James next to the Pauline letters, and the Johannine eschatology next to that of Revelation to name just a few other instances of diversity. Käsemann comes to the conclusion that "the variability of the kerygma in the New Testament is an expression of the fact that in primitive Christianity a wealth of different confessions were already in existence, constantly replacing each other, combining with each other, and undergoing mutual delimination." [12] It is no longer possible, Käsemann contends, to regard the canon as the bastion dividing Judaism from early Catholicism. On the contrary, it affords a foothold to both Judaism and early Catholicism.[13] The church tended to confine God to the canon and therefore established the unity it seeks through the canon. But such unity does not exist in something as tangible as the canon. It exists only in faith.[14]

We must agree with Käsemann that the New Testament canon as such did not safeguard the unity of the church as a monolithic block. Different denominations and confessional families do indeed exist. Yet we should not overlook that for each of them the canon is the common meeting place for dialogue with other Christians. It is the source from which they can distinguish true doctrine from heresy. Once the canon was established only those doctrines were supposed to find their way into the church that could be "proved" by Scripture.[15] It is also significant that attempts to establish a uniformity within the canon did not find general acceptance. Marcion's attempt to eliminate the Old Testament references and Tatian's endeavor to present one Gospel instead of four did not find general approval. The more recent American enterprise of the Scofield Reference Bible (1909) has not met with more favor. The Presbyterian pastor Cyrus Ingerson Scofield wanted to provide in one book the proper salvation historical interpretation of the Bible together with its texts. Similarly, many other attempts, that were at one time or another preferred by certain groups, were rejected by the church in general. No denomination that can be called Christian accepts only a certain portion of the Bible while disregarding the rest.

Perhaps the church was wise when it balanced one portion of the canon by contrasting it with another scriptural segment. Of course, since this procedure always kept a certain tension within the canon, it could not create unity. Even the adoption of the doctrine of inspiration would not have guaranteed unity. As history shows, those who emphasize the Bible as the inspired word of God and those who treat it less reverently are both prone to theological escapades. The unifying power, however, came in part from that which served to select the canonical writings from what was not accepted into the canon, the creed, or the rule of faith. This means that the confession of God in Christ Jesus assured that the church preserved its sense of unity, its scriptural diversity notwithstanding. Of course, even this confession needed elaboration and could not be used as a foolproof objectification of the universal (i.e., catholic) Christian faith. In order to express the unity that was sensed and to distinguish it from deliberate or thoughtless perversions, the necessity emerged for the development of the catholic dogma.

2. The catholic dogma

In his discussions with Augustine, Vincent of Lerins summed up well the prevalent understanding of catholic dogma when he said: "In the Catholic Church itself, every care should be taken to hold fast to what has been believed everywhere, always, and by all."[16] While the catholic dogma does not exclude advancements in dogmatic reflections, it does not allow for innovations. Since there is no possibility, however, to deny that a development of the dogma has taken place, the decisive question is, what can be called legitimate development and what cannot. Is the development of the dogma simply an adulteration and distortion of the Christian faith or do we encounter here an organic and consequent growth process? It seems to border on unwarranted optimism to answer this question with an unqualified yes or no. Yet we must bear in mind the formative character of the first centuries. Whether Eastern Orthodoxy, Roman Catholicism, or Protestantism, all major confessional groups recognize in one way or another the unique authority of the Ecumenical Creeds.

The creeds constitute genuine foundation on which each ecclesiastical and theological tradition has been built and they serve as a strong bond of unity among major confessions. Small wonder that in the post-Reformation period the Lutheran theologian Georg Calixt advanced the idea of a consensus in the first five centuries, meaning that Protestants and Roman Catholics agree on the fundamental creeds of the first five centuries. The creeds are certainly interpreted differently by different traditions. For instance, Eastern Orthodox Churches grant full recognition only to the so-called Nicene Creed, while the Roman Catholic Church also embraces the Apostles' Creed and the Athanasian Creed. But the differing interpretations are not so diverse as to remove all resemblance of agreement.[17]

a. Development and function of the creeds

It would be oversimplified to reduce the Catholic dogma to one or all of the ecumenical creeds. Yet the creeds offer a well-defined and easily intelligible description of the main points of the teaching of the church. While the whole Catholic dogma as the official doctrine of the church is more comprehensive than a creed, the latter contains "a brief summary of all that you believe for eternal salvation," as Augustine rightly said.[18] Summarizing the whole biblical doctrine, the creed helps the believers to express their faith in common formulations and is a means that helps them to recognize each other as a community of believers through this commonly expressed faith.

A creed is not a timeless formulation but it is conditioned by the language and concepts of the period in which it was formulated. Since it is a response to the Christian proclamation and a summary of Scripture, the need of reformulation or adaptation does not arise from its historical and incidental origin. But it does not just function as a summary exposition of the Christian faith. In summarizing the Christian faith, it also characterizes other religious expressions as deficient or even heretical. A creed therefore contains both a profession and an apology of the Christian faith.

Since a creed could not retell the whole history of God with his people, it had to be carefully determined what should be included in such a statement. It would then serve a red thread by which one could find one's way through the entire biblical witness and a means by which one could distinguish between the center and the periphery of Scripture. Thus we find confessional formulas used in connection with baptism (cf. Acts 8:37; though lacking in some manuscripts this verse is especially well attested in Western texts) and with the regular worship service of the Christian community (cf. Phil. 2:6-11).[19] They are also used, however, when the apostles performed miracles (Acts 3:6), in situations of persecution (Acts 17:7 and 4:10), or, apologetically, when Paul attacks pagan polytheism (1 Cor. 8:5f.).

It is significant that none of the creedal statements contains sayings *of* Jesus but rather are *about* him. This means that they are not a continuation of the proclamation of Jesus, but a response to him. There is also initially a dominance of purely christological formulas, such as: "If you confess with your lips that Jesus is Lord and believe in your heart that God raised him from the dead, you will be saved" (Rom. 10:9). Standing in continuity with the Old Testament covenant community it was self-evident for the Christians to profess faith in God. Yet the Christian community was set apart from other communities of believers by their faith in Jesus as the Christ. Thus the "proclamation of Christ is the *starting-point of every Christian confession."* [20] When we encounter bipartite formulas, confessions of God and Christ, or tripartite statements that confess God, Christ, and the Spirit, both in length and in correlation to each other the confession of Christ has clear priority. For instance, God is introduced as the father of Jesus Christ and the Spirit as the prophetic voice pointing to and announcing Christ.

In the later official creeds, such as the Apostles' Creed or the Nicene Creed, the three parts referring to God, Christ, and Spirit seem to enjoy relative independence. Yet we need not be afraid that introducing God the Father before any mention is made of the Son would lead us back to a Jewish representation of Christ as secondary to God. Such suggestion would not take account of the fact that the creeds are closely tied to the development of the Christian dogma.[21] For instance, the so-called Nicene Creed, officially recorded at the Council of Chalcedon (451) and only slightly modified since the Council of Nicea (325), is of clearly anti-Arian persuasion.[22] It exhibits the intrinsic christological concern, the emphasis on the true humanity and true divinity of Christ. The so-called Athanasian Creed functions in a similar way. Contrary to its name, it cannot be traced back to Athanasius, but originated somewhere in southern Gaul or Spain around A.D. 500. Its intensely doctrinal declarations, however, do not espouse an isolated doctrine of God or of the Holy Spirit. Its concern is Christ whose significance is explained with trinitarian and christological formulations. As an exception we could list the Apostles' Creed, the earliest of the three ecumenical creeds. Here the predominance of christological interest mainly shows in the length of space devoted to Jesus Christ.

We must conclude that the main concern of the creeds is christological, to assert Jesus as Lord. The very fact, however, that we have more than one officially recognized ecumenical creed indicates that the Catholic dogma is not synonymous with one or all of the creeds. They differ considerably in their wording and are historical, and thus circumstantial pointers to the dogma. Clothed in the respective and necessary conceptuality of their time they express and direct us to the dogma. Even the creeds have a history of development. The Apostles' Creed though widely used in the second century as Irenaeus attests, received additions for several centuries thereafter.[23] We see this when the presbyter Rufinus of Aquileia writes at the beginning of the fifth century that the version used in Aquileia included "the descent to the dead," a part not heard of until then. We should not leave the impression that everything was in flux until the text of the creeds received official sanction in the fifth and sixth centuries. Though the precise text was not yet finalized in the second century, the principle of a common rule of faith was acknowledged. At the beginning of the third century the chief articles of faith had been settled so that Tertullian could state that "this rule . . . was taught by Christ, and raises amongst ourselves no other questions than those which heresies introduce, and which make men heretics." [24]

If the creeds are indeed the living expression of the church's faith and pointers to the common dogma, we cannot expect them to advance faster than the deliberations of the councils. It took the councils approximately five centuries to clarify the christological and trinitarian issues contained in the confession that Christ is Lord. This was exactly the timespan that it took to arrive at the final formulations of the ecumenical creeds.

b. God in Christ Jesus

At the center of each Christian creedal formulation stands the assertion that Jesus is Lord. Such a short confession needs clarification and expansion. Though the parameters for expansion of the creed coincide with the New Testament canon, not everything that we find in the New Testament is contained in one of the creeds. For instance, in none of the ecumenical creeds do we find reference to Jesus' wonder-working power. On the con-

trary, to fight the docetic and Gnostic ideas of people such as Marcion and
Valentinus, we hear in the Apostles' Creed that Jesus Christ was born of
a woman, was crucified under Pontius Pilate, died and was buried, and
was resurrected in the flesh.[25] The assertion that Jesus is Lord means first
of all that as a fully human being he effects our resurrection not in such
a way that part of us is redeemed, as was to be expected according to
Platonic or Gnostic thought, but that we are resurrected in our totality.
Yet the Apostles' Creed also affirms that Jesus was not simply a human
being adopted by God. The creed makes the claim that the Son of God,
born through the Holy Spirit, resurrected from the dead, and ascended
into heaven, is now sitting at the right hand of the Father and that he will
come to judge the living and the dead. While it was maintained that Jesus
was true man and also God, neither the New Testament nor the early
creedal formulations provide an explicit doctrine of the two natures of
Christ.

The question now addressed by believers and skeptics alike was how
the human being Jesus could be called God. The Jewish apologist Celsus
put the issue very poignantly when he declared: "Either God really does
change, as they say, into a mortal body. . . . Or He does not change, but
makes those who see him think He does so, and leads them astray and tells
lies." [26] Thus he posed the alternative that God must either become a human being by renouncing his divinity or that he remains divine by only
appearing in human gown. The emphasis on the true humanity and the
divinity of Christ does not remove an adoptionistic or a docetic model of
christology for Celsus. Even Origen who attempted to refute Celsus did
not sufficiently clarify the issue. In his writings he declared on the one
hand that the Son proceeds eternally from the Father, being equal with
him, while on the other hand he affirmed that the Son, in his very being, is
different from the Father.[27] While Origen maintained the dialectic tension of unity and distinction between God the Father and Christ, theologians after him were less inclined to pursue this kind of reasoning. Thus
the humanity of Christ was either swallowed up in the divinity or vice
versa to guarantee the unity of the person—the issue which largely kin-
dled the fight between Arius and Athanasius. Or in another case humanity and divinity were separated to such an extent that reality of the incarnation was sacrificed—the issue which largely caused the controversy with
Apollinaris of Laodicea and the theologians of the Antiochian school.

The first step in settling the issues, at least as far as the relationship between God the Father and Jesus Christ was concerned, was taken at

Nicea in 325. The fourth century marked the starting point of a new era for the Christian faith. In 311 Emperor Galerius had grudgingly granted toleration for the Christian faith and in 312 the new Emperor Constantine had publicly professed Christianity. Soon afterwards, Constantine himself took over the direction of church matters. He felt it was his duty to remove error and to propagate the true religion. He also feared that a divided church would offend the Christian God and bring vengeance upon the Roman Empire and its Emperor. Constantine was present at the Council of Nicea and even participated in the debates.[28] He instructed the bishops to reach unanimous agreements, not motivated by hate or partiality, but by a desire to seek out the principles of the church and of the apostles. When we compare his own theology with the decisions of the council, we notice at once that his interest was to bring unity to the church, but not to impose his theological preferences upon the council's statements of faith.[29]

Nevertheless, we encounter a new situation. Up to the fourth century all the creedal formulations, the Apostles' Creed included, were local in nature, though expressing the universally accepted catholic faith. Now the situation had changed. Beginning with the Council of Nicea, the synodical or conciliar creeds no longer had a local character. Under imperial auspices representatives of the whole church convened and their decisions became a test of the orthodoxy of Christians everywhere. The Creed of Nicea was the first creedal formula issued by an ecumenical synod and therefore it was the first that could in a legal sense claim universal authority.[30] Expanding considerably on earlier creeds, the Council professed faith in

> one Lord Jesus Christ, the Son of God, begotten from the Father, only begotten, Christ is, from the being of the Father, God from God, Light from Light, true God from true God, begotten not made, of the same being with the Father, through whom all things were made, those in heaven and those on earth, who because of us humans and because of our salvation came down and became flesh, becoming human, suffered and rose again . . .

We hear that three hundred and eighteen bishops had assembled at Nicea and signed the creed. Only a few refused to sign, among them Arius and his friends, who preferred instead to go into exile.

The Nicene Creed was mainly a reply to the Arian position. Unlike the Apostles' Creed, biblical terminology no longer sufficed to clarify the issue of how God was related to the Father without compromising the Christian faith with heretical positions. Thus the phrases, "from the being of the Father," "true God from true God," "begotten not made," and "of the same being with the Father," were designed to assure that Jesus Christ was not inferior to God. The council fathers knew too well that semi-gods or apparitions of gods could not change our situation. As Greek and Roman mythology showed, at the most they could offer only temporary comfort, since they were either subjected to human destiny or could not appropriately guide it. Thus the council insisted that God had to dwell fully in Jesus Christ to offer salvation to humanity.

Yet did not such an identity of Christ with God that the Nicene Creed professed jeopardize Christ's full humanity? Was he still considered a human being who once lived among us and with us? Even Athanasius was reluctant to admit that Christ was "of the same being with the father." [31] Moreover, it seems that the Nicene Creed, its ecumenical status notwithstanding, was far less known than we might assume. It took a good 30 years until Latin translations were published when Bishop Hilary of Poitiers introduced the West to the crucial text of the Arian controversy.

Even the Creed issued by the Ecumenical Council of Constantinople in 381 became only slightly better known. It contained significant clarification of the original Nicene Creed, for instance, when it expanded the brief comment, he "became incarnate" into he "was incarnate from the Holy Spirit in the Virgin Mary." But now it was also time to consider christology in the context of the Trinity. Therefore we hear that the Holy Spirit is "the Lord and life-giver, who proceeds from the Father, who with the Father and the Son is together worshiped and together glorified." While elevating the Holy Spirit to the same level as Father and Son, the Creed refrains from saying that the Spirit is "one in being with the Father and the Son." These important formulations did not gain wide circulation. Until recently scholars were not even sure that this creed had indeed been issued at the Council of Constantinople.[32] When it was officially read at the Council of Chalcedon in 451 and received into its minutes, together with the Nicene Creed, many of the council fathers probably heard it for the first time. Yet soon it became the baptismal creed of the Eastern Churches, and, for a while, also enjoyed popularity in the West. For the Eucharistic liturgy which traditionally had not used a creedal statement it would become the creed in both East and West. This shows that we have now arrived at a truly ecumenical and therewith catholic summary of the Christian faith.

The same cannot be said of the Apostles' Creed. Originating largely from the Roman Symbol, the Apostles' Creed remained largely the baptismal creed in the West, while the Eastern Churches were not acquainted with it until relatively recent ecumenical encounters. This became painfully clear in the discussions between representatives of the Eastern Churches and the See of Rome in Florence in 1449. It was at that meeting, to the amazement of the Roman delegates, that the Eastern representatives confessed that they did not know of an Apostles' Creed.[33]

The Council of Chalcedon, however, did more than simply sanction the creeds of Nicea and Constantinople. Though it should have been clear by now that Christ was true God and equal with him, the notion had emerged more than once before that this required either a separation of the divine and human natures in Jesus or an absorption of the human into the divine. When the assembly at Chalcedon had publicly read the creeds of Nicea and Constantinople, it professed that it did not want to change these great creeds. But they became even more explicit in their understanding of Christ when they added that they believed in

> one and the same Christ, Son, Lord, Only begotten, made known in two natures [which exist] without confusion, without change, without division, without separation; the difference of the natures having been in no wise taken away by reason of the union, but rather the properties of each being preserved, and [both] concurring into one Person *(prosopon)* and one *hypostasis*—not parted or divided into two persons *(prosopa)*, but one and the same Son and Only-begotten, the divine Logos, the Lord Jesus Christ.[34]

The phrases may sound dry and formal for us, but for the members of the Council they clarified the vital issue: Jesus Christ is both true God and true man. Both aspects can neither be mixed into a superhuman, semi-divine being, nor can they be separated into a partly human and partly divine, or sometimes human and sometimes divine being. While emphasizing the unity of the person of Jesus Christ, the council members affirmed that he is both God and man. Of course, they did not and could not answer the question how anyone could be both God and man. Attempts to solve this question would not only have transcended the concepts that language made available to the council members, but endeavors in that direction were recognized as futile since they first required a definition of God. Thus the attempt to understand Jesus Christ was pushed to its utmost limits. Yet it was not a speculative attempt. They wanted to profess the catholic faith in Jesus Christ in the face of repeated distorted and truncated views of the Lord of the church. The council fathers had no intention of becoming theological innovators. They explicitly stated in their creedal statements that they followed the holy fathers and that they said nothing but what "the prophets from of old [have spoken] concerning him, and as the Lord Jesus Christ himself has taught us, and as the Symbol of the Fathers has delivered to us." [35] While they endeavored to stay within the limits of that which was regarded catholic, what has been believed everywhere, always, and by all, they showed that catholicity did not exclude theological advancement.

The concerns of Chalcedon were introduced to the West in the so-called Athanasian Creed, first quoted in part by Caesarius of Arles (470-552). Though bearing the name of Athanasius it goes beyond him in its formulations and very likely originated in Gaul. In 40 brief sentences it summarizes the catholic dogma of the unity of the person of Christ and of the trinity of the godhead. But the Athanasian Creed also contained a phrase that eventually jeopardized the unity of the church. It stated that "the Holy Spirit is from the Father and from the Son, neither made nor created nor begotten, but proceeding." The intention of this *filioque* (i.e., and the Son) was originally to underscore that Christ was of the same being with the Father. It does this by saying that the Spirit proceeds equally from the Father and the Son. This was different from the usual affirmation by Eastern theologians that the Spirit proceeds from the Father through the Son and is shared by all creation.

The issue was not only one of theological method, whether to start with the unity of the Trinity, as the East preferred, or to start with the Father and the Son and conceive the Spirit as the unifying factor, as Western theologians stipulated. Underlying all of this was the fundamental issue whether in unilateral action one group of churches could change a creed, if the creed had been formulated by an ecumenical council. It was in the Nicene Creed that the Eastern theologians first discovered the insertion of the *filioque* by Western authorities. In other words, only a general council of the Eastern and Western Church could expand a creed decided upon by a council. But such a council was never summoned, neither by the Pope, who was at first reluctant to change the Nicene Creed, nor by the Emperor who advocated such an amendment to avert the Spanish adoptionistic heresies. Thus the East continued steadfastly to refuse the "heresy" of the *filioque,* while it was gradually accepted in the West.[36]

The refusal of the *filioque* by the East and the acceptance by the West was also indicative of a differing self-understanding.[37] If the Spirit proceeds from the Father through the Son, then world and humanity are immediately confronted with the Spirit of God, but only in a mediated way with the Son. As the administrator of the work of Christ, the church is therefore not immediately concerned with the world. The church is free to go its own way without being bothered by the affairs of the day. That the East could so easily be captured by Islam and that today the Orthodox Church is able to survive spiritually under Marxist regimes, may at least to some extent be indicative of this self-understanding of Christianity. If the Spirit, however, is understood to proceed from the Father and the Son, the world is confronted with the Spirit of God as much as with the Spirit of Christ. As the administrator of the work of Christ, the church is then not just in a mediated way concerned with the world and its affairs. The history of the Western Church bears witness to this continuous struggle. The church wanted to limit the powers of the State and make it amenable to the Spirit of Christ that should pervade its affairs.

3. The apostolic office

The question of the apostolic office was first raised when Paul claimed to be an apostle, though he had not been one of Jesus' original disciples. While he could still qualify as an apostle because of his Damascus experience, the issue was more complicated when the first generation of followers died and the growing church needed reliable leadership. As any human grouping, the church needed a group of leaders who would direct and guide the affairs of the growing number of Christians. While the apostles were alive they could be relied on for true apostolic teaching that stood in continuity with the risen Lord. But once they were dead, who would guard the church against the numerous new and dubious interpretations of the Christian faith? The necessity arose of developing leadership that stood in true succession to the apostles.

a. The ministerial office

At the close of the first century Ignatius of Antioch tells us that bishops have been appointed throughout the world by the will of Jesus Christ

(Eph. 3:2). Therefore, one should live in harmony with the will of the bishop (Eph. 4:1) and one should regard the bishop as the Lord himself (Eph. 6:1). The church finds its unity in Christ who is represented in the local congregations through the bishop. Around the same time as Ignatius, Clement of Rome writes to the Christians in Corinth and mentions a whole line of succession: Jesus Christ was sent from God, the apostles received the gospel from Jesus Christ, the deacons and bishops were tested and appointed by the apostles from the first converts (1 Clem. 42:1-4). If the bishops should die, the apostles made provisions that "other approved men should succeed their ministry" (1 Clem. 44:2). This means that bishops are not automatically appointed, but that they are either chosen by the apostles or later "by other eminent men with the consent of the whole Church [i.e., congregation]" (1 Clem. 44:3). Since they are that carefully chosen and elected by the church, there is no reason to remove them from office if they pursue their call without blame, humbly, peaceably, and without showing favors. Clement is upset with the situation in Corinth where bishops or presbyters are being deposed, and asks the congregation to reconsider this action. Clement uses here the terms bishop and presbyter indiscriminately, which indicates that the function of their office(s) is essentially the same.

According to Clement, the bishops do not just teach. They minister to the people and offer the gift of the people during worship (1 Clem. 44:4). Clement draws heavily on Old Testament imagery to exemplify their ministerial and sacerdotal function. Bishops also supervise the congregation and therefore are called "rulers" (1 Clem. 1:3f.). We are told by Clement that once the elders or bishops are removed, others will strive to assume their positions and disorder and sedition will arise (1 Clem. 3:2f.). Thus the episcopal office assures order both in congregational affairs and in worship. Next to the bishops deacons are mentioned by Clement and again their origin is traced both to the apostolic time and beyond (1 Clem. 42:4f.). Perhaps it was not necessary for Clement to reflect on the continuity of the doctrine of the apostles with that of the bishops or presbyters. It seemed to suffice for him that they were in true succession with the apostles, which implied that they represented the true doctrine. This is essentially the way Ignatius viewed apostolic succession also.

Ignatius, however, also describes the bishop as presiding over the presbytery. Perhaps this notion of a more monarchic position arose first in Jerusalem where James, the brother of Jesus, and then Symeon, a cousin of the Lord, supervised the affairs of the congregation.[38] Ignatius sums up very succinctly the function and position of the bishop at his time when he writes:

> See that you follow the bishop, as Jesus Christ follows the Father, and the presbyters as if it were the Apostles. And reverence the deacons as the command of God. Let no one do any of the things appertaining to the Church without the bishop. Let that be considered a valid Eucharist which is celebrated by the bishop, or by any whom he appoints. Wherever the bishop appears let the congregation be present; just as wherever Jesus Christ is, there is the Catholic Church. It is not lawful either to baptize or to hold an "agape" without the bishop; but whatever he approves that is pleasing to God, that everything which you do may be secure and valid (Letter to the Smyrnaeans 8:1f.).

The whole religious and moral life of the congregation revolves around the bishop as the representative of God in Christ. Christ is the invisible bishop of the whole church, similar to the bishop being the leader of the individual congregation. Once a congregation has lost its bishop (through persecution), it still has Christ as its heavenly bishop (cf. Ignatius, Letter to the Romans, 9:1). Yet there is nothing which only the bishop can do; he can always appoint someone to act on his behalf. This means that, the elevated status of the bishop notwithstanding, the fundamental continuity between laity and bishop is maintained.

At the beginning of the fourth century, however, the Synod of Arles (314) considerably reduced the power to delegate priestly functions when it declared that deacons should not administer the Eucharist to the faithful.[39] The Council of Nicea specified this issue when it stated: "The deacons must remain within the limits of their functions, and remember that they are assistants of the bishops, and only come after the priests. They must receive the Eucharist in accordance with the rule, after the priests— a bishop or a priest administering it to them." [40]

In the second century Justin Martyr still mentions that "the one presiding over the brethren" (bishop) consecrates bread and wine and "they whom we call deacons permit each one present to partake of the Eucharistic bread, wine and water; and they carry it also to the absentees." [41] In the third century this was already changed to the deacons fulfilling the subservient role of administering the wine after the elements were consecrated.[42] Yet at the same time Tertullian reminds us that "it is the authority of the church . . . which has established the difference between the Order and the laity." [43] In other words, the church and not God through some divine decree introduced the distinction between ecclesiastical orders and laity. Tertullian even asserts that if no clerics are around we can "offer, and baptize, and are priests, alone for yourself. But where three are, a church is, albeit they be laics."

Though the church increasingly emphasized that there are two distinct classes, priests and laity, it did not forget that the priests are always to be related to a special congregation which they represent and over which they preside. Thus the Council of Chalcedon declared void any ordination to a general priesthood when it stated: "No one shall be absolutely ordained either priest or deacon, or to any other clerical order, unless he is appointed specially to the church of the city or of the village, or to a martyr's chapel or monastery." [44] Similarly, if a cleric espouses wrong doctrine, he loses his privileges as an ordained person. This means, that the priest can only function in a ministerial office if he is related to the people he serves and if he serves within the church, i.e., within and in accordance with the community of believers. Augustine put it well when he said: "We are not bishops because of ourselves, but because of those to whom we administer the Word and the Lord's Sacrament." [45]

At the same time Augustine mentions an indelible character of the priest, a feature that was introduced not for the priest's sake, but for the sake of the people he serves. For a man to be a true priest, Augustine asserts, "it is requisite that he should be clothed not with the sacrament alone, but with righteousness." [46] But if a man is a priest in virtue of the sacrament alone, he gives not what is his own but what is God's. This means that on account of his qualifications or his ordination a priest is not better or higher in rank than the laity. To insure for the laity the validity of his priestly functions, these functions must be conceived of as being independent from the variable personal dignity of the priest. Thus the notion was introduced that there was something connected with the ministerial office that remained indelible in spite of the shortcomings of the individual priest. Of course, such notion always bore the danger that it could be understood as a class privilege and a personal distinction. In the Middle Ages, for instance, we encounter a priesthood that is essential for the laity and beyond reproach.

In the East one recognized also that "the things which are placed in the hands of the priest it is with God alone to give." [47] A faithless priest, though certainly a distracting example, cannot invalidate by his own action the services he renders on God's behalf. Nevertheless Chrysostom admonishes those who rule to be watchful and sober as their subjects should be obedient.[48] If we are not watchful as leaders, we imperil our own head because we have to give account of all over whom we rule, women, children, and men. This awesome responsibility occasionally led priests to run away from their office. It also often led in the Eastern Church to ordain a candidate by force against his will. Yet the church did not see anything wrong in the awe-inspiring status of the office and Chrysostom encourages us "to fear and to tremble, both because of conscience, and because of the burden of the office." [49]

What is the cause of this immense fear that Chrysostom describes and that made it necessary for the people to ordain to the priesthood by force? We remember that the East was much more interested than the West in the true and undiminished godhead of Christ. Eastern theologians were convinced that God would not redeem what he had not assumed and permeated. Representing the church before God in worship or presenting the external sacrifice as the antitype of the great mystery of the sacrificial death of Christ, a priest cannot encounter God in a carefree attitude or half-heartedly. Gregory of Nazianzus put the situation very well when he said: "No one is worthy of the mightiness of God, and the sacrifice, and priesthood, who has not first presented himself to God, a living, holy sacrifice, and set forth the reasonable, well-pleasing service, and sacrificed to God the sacrifice of praise and the contrite spirit." [50] Gregory himself fled when he was asked to be ordained.

How can one become worthy and holy enough to clothe oneself with a garb and name of priest? Strangely enough, for Eastern theologians it was thought to come through ordination. Gregory of Nyssa, for instance, explains that similarly as the common bread

> when the sacramental action . . . . consecrates it, it is called, and becomes, the Body of Christ. . . . The same power of the Word, again, also makes the priest venerable and honorable, separated, by the new blessing bestowed upon him, from his community with the mass of men. While but yesterday he was one of the mass, one of the people, he is suddenly rendered a guide, a president, a teacher of righteousness, an instructor in hidden mysteries; and this he does without being at all changed in body or in form; but, while continuing to be in all appearance the man he was before, being, by some unseen power and grace, transformed in respect of his unseen soul to the higher condition.[51]

It is not the call through the congregation, but the divine grace "infused" at ordination that sets the priest apart from all other people and makes him inwardly a new person. There is certainly an attractiveness in the understanding that the grace of God actually transforms a human being and makes one worthy of assuming the priestly office. Yet the almost exclusively cultic emphasis on the ministerial office in the East is at least as serious a shortcoming as the formalistic understanding of succession in the West. Perhaps both aspects together, sacramental transformation and succession in history and doctrine might have something valuable to offer for the rediscovery of the ministerial office today.[52]

b. Collegiality and the papal primacy

The ministerial office may suffice to give guidance and continuity on the local level. But that office is insufficient once we go beyond an individual congregation or a certain region. We have heard that the apostles chose bishops in each of the congregations they established. Soon the bishop became the presider of a congregation with a council of presbyters under him. At the beginning of the second century Tertullian mockingly asked heretical churches to produce bishop lists that reliably show the correct succession in office with their first bishop having been installed by an apostle or someone who continued steadfast with the apostles.[53] He knew that these churches cannot meet the criterion of true succession. Yet congregations that had emphasized true doctrine had also looked for an uninterrupted line of succession in their leadership and not allowed foreign elements to intrude. For instance, Smyrna could prove that Polycarp was installed by John and Rome could show that Clement was appointed by Peter. Churches in Ephesus, Corinth, Philippi, Thessalonica, Jerusalem, and many other places could similarly prove that they stood in true apostolic succession. It was clear for Tertullian that if one held communion with the apostolic churches, this would be expressive of also sharing apostolic doctrine.[54]

Their prestige elevated the apostolic congregations to a peculiar status. Thus Tertullian exclaimed that if one wanted to get at the roots of apostolic teaching one must refer to these apostolic congregations—in Achaia there is Corinth, and not far from Macedonia there are Philippi and Thessalonica. In Asia there is Ephesus, and, of course, in Italy there is Rome.[55] Especially Rome, the capital of the Roman Empire, rose to leading status claiming two apostles as its ancestors. Thus Irenaeus writes:

> [We point to] that tradition derived from the apostles, of the very great, the very ancient, and universally known Church founded and organized at Rome by the two most glorious apostles, Peter and Paul. . . . For it is

a matter of necessity that every Church should agree with this Church, on account of its preeminent authority, that is, the faithful everywhere, inasmuch as the apostolic tradition has been preserved continuously by those [faithful men] who exist everywhere.[56]

Irenaeus does not imply that Rome's voice must prevail everywhere. Yet he assumes that Christians everywhere, who stand in apostolic succession, would naturally agree with Rome. As history tells us, Rome was not timid either in exerting its leadership role even when others differed with the Roman Church. This first appeared in the so-called Passover dispute.[57] When Polycarp of Smyrna visited Bishop Nicetus of Rome in the middle of the second century they could not agree on a common practice to establish the date for the Easter celebration. Yet they allowed their respective practices to continue and parted peacefully. Toward the close of the second century, however, Victor of Rome was less tolerant. When he discovered the divergence, he convened a conference of bishops which issued a decree declaring that the Western practice must be followed. On his instigation similar conferences were held by the bishops of Caesarea, Jerusalem, and others who arrived at the same conclusion. Since the Asia Minor churches insisted on continuing their practice, Victor of Rome wanted to sever his ties and excommunicate the dissident churches. Yet Irenaeus, bishop of Lyons and responsible for the Christians in Gaul, rebuked the bishop of Rome and admonished him not to jeopardize unity.

Even much earlier the Roman Church had already attempted to exert influence beyond its own boundaries. We have seen that at the close of the first century, Clement of Rome wrote a letter to the congregation at Corinth in the name of his congregation. He rebuked the congregation for deposing some of its presbyters and he announced that Rome would send representatives to settle the dispute in Corinth according to Roman terms (1 Clem. 63:3).

Another instance that strengthened the position of Rome and of a central church government was the dispute regarding the possibility of a second repentance and the readmission of those who had lapsed from their faith during times of persecution. At first it was clear for the church that grave sins, such as adultery, apostasy, and homicide, were unforgivable and excluded one permanently from the church if they were committed after baptism. Yet the stronger the persecution of the church became and the more people flocked to the church, the greater the need became to reconsider whether any exceptions could be granted.

At the beginning of the third century, Bishop Callistus of Rome declared to the surprise of many that he would and could forgive persons who had indulged in sensual pleasures.[58] His presbyter Hippolytus protested strongly and claimed that the church was a community of those who lived in righteousness. By admitting even repentant sexual offenders the church could no longer be the body or bride of Christ. Callistus on the other hand applied to the situation the parable of the wheat and the tares and explained that the church is always a composite body. For him the holiness of the church was based on forgiveness rather than on its empirical sanctity. The issue spilled over into Africa. Tertullian opposed the official Roman attitude and rejected any possibility of a second penitence for deadly sins. Tertullian asserted that only God or the spiritual church could forgive sins, but not "the church that consists of a number of bishops" or the successor of Peter. Christ, he declared, only conferred upon Peter the power to forgive sins, but not upon his successors.[59]

Soon the issue of a second repentance gained even more prominence. During the persecution of the Christians under the Emperor Decius (249-251), so many believers failed and temporarily denied the Christian faith to save their physical life that one could no longer ignore them. It was widely felt that the church must open a possibility for them to return. Bishop Cyprian of Carthage assembled a council composed of bishops, priests, deacons, confessors of faith during the persecution, and laity, and came up with a resolution that after a certain period of repentance lapsed believers could be readmitted to the church.[60] Cyprian mentions that he sent a copy of the resolution to his colleague Cornelius of Rome and that a council held there came to similar conclusions. Yet in both places there was also opposition to this plan. In Africa a group went so far as to demand that the lapsed should be readmitted immediately, while under the leadership of Novatian a segment of the congregation in Rome opted for the rigorous position that none of the lapsed should be readmitted. Novatian and his party gained wide recognition throughout the empire.[61] Small wonder that the concord between Carthage and Rome did not last long.

Soon followers of Novatian began to rebaptize those who had joined his rigorous movement. Now the question arose what the church should do with those who had been baptized by these heretics, but later repented and wanted to return to the church. Bishop Stephen of Rome decided that there was no need to rebaptize heretics who repentantly wanted to return to the Catholic Church, since the baptism did not depend on the sanctity of the person who administered it. Cyprian, however, argued that since there is no church outside the true Church, there can also be no baptism outside it. A heretic seeking admission to the Church Catholic must therefore be baptized.[62] If one would opt for Stephen's solution, Cyprian argued, one would destroy the unity of the church. He claimed that such practice would introduce many other foundations besides the rock of Peter on which alone the church is built. Cyprian was especially outraged that Stephen did not allow bishops who disagreed with his position to speak at a common conference. Stephen had even called Cyprian "a false Christ and a false apostle and a treacherous laborer" and thereby destroyed the unity with many congregations.[63]

Undoubtedly Cyprian's claim that "he cannot have God as a Father who does not have the Church as a mother" was also accepted by Stephen.[64] He agreed that baptism was not effective as long as one dwelled outside the church, but he did not go so far as to say that it did not even exist there. But the real question was not whether a sacrament is dependent on its administrator. It was rather the juridicial question that was important. Had a local bishop ultimate jurisdiction or was he able to act only in conjunction with and under the leadership of Rome? Cyprian had claimed that the rest of the apostles together with Peter were "endowed with an equal partnership of office and of power." Therefore the bishops watch over the church and its unity and hold the episcopate as one and undivided.[65] There is not even need for the "heretics and blasphemers" to appeal "to the Chair of Peter and to the Principal Church," because the case had been "decided by all of us and [it] is equally fair and just that the case of each one be heard there where the crime was committed and that a portion of the flock be entrusted to each pastor which each one should rule and govern." [66] But the Bishop of Rome disagreed. Though there is an episcopate and a council of bishops, Stephen demanded that the decision must be reached in consultation and in harmony with the bishop of Rome. The unity of the church in the Bishop of Rome was just not a symbolic gesture for him. Stephen contended that the Bishop of Rome could approve or disapprove of council decisions. The dissension with Africa about the rebaptism of heretics continued well into the fourth century.

The church, however, was not quite ready to grant such far-reaching primacy to the Bishop of Rome. The Council of Nicea in its famous canon six stated: "The old customs in use in Egypt, in Libya, and in Pentapolis, shall continue to exist, that is, that the bishop of Alexandria shall have jurisdiction over these [provinces]; for there is a similar relation for the Bishop of Rome." [67] The Bishop of Rome was only one of the patriarchs, presumably exercising jurisdiction over Italy, but he did not rule the whole church. A few years later the Synod at Sardica (347) in its canons gave more power to the Pope. It declared that a bishop can appeal to the Pope if he was deposed by a provincial synod. The Pope then either had to convene a new synod to investigate the case or he could approve the judgment made earlier.[68] The Ecumenical Council at Constantinople (381) finally recognized the fact of Rome's primacy saying: "The Bishop of Constantinople shall hold the first rank after the Bishop of Rome, because Constantinople is New Rome." [69] Rome had now become the actual and officially recognized focal point of the church catholic. But the battle was not yet won. Constantinople had become the New Rome, the seat of the emperor. The Council of Chalcedon duly recognized this by attributing to the See of Constantinople similar juridicial power in deciding conflicts between bishops and metropolitan bishops.[70] Such balance of power between Rome and Constantinople could easily create new tensions over which See had ultimate jurisdiction. This also shows the risk that the church took in associating itself so closely with the center of imperial power.

We have now come to the end of our brief investigation into the origin of the one, holy, catholic, and apostolic church. We find that the apostolic tradition is determined through the canon. The interpretation of this tradition is safeguarded through the decision of synods and councils and through apostolic succession. Each congregation is shepherded by a bishop in apostolic succession, the bishops are gathered into provinces, and provinces into larger areas headed by the patriarchs. Finally the Bishop of imperial Rome is considered the supreme guardian of the tradition and the ultimate authority for synods and councils. One wonders whether an institution that takes such great caution to safeguard the divine Word, does not treasure the Word so much that it becomes a relic instead of a guiding light.

Vincent of Lerins in his *Commonitory* (434) disperses our fear to some extent when he says: Of course, the canon of Scripture is complete and sufficient of itself for everything. Since, however, not everyone accepts Scripture in one and the same sense, we should take greatest care to follow in our faith universality, antiquity, and consent.

> We do so in regard to universality if we confess that faith alone to be true which the entire Church confesses all over the world. [We do so] in regard to antiquity if we in no way deviate from those interpretations

which our ancestors and fathers have manifestly proclaimed as inviolable. [We do so] in regard to consent if, in this very antiquity, we adopt the definitions and propositions of all, or almost all, the bishops and doctors.[71]

The claim is made here that the church always preaches the same gospel, while the councils only give a more precise definition of the same truth. Heresies, on the other hand, are innovations. Vincent rejects progress if it leads to alteration of faith. Yet he is confident that individuals as well as the whole church progresses in intelligence, knowledge, and wisdom. The growth of faith must be analogous to that of the body; it develops and attains its full size yet still remains the same. Vincent acknowledges that "much happens between the prime of childhood and the maturity of old age. But . . . the old men of today who were once the adolescents of yesterday, although the figure and appearance of one and the same person have changed, are identical."[72] To follow Vincent's words, we encounter in the first centuries not only a growth process towards a populous church, but a maturation process toward the one, holy, catholic, and apostolic church.

NOTES

1. Cf. Adolf von Harnack, *History of Dogma,* trans. N. Buchanan (New York: Russell & Russell, 1958), 2:174f.
2. Edwin Hatch, *The Influence of Greek Ideas on Christianity* (New York: Harper Torchbook, 1957) 350f.
3. Cf. Karl Hefele, *A History of the Councils of the Church from the Original Documents,* trans. H. N. Oxenham (Edinburgh: T. & T. Clark, 1896), 2:322f., in canon 59 and 60 of the Synod of Laodicea.
4. Cf. David L. Dungan, "The New Testament Canon in Recent Study," *Interpretation* 29 (October 1975): 340f.
5. Justin Martyr, *Dialogue with Trypho* 103, FaCh 1:310.
6. Justin Martyr, *The First Apology* 66f., FaCh 1:106.
7. Argued convincingly by Alfred Adam, *Lehrbuch der Dogmengeschichte.* Vol. 1: *Die Zeit der alten Kirche* (Gütersloh: Mohn, 1965) 87.
8. Theodor Zahn, in his stupendous work, *Geschichte des neutestamentlichen Kanons. 1: Das Neue Testament vor Origenes,* Part 1 (Erlangen: Deichert, 1888) 363, shows that Origen's remark, "divine scripture teaches us to accept all things that happen to us as sent by God, because we know that nothing happens without him" (*On First Principles,* 3.2.7) is a quote from the Didache 3 and indicates that Origen regarded the Didache as divine scripture.
9. So Conzelmann, *1 Corinthians,* 63 and n. 70, to this passage.
10. The text of the letter is edited by Zahn, *Geschichte. 2: Urkunden und Belege zum ersten und dritten Band,* Part 1 (1890) 210ff.
11. Cf. Zahn, ibid., 110ff., where he analyzes a reference in the Canon Muratori that seems to point to 2 Peter or to the Apocalypse of Peter. If it would point to the latter, we would encounter a book that was not received into the final canon.

12. Ernst Käsemann, *Essays on New Testament Themes*, trans. W. J. Montague (Naperville, IL: Allenson, 1964) 103f.
13. Ibid., 103.
14. Ibid., 106.
15. Cf. Adam, 1:90.
16. Vincent of Lerins, *The Commonitories* 2, FaCh 7:270.
17. So also B. A. Gerrish, ed., *The Faith of Christendom. A Source Book of Creeds and Confessions* (Cleveland: World, 1963) 49.
18. Augustine, *Sermons* 212, FaCh 38:117.
19. For this and the following, see the excellent remarks in Oscar Cullmann, *The Earliest Christian Confessions*, trans. J. K. S. Reid (London: Lutterworth, 1949) esp. 19-23.
20. Ibid., 39.
21. Cullmann, *Confessions*, 50, mentions that this runs contrary to the whole New Testament, since it presents a Jewish representation of Christ. This kind of argument comes close to a latent anti-Semitism.
22. J. N. D. Kelly, *Early Christian Creeds*, 3d ed. (London: Longman, 1972) 215f.
23. Irenaeus, *Against Heresies* 1.10.1, ANFa 1:330; and Rufinus, *A Commentary on the Apostles' Creed* 18, ACW, 20:52, where Rufinus mentions that this clause is missing in the creeds of the Roman Church and the Eastern Churches.
24. Tertullian, *The Prescription Against Heretics* 13, ANFa 3:249.
25. DS, 20, in a creed that dates back to the beginning of the 3rd century.
26. According to Origen, *Contra Celsum* 4.18, trans. with introduction and notes by Henry Chadwick (Cambridge: University Press, 1953) 195.
27. Cf. Origen, *On First Principles* 1.2.4. and 1.2.2, trans. G. W. Butterworth, introduction by Henri de Lubac (New York: Harper, 1966), 18 and 16.
28. So Aloys Grillmeier, *Christ in Christian Tradition. 1: From the Apostolic Age to Chalcedon (451)*, rev. 2d ed., trans. J. Bowden (Atlanta: John Knox, 1975) 258.
29. Cf. ibid., 261f.
30. So Kelly, 207.
31. Cf. for the following ibid., 257ff.
32. For the discussion of its origin, cf. ibid., 305-331.
33. According to Adam, 1:200.
34. According to Grillmeier, 1:544.
35. Ibid.
36. For details cf. Jaroslav Pelikan, *The Christian Tradition. A History of the Development of Doctrine*. Vol. 2: *The Spirit of Eastern Christendom (600-1700)* (Chicago: Univ. of Chicago Press, 1971) 183-198.
37. For the following cf. Adam, 1:375f., who briefly mentions these implications.
38. Eusebius, *The History of the Church* 4.22.4, p. 181.
39. So canon 15 in Hefele, 1:193, where Hefele also carefully interprets this text.
40. Canon 18 in ibid., 1:427.
41. Justin Martyr, *The First Apology* 65, FaCh 1:105.
42. Cyprian, *The Lapsed* 25, FaCh 36:79.
43. For this and the following quote see Tertullian, *An Exhortation to Chastity* 7, ANFa 4:54.
44. Canon 6 as quoted in Hefele, 3:391.
45. Augustine, *Contra Cresconium Grammaticum Partis Donati* 2.11.13, PL 43:472.
46. Augustine, *Answer to the Letters of Petilian, the Donatist* 2.30.68, NPNF (FS) 4:547.
47. Chrystostom, *Homily* 86.4 on John 20:10f., in ibid., 14:326.
48. For the following see Chrysostom, *Homily* 34:2 on Hebrews 13:17, in ibid., 14:519.
49. Chrysostom, *Homily* 34.3 in ibid., 14:519.
50. Gregory of Nazianzus, *In Defense of His Flight to Pontus* 95, NPNF (SS) 7:223.

51. Gregory of Nyssa, *On the Baptism of Christ*, NPNF (SS) 5:519.
52. For the origin of the priestly office, cf. the excellent article by Hans von Campenhausen, "The Origins of the Idea of Priesthood in the Early Church," in his *Tradition and Life in the Church, Essays and Lectures in Church History*, trans. A. V. Littledale (Philadelphia: Fortress, 1968) 217-230.
53. Tertullian, *The Prescription Against Heretics* 32, ANFa 3:258.
54. Ibid. 20, 3:252.
55. Ibid. 36, 3:260.
56. Irenaeus, *Against Heresies* 3.3.2, ANFa 1:415f.
57. Cf. for the following Eusebius, 5:23ff., pp. 229-234.
58. For the following cf. Jaroslav Pelikan, *The Christian Tradition. A History of the Development of Doctrine*. Vol. 1: *The Emergence of the Catholic Tradition (100-600)* (Chicago: University Press, 1971) 157ff.
59. Tertullian, *On Modesty* 21, ANFa 4:98ff. and cf. Reinhold Seeberg, *Lehrbuch der Dogmengeschichte*. Vol. 1: *Die Anfänge des Dogmas im nachapostolischen und altkatholischen Zeitalter* (Darmstadt: Wissenschaftliche Buchgesellschaft, 1965) 605ff., for the controversy.
60. Cyprian, *Letters* 55.5f., FaCh 51:136f.
61. For details of the controversy cf. Hefele, 1:93-98.
62. Cyprian, *Letters* 75.17, FaCh 51:306f.
63. As quoted ibid. 75.25, 51:312.
64. Cyprian, *The Unity of the Church* 6, FaCh 36:100.
65. Ibid. 4, 36:99.
66. Cyprian, *Letters* 59.14, FaCh 51:186.
67. As quoted in Hefele, 1:389.
68. Cf. to the whole issue ibid., 2:112-120, in Hefele's discussion of the Sardican canons 3f.
69. Canon 3 according to ibid., 2:357.
70. Cf. canon 9 according to ibid., 3:394.
71. Vincent of Lerins, *The Commonitories* 2, FaCh 7:270f.
72. Ibid. 23, 7:309.

PART II:

The Great Transformation

The apostolic church is often regarded as the ideal while everything that follows is marred by apostasy and decay. Yet as little as we can neatly perceive the dividing line between the apostolic and the post-apostolic church, so little can we regard the centuries that separate us from the New Testament time simply as aberration. We have seen that, true to the great commission, the church moved into the world. Yet once there, initially as a persecuted minority cult and later as the established church, the continual quest for the church was how to win the world without losing itself.

The many twists and turns that mark the church's road to modernity are not always adorned by victory signs. More than once the church was courting disaster, about to forget its call and surpass the world in idolatry. Yet there were always faithful servants, such as Boniface, Bernard of Clairvaux, or Girolamo Savonarola, who called the church back to its true purpose. After quickly traversing the centuries and noting the major turning points, we will notice that the church received many bumps and bruises, but it did not lose its vitality. On the contrary, without the church's involvement the world would be much poorer in spirit and without direction.

4

The Church as
Institution and Ferment

DEVELOPING A CHURCH-CONSCIOUSNESS: In our rapid review of the first centuries we could not but notice the immense struggle within the church to clarify its basic beliefs and to arrive at a structure commensurate with its task. But what is the church? Is it, as some scholars suggest, a pastoral institution founded by Paul, or a brotherhood of men under the fatherhood of God, or is it an aggregate of originally separate groups of followers of Jesus? Perhaps it was a community established by the historical Jesus, the resurrected Christ, God himself, or the Spirit at Pentecost, or a response of people to God's activity in history, or the community of those that followed the call of Jesus the Lord, or even a paradoxical unity of social institution and eschatological community![1] Whatever opinion we follow, the understanding that there is but one community or one church of the Lord is not the result of later merger negotiations. The sense of unity is as old as the Christian church.

Similarly, the apostolic tradition was never understood as a supplement to Scripture, but as a verification of that which Scripture contained. The formation of the canon too did not lead to a collection of sacred writings, but to reflection upon that which had to be added or subtracted from already existing collections to make them expressive of the faith of the believing community.[2]

The Didache instructs us that the church is gathered from the ends of the earth (Did. 9:4), and Ignatius expresses its basic oneness when he says: "Wherever Jesus Christ is, there is the Catholic Church" (Smyr. 8:2). Those who believe in Christ are one soul and one church; they are brought into being through him and share his name, since they are called Christians.[3] Since the Christians show this coherent unity centered in their Lord, they are even called "this new race," next to the Greeks or pagans, and the Jews (Ep. to Diogn. 1). But the church is not just a visible and empirical entity. As we read in 2 Clement, soon the notion emerged that

111

the church is also a spiritual entity, existing before the sun and moon were created and made manifest in those last days for our salvation in the flesh of Jesus Christ (2 Clem. 14:1-3). The church is an institution made manifest for our salvation through Jesus Christ. Since the church is an institution in our visible world, one cannot simply divide the human family into three races, with one being responsible for salvation. One must also relate the salvational aspect of the church to the two other races. This is where the transforming power of the church becomes visible.

1. Administration of word and sacrament in the West

The church as the institution founded for our salvation nowhere becomes more tangible than in the administration of word and sacrament. It is relatively easy to elucidate the understanding of the sacraments, they being external rites or signs conveying a sanctifying grace. But it is much more difficult to discover the church's understanding of God's word. We could equate the word with the canon, the rule of faith, or the Catholic doctrine. Each of these vital items is closely related to the word and to some extent even expressive of it. But the word as that which conveys grace and judgment cannot be captured with these labels. Perhaps it would be good to listen to the early Christian apologists who understood the Logos, i.e., word, as identical with Christ through whom God works in the world. Thus each manifestation of God in the world is a manifestation of his word, whether it is a saving action, a conserving act, or a condemning gesture.[4] If the church is the institution founded for our salvation, the word should be most prominent when salvation is announced and when whatever hinders salvation is condemned. It would best come to expression in the understanding of the dialectic between sin and grace.

a. Sin and grace

As we hear from Justin Martyr, it was clear for the church that through baptism we "obtain in the water the forgiveness of past sins" after we repent of them.[5] But we still find the same catalogues of virtues and vices in Justin Martyr as in the New Testament. Though the believers are a new creation, the church still exhorts them to "do all the deeds of sanctification, fleeing from evil speaking, and abominable and impure embraces, drunkenness and youthful lusts, and abominable passion, detestable adultery, and abominable pride" (1 Clem. 30:1). It is important to fear the Lord and to keep his commandments. Only those who keep them will live with the Lord. The fear of the Lord will even aid one to do the good and reject evil (Herm. Mand. 7:1-5). The question, of course, is whether such life-style of continuous sanctification is possible. Is it possible to consistently reject the bad and choose the good? There is no doubt that some held that the only way to salvation is through remission of sins through baptism and living a sinless life ever thereafter.[6] Such understanding may also have been encouraged by New Testament passages such as "it is impossible to restore again to repentance those who have once been enlightened . . . if they then commit apostasy, since they crucify the Son of God on their own account and hold him up to contempt" (Heb. 6:4-6).

In their rejection of the power of the church's ministers to forgive sins incurred after baptism, the Montanists indeed found some backing in Scripture.[7] But there only certain types of sin are mentioned for which a second chance does not seem to apply. The rigid position of the Montanists could only emerge because the church knew that ideal sinlessness after baptism, though desirable, was in fact attained by few. For instance, Clement mentions that "generation after generation the Master has given a place of repentance to those who will turn to him" (1 Clem. 7:5). The Didache also admonishes the Christians that "in the congregation you shall confess your transgressions, and you shall not come to prayer with an evil conscience. This is the way of life" (Did. 4:14).

Hermas provides us with interesting information about the church's attempt to address the issue of a second repentance. He insists that there is no chance to repent for those who are baptized, since sins committed after baptism will not be forgiven (Herm. Mand. 4.3.6). But he also announces that in a special revelation the Lord told him that for the baptized all their sins committed "up to this day" shall be forgiven, "if they repent with their whole heart" (Herm. Vis. 2.2.4). He limits, however, the chance of a second repentance for the just by saying that this is only a one-time chance. We notice with this example that the ideal of not sinning after baptism was impossible to attain, especially since the Lord did not return as soon as some expected. In view of later controversies it is interesting that even denial of Christ in term of persecution (apostasy) is explicitly mentioned as pardonable in this special act of forgiveness (Herm. Vis. 2.2.8). We should also note that Hermas considers Christ the law of God which was given to all the world and which is preached to the ends of the earth (Herm. Sim. 8.3.2.). Therefore we are watched to see if we really keep the law. Only through the remission of sins through which the Lord created us new (Barn. 6:11) can we begin to obey the will of God.

The more seriously one attempted to keep God's will, the more necessary became the continuous repentance and forgiveness.[8] Toward the end of the second century a public service of penance had already emerged, consisting of confession, a period of penance, and exclusion of the sinner from communion, then formal absolution and restoration.[9] For instance, Tertullian, before he joined the Montanist movement, and Clement of Alexandria mentioned that there is a second repentance for those faithful who fall into transgression. Clement admits that God knows the human heart and that since God foreknows the future, he knew from the beginning the weakness of humanity and the cunnings of the devil.[10] Tertullian is quick to add, however, that the possibility of a second repentance is not granted because the first one was not effective enough, but because of the Lord's indulgence.

As the notion of a second repentance won general approval, it was still thought that certain sins were excluded from such repentance. We notice in the controversies surrounding Hippolytus of Rome and Cyprian that sins such as idolatry, adultery, and homicide, were reckoned among them. Yet Pope Callistus refuted Hippolytus and took a more conciliatory stand against the sins of the flesh. After the persecution under Emperor Decius even idolatry or paying tribute to the gods became a pardonable sin, provided there was appropriate penitence. We would be wrong, however, to assume that the church simply relaxed its moral standards.

The Apostolic Constitutions, perhaps written in the middle of the fourth century, alleviate any fears we might have in this direction: On the one hand the believers are admonished that those who sin after baptism "shall be condemned to hell-fire" unless they repent and forsake their sins.[11] The bishop has the duty to give remission to the penitent. "If he is pitiless, and will not receive the repenting sinner, he will sin against the Lord his God, pretending to be more just than God's justice, and not receiving him whom He has received." Since the office of the keys places the bishop in a very high and precarious position, he is admonished to serve as an example to others and not make them fall. Even bishops are not exempt from the possibility of sinning. Therefore they too should repent and hope that they obtain forgiveness. Since repentance and forgiveness has gradually become part of the Christian life, we might assume that one simply needs to repent in order to obtain forgiveness. Yet the Apostolic Constitutions point out that forgiveness is not granted automatically. On the contrary, "if any one sin in direct opposition, and on purpose to try whether God will punish the wicked or not, such a one shall have no remission." In other words, precondition for remission of sin is a contrite heart and the sincere intention to amend one's ways. Then the grace of God is effective and the sin will be counted no more.

In the East, it was not considered to be the exclusive privilege of the bishop to oversee the penitential rite. Even presbyters could fulfill this function. To the dismay of many, presbyters were reluctantly withdrawn from this function and it was left up to the individuals to examine themselves before participating in the Eucharist.[12] In the West, however, the bishop was found more proper to oversee penitence. When Tertullian mentions that those seeking penitence "bow before the feet of the presbyters," he indicates that originally the custom may have been the same in the East and the West.[13] It is also noteworthy in the light of later developments that the martyrs, i.e., those who sacrificed their lives, are almost put into an intercessory role as those who "share His [Christ's] authority, and are His fellow-judges" and who open their arms to their fallen brethren.[14]

The notion of penitence always presupposed a gracious God. But the insistence on works of repentance tended to emphasize more the juridicial aspect of God than the benevolent one. Cyprian, for instance, claims that "there is a need of righteousness, that one may deserve well of God the Judge; we must obey his precepts and warnings, that our merits may receive their reward."[15] Our relationship with God is here described with judicial or contractual terminology. If we live up to God's decrees, he will reward us according to his promises. Yet the idea that good performance merits rewards could easily lead to the notion that one can do even more than is expected. Indeed, Cyprian tells us that if one lives a life of celibacy one obtains "the reward of a greater grace."[16] The idea of penitence finally resulted in different classes of Christians, those who have no need of a second penance, those who perform the works necessary to obtain God's forgiving grace, and those who do more than is required.

The danger is evident that the Christian faith would become a faith centered not in God's free and undeserved grace but in the calculated grace dependent upon one's own behavior. Cyprian sums up the whole issue precisely when he rejoices that Christ will "present us to the Father, to whom He has restored us by His sanctification; to bestow upon us immortality and eternity, to which He has renewed us."[17] Through Christ's death and resurrection we are eligible to inherit the kingdom.

But the tone is quite different when Cyprian exhorts the fellow believers in the same paragraph:

> An illustrious and divine thing, dearest brethren, is the saving labor of charity; a great comfort of believers, a wholesome guard of our security, a protection of hope, a safeguard of faith, a remedy for sin, a thing placed in the power of the doer, a thing both great and easy, a crown of peace without the risk of persecution; the true and greatest gift of God, needful for the weak, glorious for the strong, assisted by which the Christian accomplishes spiritual grace, deserves well of Christ the Judge, accounts God his debtor.

Christ is seen here as judge and God as our debtor. Charity is no longer a virtue but a saving labor. There is no uncertainty whether works are sufficient for salvation. They can act as a theological security blanket that gives credence to our hope. Since repentance and good works are only possible under the auspices of the church, the latter becomes the institution that enables and safeguards our salvation.

Yet the understanding of grace as an undeserved act of God was not permanently lost. In the latter part of the fourth century Bishop Ambrose of Milan tells us that we are "not bound to obedience out of servile necessity, but by free will we either incline to virtue or lean to vice." [18] But Ambrose concedes that reason, from which our free will stems, cannot master our passions completely; it can only restrain them. Since God has created humanity and implanted in it moral laws and feelings, all passions can be ruled and governed by a prudent mind. We can attribute our trouble to nothing but our own will. But then Ambrose cautions: "Don't you know that the guilt of Adam and Eve sold you into servitude? Don't you know that Christ did not buy you, but brought you back?" [19] This means that we are in an obvious dilemma. On the one hand we have free will to do the good or the bad and on the other hand we are in the bondage of sin together with all of humanity. Ambrose, however, did not sense this dichotomy between freedom and bondage to sinfulness. It was rather his intent to emphasize the inexcusable nature of human sinfulness.

For Ambrose it is not our doing, but Christ's work that endows us with righteousness. God himself is the author of our good will and the one who illumines our heart.[20] Ambrose even names the Holy Spirit as the one effecting forgiveness of sin and renovation.[21] Grace always comes first, and from this human works follow. Optatus of Mileve went a step further in the Pauline direction when he said: Perfect sanctity is not given but promised, "therefore we are imperfect, since it is up to us to want and to run, but it is up to God to perfect."[22] The primacy of God's grace led Ambrose to the acknowledgment that we need daily repentance for our daily faults, yet for the graver sins, he thought, there is just one penance as there is only one baptism.[23] But Ambrose's rediscovery of God's prevenient grace coupled with his insistence on humanity's freedom of choice could easily deteriorate into a shallow moralism. It was Augustine who, largely in confrontation with Pelagius, averted this danger and shaped the church's understanding of sin and grace.

Similar to Ambrose, Augustine asserts that the power of our mind is stronger than any desire.[24] If the will to do something is not in our power, our will is not free.[25] Even the idea that God foreknows everything does not impede our freedom, it rather presupposes it, since God foreknows both our will and our power to do something. This means that sin, if it arises from human freedom, is contrary to God and must be punished. As soon as we turn away from God's natural rule, we immerse ourselves in sinfulness. Augustine finds sin primarily expressed in covetousness, pride, and disobedience.[26] Salvation is then a reversal of these trends through unreserved submission to Christ's authority.[27] However, the Lord is not a tyrant, but a savior who intends to redeem the world and help those who are weak.[28] We need the grace of God to inspire us with divine love and subject us to his will so that we can accomplish the good.[29]

At the same time as Augustine emphasized total reliance on God's grace, the British monk Pelagius seemed to preach a totally different gospel to his audience in metropolitan Rome. Being confronted with the sinfulness of a metropolis, the ascetically-minded Pelagius thought it best to appeal to the natural possibilities of humanity. He asserted that "we have implanted in us by God a capacity for either part," to do good or to do evil.[30] Of course, Pelagius does not relegate God's grace to superfluity. He distinguishes now between ability, volition, and actuality.[31] Since volition and actuality are up to us, Pelagius asserts that "for his willing, therefore, and doing a good work, the praise belongs to man." Since God enables us in our willing and doing, Pelagius immediately corrects himself by saying: "Or rather both to man, and to God who has bestowed on him the 'capacity' for his will and work, and who evermore by His grace assists even this capacity." He even goes on to say: "That a man is able to will and effect any good work, comes from God alone."

We may at first wonder why Augustine objected to a view that seemed to express the necessity of God's grace for good action. Perhaps the issue becomes clearer when we hear Pelagius insist "that it is possible for man to be without sin," though he does not admit "that there is a man without sin."[32] Of course, Augustine vehemently opposes the idea of a sinless human being. Unlike Pelagius, Augustine views sin not as an accumulation of sinful acts, but an attitude in which we are all caught, since we are part of humanity. But Pelagius and his followers do not see sin as a universal human condition. For instance, Coelestius, one of Pelagius' ardent followers, does not find it necessary "that infants must be baptized for the remission of sins."[33] In his mind such move would affirm that sin is transmitted from one generation to another. Coelestius insists that sin is not a condition, the encounter with which we could not avoid, but it is a wilfully committed act and therefore he concludes that nobody has to sin.[34]

Since Tertullian, the idea had gained more and more prominence in the church that sin is handed on through the procreational process—from one generation to another. This idea was certainly not a boon to the church, especially when it cast a negative light on sexuality. For us today it also seems to imply that sin is a genetic defect. Yet the intention of this notion was not to cause these unfortunate misconceptions. It was designed to reinforce that sin is not an individualized act or an accumulation thereof. This was the main point that Augustine brought forth against the Pelagians. To underscore this point humanity was conceived of as a corrupt entity of which we are part. From the moment when by one man sin entered the world, "the entire mass of our nature was ruined beyond doubt, and fell into the possession of its destroyer."[35] Of course, Augustine admits that humanity was created good and its free will was directed toward the good.[36] Humanity could have relied on God, remained good, and have been rewarded for this.[37] As humanity had the ability not to sin, it also had the ability not to die, though it did not enjoy the inability to sin and to die. Such inability will only be an eschatological gift.[38] Once the ability to sin was actualized, humanity as a whole became a corrupt entity.[39] In turning away from God, humanity was deserted by God.

Since the activities of a sinner are conducted without reference to God they are sinful even if they show phenomenologically "good" results. On the other hand the sinner commits freely what is evil, following his evil inclinations.[40] Augustine concludes that the virtues of the pagans are splendid vices. Unlike Pelagius, it is insufficient for Augustine to reflect simply on the motivation or the obvious outcome of an action. Augustine insists that we must ask whether it is done in congruence with God's will or against it. Furthermore, he does not want to consider just one single act, but to consider its context too, and to determine whether the congruence with the will of God was of accidental or fundamental nature. Only an attitude of total reliance on God can result in a good act. Therefore grace cannot be conditional. It is not grace if it is not freely given. It is God then "who both makes the will of man righteous, and thus prepares it for assistance, and assists it when it is prepared." [41] God's grace prevenes to prepare our will and it assists to bring to perfection what he has started in us.[42]

Augustine is aware that the total reliance on God's saving activity could be interpreted as depriving us of a free will. But he does not agree with such a notion.[43] Of course, he insists that no one can withstand the will of God.[44] If it were otherwise, our salvation would be in constant jeopardy, because even the grace received in baptism does not do away with our sinful concupiscence. It is only no longer dangerous to us because now, with God's help, we can overcome it.[45] Augustine recognizes that in this life our righteousness "consists rather in the remission of sins than in the perfecting of virtues." [46] Perseverance of our faith in Christ is essentially a gift of God.[47]

Augustine's emphasis on the all-embracing grace of God leads to the acknowledgment that we are saved through God's undeserved grace. But why are some condemned, Augustine is asked? Augustine responds by referring to the total lack of antecedent merits. Since no one deserves to be saved, we should not boast if we are saved or complain if we are not saved.[48] Thus our election is by God's grace and our condemnation by our own works.[49] But Augustine's extensive deliberations did not convince others, why God predestines some to be saved and actually does save them, while others remain in their self-inflicted misery. Perhaps it would have been wiser if he had stayed with his insight: "Since the judgments of God are exceedingly deep and incomprehensible and His ways unsearchable, let man meanwhile hold that there is no injustice with God; let him confess that as man he does not know with what justice God has mercy in whom He will and hardens whom He will." [50]

At the Synod of Orange in 529 the church decided to adopt officially Augustine's emphasis on the primacy of grace. It stated that all people are born in sin and cannot free themselves from their sinful context. Divine grace has to precede good works and divine assistance must accompany our whole life to make it acceptable to God. Without illumination and inspiration of the Holy Spirit we can do nothing which pertains to our salvation. Yet the idea was explicitly rejected that divine power could truly destine anybody to do evil and no mention was made either of God's irresistible grace.[51] But already Augustine claimed that no one can be sure that one is predestined to God's kingdom.[52] Thus the emphasis on the primacy of grace still left the people with a certain degree of uncertainty about whether or not one actually could rely on God's grace.

b. Baptism and Eucharist

Perhaps to overcome the latent uncertainty over one's final destiny, the Synod of Orange concluded that "we may both faithfully seek the sacraments of baptism, and after baptism with His help be able to perform those (acts) which are pleasing to Him." [53] Since repentance is part of the baptismal ritual, repentance and baptism have always been closely associated with each other.

BAPTISM: Though the Didache mentions that baptism is administered in the Lord's name (9:5), it also reminds us that baptism should be performed in the name of the Father, Son, and Holy Spirit (7:1-3). This means that baptism is instituted by Christ and done in his name. Yet baptism involves the whole Trinity. We prepare for the sacrament through fasting (7:4) and once we are baptized, we are allowed to participate in the Eucharist (9:5). Of course, baptism presupposes listening and believing and we are sealed in baptism with the seal of Christ (Herm. Sim. 8.6.3) and there we receive forgiveness of all our former sins (Herm. Mand. 4.3.1). Though we hear that our life is saved through the water of baptism (Herm. Vis. 3.3.5), it was initially left open whether baptism is the end of our sinful life or the beginning of a new life under grace and repentance. Thus it was undecided whether the sealing with the seal of Christ did indeed mandate and enable a life of holiness, or whether such life was more an aspiration than a reality.

The Egyptian Church Order—presumably written by Hippolytus and Tertullian—gives us detailed insights in the rite and significance of baptism during the third century.[54] Though any believer could administer baptism, Tertullian tells us that the prime right to baptize belongs to the bishop. A suitable day on which to be baptized is the passion day (Friday) to remind us of the Lord's suffering and death into which we are baptized. Of course, other days may be chosen too. One enters baptism with repeated prayers, fasts, and vigils lasting all night. It is important that one publicly confesses one's sins. Also the anointing with oil is part of the baptismal rite.

According to Tertullian we do not obtain the Holy Spirit through the baptismal water since its purpose is to cleanse and to prepare us for the Holy Spirit. Not until the laying on of hands and the invoking and inviting of the Holy Spirit, "that Holiest Spirit" descends from the Father willingly upon our cleansed and blessed bodies.[55] We almost get the impression here that there is a twofold baptism, one with water and another with the Spirit. When Tertullian talks about the Spirit as the substance of baptism, he implicitly affirms the oneness of baptism.[56] He also implies that we do not only encounter a spiritual process in baptism, but a physical change. As we will see, this line of thought gained special prominence in the Eastern churches. We should also not forget that baptism was understood to grant both remission of sins formerly committed and actual regeneration. There are several lines that converge in baptism: (1) moral education, culminating in the confession of sins; (2) religious education, leading to the conviction of the Christian gospel; (3) confession of the Christian faith, and renunciation of everything evil; and (4) the conversion which allows the new Christian to participate in the Eucharist.[57]

When we see these different components of baptism, we wonder to what extent such a sacrament is inclusive of both infants and adults. While Tertullian, for instance, does not deny infant baptism, he makes it clear that "the delay of baptism is preferable; principally, however, in the case of little children."[58] If baptism should lead to a life of holiness and if it is the one chance to obtain remission of all sins, it should be performed as late as possible. Thus Tertullian and the people of his time are not against infant baptism as such, but against early administration of baptism.

Later in the third century, however, the sentiment had changed and we hear from Cyprian almost the opposite argument from that of Tertullian. If God can forgive sinners who have accumulated the sins of a whole life, how much easier should it be for God to forgive an infant who has no other sin than being born into a sinful context?[59] There should be no discrimination of age, Cyprian argues, and God's grace and mercy must not be denied to anybody. We must conclude that infant baptism as a prevalent practice did not just result through the change from a missionary to an established church.[60] There were other factors involved too, such as the general use of a second penance and the growing emphasis on the gravity of original sin. For instance, Tertullian still holds that the blood baptism of a martyr can be substituted for water baptism, and he surmises that baptism is not indispensably necessary for salvation.[61] We might even venture to say that the predominant practice of infant baptism led away from the heavy emphasis on law and holiness. It brought the church back to a more dynamic and more New Testament-oriented understanding of the continued necessity of grace and forgiveness.

When we now briefly consult Augustine on his understanding of baptism, we notice that he distinguishes two facets of a sacrament, the external gift administered by the priest and the invisible grace conveyed by God. A sacrament is true and valid because God's free gift cannot be hindered by fallible human beings.[62] In order to insure effectiveness of the sacraments we should not look at the one who administers them, but draw our attention to God.[63] Since God causes the effectiveness of baptism, Augustine argues against the Donatists, claiming that baptism can even be administered by people outside the church, though it shows its benefits only within the community of saints.[64] "God gives the sacrament of grace even through the hands of wicked men, but the grace itself only by Himself or through His saints." [65] The signs are present outside the church, but not God's grace. Since for Augustine the outward sign is holy, he cannot admit that it may be performed without validity. Yet validity does not automatically imply effectiveness. Only those who stand within the Christian community receive the sacramental gift, forgiveness of sins and the Holy Spirit.

We should note here that, similar to Eastern theologians, Augustine does not restrict the term sacrament to the two main sacraments, baptism and Eucharist. Many other liturgical acts, such as anointing before baptism, ordination, and exorcism are called sacraments.[66] Yet there is no doubt that baptism and Eucharist enjoy special status.

Our baptism is not simply validated when we join the Christian community. Augustine asserts "that the sacrament of baptism is one thing, the conversion of the heart another; but that man's salvation is made complete through the two together." [67] Being part of the community of believers is not analogous to holding a membership in a club. Decisive is one's intention in being part of this community. But Augustine assures us that if either baptism or conversion is missing, the other may still be present. Especially if one of them is involuntarily absent we should not despair. God's grace can make up for it, for instance, in case of an infant who died without being baptized. Yet God will not leave intentional despising of one of the two components without consequences.

As we have noticed Augustine strictly distinguishes between the sacramental action and the grace conveyed through this action. "The sacrament," Augustine says, "is one thing, the virtue of the sacrament another." [68] The baptismal action is only a symbolic cleansing act, while its efficacy comes through the word.[69] Augustine even concedes that the word is only a passing sound and not in itself efficacious. Decisive is not the utterance of the words but that we believe the word. When we hear Augustine ask: "Whence has water so great an efficacy, as in touching the body to cleanse the soul, save by the operation of the word; and that not because it is uttered, but because it is believed?", we are almost reminded of Luther's statement in his Small Catechism when he explains why water can do such a great thing. "The word is added to the element," Augustine says, "and there results the sacrament." Therefore Augustine can call the sacrament a kind of visible word. Since Augustine strictly distinguished between outward sign and inward grace and also insisted that one does not automatically coincide with or follow the other, he avoided a magical or manipulative understanding of baptism.

EUCHARIST: When we now consider briefly the other main sacrament, the Eucharist, as it developed during the first centuries, we at once are told by the early church fathers that "the Eucharist is the flesh of our Savior Jesus Christ who suffered for our sins" (Smyr. 7:1). Ignatius even goes so far as to say that the breaking of the bread, meaning the Eucharist, "is the medicine of immortality, the antidote that we should not die, but live forever in Jesus Christ" (Eph. 20:2). Of course, we could interpret Ignatius as wanting to say that by receiving Christ we receive his Spirit, eternal life, and the hope in the future resurrection. Yet especially in the East where Ignatius was at home, the notion that the Eucharist is the medicine of immortality did not simply stay within this New Testament understanding. Soon the idea emerged that in the Eucharist we are actually transformed into the divine entity in which we participate. Thus we must conclude that with Ignatius at least the groundwork was laid, whether intentionally or not, toward understanding the Eucharist as a physical medicine effecting immortality. It is also noteworthy that Ignatius already claims that a valid Eucharist can only be celebrated under the supervision of a bishop, thereby emphasizing the jurisdictional order (Smyr. 8:1). But he also calls the Eucharist an *agape* (love feast, Rom. 7:3) which indicates either that Eucharist and *agape* were still synonymous or at least celebrated in close conjunction. This would then reflect the practice of the New Testament time while the insistence on the presence of a bishop would be a new development.

When we read the Didache, we again get the impression that this document has preserved the New Testament heritage. And yet in the Didache are the first signs of new developments. For instance, we hear that the Eucharist is (connected with) an actual meal (Did. 10:1). It is celebrated on the Lord's Day and is preceded by the confession of sins, "that your offering may be pure" (Did. 14:1). This does not mean that we may be pure as through the sacramental union between the divine and us, but that our offering or sacrifice may be pure. Two movements come together here, one from God to humanity and another from humanity to God.

Offerings or sacrifices, however, were not thought of in Jewish or pagan terms as giving items to God, but as dedications to God (Bar. 2:10), prayers (Herm., Mand. 10:3), and fasting (Herm., Sim. 5:3.7). In contrast to the Jewish notion of sacrifice we hear Justin Martyr argue that prayers and giving of thanks (Eucharist) are the only perfect and well-pleasing sacrifices to God.[70] He underscores that this is a genuine Christian practice by saying: "For such alone Christians have undertaken to offer." But when he continues, "And in the remembrance effected by their solid and liquid food, whereby the suffering of the Son of God which he endured is brought to mind," we wonder whether the idea has not been introduced that offerings of food (presumably bread and wine) do indeed influence or persuade God to certain actions. This would mean that the retention of the term sacrifice for sacramental "dedications" was prone to induce certain connotations which were contrary to the intention of its users. Once the idea of sacrifice had been accepted, it seemed only a matter of time until the presiding priest became the sacrificing priest in analogy either to Jewish or pagan customs.

Towards the end of the second century Irenaeus goes one step further than Ignatius. He first acknowledges that God does not need any sacrifices from us, but then goes on to say that "the oblation of the Church, therefore, which the Lord gave instructions to be offered throughout all the world, is accounted with God a pure sacrifice, and is acceptable to him."[71] For him the eucharistic sacrifice is not limited to prayers, but includes also the elements of bread and wine which, as created things, are given back to the creator for his use. Even other gifts are offered as sacrifice.[72] But again Irenaeus contrasts this idea of sacrifice with its Jewish counterpart. He contends that the Jews had bloody and mandatory sacrifices, whereas the Christian sacrifices are voluntary and bloodless.

For Irenaeus it is not simply the Eucharist that induces immortality, but more specifically the union of flesh and spirit taking place in the eucharistic communion. "For as the bread, which is produced from the earth, when it receives the invocation of God, is no longer common bread, but the Eucharist, consisting of two realities, earthly and heavenly; so also our bodies, when they receive the Eucharist, are no longer corruptible, having the hope of the resurrection to eternity." [73] There are two realities in the Eucharist, the earthly and the spiritual. The spiritual element is introduced at the point of the *epiklesis* (i.e., invocation of Spirit) when the Spirit becomes present in the elements and effects eternal life in us.

When we come to Cyprian another step is taken to reinforce the idea of sacrifice. Now only bishops and priests can serve the altar and conduct the sacrifice.[74] The priest has assumed a completely sacerdotal role as Cyprian notes:

> For, if Christ Jesus, our Lord and God, is Himself the High Priest of God the Father and first offered Himself as a Sacrifice to His Father and commanded this to be done in commemoration of Himself, certainly the priest who imitates that which Christ did and then offers the true and full sacrifice in the Church of God the Father, if he thus begins to offer according to what he sees Christ Himself offered, performs truly in the place of Christ.[75]

The priestly sacrifice is no longer confined to the prayers or the gifts of creation that God uses. The object of the sacrifice is the passion of Christ. Christ sacrificed himself on the cross. The priest does not repeat Christ's sacrifice, but he imitates it by offering to God the body and blood of Christ. Yet the object of the sacrifice is not simply the body of Christ. It is rather its redemptive effects. Cyprian emphasizes that we should do everything the way Christ himself did it. The oblation and our sacrifice correspond to his passion. We should even mix water with wine since Christ has taught it this way.[76] In faithful obedience to Christ, he and his passion are commemorated and its benefits are brought upon those who participate in the Eucharist.[77] We encounter here an interesting mixture of imitation, commemoration, and representation. Needless to say, the priest gains in status as the one who represents Christ to the people.

But what does the eucharistic sacrifice effect according to Cyprian? We hear that the Holy Sacrifice can be offered for the repose of the soul of a deceased person or for those who are still among the living.[78] Of course, Cyprian does not advocate automatic efficacy. The one who has lapsed from faith or who has died in defiance of the rules of the church is excluded from the benefits of the eucharistic sacrifice. Yet for those in good standing it brings upon them the blessings of eternal life and forgiveness of sins.

When we come to Ambrose we notice again continuity and further development. According to Ambrose the Eucharist offers the prospect of eternal life.[79] Unlike the understanding of Irenaeus, there are no longer two ingredients in the Eucharist, an earthly and a heavenly reality. For Ambrose, "nature itself is changed" through the power of blessing.[80] In partaking of the Eucharist we do not eat bodily but spiritual food. When Ambrose declared that "the Body of Christ is the body of the Divine Spirit, for the Spirit is Christ," [81] he escaped the consequence of asserting that we actually eat the body of Christ. Yet Ambrose certainly believed that the nature of the elements was changed into the spiritual body of Christ.

When we consider the results of the Eucharist, we notice a strengthening of the soul and a continual progress in grace. However, one further point needs mentioning. Though Ambrose did not yet take the step toward transubstantiation of the elements, he certainly furthered the power of the priest. The priest not only imitates Christ, but he has the power to change nature.

Looking at Augustine, Ambrose's most famous student, we observe several significant developments. For instance, the New Testament understanding of the community of believers as the body of Christ is now applied to the Eucharist. "Believers know the body of Christ," asserts Augustine, "if they neglect not to be the body of Christ. Let them become the body of Christ, if they wish to live by the Spirit of Christ. None lives by the Spirit of Christ but the body of Christ." [82] The community of saints is the body of Christ and for its strengthening it receives the Spirit of Christ in the Eucharist, since "the body of Christ cannot live but by the Spirit of Christ." In analogy to Augustine's understanding of the benefits of baptism, he now asserts that a heretic will not receive any benefits from the Eucharist. Moreover, if one is not clean and not a member of the body of Christ, the sacrament can only do harm.[83]

Since Augustine also identifies the body of Christ with the community of believers, he can understand the presence of Christ in the sacrament in a more symbolic way than did Ambrose. For instance, Augustine says: "This is, therefore, for a man to eat that meat and to drink that drink, to dwell in Christ, and to have Christ dwelling in him." [84] Again he writes, "We are made better by participation of the Son, through the unity of His body and blood, which thing that eating and drinking signifies. We live then by Him, by eating Him; that is, by receiving Himself as the eternal life, which we did not have from ourselves." [85] He can even talk about "the figure *(figura)* of His Body and Blood" that he committed and delivered to his disciples in the Lord's Supper." [86] Augustine asserts that even the heretic, if admitted to the Lord's Supper, receives, "none the less the body of the Lord and the blood of the Lord." [87]

But Augustine also says that as God, Christ is everywhere wholly present, "while in His true Body He is in some part of heaven." [88] Does this mean that Augustine is either inconsistent in his approach to the Eucharist or that he ultimately assumes a symbolic interpretation of the presence of Christ? [89] Similar to his understanding of baptism, Augustine does not reflect on the action of the presiding priest in the Eucharist. God's action in the Eucharist is what matters: God doing something for us. With this approach, the issue of the eucharistic sacrifice becomes secondary. There is also no doubt for Augustine that Christ is truly present in the Eucharist, since in this sacrament God does something for us. That Augustine does not speak of Christ's presence in human form, but in divine form only, indicates that he has not yet conceptually developed the ubiquity of the person of Christ. He conceives only of the ubiquity of Christ's divine nature with the human nature necessarily locally confined as human nature always is.

The important point in Augustine's understanding of the Eucharist is that he pays primary attention to what the Lord's Supper means and effects for us, instead of devoting predominant attention to the sacrament itself. Similar to the New Testament, the soteriological aspect of this sacrament reigns supreme and the speculative aspect becomes incidental. The Reformers attempted to pick up this emphasis almost a thousand years later against the rationalistic speculation of medieval scholasticism.

Augustine's understanding of sacrifice moves away from the priest to the true sacrifice "which Christ alone offered on his altar. This sacrifice," we hear, "is also commemorated by Christians, in the sacred offering and participation of the body and blood of Christ." [90] Instead Augustine designates as true sacrifice every work "which is done that we may be united to God in holy fellowship, and which has a reference to that supreme good and end in which alone we can be truly blessed." [91] Since Christ is both the priest who offers the sacrifice and the sacrifice to be offered, "He designed that there should be a daily sign of this in the sacrifice of the Church, which, being His body, learns to offer herself through Him." [92] For Augustine sacrifice is not a manipulative or repristinating act, but a daily commemoration of Christ's sacrifice in the worshiping and self-giving community. He does not reflect on the action of the eucharistic sacrifice, but rather emphasizes that it becomes the source of action for the upbuilding of the body of Christ, namely the church. Augustine's reflection on the christocentricity and ecclesiological structure of the Eucharist, however, could not stem the tide of popular piety.

Barely a century later, Pope Gregory the Great claimed that Christ, though living in himself immortally and incorruptibly, "is again immolated for us in the mystery of the holy Sacrifice." [93] In other words, the Eucharist is a repetition of the sacrifice of Christ. Gregory even speculates that sometimes the souls of the dead "beg to have Masses offered for them," and that the Mass can be said to spare people in dangerous situations. [94] Here pagan superstition was paired with Christian elements to turn the Eucharist into an apotropeic means by which one could secure certain advantages in this life and in the hereafter. Yet Gregory the Great was not an exception. His line of thought was the course that eucharistic practice would take through the centuries moderated on occasion with reforming movements.

2. The piety of Eastern Christendom

The following reflections on the piety of Eastern Christendom are not meant to be exhaustive. We are merely attempting to indicate some major points at which Eastern and Western piety differ.

a. The means of grace

True doctrine and the means of grace are the focal points of Eastern Christendom. The means of grace, however, are conceived of much more broadly than we would assume. For instance, John of Damascus tells us that "the Master Christ made the remains of the saints to be foundations of salvation to us, pouring forth manifold blessings." [95] Then he asks rhetorically: "Are not those, then, worthy of honor who are the patrons of the whole race, and make intercession to God for us?" John encourages us "to give honour to them by raising temples to God in their name, bringing them fruit-offerings, honouring their memories and taking spiritual delight in them." Besides the worship of saints and their remains, John also encourages us to worship the paintings of saints, the Gospels, the cross, the mother of the Lord, and the like.[96] Yet he does not want us to worship graven images as the pagans do. Since God cannot be depicted, John expressly refutes the idea that we should worship idols.

Yet John of Damascus reminds us that we are created in God's own image. Because of this fact we show reverence to each other. The reason for this is, he says, quoting Basil the Great, that "the honour given to the image passes over to the prototype." A prototype is that from which the image is made. When we worship the cross of Christ, the nails, the spear, the clothes, the manger, and the tomb, we do not honor the objects, but the objects are understood as symbols of Christ. "For wherever the sign may be, there also will He be." [97] John can even say that the honor we give to Mary, the mother of the Lord, "is referred to Him Who was made of her incarnate." [98] All these various means of grace are understood as essentially pointing to Christ, the incarnate representation of God. The idea that the symbol represents that for which it stands and that one obtains with it access to the thing itself led to a multitude of ways in which one could assure divine presence and help.

This understanding of divine presence influenced the sacramental practice. Again we refer here to John of Damascus who gave Eastern Christendom its most prominent and coherent theological system.[99] With regard to baptism we notice some very interesting reflections and actions. In analogy to the three days that passed between Christ's death and resurrection, John mentions a three-fold immersion in baptism. He also mentions anointing with olive oil, again a reminder of Christ's passion which announces us to God's pity. Coming from the Greek tradition, John distinguishes between two sides of human nature, body and spirit. Consequently he finds that God bestows on us "a twofold purification, of water and of the Spirit: the Spirit renewing that part in us which is after His image and likeness, and the water by the grace of the Spirit cleansing the body from sin and delivering it from corruption." While remission of sins is granted alike to all through baptism, "the grace of the Spirit is proportional to the faith and previous purification."

We conclude that the effects of baptism are twofold. We receive the forgiveness of sins and we stand with the help of the Holy Spirit at the beginning of a new life. Thus gift (remission of sins) and task (regeneration and sanctification) are equally present in baptism. Since the Spirit is the active agent in baptism, we are not confronted with a simple moralism. This becomes obvious when John warns against postponing baptism so that the faith of those aspiring to baptism may first be testified by works. Since the life after baptism is understood as a dynamic progression toward holiness, we need not wait with the inception of new life until the end of our earthly days. In the West, however, the aspect of forgiveness in baptism was emphasized to the detriment of sanctification. It was thought there that one should wait with baptism until the last possible moment so that all the sins could be forgiven.

John of Damascus would agree that in baptism we receive remission of sins so far committed. It is also clear for the Eastern tradition that there is no second remission by another baptism.[100] Yet there is remission of sins even after baptism. Though John admits that this is a difficult process involving "tears, repentance, confession, almsgiving, prayer, and every other kind of reverence." But we should remember that in baptism we receive the Holy Spirit who helps our infirmities and aids our mind against "the law that is in our members," it is realistic to encourage the baptized to sin no more.[101] For instance, Ignatius called his fellow Christians carriers of God, carriers of the temple, carriers of Christ, and carriers of holiness, since they are in all their ways "adorned by commandments of Jesus Christ" (Eph. 9:2). Irenaeus too emphasized that "the Word of God, our Lord Jesus Christ, who did, through His transcendent love, become what we are, that He might bring us to be even what He is Himself."[102] In the same vein, pointing out that God had to become a human being, Athanasius explained: "For He was made man that we might be made God."[103] These statements describe the divine-human encounter with a twofold movement. God comes to us so that we may come to him and become like him. If we consider this movement, perhaps we understand that baptism is the first step, nay the initiation, into the divinization process.[104]

b. The emphasis on divinization

Actually, the notion of a divinization of humanity should not surprise us. As we hear from John of Damascus, "Man, however, being endowed with reason and free will, received the power of continuous union with God through his own choice, if indeed he should abide in goodness, that is, in obedience to his Maker."[105] Since humanity abandoned its primordial union with God through its sinfulness, it has become unable to return to this union on its own. But the estrangement can be overcome. Through the salvational process in Jesus Christ, i.e., incarnation, passion, and resurrection, "we, too, following in His footsteps, may become by adoption what He is Himself by nature, sons and heirs of God and joint heirs with Him."

We have been given a new birth through baptism and now we obtain a new (spiritual) food through the Eucharist. John of Damascus insists that in the Eucharist the body of Christ which was received up into the heavens does not descend. Yet the Word of God is true and energizes, and it is omnipotent in a manner which cannot be explained. "So the bread of the table and the wine and water are supernaturally changed by the invocation [*epiklesis*] and presence of the Holy Spirit into the body and blood of Christ, and are not two but one and the same." The power of the word in the *epiklesis* induces an actual change of the elements and as John explains, this is done through the Spirit in analogy to Jesus becoming man. Bread and wine are united with the divine that they have not just their earthly nature, but also a divine. "The bread and wine are not merely figures of the body and blood of Christ (God forbid!) but the deified body of the Lord itself."

John's emphasis on the real presence becomes understandable when we consider the twofold effects of the Eucharist on those who partake of it worthily and with faith. First, we receive remission of sins and assurance of life everlasting. Secondly, the divine coal of the elements consumes our sins and illumines our hearts "that we may be inflamed and deified by the participation in the divine fire." Being purified through the Eucharist, we are united to the body of Christ and to his Spirit and actually become the body of Christ. This unification process must be seen in three ways:

(1) The body and blood of Christ support our body and soul in a very dramatic way. We are protected against all kinds of injury, purged from all uncleanness, and purified "from diseases and all kinds of calamities." This means that Eucharist is becoming an apotropeic tool through which we can protect ourselves against undesirable events.

(2) Having communion with Christ and sharing in his flesh and in his divinity, "we have communion and are united with one another through it. For since we partake of one bread, we all become one body of Christ and one blood, and members one of another, being of one body with Christ." Here the Augustinian notion surfaces that Christ's real presence

enables the Christians to become the body of Christ and therewith his church in being united with one another and with him.

(3) There is also a third aspect which seems to bear special merit. John recognizes the life-giving and divine power of the sacrament when he says that the Eucharist becomes necessary for existence, either for a future age or "for the preservation of our essence." The life-giving spirit of the elements preserves us toward our eschatological perfection and is also essential to preserve our humanity. Only in union with the divine and empowered by it can we be truly human, fulfilling our function as the image of God. In its desire for deification Eastern Christendom may have sensed something of the necessity of the divine presence if we want to remain human.

We would misinterpret Eastern Christendom if we would assume that, in contrast to the West, it does not consider the forgiveness of sin but immortality as the real effect of the Eucharist. Certainly, the forgiveness of sin is central, but also important is the next step, union with Christ and the ensuing deification. Except for mystic and pietistic circles, the West could not quite take this second step, since it knew about the immensity of human depravity. In Eastern Christendom, however, original sin was seldom emphasized to the same extent as in the West. It was taught in the East that we have come into this world sinless, that we can choose to sin of our own free will, and therefore we are sold by ourselves.[106] Small wonder that Eastern Christendom was free to admit that deification was a goal to be attained. Eastern theologians had even initially accepted Pelagius and his followers rather favorably. But they could not admit with the Pelagians that humanity still had an either/or choice, to sin or not to sin. Human weakness, the Eastern theologians taught, had succumbed to sin freely and was now enslaved to sin. Yet through the aid of the Spirit of God, the mind could regain control over the desires of the flesh.

Eastern anthropology may prove more beneficial for the assurance of salvation for the individual than the sin-ridden anthropology of the West. It allows the believers to recognize that they are on the way to deification. Under the Western dialectic of sin and forgiveness, however, no actual progression is attained, and therefore uncertainty rules supreme. Yet the Eastern anthropology proved extremely dangerous when the positive evaluation of humanity was applied to the universal and political scene. Then the earthly empire became a replica of the heavenly city and the emperor was designated as the viceroy of God. Unlike in the West, where the Pope continuously attempted to check the sanctity of the earthly ruler, the East trusted in one kingdom and thought it did not need such checks. As history showed, the church there depended more and more on the mercy of a state that often did not resemble the theocracy it was intended to embody.

3. Church and state

The relationship between church and state is relatively easy to define if we would start with the church as an established religious institution. But the beginnings of the relationship were of rather modest dimensions. Before the church could establish itself it had to win a whole empire.

a. The emerging majority religion

When Jesus admonished the people to give Caesar what is Caesar's and to God what is God's, he did not regard the state as a permanent institution. As soon as the kingdom of God has arrived in fullness, the state would disappear from this world. Yet as long as the present age continues, God wants the state to exist, even the Roman state. This is also basically the attitude of Paul when he says: "Let every person be subject to the governing authorities. For there is no authority except from God, and those that exist have been instituted by God. Therefore he who resists the authorities resists what God has appointed, and those who resist will incur judgment" (Rom. 13:1f.). When Paul calls the authorities "ministers of God" (Rom. 13:6), it should become clear that the state can never usurp the position of God, but it exerts its authority under God's supervision and on his behalf.[107]

Important also is Revelation 13 in which the state is compared to a beast arising from the sea. We might at first assume that Revelation presents a totally different attitude toward the state, perhaps under entirely new conditions. But the seer of the Book of Revelation looks at the same state as did Paul, the Roman Empire. Now it is no longer the state's reign on God's behalf that is addressed, but its attempt to extricate itself from God's supervision and to set itself up as a divine entity. This pursuit is interpreted as a demonic enterprise and is described with imagery taken from Jewish apocalyptic. We also notice that people are tempted to follow the beast and "all who dwell on earth will worship it" (Rev. 13:8). This provides a vivid description of the church's struggle to withstand the demands of the Roman State for adjuring allegiance and sacrifice to the emperor. For instance, we read in the exchange of letters between the imperial administrator, Pliny the Younger, and Emperor

Trajan that the Christians were ordered "to curse Christ" and to worship Rome's gods. If they did not comply they were slain, but if they did conform they were freed. Once the state takes on these totalitarian and demonic features, it can no longer be recognized as God's representative.

The Christian religion as nuisance and challenge: During the centuries of latent or outright clashes between church and state, the church never resorted to revolt against the state. Of course, the church tried every legal means to free its people from prison once they were imprisoned for their Christian affiliation, but it always accepted the verdict of the state.[108] For example, Paul claimed his Roman citizenship when he was about to be treated unfairly (Acts 22:25). And then we read in the pastoral letters: "First of all, then, I urge that supplications, prayers, intercessions, and thanksgiving be made for all men, for kings and all who are in high positions, that we may lead a quiet and peaceable life, godly and respectful in every way" (1 Tim. 2:1f.). Even in times of trial and persecution the church does not reject the state as an institution of God. It continuously prays that this institution will not be perverted into a demonic tyranny. But unlike Judaism, the Christian church did not rise up against persecution or suppression of its adherers. On the contrary, occasionally its faithful are even admonished not to seek the martyrdom on their own. This means that the church attempted to win the world by love and prayer and not by resistance and force. Yet what made the Christians so despicable in the eyes of most people and of the state?

To understand the tension between the church and the Roman state we must be aware of the intimate connection of the official Roman state religion to Roman citizenship. Participation in the Roman cult and Roman citizenship were nearly synonymous. As a Roman citizen one worshiped the gods of Rome. Roman citizenship excluded any other citizenship and the worship of Roman gods excluded worship of other gods. Of course, we know that Paul was a Roman citizen and that he had certainly been a worshiping Jew prior to his conversion. This indicates that the term "gods of Rome" was not very narrowly conceived. For instance, the worship of the Egyptian gods Isis and Serapis, and the Phrygian goddess Cybele enjoyed to some degree the status of a licensed and consecrated state religion, subject to certain restrictions in membership and conduct. We may assume a similar status for Judaism.[109]

Certain nations could continue to exercise their own religion as long as its worship did not include offensive elements such as human sacrifice, orgiastic feasts, etc. Since the Jewish people were a nation in the Eastern part of the Roman Empire their religion was regarded there as a licit religion. In the West, however, where they had colonies and proselytes in every major city, their religion was simply a tolerated or licensed one. The Christians initially enjoyed freedom of worship under the umbrella of Judaism. Tertullian refers to this when he states that Christianity was hiding "under the shadow of an illustrious religion [Judaism], one which has at any rate undoubted allowance of the law." [110] Yet soon it must have become obvious even to outsiders that Judaism and Christianity were two separate movements.

Since Christianity was not a licensed religion, its adherers transgressed the Roman law which stated "that no god should be consecrated by the emperor till first approved by the [Roman] senate." [111] Of course, the Christians could have fulfilled the letter of the law by also worshiping the gods or offering sacrifices to the emperor.[112] Yet the Christians refused to offer sacrifices to the gods. They claimed that there were no other gods and neither could they offer sacrifice to other people, i.e., the emperor. The verdict against the Christians was sacrilege and high treason, sacrilege because they worshiped an unlicensed god and denied homage to the licensed ones, and high treason because they did not acknowledge the supposedly divine attributes of the emperor. Small wonder that they were regarded as "public enemies" and "enemies of Rome." [113]

The measures against the Christians were predictable. If they were Roman citizens they were either sent to Rome for trial, which usually resulted in the death penalty, or they were decapitated in the city in which they were apprehended, pending approval by the emperor.[114] If they did not have Roman citizenship they usually died in the arena, or often in case of women, were sent to the brothel. There were many rumors and charges brought against the Christians, such as conspiratory oaths, black magic, and even cannibalism.[115]

The issue mitigating against Christianity was not simply that it was an unlicensed religion or that it refused to include in its cult some sign of allegiance to the emperor. Especially since Julius Caesar and Caesar Augustus, the emperor had become both the high priest and an object of religious devotion. The emperor himself was not adored, however, as a divinity, but libations were offered to his imperial genius. In areas, however, that were more used to the idea of divine kingship, the fine line between the divine genius of the emperor and the emperor as deity was hardly noticed and altars were erected to Augustus.[116] While the Jews found it possible to offer prayer and sacrifice in the Jerusalem temple on behalf of Augustus and his successors, the Christians did not want to compromise their undivided allegiance to their Lord. Yet they were not simply indifferent to the state.

Mindful of 1 Timothy 2:1f. and its exhortation to pray for all in authority, Christians offered prayers on behalf of the emperor.[117] Origen, for instance, rejects the accusation that Christians do not accept public office or fight in wars. Indeed it was initially impossible for Christians to aspire to public office since that meant sacrifice to the emperor and they also abhorred the idea of war. But Origen argues that we Christians

> do take our part in public affairs, when along with righteous prayers we join self-denying exercises and meditations, which teach us to despise pleasures, and not to be led away by them. And none fight better for the king than we do. We do not indeed fight under him, although he require it; but we fight on his behalf, forming a special army—an army of piety —by offering our prayers to God.

According to Origen the Christians understood themselves as the moral and spiritual backbone of the state. They bring the affairs of the day to the attention of the Lord and by their prayers "vanquish all demons who stir up war, and lead to the violation of oaths, and disturb the peace." Yet their obvious noninvolvement in public office and positions of leadership led many people to contrary conclusions. The suspicion about the Christians was nourished even more when Origen claimed that "we recognise in each state the existence of another national organization, founded by the Word of God." Such a statement not only indicates the autonomy the early church felt over against the nation in whose midst it lived, but it can also be interpreted as a call for subversion.

The Jewish authorities were initially eager to lend a helping hand to the state in persecuting the Christians and "through jealousy and envy the greatest and most righteous pillars of the Church were persecuted and contended unto death" (1 Clem. 5:2). Unlike the Jews, the Christians never caused actual problems in the Roman Empire. They did not stir up revolts and they did not defend their national autonomy with utmost tenacity. At the most, the Christians were a nuisance and an enigma. As Clement, for instance, shows, they prayed for those in authority that God may "direct their counsels according to that which is 'good and pleasing' before him, that they may administer with piety in peace and gentleness the power given to them by him, and may find mercy in his eyes (1 Clem. 61:2).

Nevertheless, we hear from Pliny the Younger's letter to Trajan that merely belonging to the Christians was sufficient for a trial since this was considered a "madness." [118] As a remedy one was forced "to curse Christ" and to sacrifice through a libation of incense and wine before the imperial statue. Pliny already admitted that the Christians were not conspirators. On the contrary, they bound themselves by a sacred oath never to commit fraud, theft, adultery, and other crimes or bear false witness. Why were the Christians then persecuted if they did not pose a threat to anyone? The reason, as we see from Pliny, is that with the increasing number of Christians, the temples became less and less frequented and there was no longer much demand for sacrificial animals. So what was at stake was in essence the popular Roman religion and, as many people and the state authorities felt, the existence of the Roman state. We are not surprised that usually "better" emperors persecuted the Christians in order to restore the Roman religious cult and to instill peace and order in the communities. The Christians had become such a disturbing and annoying factor for the traditional Roman way of life that they were often denounced to the authorities.

Yet the Christians were not simply persecuted for persecution's sake. For instance, Samaritans who practiced circumcision were put to death, even if they fell away from their faith, because in violation of Roman law, they mutilated themselves. [119] Yet Christians were always given a second chance to offer sacrifice and to repudiate their religion. This means they were never persecuted as radically and relentlessly as Jewish sects, or even, at times, as the Jewish people themselves. If they "repented" and returned to the pagan religion, they could return to their homes and live in safety. As the ranks of the Christians increased and the persecutions against them became more intense and more systematic, the large number of lapsed Christians indicates that the route of apostasy was taken by many.

The Christian faith as marvel and attraction: The Christian faith was a relative novelty and did not have the sanction that the Jewish religion usually enjoyed. The Christians were not inclined to compromise the faith and their insistence on one God to the exclusion of any devotion to the emperor or his genius was viewed by many as a potentially subversive act and also as arrogance. There were positive things too that the pagans observed from the Christians. For instance, Tertullian tells us that the pagans say: "See, how they love one another." [120] The pagans obviously had observed that the Christians called each other brothers and sisters and showed concern and interest for each other. In a selfish, self-centered

society in which especially those in prominent positions were never sure
that the status they had attained would survive until the next day, such
mutual concern as existed in the Christian community was unheard of.
It often encountered surprise and sometimes even ridicule, since it seemed
a sign of stupidity to some pagans. As Dionysius of Rome tells us:

> From the start it has been your custom to treat all Christians with unfail-
> ing kindness, and to send contributions to many churches in every city,
> sometimes alleviating the distress of those in need, sometimes providing
> for your brothers in the mines by the contributions you have sent from
> the start.[121]

The love among Christians went so far as to support Christians in other
cities and also to support, at least occasionally, those who had been condemned to work in the mines because of their Christian affiliation.

As we see from the account of Polycarp's trial, the steadfastness, gentleness, and perseverance of the Christians impressed quite a few who did
not impulsively follow the agitations of the mob. Often the authorities
played down the significance of sacrificing to the emperor, trying to make
it more palatable to the Christians.[122] Justin tells us that he was finally
converted from Platonism to Christianity by the sight of the steadfastness
of the martyrs and he concluded that the accusation of moral depravity
of the Christians could simply not be true.[123] He observed that hatred,
lust, strife, envy, and continuous warfare so vividly depicted and extolled
in the pagan myths is replaced in the Christian teaching by virtue, love,
and serenity.[124] No wonder that more and more people flocked to the
Christian church.

At the middle of the third century the Christian faith was one of the
major religions of the Roman Empire. Yet notoriety was not necessarily
beneficial. As Tertullian reminds us: There were still enough people left
to think that the Christians were

> the cause of every public disaster, of every affliction with which the people
> are visited. If the Tiber rises as high as the city walls, if the Nile does not
> send its water up over the fields, if the heavens give no rain, if there is an
> earthquake, if there is famine or pestilence, straightway the cry is, "Away
> with the Christians to the lions!" [125]

As we will see later, this superstition that the gods are enraged about the
growing number of the Christians and the increasingly deserted temples

eventually helped to turn the tide in favor of the Christians. The Christian God proved to be stronger than all other gods. Meanwhile acceptance as Christians stood on shaky ground.

There are many items, however, that contributed to the eventual victory of the church in the pagan state. When Christ could be depicted in a mosaic in one of the tombs underneath St. Peter's in Rome as *sol invictus* (i.e., the invincible sun god), riding in a heavenly chariot, we realize that he is no longer a complete foreigner in the religious world of Rome. He has become part of it, occupying a prominent place. Other gods too could assume features that today we would call decidedly Christian. For instance, Hermes Trismegistos could be represented as guide and instructor for the soul, Heracles could symbolize the salvation of humanity by overcoming the evil powers, and Attis could be depicted as the good shepherd. We notice a remarkable confluence of religious motifs in the third century. But Christianity was here in an advantageous position since its God had really lived, performed miraculous deeds, and had died for all people.

At the beginning of the third century we also hear the church in Rome had a cemetery (at the Via Appia) of which Callistus, later to become pope, was in charge.[126] This meant that the church was legally entitled to obtain and hold property. A generation later Christians were even so much recognized that Mammaea, the mother of Emperor Antoninus Pius, secured an interview with Origen and sent a bodyguard of soldiers to escort him to Antioch and to test "his universally admired skill as a theologian."[127] Yet at mid-century the tide had changed again and Origen died from the results of an interrogation by the authorities on the charge of being a Christian. The fortunes swayed back and forth several times and on each occasion the Christians came out stronger than before.

Even before the church was officially recognized the emperors were not oblivious to the church's own affairs. For instance, Paul of Samosata had finally been condemned by the Synod of Antioch (268) because of his Origenist tendencies and had lost his bishop's seat. Now the question was raised whether he also had to vacate the bishop's residence. Eusebius tells us that in this matter "the Emperor Aurelian was appealed to, and he gave a perfectly just decision on the course to be followed: he ordered the building to be assigned to those to whom the bishops of the religion in Italy and Rome addressed a letter."[128] This meant that the emperor decided that those who made known the decisions of the synod to the whole church should be the owners of the bishop's mansion. Here the first appeal was made to the emperor in church matters—and the church was not even officially recognized. Small wonder that the imperial influence in church matters would soon become even more visible.[129]

When the last all-out attempt was launched under Emperor Diocletian to persecute the Christians and to restore the old-time religions, the same day his edict appeared, a Christian tore it down with the comment "that victories of the Goths and Sarmatians were proposed in it." [130] To make Diocletian continue the persecution, Lactantius alleges that Caesar Galerius had to set fire twice to the imperial palace in Nicomedia and attribute the cause to the Christians.[131] Even if the Christians had started the fire as a warning to the emperor it would show how difficult his persecutions of the Christian cause had become. Galerius, the successor to Diocletian, continued to persecute the Christians for another ten years. But then he was afflicted with a fatal disease that Orosius savoringly describes in all details. One physician finally took courage to tell him "that his punishment was the anger of God and so he could not be cured by physicians." [132]

In 311 Galerius, perhaps as a last attempt to escape from his illness, drafted an edict in which he decreed that the Christians were free to live as they pleased and were able to restore their churches, provided they would do nothing contrary to public order. They were also encouraged to ask their God for the well-being of the emperor, the state, and for themselves.[133] The actual reason given for allowing them to worship as Christians is that once their worship was outlawed they did not flock to any other religion, but simply ceased to worship God. Yet worshiping the Christian God is still better in the eyes of the emperor than having such a large group not worshiping any god at all. Finally, in 313 the famous edict signed by the emperors Licinius and Constantine was published which decreed that the Christian church had equal footing with all other cults. The church property should be completely restored and those who had purchased any would be compensated by the imperial treasury. The reason for this edict seemed clear, namely that "by this provision, as was mentioned above, the divine care for us of which we have been aware on many earlier occasions will remain with us unalterably for ever." [134]

Constantine intended to repay the (Christian) God for the advantages he had received and he wanted to insure that they continued. Under the sign of the cross he had defeated Maxentius in the battle at the Milvian Bridge against great odds. Now it was time to repay. Among other things Constantine made cash contributions to the church and exempted the clergy from municipal obligations.[135] This means that the church and its clergy were no longer assessed for road repair, building and oversight of public edifices, and taxes. Under the guidance of Bishop Ossius of Cordova, his close advisor in church matters, Constantine was also concerned about internal ecclesiastical affairs. For instance, he wanted to settle the disturbances in Africa that the rigorist faction had caused. His rationale was that "I shall really fully be able to feel secure and always to hope for prosperity and happiness from the ready kindness of the most mighty God, only when I see all venerating the most Holy God in the proper cult of the catholic religion with harmonious brotherhood of worship." [136] Constantine reasoned that if the cult mattered, it should be performed properly and in unity. Otherwise God might feel angry about the squabbles of the worshipers and withdraw his protection from the emperor, who, as the supreme ruler, was obviously responsible and liable in religious matters. But his attempts to arrive at a lasting solution in church affairs were largely futile.[137]

The decisions of the Council of Nicea (325) at which Constantine again attempted to emphasize the necessity for unity in the church did not seem to have lasting effects. Their implementation had driven too many into exile or permanent alienation. Referring to the Council of Nicea, however, Constantine rejoices that he was present "as one of you" [the bishops] and he considers himself as "your [the bishops'] fellow-servant." [138] Of course, we hear of the articles of faith proposed at the Council that

> our most pious emperor himself was the first to admit that they were perfectly correct, and that he himself had entertained the sentiments contained in them; exhorting all present to give them their assent, and subscribe to these very articles, thus agreeing in a unanimous profession of them.[139]

Constantine seemed to serve more in the role of a universal bishop than just as a fellow servant. Many seemed to rejoice in the prospect that the dreaded Roman Pontifex Maximus had become the benevolent supreme overseer. But others frankly admitted that "the state is not in the Church, but the Church is in the state, that is, the Roman Empire which Christ in the Song of Songs calls Lebanon, where there is a holy priesthood, and chastity and virginity which does not exist among barbarian nations, or if they do, do not exist in safety." [140] Here the benefits of the Christian state are clearly recognized: the Roman Empire is the protector of the church and its clergy and in exchange the Empire can expect their service and obedience. Yet it was also noted that church and state are two distinct though interdependent entities.

b. Transformation without surrender

The idea that church and state are affiliated with each other had been expressed longe before the Constantinian turning point. For instance, with reference to Romans 13 Irenaeus claimed that earthly rule "has been appointed by God for the benefit of nations, and not by the devil . . . so that under the fear of human rule, men may not eat each other up like fishes; but that, by means of the establishment of laws, they may keep down an excess of wickedness among the nations."[141] This means that God has instituted the earthly rulers to provide peace and order among the people. Yet Irenaeus also adds the warning that magistrates will not survive if they exercise their power to the perversion of justice, iniquitously, impiously, illegally, and tyrannically. The worldly authorities are therefore responsible to God. Origen used a similar argument when he claimed that the worldly authorities had no right to persecute the Christians, because such action violates the natural law.[142]

The Eastern experiment in theocracy: Especially the identification of the *logos* with both the Lord Jesus Christ and world reason at work in the whole universe made it possible to fuse the destiny of the believers and of the world. World history and salvation history became synonymous, since "our Instructor is the holy God Jesus, the Word, who is the guide of all humanity."[143] "All things are arranged with a view to the salvation of the universe by the Lord of the universe, both generally and particularly."[144] Since everything moves toward salvation, a Christian should actively engage in this process and anticipate its conclusions as much as possible. But the state is involved in this process too. For instance, Origen claimed that the unification of the Roman Empire under Augustus and the resulting *Pax Romana* (Roman peace) was a preparation for the spreading of the gospel.

> God preparing the nations for His teaching . . . the existence of many kingdoms would have been a hindrance to the spread of the doctrine of Jesus throughout the entire world; . . . on account of the necessity of men everywhere engaging in war, and fighting on behalf of their native country which was the case before the times of Augustus.[145]

Similarly, Eusebius can call Constantine "God's friend" who with "God the universal King, and God's Son the Savior of all, as Guide and Ally" defeated Licinius, every detail of the battle made easy for him "by God, in fulfillment of His purpose."[146]

When we hear this outpouring of praise, we are not surprised that half a century later the historian Socrates criticized Eusebius that he was more interested in the "rhetorical finish of his composition and the praises of the emperor, than on accurate statements of facts." [147] Even if Eusebius was too enthusiastic about the fact that Constantine had set an end to the persecution under Licinius, the idea that the emperor enjoyed special favor in the eyes of God became increasingly common. For Constantine, being the emperor and being a Christian were not two separate matters.[148] Constantine wanted to be a Christian emperor, and he feared the wrath of God if he did not fulfill his imperial task to the satisfaction of his Lord. Yet he also knew about his exceptional status, being made an emperor by his Lord. Once Constantine moved the imperial residence permanently to Constantinople, he and his successors never lost close contact with the patriarchs of Constantinople. It was in the interest of the emperor that the patriarch of Constantinople would gain more and more power, second to or even on equal footing with the pope in Rome. A church administration in such close proximity to the court could become much more easily a department of the Byzantine state and be subject to its supervision and laws than the papacy in faraway Rome.

Especially Justinian, in his attempt to reestablish one unified Catholic church, strengthened the patriarchate in Constantinople. He felt that church and state were alike creations of God and it was the duty of the latter to direct the former.[149] Yet he overestimated the difficulties of bringing together the Nestorians of Syria and Persia, the Monophysites of Egypt, Syria and Armenia, Western Christendom under the leadership of Rome, and the Orthodox Church of the East. While it was still possible to heal the breach between East and West, the imperial hand had rested too heavily on those outside the orthodox faith that they would return for a lasting peace with the church universal. Through Justinian's energetic insistence on one Christian Church in one Christian Empire, he assumed so much the leadership in church matters that he paved the way for what became known as caesaropapism (exercise of supreme authority over church matters by the emperor). How far the influence of the emperor had spread becomes evident when we hear from a recent commentator that "in the East the patriarchs, like modern English bishops, were elected by the Church, but not until they had been nominated by the government. At Rome the Pope was elected by the Romans, but their choice had to be ratified by the Emperor." [150]

Such a close connection between church and state could have dangerous effects, particularly when a strong emperor emerged who sought to dominate the church and installed compliant patriarchs instead of critical ones.[151] This certainly happened occasionally. But on the whole, the patriarchs were chosen wisely and usually were qualified for their task. The Eastern Church even welcomed such dominance, since the emperor was the accepted and welcomed earthly manifestation of the divine reason which guided, instructed, and chastened the world and which would finally save the human race. Just as God ruled in heaven, so the emperor, made in his image and being his viceroy on earth, should subdue the earth and carry out his commandments.[152] Likewise, for the Orthodox Church, the emperor's reign should embrace all people on earth and foreshadow the heavenly city. Upon suggestion of councils or patriarchs, the emperor put forth the decisions of faith and even after the Muslims swept through Syria and Egypt, the orthodox believers there, though having to obey the laws of the land, still regarded the emperor as their sovereign lord.

At the eighth session of the Sixth Ecumenical Council in Constantinople (681) the supreme role of the emperor became evident when the synod hailed him: "Long live the preserver of orthodox faith, to the new Constantine the Great, to the new Theodosius the Great, to the new Marcian, to the new Justinian many years. We are *douloi* [slaves] of the Emperor." [153] The emperor was regarded as the defender of faith who ruled the destiny of the church and safeguarded its orthodoxy. During the iconoclast controversy—the issue whether icons of saints could be venerated— in the 8th century, Emperor Leo III finally considered himself pontifex and priest-king.[154] With this understanding the epitome of the wedding between state and church had taken place.

Even then Leo III and his successor Constantine II learned that they could not force upon the people permanently a theology that they disliked. When Leo V pushed too much the idea of banning icons, Theodore of Studion challenged him with the words:

> Do not undo the status of the Church; for the Apostle spoke thus: "And he gave some apostles, and some prophets, and some evangelists, and some pastors and teachers, for the perfecting of the saints" (Eph. IV. 11), but he did not speak of Emperors. To you, Emperor, has been entrusted the political system and the army. Take care of them, and leave the Church to its shepherds and teachers according to the Apostle. If you do not agree to this—even if an angel from Heaven should give us a message about a deviation from our faith we shall not listen to him, and certainly not to you.[155]

The message was clear: the emperor should not meddle in the affairs of the church.

The emperors, however, continued to appoint patriarchs and depose retinent bishops. When John Tzimisces announced the appointment of a new patriarch, he made the general policy clear: There are two powers, the priesthood and the kingship. Since the head of the priesthood had died, he was appointing with imperial authority a person to the ecclesiastical throne whom he considered worthy.[156] Around 1180 the great canonist Theodore Balsamon even stated that the emperor was above the law, both secular and religious. He alone could introduce religious and secular legislation. It was his task to care for the souls and the bodies of his subjects. But he still had no power to dictate doctrine.[157] Once the emperor transgressed these limits, the whole empire might arise against him. For instance, when Michael had blinded the infant emperor John, who had been committed to his care, and put himself in his place, Patriarch Arsenius excommunicated the emperor. Even deposing the patriarch and appointing another one in his place and then still another one did not improve the emperor's chances. His political victories on the battlefield did not help either to improve his situation. "On 2 February 1267, the Emperor knelt bare-headed in front of the Patriarch and the Holy Synod and confessed his sin. The ban of the Church was then lifted from him." [158] The church as the guardian of morality had triumphed.

Another famous incident at which the Patriarch of Constantinople spoke out against the lax morals of the court had occurred almost 800 years before when John Chrysostom had attacked the splendor-loving Empress Eudoxia. Though John too was deposed from his position, it was clear that the public mind was behind him. The people venerated the emperor for his divine authority. But that did not prevent them from rebelling against him as a human being—especially if he did not fulfill his role. When he overstepped his boundaries in religious matters, such as pushing through the union with the West of 1274 and 1438 (finally proclaimed in 1452), he soon felt that the people backed the clergy against him and he had to pursue a different course. Conversely, when the patriarch such as John XIV Calecas overstepped his boundaries in secular matters and deposed Cantacuzemus and took over the government, he did not find unanimous support. He caused a devastating civil war that, in the end, saw the emperor victorious.

On May 29, 1453, the image of the heavenly kingdom finally came to an end when Constantinople fell into the hands of the Muslims. One may be correct in assuming that the roots of this divine monarchy were grounded in late Roman ideas. Essentially the Christian emperor continued in the pagan role of the pontifex maximus (high priest). If we would ignore these obvious historical connections, we could also find biblical parallels in the Old Testament understanding of kingship. As did the Old Testament prophets, the clerics and especially the monks often functioned as the conscience of the emperor.

Toward the close of the Eastern Empire, the territory of the patriarchate was by far larger than the continuously shrinking earthly empire. The Orthodox Church had to live under the domination of "unbelievers." Since the church, however, had always assumed the essential oneness of church and state, it was rather helpless in coping with this new situation. Despite a mass exodus of believers to areas still under political control of the emperor, the church attempted to survive under the leadership of its patriarchs in Constantinople, Alexandria, Antioch, and Jerusalem. Though the church endured in these Muslim areas, it had clearly become a minority religion, confined to its own affairs.

To some extent the Byzantine ideal found its continuity in the Russian Orthodox Church which had resulted from the efforts of orthodox mission. The Church of Constantinople had become the mother church of Russia. But the Church of Russia was not just an offspring like others. The Church of Russia eventually became the successor to the Byzantine Church when Constantinople declined in power and was finally occupied by the Muslims in 1453. The end of the imperial city almost coincided with the proclamation in 1480 by John III, Prince of Moscow, of Russia's independence from the Tartars, the Asian hordes who had devastated large parts of Europe including Southern Russia. Moreover, in 1472 John had married Sophia Baleologus, niece of the last emperor of Constantinople. After that Russia adopted the Byzantine coat of arms with the two-headed eagle.

That the Russian Church should become the heir of the Byzantine Church was also plausible since the emperor of Constantinople and the ecumenical patriarch had committed the worst crime possible. In a last desperate attempt to obtain military help against the Muslims, they had engaged in negotiations with the West, even submitting themselves to the papacy. The people back East interpreted this as apostasy, betraying the faith of their ancestors. God had rightly punished them through the fall of Constantinople. But he had selected another nation to continue the tradition of the New Rome and he would eventually restore the empire and deliver the Christians from oppression. Thus Moscow became "the Third and last Rome, the successor and spiritual heir of Rome and Constantinople." [159] Yet there too the tsar, meaning the autocrat, a title which had belonged to the Byzantine emperor, was eventually replaced by "unbelievers." Again the church managed to survive the onslaught of Marxist-Leninist propaganda, though at the expense of being reduced to a "fringe phenomenon in society." [160]

We must admire the ability of the Orthodox Church to survive under such adverse conditions; but we must also ask what caused these conditions. Truly, the patriarchs were supposed to function as the conscience of the emperors and they indeed fulfilled this task. Yet in the West it was clear that church and state were two distinct and entirely different entities. The basic unity between church and state in the East, however, made any criticism of the emperor one "from brother to brother" and therefore usually soft-spoken and ineffective. Moreover, the church as guardian of true doctrine was more associated with the emperor than with the people it served. Thus the self-understanding of the church harbored the danger of losing touch with its members and instead serving those in authority. Any thoroughgoing reform of church or state was therewith excluded. In the long run this meant alienation from and betrayal of the people. Small wonder that they felt that a different regime could perhaps serve better their spiritual and physical needs.

Demarcation between church and state in the West: The West was never much tempted with the idea of oneness between altar and throne. The ecclesial power was located in Rome and the emperor ruled in far-away Constantinople. Thus it was difficult for the emperor, if not outright impossible, to be directly involved in church affairs. For instance, when Valentinian II wanted to reserve for himself the final decision in the appointment of judges in church matters, Bishop Ambrose of Milan told him in no uncertain terms: "If we examine the context of holy Scripture or of times past [i.e., tradition], who will deny that in a matter of faith, in a matter, I say, of faith, bishops usually judge Christian emperors; not emperors, bishops." [161] Later, when Theodosius had become emperor of the whole empire, he too had a very serious clash with Ambrose. After the massacre at Thessalonica, where Theodosius had secretly ordered the killing of people attending games at an amphitheater as a punishment for starting riots, Ambrose told the emperor in writing that "you will make your offering then when you receive permission to sacrifice, when your offering has been acceptable to God." [162] In other words, the emperor was excommunicated because of the crime he had ordered committed and he would only be admitted to the sacrifice (Eucharist) after he had repented. Only after penance, lasting several months, was the emperor readmitted to communion.[163]

The notion that the church was not simply the conscience of the empire but that the church had a role to play within and independent of the state was especially well pronounced in Augustine's writings who had learned much from Ambrose as we have seen in other places. In his great work, *The City of God,* Augustine distinguishes between the city or the society of God and the society of this world. The city of God is not a purified church but it has among it some who shall not eternally dwell with the saints.[164] Yet it is the pilgrim city of Christ the King and a stranger in the world. At the same time it is entangled and intermixed with the city of the world until both are separated in the last judgment. Christ has built the city of God and he has inspired us with a love that makes us covet its citizenship. The city of God or the new Jerusalem has as its goal peace and life eternal. This promised goal already determines the action of the members of the city of God now, since we should walk in hope and mortify the deeds of the flesh through the Spirit and make progress from day to day.

The City of God was written to refute the accusation that the devastation of Rome by the Gothic hordes of Alaric in 410 was due to the worship of the Christian God in place of the gods of Rome. To accomplish his goal Augustine often juxtaposes the city of God to the city of this world. The citizens of the earthly city, for instance, prefer their own gods instead of the true God; they wish to live after the flesh instead of after the Spirit; they hate the Christians with deadly malice, and they glory in themselves instead of God, seeking self-love instead of love of others.[165] Yet Augustine does not reject the earthly city in Manichaean fashion, since he knows that we all are members of the earthly city by birth and become members of the city of God only by rebirth or regeneration. Augustine leaves no doubt that the gods increase demoralization and corruption in a city, while Rome has attained its greatness by the power and providence of God. It is also due to the influence of Christ, he says, that the barbarians who sacked Rome behaved much more moderately than is customary in wars.

The goal of the earthly city is civil obedience in an attempt to attain the things that are helpful for this life.[166] Since Christians live in the earthly city, they make use of its peace and obey its laws so that the things necessary for the maintenance of this mortal life can be administered. Augustine even ventures to say that since this life is common to both cities,

> there is a harmony between them in regard to what belongs to it . . . This heavenly city, then, while it sojourns on earth, calls citizens out of all nations, and gathers together a society of pilgrims of all languages, not scrupling about diversities in the manners, laws, and institutions whereby earthly peace is secured and maintained, but recognizing that, however various these are, they all tend to one and the same end of earthly peace.

This means that the city of God respects the different political entities in their pursuit of peace. But it also transcends them in its vision of the unity and common eschatological destiny of all humanity.

Augustine praises Christian emperors who use their power as the hand-maid of God's majesty, being slow to punish and ready to pardon.[167] They punish as it is necessary for the government and the defense of the republic. They do not gratify their own enmity and grant pardon, not that iniquity may go unpunished, but hoping that the transgressor may amend his ways. Augustine, however, is realistic enough to concede: "The fact is, true justice has no existence save in that republic whose founder and ruler is Christ." [168] Yet Augustine is not afraid to suggest that the earthly pow-ers should serve very openly the city of God "by making laws in behalf of Christ" in furthering the unity of the church and bringing sectarian spirits back into the harmony with the church.[169]

If we want to sum up the main points in Augustine's understanding of church and state,

(1) We are struck with his profound eschatological vision of the church. Though the church is a present reality, it strives and yearns for eschato-logical perfection.

(2) The state as a non-Christian entity is not a viable option. Wherever the state pursues that which is good, true, and beautiful, the active presence of God is (un)willingly acknowledged.

(3) Therefore the best state is one that is under the corrective and direc-tive guidance of Christ. Augustine envisioned that the Christians actively transform the earthly city to make it more Christ-like in its actions.

(4) He also summoned the aid of the earthly authorities to further the unity of the church. If the earthly authorities would do this only by invita-tion, the distinction between church and state could be preserved. But there was tremendous temptation for worldly authorities also to intervene in church matters if they were not invited to do so. The worldly powers

did not simply recede when no longer needed by the church. Up to the present, the church in the West has been involved in a continuous struggle to preserve its autonomy.

Gelasius I attempted to draw a strict line of demarcation between church and state when he intentionally neither informed the Emperor Anastasius of his election as Pope in 492 nor asked for confirmation of his election. When the emperor objected, Gelasius replied: "There are two powers, august Emperor, by which this world is ruled from the beginning: the consecrated authority of the bishops, and the royal power." [170] In matters relating to public law and order, Gelasius asserted, the priests obey the laws of the emperor, knowing that the empire is conferred upon him by God. The emperor's judgment is unchallengeable in worldly affairs. But the emperor "is permitted to judge only human affairs and not to take the lead in things divine." It would be presumptuous for him to judge those through whom divine affairs are administered. On the contrary, the faithful should submit themselves to the bishops who rightly conduct the religious affairs, and above all they must give support to the bishop of Rome.

Since Christ, the true king and pontiff, did not lay claim to royal supremacy, the emperor should refrain from calling himself pontiff (a standard procedure in the Eastern Empire). Christian emperors need bishops for the sake of eternal life and in turn the bishops avail themselves of imperial decrees for the good order of temporal affairs. Thus the spiritual function shall be free from worldly interference and nobody involved in the affairs of this life shall take charge of things divine. Gelasius sums up the theory of two powers saying: "Both orders might be restrained and neither be boasted and exalted above the other, and each calling might become specially competent in certain kinds of functions." [171] Yet Anastasius replied that he would not take orders from Rome and continued to use the title pontifex (bishop) for himself. Thus the definitions were clear, but even in the West, their execution caused continuous strain.

Four phases in the continuous struggle between church and state in the West: There are roughly four phases that can be distinguished in which the struggle between church and state was conducted in the West. The first phase culminates in the unity of church and state under Charlemagne. In the second phase the church strives to attain independence from the state, and in the third the church in turn asserts the powers of a universal monarchy. This leads to the fourth phase in which the unity of church and world disintegrates and modern pluralism emerges. Without going into details we should at least note the most decisive points of each phase.

(1) When the Roman Empire collapsed in the West in the 5th century, the church remained the only continuing link with the culture and governmental style of antiquity. Though Pope Gelasius I showed a rather audacious attitude against the emperor in faraway Constantinople, his own surroundings and those of his successors were not very pleasant and tranquil. Most of Western Europe was either totally Arian or at least heavily influenced by this "heresy" through the Germanic tribes of the Vandals in Northern Africa, the Visigoths in France, the Suebi in Spain and Southeastern France, and the Ostrogoths in Italy.

The big breakthrough, however, for Rome and the church, came in 496 when King Clovis was baptized and in turn convinced his Franks, who had settled in Northern France, to adopt Christianity. Since the Franks obtained victories over most of the Arian tribes, they helped to establish the Catholic faith in Western Europe. This means that the baptism of Clovis was at least as important for the Western Church as the conversion of Constantine had been for the future of all of Christendom.[172] It soon became evident that in the Frankish kingdom the king considered himself lord of "his" church. He called or at least installed the bishops and called and gathered synods. Yet the kings did not meddle with doctrine. Though the pope was not accepted as the ruler of the church, he was respected in doctrinal affairs. Yet the worldly authorities were unable to eliminate some of the crass abuses of the church, e.g., robbery of church property by those who needed money, and the buying and selling of bishoprics.

The renewal of the church finally came through the church itself. Anglo-Saxon monks worked among the Franks with papal approval and introduced more stringent morals. Especially Boniface who was supported by the Frankish kings Carloman and Pepin and by Pope Zacharias achieved lasting reforms. Since Boniface had been invited to reform the church and since he had done this under the auspices of Rome, the papacy grew in esteem among the Franks. When Pepin was chosen by the Franks as their king, Archbishop Boniface anointed him. And when Pope Stephen escaped from the Lombards and fled to France, King Pepin received him with all honors and devotion. He promised him in the so-called Donation of Pepin to restore the Exarchate of Ravenna—an area that had always belonged to the Eastern Church and not to Rome—and the rights to the Roman territories.[173]

When Charlemagne came to reign in 768 the papacy soon ceased to be an equal partner. Charlemagne had been victorious over the Lombards and had eliminated the "neutral zone" between the Frankish Empire and

the papal territories. Though he renewed the Donation of Pepin, the papal
territories were now supervised by royal administrators. Leo III may have
surprised the king when he knelt at the tomb of St. Peter in Rome on
Christmas Day 800 by crowning him emperor. Charlemagne received
from the hands of the pope the imperial crown of the old Western Empire.
But by doing so the pope inadvertently gave the empire also a spiritual
prestige. Soon it was to become synonymous with the Western Church.
The pope was a necessary ingredient of this newly established theocracy,
but he was not its mastermind. Often the king acted on his own, establishing a new regional structure of the church, making the bishops the rulers
in their dioceses, adopting and adapting in a unified way the Roman
liturgy, emphasizing the sermon within the main worship service, establishing parochial schools connected with monasteries or bishoprics, and
requiring from the laity a minimum knowledge of the Lord's Prayer and
the Apostles' Creed. While in these reforms the voice of the pope was
heard, he had no legislative power.

How important the emperor had become in deciding church matters
we see when Charlemagne introduced the *filioque* into the Nicene-Con-
stantinopolitan Creed, i.e., that the Spirit proceeds from the Father and
the Son. Of course, Charlemagne did not make these decisions on his own.
He relied for advice on his court theologians, such as Alcuin and Paul
the Deacon. At another instance, he disagreed with both the iconoclasts
and their opponents in the East, declaring that pictures had no religious
significance whatsoever. They remind us of important events and persons
and also serve as ornaments. This imperial opinion then informed the
decision of the general council in Frankfurt of 794 and again the pope
had no choice but to agree. The empire of Charlemagne soon crumbled
after his death and therewith the domination of the church by the emperor. But the unification of the church that he fostered far outlasted
his reign.

(2) Under the Roman papacy as its central administration, the church
was not satisfied with being simply an essential ingredient of the Frankish Empire. The search for independence becomes evident from the so-
called Donation of Constantine. This document was allegedly issued by
Constantine upon his conversion in 317, but most likely was produced
by the papal curia in the middle of the 8th century.[174] It states that Constantine donates to Pope Silvester and all his successors his own Lateran
palace and various insignia pertaining to the imperial office. The pope,
however, will have dominion over "the provinces, territories and cities of

the city of Rome and all of Italy and the western regions." They shall be irrevocably administered "by the dominion and government of Silvester and of the pontiffs who succeed him" and "remain the lawful property of the holy Roman church." These privileges are granted by the God-fearing emperor so that the honor, power, and glory of the pope may surpass that of the earthly empire. Since "it is not right that an earthly Emperor shall have power in a place where the government of priests and the head of the Christian religion has been established by the heavenly Emperor," Constantine ceded his power and his residence in the West to the pope. With this document the church attempted to establish its supremacy over earthly rulers and it thereby became an earthly and political institution.

The church had not much success to put its earthly claims into reality under Charlemagne, and it fared worse under his successors. It had become so much a part of the Frankish Empire that the decline of the latter also resulted in the demise of the former. When the Frankish kings lost their power in Italy, the pope became a prodigy of the Roman nobility that installed and removed the popes at will.

The church's predicament changed in the 9th century when Otto I began to elevate bishops into prince-bishops and administrators in his kingdom. He also installed the bishops and endowed them with considerable land holdings. Since the position of a bishop was not handed on to the next generation, the king felt that bishops could be more trusted than worldly princes who were mainly interested in securing power for their descendants. The bishops, however, did not only feel allegiance to the king but also to the pope. Yet this did not cause an immediate danger for the king, since the pope was still without much power. Otto went to Rome to unite northern Italy with Germany and he also installed a pope he saw fit for this office. But then he renewed the Donation of Constantine and was crowned emperor by the pope. Otto still had sufficient power though to treat the pope like one of his bishops. The same constellation of power continued to prevail for another century.

Later, the influence of the reform movement was felt, a movement started by the monastery of Cluny. A pope was subsequently elected who was determined to take the reform of the church in his own hands. The new Pope, Leo IX, personally conducted reform synods in various parts of Europe. Eventually the idea was questioned that popes and bishops could be in the service of a worldly government. Yet it took another generation until it came to an outright clash between the Emperor, Henry IV, and Pope Alexander II. When the emperor installed his own candidate in the strategically important archbishopric of Milan, the pope certified someone else. Since the emperor did not accede, the pope excommunicated the advisors of the emperor. Only the sudden death of Alexander II avoided a prolonged battle. His successor, Gregory VII, still announced to the emperor his election and was certified by him. Yet he resumed the argument of Alexander II and convinced the emperor that he had acted incorrectly. This victory considerably increased the power of the papacy and set a precedent for the investiture of bishops. Now the pope went a step further and wanted to abolish completely the custom that a layperson, the emperor, would invest ecclesiastics with the emblems of the spiritual office. He argued that bishops should be obedient to the church alone.

Since the church had amassed considerable land holdings, the emperor could not simply forfeit the influence and services of the bishops. Since neither side was willing to give in, Henry IV summoned a synod of German bishops in 1076 and declared the pope deposed. Unwilling to compromise, the pope immediately excommunicated the emperor. The results were evident. The voice of the pope had a stronger effect in ecclesiastic matters than that of a synod summoned by an emperor. An excommunicated emperor could not even function politically. Thus Henry IV had to conduct his famous penance, appearing before the pope at the fortress of Canossa in the Apennines. Yet even a pope could not do whatever he pleased. Though he disliked it, as the head of the church and its supreme bishop, Gregory VII had no choice but to absolve the emperor. Again the struggle was not over. Rudolph of Swabia had usurped Henry's throne and a civil war ensued in which the pope sided with Henry's opponent. Henry won but was promptly banned by Gregory VII. A second excommunication, however, was not quite as debilitating as the first. Henry besieged Rome and Gregory fled and died in exile. Henry installed a new pope and crowned him with the imperial crown without questioning.

The struggle between church and state was of prime importance for the Holy Roman Empire of the German Nation because of its right to territories in Italy. But other countries were not exempt from this struggle. For instance, in England it came to a confrontation between Anselm, Archbishop of Canterbury, who was backed by the pope, and King Henry I. The reasons were similar to those in Germany. When Henry II had Thomas Becket murdered in his cathedral for standing up to him, the king again experienced the power of the church. In penance the king knelt barefoot at Becket's shrine and was scourged by seventy monks of the cathedral chapter. Throughout the 11th and 12th centuries the struggle of the church for independence was waged with various success on both sides. Yet with Innocent III (1198-1216) a new phase commenced. Now the church and the papacy were not only independent from the state, but they in fact attempted to rule the world.

(3) In Germany Pope Innocent III installed the bishops or at least ratified their election. He also played one prince against the other to secure the most favorable conditions for his own pursuits. In France he made Philip reconcile himself with his wife from whom he had separated, and in England he deposed John Lackland when he refused to acknowledge Stephen Langton as Archbishop of Canterbury. Of course, he consolidated and expanded the papal land holdings in Italy.

The reason for the papal involvement in the affairs of other countries was justified with the paradigm that pontifical authority and royal power correspond like sun and moon. The superior dignity of the pope endows the worldly powers with dignity that they would not have on their own.[475] The two swords in Luke 22:38 are now interpreted as denoting the authority of the bishop and the power of the king. Only if the two work together, under the guidance of the church, can the evil in the world be overcome. The pope had gained so much independence and power that it could not even be taken for granted that he would crown the emperor. He insisted now that the princes either "agree upon a suitable person or submit themselves to our judgment or decision."[176] Of course, the pope decides who is a "suitable person" and who is not. Yet his intention was laudable; he wanted the church to aide the state in combating the forces of darkness.

A century later Boniface VIII in his bull *Unam sanctam* (1302) summarized the development and declared: There are two swords and

> each is in the power of the Church, that is, a spiritual and a material sword. But the latter, indeed, must be exercised for the Church, the former by the Church. The former (by the hand) of the priest, the latter by the hand of kings and soldiers, but at the will and sufferance of the priest . . . It is necessary that we confess the more clearly that spiritual power precedes any earthly power both in dignity and nobility, as spiritual matters themselves excel the temporal.[177]

In this claim reverberate the words of Augustine's *City of God* that the city of God precedes and is superior to the earthly city and that only a christianized earthly city could lead to true humanity. But for Augustine the members of the city of God were pilgrims on this earth. For the medieval church, however, they had become full-fledged members in the worldly city. The pope had become the emperor of the world and the princes and kings his servants.

Since the pope still lacked sufficient earthly power, he had to rely on the earthly authorities to pursue his (earthly) goals. For instance, Western kings and noblemen were enlisted in the crusades to free by force the holy sites from the occupation by "infidels." Usually worldly authorities were not much inclined to subject themselves to the demands of the papal (political) authority. But to achieve his goals the pope played one contender for the crown against another, and one nation against another. This maneuvering immensely harmed the unity of the Holy Roman Empire. But it also hurt the church. In order to free itself from its dependency on the empire, the papacy relied even more strongly on France, a relationship that ultimately resulted in the captivity of the papacy at Avignon, France (1309-1377). Thus the ultimate triumph of the church had become its stumbling block. The church's attempt to acquire earthly dominion did not remedy its situation. The huge tracts of land that papal see and the local bishops and prince bishops administered focused the attention of the spiritual leaders more and more on earthly concerns. The more earthly goods the church accumulated the more it was envied by less fortunate princes and authorities so that the tension between church and state continued to increase. Yet the idea of the church's domination over the earthly rulers had solid theological backing.

Like all medieval theological systems, the *Summa theologica* of Thomas Aquinas did not contain a separate section devoted to the doctrine of the church. The church as the institution of salvation was simply taken for granted. Yet the overarching aspect of the church was evident for him when he stated that "the end of human life and society is God."[178] While Aquinas recognizes that arbiters do not enjoy coercive power but are subject to the law, he grants the bishops as much power of arbitration as the princes to judge offenses committed in their respective territories.[179] This means that the church does not just have spiritual power, but through its earthly involvement also enjoys earthly power. This becomes especially prominent in the exercise of the most severe spiritual punishment, excommunication. We hear that "as soon as sentence of excommunication is passed on a man on account of apostasy from the faith, his subjects are *ipso facto* released from his authority and from the oath of allegiance binding them to him."

Not only infidelity can lead to excommunication and loss of dominion. On occasion, we hear, other faults can have the same consequences. This means that an ecclesial punishment can have drastic consequences in the world. For instance, the pope could depose at will any emperor or king who disagreed with him. How cautious worldly authorities had to be, becomes clear when we hear that "every question arising out of faith were resolved by the one [the pope] having care over the whole Church, whose decisions therefore are followed by the whole Church." [180] For instance, the pope can introduce a new version of the creed, summon or dismiss a general council, etc., without anybody being able to stop these actions. In a hierarchy of power, in which all power stems from God, the worldly authority is controlled by the church. Yet the centralization of the church's power in the papacy and the continual interference of the papal office and its regional extensions with the affairs of the day caused increased dissatisfaction among many faithful.

(4) In the 14th century, the complaints about the tyranny of Rome and its insatiable hunger for money, and the widespread spiritual and moral decay of the clergy led to the first vigorous calls for reform. How far the things had drifted can be seen from Dante's *Divine Comedy* in which he alludes to the Donation of Constantine as one of the great calamities that befell the church. Dante characterizes the church in allusion to the Book of Revelation as the seven headed monster, and even calls her an "ungirt harlot." [181] Such assessments were no exception and certainly helped to shape the public mind.

It was not only the decadence of the centralized church that made people wonder about the role of the church. As the church amassed more and more riches, the question was asked repeatedly why its fortunes always had to be transferred to Rome and could not stay within one's own country. Especially when the leadership of the Holy Roman Empire began to crumble in Europe in the late Middle Ages, other major monarchies, such as England, France, and Spain, were calling for more independence from Rome. They thought that the unity of the church ought to be expressed more on a national basis. Theologians too had become more hesitant in advocating a centralized church. Yet above all we must mention here the political philosopher Marsilius of Padua.

In his seminal work, *Defender of Peace*, Marsilius radically challenged the prevailing notion of how church and state ought to be related and he can rightly be called a forerunner of the Protestant Reformation.[182] Marsilius wrote his *Defender of Peace* in 1324, 50 years after the death of Thomas Aquinas and three years after Dante had died. The basis for his argumentation is no longer the Bible but Aristotle's philosophy when Marsilius asserts that the state came into existence for the sake of living and exists for the sake of living well.[183] Since a future world is promised to us through God's "supernatural revelation" and since this revelation is also useful in the present, the state must designate certain people as teachers, so that God is properly worshiped, honored, and given thanks. This means that the function of the church is restricted to its spiritual role, to teaching, preaching, and administering the sacraments.

With extensive references to the New Testament, Marsilius shows that Christ refused to be a ruler or a coercive judge in this world, "whereby he furnished an example for his apostles and disciples and their successors to do likewise." [184] Moreover, Christ demonstrated through word and deed that all people, both priests and lay, "should be subject in property and in person to the coercive judgment of the rulers of this world. This would mean that the state exerts coercive jurisdictional power even over the church. Marsilius, however, is quick to add that this power is not given to the worldly authorities by others or by birth, but by God. The only power that remains for the priests is to administer the Eucharist and to bind and loose people from sins. Yet in these matters one priest has not greater power than another, a fact which he also finds documented in the originally interchangeable use of the terms priests and bishops. If one is elected or appointed to be overseer over other priests, one does not obtain greater merit or priestly authority, but only power and authority for which it was granted, the overseeing and ordering of other priests. Moreover, the power thus delegated is not coercive "unless the authority for such coercion shall have been granted by the human legislator to the person thus elected." We are not surprised that Marsilius applies his conclusions especially to the Roman bishop disclaiming that he could enjoy more priestly authority than any other bishop.

The worldly authorities administer all coercive power, unless they delegate some to church authorities for the sake of enforcing church order. To strengthen its power Marsilius suggests that the surplus revenues which the church does not need for the gospel ministry should be taxed. This would then help the state in carrying out its public services.[185] Marsilius opts here for a clear distinction and separation of the power of church and state. Yet he also does not leave untouched the structure of the church, when on the basis of Scripture, he advocates a strictly conciliar arrangement between bishops. According to him all power ultimately comes from God and must be used for the benefit of all people, and not to increase the privileges of individuals. Since Marsilius' proposals severely jeopardized the worldly interests of the church and its papacy, we are not surprised that his book was banned by the pope within two years of its first appearance. Yet his concerns could not be suppressed. They were soon picked up by other scholars.

We must mention here especially William of Ockham who lived a major portion of his life in exile in Munich, Germany, and who was also of considerable literary influence on Luther. Ockham was certainly familiar with Marsilius. But he was more a theologian than a political philosopher and therefore did not follow him very closely.[186] As did Marsilius, Ockham claimed that Sacred Scripture cannot err, while the pope can err. Therefore a pope cannot issue new articles of faith or excommunicate someone by his own power, unless his decrees are based on Scripture. If a pope would obstinately err, Ockham even suggests that one has the obligation to remove him from office. Of course, he concedes that God promised to guide the church in all truth. But it would be dangerous to interpret this as meaning through the pope, or through the cardinals, or through a general council, or even through the church itself. Only as the totality of all believers, even if this were just one faithful Christian, can the church be infallible. Ockham claims that it might be the simple laity instead of the clerics that could form the core of true believers.

Ockham also invokes the conciliar theory when he suggests that the church is truly represented in the general council, since it is called by the whole church.[187] Yet unlike Marsilius, he concedes that usually the pope exercises the functions of the council. Since for Ockham the church consists of all believers, he asserts that princes and other representatives of the laity, women included, could and should be present at a council. Again we hear that if the pope is an acknowledged heretic, the council must depose him and select a new one. Yet we notice in Ockham an emphasis different from the consideration of Marsilius. For Ockham, unlike Marsilius, the church is not a state institution for the benefit of the state and its citizens, but it is a community of believers. Therefore there is no place in its ranks for ecclesiastical hierarchy or for worldly power. It is important that at the eve of the Reformation both ideas had been expressed, the church as an institution for the benefit of the state and its citizens, and the church as a community of believers. During the Reformation period these two ideas were picked up time and again. Even as late as in the 18th century the Prussian King Frederick the Great picked up one of these ideas when he declared that one pastor replaces seven policemen.

NOTES

1. For the origin of the church cf. the comprehensive work by Gerhard Heinz, *Das Problem der Kirchenentstehung in der deutschen protestantischen Theologie des 20. Jahrhunderts* (Mainz: Matthias Grünewald, 1974).
2. Cf. the remarks by Tertullian, *On Prescription Against Heretics* 38, ANFa 3:261f.
3. Justin Martyr, *Dialogue with Trypho* 63, FaCh 1:248, uses the term Christians.
4. Ibid. 61, 1:244f.
5. Justin Martyr, *The First Apology* 61, FaCh 1:100.
6. Justin Martyr, *Dialogue with Trypho* 44, FaCh 1:214.
7. Cf. Tertullian, *On Modesty* 21, ANFa 4:99, who even rejects the right of the priest to forgive sins, but still admits that God himself will forgive.
8. So rightly Reinhold Seeberg, *Lehrbuch der Dogmengeschichte,* 1:177.
9. For this and the following see the enlightening remarks by J. N. D. Kelly, *Early Christian Doctrines,* rev. ed. (New York: Harper, 1978), pp. 216ff.
10. Clement of Alexandria, *The Stromata* 2.13, ANFa 2:360; and Tertullian, *On Repentance* 7, ANFa 3:663.
11. See for this and the following quotes *Constitutions of the Holy Apostles* 3.7, 24, 23, ANFa 7:398, 408, 408.
12. Cf. Socrates, *Ecclesiastical History* 5.19, NPNF (SS) 2:128; and Sozomen, *Ecclesiastical History* 7.16, NPNF (SS) 2:386.
13. Tertullian, *On Repentance* 9, ANFa 3:664.
14. So Dionysius of Alexandria according to Eusebius, *The History of the Church* 6.42.5, p. 279. Tertullian's mention of "God's dear ones," *On Repentance* 9, ANFa 3:664, may also be a reference to the martyrs to whom the repentant sinners confess.
15. Cyprian, *Treatise on the Unity of the Church* 15, ANFa 5:426.
16. Cyprian, *Treatise on the Dress of Virgins* 23, ANFa 5:436.
17. For this and the following quote see Cyprian, *Treatise on Works and Alms* 26, ANFa 5:483.
18. Ambrose, *Jacob and the Happy Life* 1.1.1, FaCh 65:119.
19. Ibid. 1.3.12, 65:127f.
20. Ambrose, *Expositio Evangelii Secundum Lucam* 7.132, CSL 14:259.
21. Ambrose, *Apologia Prophetae David* 5.23, PL 14:860.
22. Optatus of Mileve, *De Schismate Donatistarum* 2.20, PL 11:973.
23. Ambrose, *Concerning Repentance* 2.10.95, NPNF (SS) 10:357.
24. Cf. Augustine, *The Free Choice of the Will* 1.10.20, FaCh 59:91f.
25. For this and the following cf. ibid. 3.3.8, 59:173, and 3.1.1, 59:165.
26. Cf. Augustine, *Acts or Disputation Against Fortunatus, the Manichaean* 2.21f., NPNF (FS) 4:120f., *et al.*
27. Augustine, *Letters of St. Augustine* 118.5.32, NPNF (FS) 1:450.
28. Cf. Augustine, *Letters* 175, FaCh 30:87.
29. Augustine, *Acts or Disputation Against Fortunatus, the Manichaean* 2.23, NPNF (FS) 4:122.
30. According to Augustine, *On the Grace of Christ. On Original Sin* 1.19 (18), NPNF (FS) 5:224.
31. For this and the following quotes from Pelagius see ibid. 5 (4), 5:219.

32. According to Augustine, *On Nature and Grace, Against Pelagius* 8, NPNF (FS) 5:123.
33. According to Augustine, *On the Grace of Christ. On Original Sin* 2.6 (6), NPNF (FS) 5:239.
34. According to Augustine, *On Man's Perfection to Righteousness* 2.4 (4), NPNF (FS) 5:160.
35. Augustine, *On the Grace of Christ. On Original Sin* 2.34 (29), NPNF (NS) 5:249. 5:249.
36. Augustine, *The City of God* 14.11, NPNF (FS) 2:271.
37. Ibid. 14.27, 2:282.
38. Augustine, *On Rebuke and Grace* 33 (12), NPNF (FS) 5:485.
39. See Augustine, *De Diversis Quaestionibus ad Simplicianum* 1.2.16, CSL 44:42, where Augustine uses the term *massa peccati* to describe humanity.
40. Augustine, *Against Two Letters of the Pelagians* 7, NPNF (FS) 5:379.
41. Augustine, *Enchiridion* 32, NPNF (FS) 3:248.
42. Augustine, *On Grace and Free Will* 17.33, FaCh 59:288.
43. Augustine, *On the Spirit and the Letter* 58, NPNF (FS) 5:109.
44. Augustine, *On Rebuke and Grace* 45, NPNF (FS) 5:489.
45. Augustine, *On the Merits and Forgiveness of Sins. And on the Baptism of Infants* 1.70 (39), NPNF (FS) 5:43.
46. Augustine, *The City of God* 19.27, NPNF (FS) 2:419.
47. Augustine, *On the Gift of Perseverance* 1.1, NPNF (FS) 5:526.
48. Augustine, *Letters* 194, FaCh 30:303f.
49. Cf. ibid. 186, 30:209.
50. Ibid., 30:205.
51. DS(E) 200, p. 81.
52. Augustine, *On Rebuke and Grace* 40, NPNF (FS) 5:488.
53. DS(E) 200, p. 81.
54. Cf. Seeberg, *Lehrbuch,* 1:441ff., for an extensive summary of the baptismal practice in the second century; and Tertullian, *On Baptism,* ANFa 3:669-679, who provides an excellent introduction to the practice in the early church.
55. So Tertullian, *On Baptism* 8, ANFa 3:672f.
56. Tertullian, *On Modesty* 9, ANFa 4:83.
57. Cf. Justin Martyr, *The First Apology of Justin* 65, ANFa 1:185, for a brief description of the transition from (adult) baptism to the Eucharist.
58. Tertullian, *On Baptism* 18, ANFa 3:678.
59. Cyprian, *Letters* 64.5, FaCh 51:218f.
60. Seeberg, *Lehrbuch,* 1:451, assumes that this transition would account for the prevalent practice of infant baptism.
61. Tertullian, *On Baptism* 16 and 18, ANFa 3:677f.
62. Cf. Augustine, *The Letters of Petilian, the Donatist* 2.30.69, NPNF (FS) 4:547.
63. Ibid. 1.3.4, 4:520f.
64. Augustine, *On Baptism. Against the Donatists* 4.1.1, NPNF (FS) 4:447.
65. Ibid. 5.21.29, 4:474.
66. So Reinhold Seeberg, *Lehrbuch der Dogmengeschichte. 2: Die Dogmenbildung in der Alten Kirche* (Darmstadt: Wissenschaftliche Buchgesellschaft, 1965), 451f.
67. Augustine, *On Baptism. Against the Donatists* 4.25.33, NPNF (FS) 4:462.
68. Augustine, *On the Gospel of St. John* 26.11, NPNF (FS) 7:171, in his treatment of John 6:41-59.
69. For the following and the quotes of cf. ibid. 80.3, 7:344f., in Augustine's treatment of John 15:1-3.
70. See for this and the following quotes Justin Martyr, *Dialogue with Trypho* 117, ANFa 1:257.

71. Irenaeus, *Against Heresies* 4.18.1, ANFa 1:484.

72. Ibid. 4.17.5 to 4.18.4, 1:484f.

73. Ibid. 4.18.5, 1:486.

74. Cyprian, *Letters* 72.2, FaCh 51:267.

75. Ibid. 63.14, 51:212f.

76. Ibid. 63.9, 51:208.

77. Ibid. 63.17, 51:213f.

78. Ibid. 1.2 and 15.1, 51:4 and 44.

79. Ambrose, *On the Mysteries* 8.47, NPNF (SS) 10:323.

80. Ibid. 9.50, 10:324.

81. Ibid. 9.58, 10:325.

82. For this and the following quote see Augustine, *On the Gospel of St. John* **26.**13, NPNF (FS) 7:172, in his comments on John 6:41-59.

83. Ibid. 26.18, 7:173.

84. Ibid.

85. Ibid. 26.19, 7:173.

86. Augustine, *On the Psalms* 3.1, NPNF (FS) 8:5.

87. Augustine, *On Baptism. Against the Donatists* 5.8.9, NPNF (FS) 4:467.

88. Augustine, *Letters* 187.41, FaCh 30:255.

89. The later position is adopted by Seeberg, *Lehrbuch,* 2:459f.

90. Augustine, *Reply to Faustus, the Manichaean* 20.18, NPNF (FS) 4:261.

91. Augustine, *City of God* 10.6, NPNF (FS) 2:183.

92. Ibid. 10.20, 2:193.

93. Gregory the Great, *Dialogues* 4.60, FaCh 39:273.

94. Cf. ibid. 4.59, 39:270; quote ibid. 4.57, 39:266.

95. For this and the following quotes, cf. John of Damascus, *Exposition of the Orthodox Faith* 4.15, NPNF (SS) 9:87.

96. For the following and the quote cf. ibid. 4.16, 9:88.

97. Ibid. 4.11, 9:80.

98. Ibid. 4.16, 9:88.

99. For the following and the quotes cf. ibid. 4.9, 9:78f.

100. So Chrysostom, *Baptismal Instruction* 3:23, ACW 31:63, and note 49 on p. 239f. to this passage.

101. John of Damascus, *Exposition of the Orthodox Faith* 4.22, NPNF (SS) 9:95.

102. Irenaeus *Against Heresies* 5 pref., ANFa 1:526.

103. Athanasius, *Incarnation of the Word* 54.3, NPNF (SS) 4:65.

104. Petro Bilaniuk, in his excellent article, "The Mystery of *Theosis* or Divinization," in *The Heritage of the Early Church. Essays in Honor of Georges Vasilievich Florovsky,* ed. by David Neiman and Margaret Schatkin (Rome: Pont. Inst. Stud. Orientalium, 1973), 337ff., points out very perceptively that the notion of divinization is the main point of contention between Eastern and Western piety and also that divinization induced a much more positive picture of humanity in the Eastern Church than became normative for the West.

105. For the quotes in this and the following paragraphs cf. John of Damascus, *Exposition of the Orthodox Faith* 4.13, NPNF (SS) 9:82-84.

106. So Cyril of Jerusalem, *Catechetical Lectures* 4.19, NPNF (SS) 7:23; and John of Damascus, *Exposition of the Orthodox Faith* 4.22, NPNF (SS) 9:94.

107. For the relationship between church and state cf. the perceptive analysis by Oscar Cullman, *The State in the New Testament* (New York: Scribner's, 1956).

108. Cf. Lucian, *The Death of Peregrine* 12f., in *The Works of Lucian of Samosata,* trans. H. W. Fowler and F. G. Fowler (Oxford: Clarendon, 1905), 4:82f.

109. Cf. the interesting study by Simeon L. Guterman, *Religious Toleration in Ancient Rome* (Westport, CT: Greenwood, 1951) 120f.
110. Tertullian, *Apology* 21, ANFa 3:34.
111. Ibid. 5, 3:21.
112. For the following cf. the arguments by Tertullian, ibid. 10, 3:26.
113. So Tertullian, ibid. 35 and 36, 3:43 and 44.
114. Cf. W. H. C. Frend, *Martyrdom and Persecution in the Early Church. A Study of a Conflict from the Maccabees to Donatus* (New York: New York University Press, 1967) 7f. and 163, in his discussion of the persecution in Lyons (177) and the procedures adopted by Pliny the Younger in 112 to handle the Christian issue.
115. Cf. ibid., 9, in Frend's profound and illustrative investigation.
116. Cf. ibid., 9f., for further details.
117. Cf. for the following and the quotes the enlightening remarks by Origen, *Against Celsus* 8.73, 75, ANFa 4:668.
118. Cf. for the following Pliny, *Letters* 96 and 97, with an Engl. trans. W. Melmoth, rev. W. M. L. Hutchinson (Cambridge, MA: Harvard University Press, 1963), 2:401ff., where he uses the word *amentia* to describe the attitude of the Christians.
119. For the following and the quotes see the interesting remarks by Origen, *Against Celsus* 2.13, ANFa 4:436f.
120. Tertullian, *Apology* 39, ANFa 3:46.
121. According to Eusebius, *The History of the Church* 4.23, p. 184.
122. Cf. the martyrdom of Polycarp according to Eusebius, ibid. 4.15, pp. 170ff.
123. Justin Martyr, *The Second Apology* 12, ANFa 1:192.
124. Justin Martyr, *The Discourse to the Greeks* 5, ANFa 1:272.
125. Tertullian, *Apology* 40, ANFa 3:47.
126. Hippolytus, *The Refutation of All Heresies* 9.7, ANFa 5:130.
127. Eusebius, *The History of the Church* 6:21, p. 262.
128. Ibid. 7.30, p. 319.
129. To see this simply as "arbitration in a civil dispute between two rival parties in a powerful sect," as Frend argues in his otherwise excellent study, *Martyrdom and Persecution in the Early Church*, 327, seems to miss the point. It was not simply a civil dispute. The question was rather why the state would want to settle the church's own affairs. This issue becomes clearer when we consider Constantine's position at Nicaea.
130. So Lactantius, *The Deaths of the Persecutors* 13, FaCh 54:152.
131. Ibid. 14, 54:153.
132. Orosius, *Seven Books of History against the Pagans* 7.28, FaCh 50:330.
133. According to the text of the edict as rendered by Frend, *Martyrdom and Persecution in the Early Church*, 381f.
134. According to the Imperial Ordinances concerning the Edict as rendered by Eusebius, *The History of the Church* 10.5, p. 403.
135. See ibid. 10.6f., pp. 406ff., for the texts of the imperial letters that contain such provisions.
136. According to a postscript in a letter of Constantine translated in Frend, 399f.
137. Cf. Ramsey MacMullen, *Constantine* (New York: Dial Press, 1969) 105ff., for a good summary.
138. According to Socrates, *Ecclesiastical History* 1.9, NPNF (SS) 2:14, in a letter of Constantine that he renders.
139. Ibid. 1.8, 2:11.
140. Optatus of Mileve, *De Schismate Donatistarum* 3.3, PL 11:999f.
141. Irenaeus, *Against Heresies* 5.24.2, ANFa 1:552.
142. Origen, *Against Celsus* 5.28 and 5.37, ANFa 4:555 and 559f., where he argues that

one has to obey the natural law more than the individual positive law of a country and that with regard to religion there are no absolute definitions of what is holy and pious. Thus there is always room for change (i.e., inclusion of the Christians).

143. Clement of Alexandria, *The Instructor* 1.7, ANFa 2:223.
144. Clement of Alexandria, *The Stromata* 7.2, ANFa 2:526.
145. Origen, *Against Celsus* 2:30, ANFa 4:444.
146. Eusebius, *The History of the Church* 10.9, pp. 412f.
147. Socrates, *Ecclesiastical History* 1.1, NPNF (SS) 2:1.
148. Cf. for the following the instructive essay by Arnold Ehrhardt, "*Constantin des Grossen Religionspolitik und Gesetzgebung,*" in Heinrich Kraft, ed., *Konstantin der Grosse* (Darmstadt: Wissenschaftliche Buchgesellschaft, 1974) 388-456, esp. 413f.
149. So Walter W. Hyde, *Paganism to Christianity in the Roman Empire* (New York: Octagon Books, 1970) 230, who outlines the basic differences between the East and West in their understanding of the relationship between state and church.
150. So Leighton Pullan, *From Justinian to Luther. A.D. 518-1517* (Oxford: Clarendon, 1930) 3.
151. Cf. for an informed discussion of the imperial powers John W. Barker, *Justinian and the Later Roman Empire* (Madison: University of Wisconsin, 1966), 97f.
152. Cf. for the following the instructive book by Steven Runciman, *The Byzantine Theocracy* (Cambridge: Cambridge University Press, 1977) 1f. and 58.
153. As quoted in Karl Hefele, *A History of the Councils,* 5:157.
154. So Runciman, 72.
155. *Vita Nicetae* according to Paul J. Alexander, *The Patriarch Nicephorus of Constantinople. Ecclesiastical Policy and Image Worship in the Byzantine Empire* (Oxford: Clarendon, 1958) 131.
156. So Leo Diaconus, *Historia* (Bonn, 1828), 101-102, according to Runciman, 104.
157. Balsamon, *Canones Constantinopolitana Prima et Secunda Synodo* ad 3 and 4, PG 137:1018-1022, and cf. Runciman, 140, who also refers to this passage in Balsamon.
158. So Runciman, 146.
159. For this paragraph see the instructive book by Nicolas Zernov, *Moscow the Third Rome* (New York: AMS, 1971 [1937]), quote on p. 7.
160. So Gerhard Simon, *Church, State and Opposition in the U.S.S.R.,* trans. K. Matchett (Berkeley: University of California, 1974), 101.
161. Ambrose, *Letters* 9, FaCh 26:52f.
162. Ibid. 3, 26:25.
163. Cf. for a good description of this incident John G. Davies, *The Early Christian Church* (London: Weidenfeld and Nicolson, 1965), 216.
164. Cf. for the following Augustine, *The City of God* 1.35, 17.15, 11.1, 19.11, 21.15, NPNF (FS) 2:21, 353, 205, 407, and 464.
165. For the following cf. ibid. 11.1, 14.1, 18.1, 14.28, 15.16, 2.23, 5.1, 2.2, 2:205, 262, 361, 282f., 298, 37, 84, and 23.
166. For the following and the quote cf. ibid. 19.17, 2:412f.
167. Cf. ibid. 5.24, 2:105.
168. Ibid. 2.21, 2:36.
169. Augustine, *Letters* 93, FaCh 18:75.
170. Cf. for this and the following the extracts from letters of Gelasius I, in Brian Pullan, *Sources for the History of Medieval Europe from the Mid-eighth to the Mid-thirteenth Century* (Oxford: Blackwell, 1966) 46f. Cf. also the incident related in Runciman, 44f.
171. In a letter of Gelasius I as rendered by Brian Pullan, *Sources,* 47.
172. So rightly Leighton Pullan, *From Justinian to Luther,* 56.
173. Cf. for the text of the promise in Brian Pullan, *Sources,* 5f.
174. For a portion of the text and the following quotes see ibid., 9ff.

175. Cf. the extract of a letter from Innocent III to Otto IV in ibid., 206.
176. So Innocent the III as quoted in ibid., 200.
177. DS (E) 469, p. 187.
178. Thomas Aquinas, *Summa Theologiae* la 2ae q100 a6r, Latin text and English trans. Blackfriars (New York: McGraw-Hill, 1969), 29:83.
179. For this cf. ibid. (1975) 2a 2ae q67 alr, 38:91, and for the following quote see ibid. 2a 2ae a2r, 32:103.
180. Ibid. (1974) 2a 2ae q1 a10r, 31:55.
181. Cf. Dante Alighieri, *The Divine Comedy,* trans. with a commentary by Charles S. Singleton, *Purgatorio* (32.124-129, 32.142-144, 32.149), vol. 1: *Italian Text and Translation* (Princeton: Princeton University Press, 1973) 359ff. Cf. also the helpful commentary, ibid., vol. 2: *Commentary,* 800-805.
182. Cf. Alan Gewirth, *Marsilius of Padua. The Defender of Peace.* vol. 1: *Marsilius of Padua and Medieval Political Philosophy* (New York: Columbia University Press, 1956), esp. 3f. and 260-302, in his chapter on "The People's Church."
183. Cf. for the following *Marsilius of Padua. The Defender of Peace.* vol. 2: *The Defensor Pacis* 1.4.1, and 1.4.4, trans. with an introduction by Alan Gewirth (New York: Columbia University Press, 1956) 12 and 14.
184. Cf. for the following and the quotes ibid. 2.4.9, 2.4.12, 2.15.3-9, 2:119, 123, 235-239.
185. Cf. for the following ibid. 2.18.17 and 2.18.8, 2:226 and 273.
186. For the relationship between Marsilius and Ockham cf. Helmar Junghans, *Ockham im Lichte der neueren Forschung* (Berlin: Lutherisches Verlagshaus, 1968), esp. 258f.
187. Cf. for the following the helpful summary of Ockham's *Dialogues between Master and Disciple on the Power of Emperor and Pope,* in Wilhelm Kölmel, *Wilhelm Ockham und seine kirchenpolitischen Schriften* (Essen: Ludgerus Verlag, 1962) 66-98.

5

Between Reformation
and Revolution

IT WOULD BE MISLEADING TO CLAIM THAT THE REFORMATION BEGAN ON OC-
TOBER 31, 1517, when Luther nailed his *Ninety-five Theses* on the door of
the castle church in Wittenberg. The start of the Reformation cannot be so
clearly dated, especially since the Reformation was not a single event. It
was instead a process that eventually became inevitable. For instance, we
know that during his pontificate, Pope John XXII spent 63.7% of his revenues on warfare.[1] The popes had excommunicated each other several times
during the Great Schism (1309-77). The Donation of Constantine was
openly declared a forgery designed to enable the papacy to amass worldly
riches. Indulgences were peddled primarily to provide revenues for papal
building plans and not to relieve the people from the threat of eternal
damnation. Under Renaissance popes Innocent VIII and Alexander VI,
Rome had become the center of simony (i.e., obtaining church offices
through payoffs), murders, and indescribable vices. The whole church,
from cardinals down to bishops, priests, abbots, and monks, resembled the
picture portrayed by Rome. These examples that could be easily multiplied
show too clearly that only drastic changes could return the church to the
apostolic tradition from which it had strayed.

1. The medieval church—The failure to keep in touch

At times Protestants have been tempted to write off the medieval church
with the argument that its doctrinal assertions are contrary to Scripture
and to the teaching of the church universal. For instance, at the Fourth
Lateran Council in 1215 the doctrine of transubstantiation was officially
declared. Now it was doctrine that the body and blood of Jesus Christ

> are truly contained in the sacrament of the altar under the species of bread
> and wine; the bread [changed] into His body by divine power of transub-
> stantiation, and the wine into the blood. . . . And surely no one can accom-

167

plish this sacrament except a priest who has been rightly ordained according to the keys of the Church.[2]

Furthermore, next to the original two sacraments, baptism and Eucharist, another five sacraments, confirmation, penance, extreme unction, (ecclesiastical) orders, and matrimony were officially sanctioned at the Council of Lyons.[3]

Yet to discount the medieval church on account of new doctrines would be ill-founded. We recall how close some of the early church fathers came to the doctrine of transubstantiation in speaking about the eucharistic sacrifice. Some of them also used rather loosely the terms sacrament and mystery. We should not be surprised then about such doctrinal developments. But we might question whether such developments were the only and most consequential ones. The widespread uneasiness with the medieval church does not stem primarily from its endeavor to express the overarching presence of God in the world. When we consider objectives of the people that are commonly called forerunners of the Reformers, or if we reflect on the various medieval reform movements, we notice immediately their deep concern that the church was abandoning its goal of being the new community of Christ and also of losing touch with its constituent membership, the people.

The failure to keep in touch with its constituency could only continue for so long. Eventually the church would collapse or a reform movement would alert the church to its actual purpose of ministering to the hoping, witnessing, and anticipating community of the new covenant. There were many incisive reform movements in the medieval period connected with names such as Bernard of Clairvaux, Francis of Assisi, Thomas a Kempis, or Catherine of Siena. Each of these persons influenced the church in a different but significant way by founding monastic reform movements, shaping the devotion and piety of the people, or reforming the structures of the church. Though influential in their own ways, these movements remained by and large without decisive popular support. They brought about reforms initiated by the clerics and often for the clerics. The so-called pre-Reformation movements, however, were of a different type. Here the people themselves seemed to take the initiative and to voice their discontent with prevalent structures and practices. There are two main currents of discontent, the one dealing with piety and humility—a sadly neglected aspect of the life for laity and clerics alike—and another seeking more national autonomy and allowing for decisions being made in the respective countries.

a. The revolt of piety and humility (Peter Waldo and Girolamo Savonarola)

Unlike the sect of the Cathari or Albigenses that originated in the East and gained fame in France, the followers of PETER WALDO had no heretical inclinations. They did not claim links with the early church, nor did they portray Manichean and Gnostic leanings. They simply wanted to make accessible to everyone the Bible and its teachings. In 1179 Waldo even went to Rome to have his teachings examined and to obtain for his followers the privilege to preach. Pope Alexander III was rather sympathetic to this new movement and praised Waldo for taking the vow of poverty and allowed him to preach upon approval by the local clergy.[4]

When Waldo, a rich merchant of Lyons, France, renounced the bonds of property and family and instructed his first followers in the teachings of Scripture, sending them out to preach and live an apostolic life, he had no intention of revolting against the church and its hierarchy.[5] The Waldensian movement was not intended to change the social conditions of the West. Perhaps poor people did not even appreciate these "poor in the spirit." The Waldensians included people from all strata of society, poor, rich, middle class, and occasionally even nobility, people who understood themselves as sinners, who repented and intended to live a life of humility. The movement was not even confined to lay people, as clerics and several monks who had left their monasteries were counted among them.

When excommunicated in Lyons and condemned by Pope Lucius III in 1184, the "poor in the spirit" continued their work uninhibited. They declared that they derived their calling from Christ's great commission (Matt. 28:18-20) which also included Waldo and his brethren. Though they obeyed the bishops as legitimate successors of the apostles, they refused to obey them if they infringed on their apostolic mission.[6] This meant that the Waldensians fought heretical movements, such as the Albigenses and attempted to alleviate the spiritual decay within the church. Their piety and humility quite often earned them the admiration of both clerics and common people. While defending the orthodox faith of the church and its leadership, they did not compromise their mission by condoning the sins of the hierarchy.

Waldo had considerable influence among the brethren and the few sisters that associated with his movement, but he refused to be considered their leader. In order to withstand the continuous harassment and persecutions, however, most of his followers opted for a more structured movement. The group met for yearly conventions in which two leaders were elected who directed the actions of the brethren for one year. They also served as ministers who administered the sacraments for a certain period. This process shows symptomatically the difficulty inherent in a grassroots reform movement. If the main pillars of the church resisted the suggested reforms long enough, the reformers either had to abandon their ideas or opt for a movement independent of the main church. But the Waldensians did not feel that they operated outside or in opposition to the church. Their demand was not to return to the apostolic church but they were genuinely concerned about alleviating the deep spiritual need among the people that was unmet by the hierarchy and its administrators. Usually they did not oppose the hierarchy or demand that it return to an exemplary life of poverty. Their only demand was that everyone, whether clergy or lay, would fulfill God's commandments in a pious life. The Waldensians withstood the clergy only if they demanded something that they understood to be contrary to Scripture.

The Waldensians diligently read the Bible and extracts of the fathers in Romance translations, sources from which they defended their stand on issues of faith and life. For instance, they rejected the then current doctrines and practices of indulgences and purgatory, and the performance of good works by the living on behalf of the dead. The ability to move, often under disguise, as itinerant preachers from France to Italy and Germany, and the fact that their strongholds were on the border between southern France and Italy enabled them to survive fierce persecutions. In the late 15th century the Waldensians living in Piedmont were discovered by the Bohemian Hussites and a relationship of mutual respect was developed. When the Waldensians joined with the rest of the Reformation movements in the 16th century, they finally discarded the notion of seven sacraments, and the invocation of the saints.[7] They adopted a Calvinistic doctrine of predestination and joined the Protestant cause. In spite of the fierce persecutions in the Counter-Reformation era, they have survived until the present with a seminary in Rome and the majority of their congregations located in the valleys of Piedmont.

The near failure of the Waldensian cause shows in a nutshell the deepest problem of the medieval church, the inability truly to reform. The Waldensians were a lay movement, sympathetic to the ecclesiastical structure, the monastic life, and the orthodox faith. But they were not obedient enough to Rome, clerical enough to overcome the suspicion against the laity, nor orthodox enough to let ecclesiastical doctrines suffice without being questioned by recourse to the Scriptures. Therefore this grassroots movement that attempted to bring back to the church a badly needed piety and humility was nearly wasted. Perhaps the church's reaction was also caused by the fear that truly sweeping reforms might ensue if one would recur to the teachings of the Bible instead of to canon law and the theory of the two swords. The study of the Scriptures eventually had to result in a vehement critique of the church, its worldly aspirations, and the exclusion of the people from its affairs. What was the basis for the authority of the church and its political aspirations? A movement that, at least implicitly, had raised such questions would have become a deadly threat to current practices and it could not have fulfilled its intentions as a reform movement without becoming revolutionary. Since the Waldensians, however, rejected assuming earthly power, they were eliminated or at least rendered ineffective.

When we look at the base of the famous monument in Worms, Germany, commemorating the Reformation movement, we see another figure next to Peter Waldo, a man wearing a tightly fitting monastic attire, GIROLAMO SAVONAROLA. Like Peter Waldo, Savonarola came from a grand merchant family. The decadence of morals had become an ever-increasing torment for him in the easy and liberal atmosphere of Ferrara, Italy.[8] As a twenty-year-old he wrote poetry deploring the lust and greed in Rome. He soon realized, however, that he was an unwelcome prophet crying out against the destruction for which Rome seemed destined.

In 1474 Savonarola concluded a long struggle over whether to become a member of a religious order by joining the Dominican convent of San Domenico in Bologna. Later, after the usual preparation and studies he was appointed lecturer at the convent of San Marco in Florence. His principal task there was to explain the Scriptures, the teachings of which he exemplified through a vigorous spiritual life. A few years later he was sent back to San Domenico in Bologna, then to Ferrara, Brescia, and Pavia, among other places. In each place he preached in a prophetic manner—a vision a few years earlier in Florence had shown him the necessity of drastic reforms in the church—becoming better known throughout Italy, at least with the superiors of his order. In 1490 he returned to Florence for a second time, oddly enough at the request of the rich and influential Lorenzo de' Medici. Pico della Mirandola, the leader of the Florentine Platonic academy, had requested this favor from Lorenzo, since Pico had earlier become acquainted with Savonarola.[9] Lorenzo was a great patron of artists, highly intelligent and witty of speech, yet at the same time cruel, vengeful, and a corrupter of morals.

Upon his return to Florence, Savonarola was no longer the soft-spoken and dull preacher that people remembered from his first stay in Florence. He had now become a powerful orator, drawing a large crowd from all classes of people, and forcefully putting forward three propositions: reform, castigation of the church, and the need for quick action. He attempted to prove his propositions with reasons, images and parables, and the authority of Scripture. He based his arguments on what was evident in the church and claimed that these matters called for the measures for which he was asking. Though he did not convince everyone, he had on his side the more pious citizens who disapproved of the depravity of the church. He also won the poor and the malcontents who felt oppressed by the arbitrary taxations and confiscations of the Medici. Giovanni Pico, who had called him back, soon sensed that trouble was brewing for Savonarola. Indeed, Lorenzo sent many warnings and even contemplated having him banished from Florence. Yet he respected Savonarola and believed him to be a man of great piety. His saintly way of life also helped elect him prior of San Marco in 1491. Lorenzo, on his deathbed, obtained the blessings of Savonarola after showing fervent piety and asking for these blessings. Savonarola then went on preaching as usual.

In 1492, the same year that Lorenzo had died, another decisive event occurred. Upon the death of Pope Innocent VIII, Cardinal Rodrigo Borgia was elected pope, taking the name of Alexander VI. This pope represents the epitome of everything distasteful about the Renaissance papacy. His life-style was totally immoral and his character without sincerity. Though calling himself Vicar of Christ, he was very likely an atheist or at least an unbeliever. The election of Alexander VI convinced Savonarola even more that reform was imminent. As prior, Savonarola introduced the strict rule in San Marco and sold all the property of the monks. To give the reforms even more vigor, he severed the ties of San Marco from the Lombard congregation to which it had belonged, and finally formed his own congregation together with a few other convents. With these moves he introduced into their studies and way of life an almost divine order.[10]

When the French King Charles VIII invaded Italy, Savonarola had attached certain prophecies to this invasion, which came true in a remarkable way. He also dealt rather courageously with the king and thereby extended his influence far beyond his convent and his newly established congregation. He rid Florence of the reign of the Medici and helped to avert the threatening destruction by the French Army. In turn he became the main influence shaping the Florentine Republic. He introduced legislation against murder and sodomy, and did away with excessive festivities giving the money instead to the poor. Of course, the pope was well aware of this monk who was prophesying that the scourge of God would descend upon Italy. He first intended to summon Savonarola to Rome, and then, when this failed he attempted to dissolve Savonarola's congregation and silence him. But Fra Girolamo continued to preach and attack the shortcomings of the papacy and the church. He was convinced that God would send a saintly pope or even convert the present one. He also left no doubt that conversion and reform were necessary.[11] The pope even offered him a cardinal's hat if he would tone down his accusations. Savonarola set the stage for his final demise when he replied that he was not seeking honors except death and the red hat of blood as a martyr.[12]

When the pope excommunicated him, both the city and Savonarola himself sought to avert the dictum and placate the pope. Savonarola assured the pope that he only preached "repentance of sin and the mending of our ways, for the sake of Our Lord Jesus Christ," but not heresy or deviation of the catholic truth.[13] He was convinced that the excommunication was invalid, since it was based on false premises maliciously put forward by his enemies. He even wanted to show the pope his loyalty. But through intrigues the pope was confirmed in his own judgment and it came to a final confrontation.

Savonarola now took an unprecedented step. He wrote letters to the King of France, the King and Queen of Spain, and the German Emperor begging them to convene a solemn concilium in a free and safe place. He argued that Alexander VI was not a real pontiff, nor ever could be, because of his simoniacal and sacrilegious election and his publicly committed sins, and especially since he was not a Christian and lacked any kind of faith. Moreover, the church could not long remain without a shepherd since in the long run this would endanger the souls of the faithful.[14] His steps implied that the power to convene a council was no longer the prerogative of the pope or of the ecclesiastical hierarchy. Yet the council never convened. Instead, the intrigues of Savonarola's enemies continued to do their work. Savonarola remained excommunicated and the pope even threatened him with an interdict against the city which would have left the people without any worship services. Intimidated by the ecclesiastical authorities, they asked him to refrain from preaching outside the convent. Then he was told to refrain from functioning in any priestly role, and finally he was apprehended. Yet the city refused to send him to Rome. They conducted their own trial and Savonarola and three of his closest followers were hanged in 1498 and their bodies committed to the flames. The church was still not awakened to the growing needs for piety and modesty. Instead it continued its path into worldly life and interests.

b. The revolt of autonomy and nationality (John Wyclif and John Hus)

JOHN WYCLIF, doctor of theology, and for some time professor at Oxford, England, is most famous for being instrumental in publishing the entire Bible in the English language between 1380 and 1384. Yet translating the Bible into the vernacular was only a means for Wyclif to enable the common people to discover the law of Christ which was supposed to transform the law of the church. Wyclif saw the main fault of the church in disobeying the laws of the Bible. Therefore, it had to be made to conform again with the biblical laws and thereby become reformed.[15]

Wyclif saw Christ as the head of the church who rules it through his law or the Holy Scripture and who is the church's patriarch and spiritual king. To add another chief ruler would mean to invest the officeholder with divine prerogatives.[16] His thoughts coincided with those of Waldo and Savonarola concerning the actual authority for what is normative in the church. Simply claiming that he was Vicar of Christ was not sufficient for the pope to give his authority credibility. It now had to be backed up by the authority of Scripture. Yet Wyclif went one step further than did either Waldo or Savonarola.

Wyclif attempted to redefine the relationship between the worldly and ecclesiastical authority. According to him worldly and ecclesiastical authority do not oppose but complement each other, since they are both instituted by Christ to preserve the church.[17] Since they work toward the same goal, the state can be understood as the actual worldly power that endows the church with worldly goods so that it can fulfill its function to proclaim the law of Christ. The proper fulfillment of this task would prevent the church from being preoccupied with worldly pursuits.[18] Wyclif argued that the property the church enjoys is not its exclusive possession but often given for a specific purpose, such as caring for the poor. Thus Wyclif advocated that the state must withdraw some of this property if the church misuses it. He also saw it as the duty of the government to supervise the clerics and, if necessary, to punish them if they go astray. Of course, this is to be done only with counsel and consent of the church, and not by the government's own volition. In matters of possessions, however, Wyclif seemed to be less hesitant to appeal to worldly authority since neither Christ nor the apostles indulged in worldly possessions. Therefore the clergy should not be preoccupied with civil matters but should renounce involvement in earthly rule and possessions.

Wyclif was well aware that the predominant involvement with worldly affairs had led to spiritual impoverishment of the church. He insisted on virtue in the life of the church, since any changes in church organization and control would be ineffective, unless they were accompanied by a new devotion to a virtuous life. "Reform must be internal and spiritual as well as external and ecclesiastical." [19] Having lived through the dark hours of the papal schism, he realized that lust for worldly power and frequent excommunications threatened to destroy the church, while studying and following the law of Christ would upbuild it. The emphasis on spiritual renewal would also change the position of the pope and the central church government which the popes were striving to maintain. If the pope wanted to be the head of the church, Wyclif insisted, it was insufficient to be elected or to claim succession to Peter. A spiritual leader must also show spiritual qualities which cannot be conferred through mere election or succession.[20]

Wyclif pointed out that the pope owes his worldly authority to Constantine and, since the measure for what the church ought to be is the Bible, Wyclif refused to attribute to the pope more than spiritual authority.[21] He does not even see the papacy as absolutely necessary. The pope may fall into sin, but Christ and his law suffice to rule the church spiritually. The primacy of Scripture that Wyclif propounded had a twofold effect on his understanding of the papacy.

(1) He saw the pope as under the judgment of the Scriptures. In his spiritual leadership the pope is authority only if he advocates the teachings of Scripture and if his decrees agree with the law of Christ. It would have been heresy for Wyclif to believe that a person could be equal to Scripture. Therefore the pope cannot correct the gospel. On the contrary, a pope can err and his dispensations are valid only if they correspond with Scripture.

(2) Since the pope should function as the spiritual leader, it is totally improper that he impose taxation upon the church. Even the frequent excommunications and the whole system of church sanctions are questionable and must be decided by the church as a whole. The pope has no other authority than the word of God. Similar to Savonarola at the end of his career, Wyclif demanded that a pope who lives in sin and who misuses his

office for worldly affairs should be replaced with a more worthy pope by the bishops and cardinals or by the worldly authorities. This means that the pope is not sacrosanct and that worldly authorities have an obligation to defend Scripture against the heretical innovations of the pope.

It is difficult to evaluate Wyclif properly. The emphasis on the primacy of Scripture as the sole norm, rule, and judge for worldly and spiritual life reminds us of Reformation concerns. His sending out disciples in pairs according to Matthew 10 to preach the law of Christ reminds us of Peter Waldo. Yet what impresses us most is his immense political realism that he undergirded with biblical theology. In essence, he advocated "a theocracy headed by a spiritual king and a pontifical monarch." [22] But therein also lies his greatest weakness. For instance, the royal confiscations of church property, for which he argued theologically, had already become a political reality in the England of his time. In many other respects too he gave theological sanction to political *fait accompli*.

When his teachings were finally condemned in 1382 and his followers, the Lollards, were persecuted by the inquisition from 1401 onward, his name was mentioned less and less frequently. His ideas, however, were not lost. For instance, when King Henry VIII pondered what stand he should take against Rome, he read Wyclif and found himself considerably strengthened in his antipapal position.[23] Also the strict supervision that the English crown began to exercise over the church of the Reformation is not unrelated to Wyclif's propositions. There exists also a close connection between John Wyclif and John Hus of Bohemia that proved to be fruitful for the future. This connection was first fostered by the ties between the universities of Prague and Oxford, Wyclif having been a professor at Oxford, and further in 1382 by the marriage between Richard II of England and Anne, sister of Wenceslas of Bohemia. Hus was considerably influenced by Wyclif, even to the point of incorporating whole sections of Wyclif's writings into his own works.

John Hus was born around 1372 in a small hamlet in southern Bohemia called Husinec after which he was named, and he taught after 1398 at the University of Prague, the oldest university in central Europe. Similar to Wyclif, Hus was not the founder of a reform movement but rather its most eloquent proponent. In addition to Wyclif, two Czech reform theologians must be counted among his spiritual ancestors, Jan Milic of Kromeriz (d. 1374) and Matthias of Janov (d. 1394). Hus was the heir of this movement.

John Hus made a name for himself in 1402 when he was appointed to

the Bethlehem Chapel in Prague, the center of the Czech reform movement.[24] Though not yet influenced by Wyclif, his sermons are characterized by earnest exhortations to follow Christ. He exposed the sins of ordinary people, kings, and noblemen, and was aware that nothing hurts the
church more than the sins of the clerics. He declared that a pope living
contrary to the word of God could be deposed, and he reprimanded the
clergy for being more interested in money than in the welfare of souls.
He reminded both preachers and hearers that their faith is grounded in
the gospel and that they ought to live in accordance with it.

John Hus and his followers soon suffered the same fate as did the other
prereformers. The church, though aware of the abuses, would not tolerate
extended denunciations of the clergy, since it would bring them into dispute and contempt before the people. Even Archbishop Zbynek changed
his stance from protecting Hus to openly criticizing him. Yet Hus replied
that he had not said anything in malice but out of love for the church.[25]
The pretense for the archbishop's concern was that Hus had advocated
the Wyclifite heresy. But the whole affair was more a struggle for influence in the church. Zbynek even excommunicated Hus and applied the
interdict against Prague. King Wenceslas, however, protected Hus and
made the archbishop declare that there was no heresy propounded in
Bohemia. But the issue was no longer a local one. By now Hus was not
just a simple preacher but had become the rector of the University of
Prague. Together with university reform, this appointment was bitterly
opposed by the German constituent of the university. Finally the German
professors left Prague and founded the University of Leipzig.

While Hus advocated a more conciliar understanding of the church,
Zbynek was relying on the pope who gladly took the occasion to intervene
in Bohemia. To heat up the issue even more, Hus spoke out boldly against
the indulgences that John XXIII freely issued to wage his war against
Ladislaus, king of Naples, who still supported Pope Gregory XII. Hus
did not flatly reject indulgences, but he denied that it was lawful for the
pope to fight with the sword. He argued that the bull with which John
XXIII had introduced the indulgences in 1411 was an appeal to violence
and murder. The pope, he argued, should conquer his enemies by prayer.
Since the pope does not know whether the purchasers of indulgences have
truly repented, he cannot usurp God's prerogative and declare the sins
forgiven.[26] As a result, Hus came under excommunication and interdict.
Consequently he could not receive any food or shelter from anyone, and
any place where he was allowed to appear would lose ecclesiastical services.

Yet he continued to enjoy the protection of powerful friends and also of King Wenceslas who seemed to perceive the issue primarily as a Bohemian affair and wanted to settle it without outside intrusion.

The situation changed when the Council of Constance was convened in 1414 and King Sigismund of Hungary invited Hus to present his case at the Council. Sigismund had guaranteed his safe journey to the Council, which also seemed to imply a safe return home, even if the Council would decide against him. Yet the latter guarantee was not explicitly specified.[27] Hus gladly accepted the invitation, because he was assured of defending himself freely before the Council, and he was confident that he would prove his innocence. Yet he never got a chance. Upon arrival he was thrown into prison. His accusers attempted to convict him as a blatant Wyclifite, but he steadfastly refused to acknowledge the charges. Even when they finally examined his own writings, he demanded that he be convicted on the grounds of Scripture. Yet his demands went unheard. He was condemned as a heresiarch and committed to the worldly authorities for appropriate punishment. He died at the stake on July 6, 1415.

Having obtained the support of his brother Wenceslas for his coronation as emperor, Sigismund was no longer interested in being favorably disposed toward Hus. Instead of demanding his release Sigismund contributed to his demise. But it is significant for later developments that John Hus found his insuperable challenge in the political constellation rather than in the strength of the ecclesiastical hierarchy. The Council even attempted initial reform of ecclesiastical authority when it began to resolve the schism between Rome and Avignon and deposed John XXIII who had called the Council. Hus too was ultimately condemned by the Council and not by the pope. We should also note that the decisions at the Council were arrived at by voting according to nationality (Italian, German, French, English, and later Spanish), and that in the case of Hus the Germans had not forgotten the reforms at the University of Prague that led to their exodus. Thus the (Western) church was no longer a monolithic block. It had become more and more conscious of its national individuality, and as Hus insisted, even autonomy based on Scripture. The emphasis on national individuality is again a major point of contention that led to the uprisings that followed Hus' death. In negotiations with the Husites at the Council of Basel (1431-1449), they were even admitted as an equal and recognized party.

For Hus the desire for individuality does not diminish the emphasis on the unity of the church. But now the unity does not manifest itself in the Apostolic See, but in the predestining grace that shows itself in the exercise of Christian virtues. For instance, in his treatise on *The Church,* John Hus states clearly "that Christ alone is the head of the universal church, which church is not a part of anything else." [28] Since Christ is the head of the church, a Christian cannot also be head of the church without the church becoming a two-headed monster. The pope then is not the head of the church, but the Vicar of Christ—provided he is a faithful minister to the glory of its head, Jesus Christ.[29] Hus also finds the unity of the church expressed in its goal: "The unity of the catholic church consists in the unity of predestination, inasmuch as her separate members are one by predestination and in the unity of blessedness, and inasmuch as her separate sons are finally united in bliss." [30] Since Christ is recognized as the head of the church, the pope does not enjoy authority automatically. If a pope teaches the doctrine of the apostles and follows them in works, he is called apostolic; "if he puts the teachings of the apostles aside, teaching in word or works what is contrary, then he is properly called pseudo-apostolic or an apostate." Therefore it is our duty as faithful disciples of Christ to consider on what authority a pope issues a command,

> whether it is the express command of any apostle or of Christ's law or whether it has its foundation in Christ's law, and this being known to be the case, he ought to obey a command of this kind reverently and humbly. But, if he truly knows that a pope's command is at variance with Christ's command or counsel or tends to any hurt of the church, then he ought boldly to resist it lest he become a partaker in crime by consent.[31]

The acknowledgement of Christ as the head of the church, leads necessarily to the apostolic tradition or the Scriptures as the repository of the word of Christ and ultimate authority in the church. An authority can then only claim legitimacy if it stands in faithful continuity with the fount of the church, Jesus Christ. Whether Wyclif or Hus, whether Savonarola or Waldo, all preformers pointed to Christ as the ultimate criterion of what the church ought to be. Yet their reform movements were unable to pick up sufficient momentum to introduce significant and lasting changes. The medieval church continued to lose touch with its own origin and with those who attempted to recover this origin with piety and humility and in autonomy and faithful independence.

2. The Reformation movement—A grass roots movement

The Reformation movement was to a large extent an outgrowth and continuation of movements prior to the 16th century. Martin Luther reinforced this notion when he remarked on the occasion of the edition of Hus' writings that he wished his name were worthy to be associated with that of Hus.[32] Yet the mainstream of the Reformation did not simply continue earlier movements. In its breadth and the sweeping reforms that the Reformation inaugurated, a new day had dawned. The Reformation marked the end of the centralized Roman domination of the Western Church. In many ways the permanence of the Reformation was due to peculiar political constellations, e.g., the pope's initial underestimation of the force of the new movement, the emperor's unfamiliarity with the German scene and his dependence on the Elector Frederick the Wise in whose territory Luther lived, and the threatening assaults of the Turks at various crucial times. But the Reformation was not a political movement. Similar to the uprising of the Husites, the Reformation was a grass-roots movement facilitated by the relatively easy accessibility of the printed word due to the recent invention of the movable type printing press.

For Luther and those who stood at his side, the end of the centralized Roman domination of the Western Church did not imply the end of the unity of the catholic church. The Reformation did not mark either the end of dogmas or of tradition. Similar to Hus, who quite frequently quoted Augustine or other church fathers to prove his point, Luther saw himself in agreement with the fathers of the church and the catholic dogma. Yet he radicalized Vincent of Lerins' insight stated 1000 years earlier that the catholic faith is what always, everywhere, and by all has been believed. He argued that the decisions of the early church councils must then be accepted without qualification, while the identification of the church with the papacy or the councils, the peddling of indulgences, the higher virtue of monastic life, and the reservation of the Scriptures for the clerics, must be rejected as innovations.

That the Reformation did not lack the moment of catholicity can be seen from the exchange between some Reformers and representatives of the Eastern Church. In 1573 some of the German Reformers had taken up correspondence with Jeremiah II, the Ecumenical Patriarch of Moscow, and even appended a copy of the Augsburg Confession in Greek.[33] Their hope was that the Patriarch might see a basic agreement in doctrine between the Orthodox and the Lutherans, in spite of an obvious divergence in their liturgical practice. Yet the response of the Patriarch, though very irenical in tone, was not what the Lutherans had hoped for. He suggested that if the Lutherans were wholeheartedly prepared to adhere to the Orthodox doctrine, he would receive them into communion, and this way the two churches could be made one. This exchange indicates how different the unity of the church was perceived before and after the Reformation. For the Reformers, unity and catholicity no longer meant organic union or accepting a certain hierarchical structure. They had rediscovered that union and catholicity depended on the unconditional and exclusive acceptance of Jesus as Lord, the founder and raison d'etre of the Christian church.

a. The rediscovery of the catholic church (Martin Luther)

The essentials of true unity were described in the Augsburg Confession (1530) when it stated: "For the true unity of the Church it is enough to agree concerning the teaching of the Gospel and the administration of the sacraments. It is not necessary that human traditions or rites and ceremonies, instituted by men, should be alike everywhere" (CA 7). This approach to church unity presents a significant reduction of other "marks" of the church, such as unanimity with the Apostolic See, observance of certain festivals, proper distinction between laity and clerics, and the like. There is also no mention of organic union or parallel structuring. The church is not completely undefined, however, since the Augsburg Confession asserts that "the church is the assembly of saints in which the Gospel is taught purely and the Sacraments are administered rightly" (CA 7).

The term assembly *(congregatio)* in the Augsburg Confession that describes the church is not to be understood as a "getting together" as in a haphazard meeting of 15 people, but rather a "gathering." This becomes evident when MARTIN LUTHER described the church in his Large Catechism (1529). He said: "There is on earth a little holy flock or community of pure saints under one head, Christ. It is called together by the Holy Spirit in one faith, mind, and understanding. It possesses a variety of gifts, yet is united in love without sect or schism."[34] We are not part of this community by birth but the Holy Spirit "first leads us into his holy community . . . where he preaches to us and brings us to Christ."[35] The church is not a sinless community of saints, but one in which we may daily obtain full forgiveness of sins through word and sacrament. Since God forgives us we in turn forgive each other. The community aspect is not just accomplished by the Holy Spirit in assembling the saints. It is also our task through forgiving, bearing with, and aiding one another. Outside the church, Luther added, there is no forgiveness and hence no holiness. These people attempt to attain holiness through their own efforts rather than through repentance and reliance on God's grace. They remain in their pride and sin and separate themselves from the church.

When we hear in the Smalcald Articles (1536) that "a seven-year-old child knows what the church is, namely, holy believers and sheep who hear the voice of their Shepherd," we may wonder whether Luther has moved away from the concept of the visible church to the idea of an elite group.[36] Yet like Augustine, Luther distinguishes between the visible and the invisible church, claiming that the visible church is a mixed group, representing the totality of the baptized and actually consists both of good people and bad ones, and even of some heretics.[37] Luther feels that this distinction was never observed and the one holy Christian church was identified with the visible church and tied to a certain person, the pope.[38] But, Christ's holy church is not a tangible entity. It is a matter of faith, built on Christ and not on temporal things.

Similarly, Luther talks about community in a twofold sense:[39] (1) One community is an external and visible one, that, for instance, decides about admission to the sacraments. Yet often this external authority is wrong when it excludes or includes someone in the community. (2) The internal community is spiritual and invisible in the heart. It can neither be taken away nor created by external or visible authority. Only God through his Holy Spirit can establish this community. This unity is not something that can be made or decreed by us. It is given to us and works through us.

Since for Luther the true church is invisible, we might get the idea that he discards the visible church in spiritualistic fashion. But this is far from the truth. The spiritual church is divine and comprises the internal person, while the human ecclesiastical structures are external and belong to the external person. Luther strictly distinguishes between the two, realizing that they belong together like concentric circles. To what extent the outer visible circle coincides with the invisible and spiritual church depends on the degree to which the visible church obeys the power of the Holy Spirit active in the invisible church. Luther is convinced that even in its greatest demise the external is not totally void of being the true church. The realm of Christ and of the true church are present as long as baptism and the gospel are still present.[40] This means that the invisible church has visible signs, namely baptism, Eucharist, and the gospel. Luther even calls them the symbols and characters of a Christian. Whenever we see that baptism and Eucharist are administered and the gospel is proclaimed at a specific place we should not doubt that the church is there too. It does not suffice that the sacraments are present without the gospel, since through the gospel we have one faith, one hope, one love, and one spirit. The unity of the spirit expressed in hope, faith, and love, is the power that makes the church one.

Luther did not perceive the catholicity to consist in the unity of the visible external church, but in the invisible, internal one. He saw this unity created through the one spirit active in every member. It follows without surprise that he did not assign exceptional status to the clergy. Christ has become the first priest of the New Testament without all the rites which a priest underwent at Luther's time. He also made his disciples priests without these rites. It is not necessary therefore, Luther argued, to become ordained to be a priest.[41] All Christians are priests through their baptism. They are part of the Christian community and participate in the signs of the community, administering the sacraments and preaching the gospel. In passages such as 1 Peter 2:9: "You are a chosen race, a royal priesthood, a holy nation, God's own people, that you may declare the wonderful deeds of him who called you out of darkness into his marvelous light," Luther finds support for his claim that the proclamation of the word belongs to all Christians. Their foremost task consists in the proclamation of the gospel. While Luther sees no justification in distinguishing between different classes of priestliness, the common priesthood of all believers does not lead to anarchy. Luther states very clearly:

> For whoever comes out of the water of baptism can boast that he is already a consecrated priest, bishop, and pope, although of course it is not seemly that just anybody should exercise such office. Because we are all priests of equal standing, no one must push himself forward and take it upon himself, without our consent and election, to do that for which we all have equal authority. For no one dare take upon himself what is common to all without the authority and consent of the community. And should it happen that a person chosen for such office were deposed for abuse of trust, he would then be exactly what he was before. Therefore, a priest in Christendom is nothing else but an officeholder. As long as he holds office he takes precedence; where he is deposed, he is a peasant or a townsman like anybody else. Indeed, a priest is never a priest when he is deposed.[42]

Luther perceived the priesthood in purely functional terms and not as an ontological characteristic that would confer upon the priest indelible status as the Roman Catholic Church declared.[43] Once the functional role ceases, the priesthood ceases too. For Luther, ordination meant being called to and entrusted with the pastoral office.[44] Since there is no distinction in authority among Christians, Luther argued that to have validity the call to service cannot come only from human beings. Ultimately it must come from God and be mediated through human beings, since they actually set someone apart for the specific task of proclaiming the gospel. Especially in his dealings with some enthusiasts who claimed to be directly called by God, it was important to insist that every call must be mediated. Conversely to counteract those who only looked at the external, visible church it was important to show that the call must be from God. Proclaiming the gospel and administering the sacraments is done on behalf of the community which one serves. But it is not the word or the sacrament of the community that is administered. Message and signs are God's and are administered on his behalf. The rejection of a special priestly class serves to further the unity of the church as the true and equal community under the headship of Christ.

One may wonder whether the emphasis on the officeholder as the only one who is called to fulfill the functions of the priestly office does not render ineffective the common priesthood of all believers. The Augsburg Confession refutes such an idea when it says that "nobody should preach publicly in the church or administer the sacraments unless he is regularly called" (CA 14). We note here that the delegation of the priestly function pertains only to the public aspect of the ministry, but not to the private aspect. Luther was very explicit at this point when he stated that a father does well when he teaches his household the word of God— Luther wrote the Large Catechism for fathers to instruct their families— because God has commanded us that we educate our children and families in the word of God. Yet for Luther the same does not pertain to the administration of the sacraments, since they are public signs and confessions.

At Luther's time the Christian church was usually coextensive with the political community in which the Christians lived. Thus the notion of home or foreign mission was not well developed. Today, however, Christians occupy minority status in many countries. Therefore the question must be raised now whether the nonordained proclamation of the gospel can be restricted to catechetical instruction in the homes or whether it should not be expanded to include evangelistic outreach to nonfamily members. Luther's concept of the pastoral office, though proper and justified at his time, proved stifling in more recent times when Christianity was relegated to minority status in many countries. Here the concept of the common priesthood evolving from "free churches" allowed for more flexibility.

It would be wrong to assume that Luther's understanding of the priesthood of all believers implied that each Christian could now stand in direct relationship with God without a human mediator.[45] Luther was not an advocate of Protestant individualism. The communal dimension was essential for him and he continually emphasized the necessity to intercede before God on behalf of the brethren and of the world. For him Christians must exercise their priestly function toward one another in the home and toward the world.[46] When Luther lists seven rights of the universal priesthood, to preach the word of God, to baptize, to celebrate the Sacrament of the Altar, to minister the office of the keys, to sacrifice, to pray for others, and to judge doctrine and distinguish spirits, we cannot miss their corporate dimension. Luther even claims that a Christian has a right and duty to teach the word of God and if he fails to do so, he would risk his own salvation. But Luther confines the public preaching of the word within the church to those who have been called through the community and he permits someone who has not been called to preach publicly only in genuine mission territory or when the called teacher fails or errs. Through his negative experience with the Enthusiasts he even qualifies the latter statement saying:

> I have no right to do this even if I hear that false doctrine is being taught and that souls are being seduced and condemned which I could rescue from error and condemnation by my sound doctrine. But I should commit the matter to God, who in His own time will find the opportunity to call ministers lawfully and to give the Word.[47]

The reason for this obvious ambivalence in Luther's argument is the realization that there are two agents to a call, God and the community. Luther says:

> God calls in two ways, either by means or without means. Today he calls all of us into the ministry of the Word by a mediated call, that is, one that comes through means, namely, through man. But the apostles were called immediately by Christ himself, as the prophets in the Old Testament had been called by God himself. Afterwards the apostles called their disciples, as Paul called Timothy, Titus, etc. . . . This is a mediated calling, since it is done by man. Nevertheless, it is divine.

That one is called in an orderly and mediated way is mandatory to preserve order in the community. But it is also significant for the ones who are called. In times of temptation and doubt they know that they did not seek the office they serve on their own. They were asked by others to fulfill this task. With regard to himself Luther confesses that he "would surely in the long run lose courage and fall into despair if, as these infiltrators, I had undertaken these great and serious matters without call or commission." [48] Luther is convinced that those who do not have this external call will not prosper in their work even if they have the right doctrine.

We might ask what happens if the community through whom the call was mediated takes it away. Should the one who was called remain silent even if the community's action does not coincide with God's will? We remember that Savonarola obeyed the authorities when they asked him to remain silent, whereas Hus did not. To address this question, we should note that Luther bases the priestly office on the presupposition of the universal priesthood and describes it as a mediated office. Yet he can also derive it directly from Christ's institution without reference to the universal priesthood. For instance, we hear that Christ has directly given and instituted this special office, and then again we hear that everyone is entrusted with this office.

God does not want chaos but order. For the sake of order the public aspect of this office is entrusted to someone called by Christ through the community. The authority that every Christian in the entire Christian community possesses is delegated to the one whom they choose from their midst or who is called by a superior with the consent of the community. Though this one person publicly proclaims the word, the other members of the community are not released from their priestly duty of speaking God's word to each other. Similarly, in the administration of the sacraments we gather beside, behind, and around the one delegated, since all of us are true and holy fellow priests. [49] We do not permit our pastor to speak the liturgy by himself as for his own person, but through his mouth we speak with him from our hearts and with strengthened faith to the lamb of God.

Through his emphasis on the headship of Christ, Luther could not tolerate the notion of a special (elevated) clerical order. Confronted with the disruptive and individualized approach to the pastoral office by the spiritualists and enthusiasts, he also could not condone an individualized understanding of being a Christian. Without diminishing the full responsibility of each Christian he attempted to emphasize that clergy like laity receive a special call from God through the community. By community

consent this call sets the clergy apart for the specific task of public proclamation of the word and administration of the sacraments, while the
private instruction remains the task of everyone. The dangers of this
approach are evident: If individual responsibility is unduly emphasized it
leads to a crisis in pastoral identity and sense of calling. On the other
hand, if the pastoral office is too much emphasized, it leads to passivity
and irresponsibility among the laity. Therefore, the pastoral office on the
one side and individual and corporate responsibility on the other must
have equal weight. The setting apart for the public office was unthinkable for Luther without adequate preparation provided by the sending
community and adequate gifts brought to the office by the one who is
set apart. One does not call lightly and hastily but after careful delibera-
tion and equipment.

Rediscovering Christ as the one who has founded the church, who
guides it through the Spirit amid all adversity and who leads it towards
its fulfillment at the last day, was not unique to Luther. As had others
before him, he led back to Jesus Christ as the only one who enables true
unity and catholicity of the church. Though Jesus Christ, the author and
agent of unity and catholicity, had never been completely forgotten, the
emphasis on outward conformity and compliance had obtained dominance over true spirituality, the Spirit that Jesus Christ had promised
his followers. When Luther was accused as an innovator and apostate, he
rightly responded that he intended to stay within the true and old
church by rediscovering it, while the church of his day was the truly
new church, departing from the old true church.[50] He did not see his
task in establishing something new, but conserving through the word
that which was in danger of being lost and destroyed.[51] Luther attempted
to recover continuity and catholicity with the early church and with whatever could be justified in the face of its biblical origin. His insistence on
Christ alone was always paired with the demand for Scripture alone, not
in terms of a purist and biblicist attitude, but to discover that which was
necessary and essential to maintain the unity of the church.

b. Structure versus Spirit (Huldreich Zwingli and John Calvin, Anabaptists, Spiritualists, and Enthusiasts)

While Luther is the most prominent figure of the Reformation, he was
not the only Reformer. There were many diverse streams noticeable in
the Reformation period, some with more social concerns than theological
ones, such as the concerns surfacing in the Peasants' Revolt (1525), and

others predating the Reformation but finally getting the upper current, such as the antitrinitarian movement. There are two major currents outside Lutheranism, however, that deserve special mention, namely Calvinism and Spiritualism. While Huldreich Zwingli, John Calvin, and Thomas Cranmer can be easily classified as the main proponents of Calvinism, the task is more difficult to name the main representatives of the spiritualistic group. It comprises the Anabaptists, the Enthusiasts, and the Spiritualists and it never succeeded in establishing sizeable churches of its own. Many of its adherents eventually moved to North America and contributed much to the growth of Protestant denominations, such as the Hutterites, Mennonites, Schwenkfeldians, and others.

HULDREICH ZWINGLI, the Reformer of Zurich, is known for his idea of theocracy. But he did not advocate the supremacy of the church or the dictatorship of the state. He was concerned that both public and spiritual things be governed by God's will. Like Luther, he recognized Christ as the sole foundation of the church, a move that led to the collapse of the Roman hegemony and the hierarchial structure of the church.

For Zwingli the church is the community of those whose faith is founded in Christ as their Lord. The church is the community of saints. Since its members are disbursed throughout the world, it is invisible. Like Luther, he distinguishes between the visible church which contains many sinners and the invisible church which, as Zwingli insists, consists of the predestined. Similar to Luther, he recognized that Christians who believe and have the spirit of Christ are also priests. Yet only those specially chosen or designated should publicly exercise their priestly function.

It is indicative for Zwingli's humanistic roots that he even counted noble pagans, such as Socrates, Aristides, and Catos, and the Scipios among the predestined whom we will meet in heaven.[52] While Zwingli is equally Bible-centered in his theology as Luther, he is not equally Christocentric in his teachings. Of course, he sees himself in agreement with the dogmatic decisions of the early church. But unlike Luther, Zwingli does not view God as the inaccessible power who can only be adequately recognized in his self-disclosure in Jesus Christ. As we can see from his emphasis on predestination, Zwingli understands God primarily as the all-determining first cause who governs the world according to his providence. Zwingli is convinced that God can be known through the orderliness of the world and he wants us to obey his laws. God remains a distant God as expressed in Zwingli's assessment of the sacraments. The sacraments are symbols endowed with meaning through God's word, but God does not come to us in them. They are signs through which we remember his deeds; they are obligatory signs that remind us to live a certain way.

The state plays an especially important role in forming the Christian life. While Zwingli distinguishes between church and state, he did not separate them. Even the distinction between the two was not a strict one, since he concluded from his experience in Zurich that a civic community is a unified whole. Such a community can be governed best when clergy and magistrate work together in harmony to realize God's will. Since the Bible is the sole norm for both church and government, it is the task of the latter to spread the knowledge of God so that all live according to his will. The best state we hear is one in which the word of God is preached most clearly.[53] "The divine word shall rule among all people, it shall be prescribed, recited, and truly revealed and opened to them, because it is our duty that we follow it."

This close interaction between church and state presupposes that the government is composed of Christians and that the biblical commandments become the supreme source of the law. It also means that the authority of the state finds its limits in the Decalogue. If the government does not follow the precepts of the Lord, Zwingli insists that it be replaced by a more obedient regime. This does not mean that the church is telling the government how to run its affairs. The church's only task is to further the faith and to increase internal righteousness. The state, however, must be concerned with external, civil justice necessary for the existence of human society. Since the public realm and the church are ordered by the same God, the government would not even be necessary if humanity were not sinful. Humanity would then follow the rules of the state by voluntarily obeying the word of God. Zwingli can therefore say that "a Christian is nothing but an honest and good citizen and a Christian state is nothing but a Christian church."[54] Since there are, however, sinners in the world and in the church, the state and its laws are a necessity to assure the peaceful living together of people.

We could reject Zwingli's notion of a theocracy by claiming that it is basically medieval and also strongly influenced by the peculiarities of the Swiss city states. In many ways it reiterates ideas advanced by Savonarola. Both wanted to reform their cities according to the divine law of the Bible and with the help of the worldly authorities. Yet both approaches contain features that are no longer medieval; the confinement of the church to its spiritual task, the rejection of papal supremacy over worldly power, and the Bible as the sole source of religious authority.[55] In our pluralistic society a theocracy that Zwingli envisioned is no longer tenable. But is Zwingli actually wrong when he asserts that both state and church are as dependent on guidance through God's spirit as our body depends on the soul?[56] Furthermore, is it not still the task of the church to function as a prophetic guardian of the state?[57] It is all too easy for the church to relinquish the public and political realm and withdraw to the spiritual sphere. Perhaps Zwingli could serve as a reminder that God is also the God of the state even if the state refuses to recognize this.

For JOHN CALVIN too, the Reformer of Geneva, the sovereignty of God was the fundamental axiom of his theology. God is the sovereign ruler, and all authority on earth is derived from this ultimate authority. In his counsel God determined some to be predestined to be saved and others he determined in his unsearchable will to eternal damnation.[58] As Calvin wrote in his Geneva Catechism of 1541, the church is "the community of the faithful which God has ordained and elected to eternal life."[59] The church includes all saints who presently live on earth plus those elect who have been from the beginning of the world.[60] The elect are those who believe in Christ, since election means incorporation into his body. Election is community-centered. The believers have God as their common Father and Christ as their Head and they form a community through which they serve each other. The church is a holy community in which the believers are connected with each other in love. In Christ they have one judgment and one will.

Calvin, however, realizes that Scripture talks in a twofold way about the church. On the one hand it is composed of those who have become children of God through the grace of adoption and are true members of Christ through sanctification in the Spirit.[61] These are the elect who constitute the invisible church. But the church also includes those who confess that they honor Christ alone and who have been initiated to faith in him through baptism and the Eucharist. Calvin realizes that there are many hypocrites among them. Yet he admits that we dare not write off the visible church. We must honor it and utilize its community structure. The preaching of the word and the keeping of the sacraments makes us aware of the invisible church, since these cannot be present without results and God's blessing.[62] As long as there is word and sacrament, we are not just confronted with the visible church, but also with the invisible one. By its very nature the invisible church is not a tangible entity and can only be grasped in faith.

> Where the preaching of the gospel is reverently heard and the sacraments are not neglected, there for the time being no deceitful or ambiguous form of the church is seen; and no one is permitted to spurn its authority, flout its warnings, resist its counsels, or make light of its chastisements— much less to desert it and break its unity.

We are not allowed to reject the visible church. We encounter in it the Christian proclamation and the community engendered by this proclamation. Yet this does not mean that Calvin would condone the Roman Church. On the contrary, he argues that we do not separate ourselves from the church of Christ if we part ways with Rome.[63] The marks of the church have been totally perverted by Rome so that it is no longer a church. If one would apply its criteria of the church, we could not even distinguish between the assembly of believers and one of Turks. The church can only be found where the gospel is proclaimed purely and the sacraments are administered according to their institution.

Calvin, however, goes one decisive step beyond Luther when he claims that as its head, Christ wants also to rule the church.[64] Since Christ is no longer visibly among us to guide us through his word, Calvin concludes that he charged certain people to act on his behalf. For instance, pastors or ministers serve as the unifying bond among the believers and as shepherds. There are also other offices instituted by Christ in the Scriptures that must be continued, namely teachers who replace the New Testament prophets, presbyters who form a trustworthy group of lay people, and deacons who are charged with the caring for the poor. The presbyters are selected from the laity and together with the bishops or pastors form a governing body that is supposed to supervise the morals of the people, and, if necessary, exercise discipline. Like Luther, Calvin sees the necessity for a call mediated through other people rather than one coming unmediated from God. He also agrees that one should call those who appear to be the most appropriate candidates according to the unanimous opinion and approval of the people. To assure orderliness and to avoid rash decisions, the supervision of such elections should be in the hands of the pastors. Unlike in later Calvinism, the individual congregation at Calvin's time did not yet enjoy complete democratic self-determination.

The order that Calvin outlines should be binding for all congregations. The ruling body of elders and bishops should supervise in this regard the whole church and not just individual congregations. Though Calvin recognizes proclamation of the gospel and administration of the sacraments as the primary task of pastors, he explicitly states that their teaching function does not exhaust itself in public sermons but must also cover personal admonitions.[65] All these notions are backed up with ample reference to Scripture. Thus the church order of the New Testament community becomes prescriptive for the reformation of the church that Calvin envisions. According to Luther, external orders were designed by humans and were changeable, but for Calvin they are of divine character, since Scripture is God's prescriptive work.

The Bible is also God's limiting word for Calvin, since it is not allowed for the church to institute a new doctrine, i.e., to teach more than what God has revealed in his word.[66] While such procedure made good sense against the innovative ideas of Rome, the situation is different when the same procedure is applied to church or the church's worship. All human traditions designed to venerate God must then be rejected, as would the useful and holy ordinances of the church that aid the sustenance of peace, honesty, and order. The law of Christ alone, i.e., the law of freedom, should rule among the Christians and not the external law. As the head of the church, Christ rules through a system of offices which are designed to preserve and proclaim pure doctrine and make effective the purifying and sanctifying order in the church.[67] In analogy to the medieval Roman Church, Calvin's church becomes inadvertently the institution designed to insure salvation. Yet not everything is law for Calvin. For instance, he argues, that there should be fixed hours of worship, but the selection of hours and the days is a matter of convenience.[68] He also can see in genuflecting, fasting, and in the lifting up of the hands appropriate aids for worship. Yet he argues that musical instruments should be banished from the churches, since they are among the legal ceremonies that Christ abolished at his coming. He also did away with choirs on grounds of vanity and only allowed the singing of psalm hymns for the edification of the congregation.

Calvin understands the Christian life as progress in the formation of righteousness, since "no one shall set out so inauspiciously as not daily to make some headway, though it be slight. Therefore, let us not cease so to act that we may make some unceasing progress in the way of the Lord."[69] Of course, Calvin recognizes that we stand in daily need of forgiveness and of free imputation of God's righteousness. But Calvin wants the church to be an aid toward this progressive justification. Geneva became for Calvin a city of God—adultery merited capital punishment, dancing and gambling were outlawed, and even houses were inspected to insure that all ordinances were followed. Though one could not eliminate all the undesirable elements in the population, by and large Geneva became a model community built on Calvin's religious and ethical premises.

To safeguard the obedience to the ordinances, Calvin needed the cooperation of the state. Since God is the ultimate authority in this world, he also works through the government. Like Luther, Calvin realizes that the spiritual, internal kingdom of Christ is different from the external government of the state. Yet unlike Luther, he enlists the government of the state very emphatically for his purposes when he says:

> Yet civil government has as its appointed end, so long as we live among men, to cherish and protect the outward worship of God, to defend sound doctrine of piety and the position of the church, to adjust our life to the society of men, to form our social behavior to civil righteousness, to reconcile us with one another, and to promote general peace and tranquility.[70]

Civil authorities are summoned to assure that the second part of the Ten Commandments is kept and they engender obedience to the first part. While only religious authorities may judge what is proper doctrine, they must also address religious, moral, and social questions. Since they have no worldly power to enforce their decisions, they rely on and enlist the civil authorities for that purpose. Unavoidably ecclesiastical authorities attempted to arrive at a position superior to that of the government. This meant that there was no room for religious freedom. State and church existed to the glory of God and were obligated to enforce pure doctrine.

John Knox, the Reformer of Scotland, developed Calvin's ideas further and claimed that the subjects of a Catholic sovereign were lawfully entitled to overthrow their sovereign by armed revolution.[71] Calvin, however, did not condone the deposing and punishment of unworthy princes. His evangelical fervor revolted against this kind of medieval authoritarianism. But his idea of the necessary complementation of church and state and the implicit superiority of the church's forces over the latter led easily to the idea of a state church. But it made a great difference to its rigor whether Calvinism obtained control of the state, as in Geneva or Scotland, or whether it was the faith of a minority as in England.[72] Everywhere, however, Calvinism exhibited a hostility to tyranny and a militant defense of what it believed to be true and just.

Thus in Holland the Dutch (Reformed) fought for independence from Catholic Spain. In France, the Huguenots were less fortunate and had to leave their country. Even in England the crown had a difficult time defending its "divine rights."

We should also note that the Thirty-nine Articles of the Church of England and its great lawgiver Richard Hooker are strongly influenced by Calvin. The influence of Geneva was especially noticeable in the Puritan Revolution of the 17th century when Oliver Cromwell and his Ironsides attempted to establish a theocratic democracy in England, one people under God. To this end Cromwell attempted to gather all the diverse religious entities into one ecclesiastical community with unity of doctrine, cult, and church order. All Christian traditions were recognized under the umbrella of Puritanism. When all citizens are Christians, their common denominator of religious and moral teachings is of authoritative significance for the state and endows the laws of the state with religious sanction. The divine law that Calvin emphasized is then advocated by the state. But it is no longer the divine law of the Bible to which Calvin could still appeal in confronting the state. Now the biblical law is replaced by the main Christian truths as they are commonly accepted by the citizens and represented in public opinion. The Christian state is sanctioned by the Christian society.

If we want to conclude by comparing Calvinism with Lutheranism, there are basically three items that stand out even today and that clearly distinguish it from Lutheranism:

(1) Among Lutherans, church doctrine is commonly adhered to, while order and polity varies according to local circumstances. But Calvinists maintain an equal emphasis on doctrine and order.

(2) Lutherans recognize the distinction between state and church without wanting to sacrifice one at the expense of the other. Calvinists feel that the church must enlist the power of the state for its purposes, and are therefore politically more active. The church is seen as occupying the frontier of history, "beckoning the world toward its appointed destiny." [73]

(3) Emphasizing the distinction between church and state, Lutherans recognize the moral depravity of the world. Yet often they perceive the world as being so godless that it should be avoided. In Calvinistic societies the state is seen as the advocate of common moral opinion. This can often lead to shallow moralism and self-righteousness, instead of recognizing the depravity of human nature and the need for renewal.

If we now want to deal briefly with the contributions to the understanding of the church by the Anabaptists, Spiritualists, and Enthusiasts, we deal with a very diverse group. The left wing of the Reformation, meaning those who made the most radical break with the tradition, is usually influenced by Luther, Zwingli, or Calvin, and in many instances by more than one of them. Some of its representatives, as we will see, only seem to take advantage of the spiritual and political turmoil of the Reformation period, having more in common with medieval trends than with the Reformation. All of them seem to emphasize the direct working of the Spirit much more than the structure-oriented Calvinists. This becomes immediately evident in the Anabaptist movement.

The ANABAPTISTS have their origin in the Zurich of Huldreich Zwingli when dissatisfied citizens decided that Zwingli was not radical enough with his reforms. They insisted that the church must follow the guidelines of the New Testament without compromise as to confession of faith and organizational patterns. The church, they believed, must also be a voluntary organization without state interference, taking its power and dedication from those who intentionally belong to this fellowship. Unlike the movements that Luther, Zwingli, and Calvin inspired, and with the exception of the short-lived experiment in Münster and some Hutterite and Amish enclaves, the Anabaptist churches nowhere became coextensive with the political communities in which they lived. They gathered as minorities with a tolerating or quite often persecuting society. They shared with the main stream of the Reformation the emphasis on the Bible as the sole norm for doctrine and organization.

To illustrate the Anabaptist position, we want to quote here from the Schleitheim Confession of 1527 which became an important document in Anabaptist history.[74] In seven articles it deals in sequence with baptism, bann, breaking of the bread, separation from evil, shepherds in the congregation, sword, and oath.[75]

(1) Infant baptism is excluded as nonbiblical and nonapostolic. Baptism should only be given to those who have been taught repentance and the amendment of their lives, and who truly believe that their sins are forgiven through Christ and who intend to walk in the resurrection of Jesus Christ. Baptism must be demanded by the believer and not by someone on his behalf. This article captures in a nutshell the essence of Anabaptist thought. Since Jesus was 30 when he was baptized, we should do likewise. The arguments of the Reformers in favor of infant baptism are declared to be

on shaky ground. One might object that the Anabaptists denied the primacy of grace extended through infant baptism and that they turned the sacrament into subjective assertion of their faith. Yet the real issue for the Anabaptists was the restitution of a vigorous congregational life, similar to what they thought had existed in apostolic times.[76]

If the Christian community consisted only of believers who had publicly confessed their faith and their intent to amend their ways, there would be no laxity among the brethren. The idea of the church as a pure community seemed to be one of the most essential elements in Anabaptist thought.[77] For the mainstream of the Reformation the church was important too. Otherwise its representatives would not have attempted to reform the church. But unlike the Anabaptists they always conceived of the church in a twofold way: as the visible institutional church, and as the invisible church of the community of saints. In their naive realism and in their attempt to recover a truly apostolic situation—if such ever existed—the Anabaptists, however, understood the church always to be a visible community of true Christians. They regarded the church, at least in part, as the nucleus of God's kingdom on earth and its attempted realization. The church is an island of grace in the turmoil and darkness of the present day. It portrays the unity of the spirit and conveys the picture of the true community as it is lived and practiced today.

Through baptism the believers come under a discipline which they themselves affirmed and enforced. By closely watching the entrance to their community of believers and by enforcing the discipline among its members the Anabaptists felt they could maintain a strong and true church. Baptism was not administered lightly and often required a long period of waiting and, once attained, membership in the community was not automatically lifelong. It could also be revoked if the member persistently lapsed.

(2) In the second article of the Schleitheim Confession we read that brothers or sisters who have sinned should be admonished twice privately. The third time they must be publicly admonished in front of the entire congregation or banned. The threat of expulsion from the congregation of believers occasionally implied social ostracism or shunning, and it usually meant exclusion from fellowship. This practice was based on a biblical precedent (Matt. 18:15-17). It was significant that admonition or banning occurred prior to the celebration of the Lord's Supper, so that those admitted could enjoy unity of spirit and one love, one bread, and one chalice.

(3) The Eucharist was understood as a strict memorial of Christ's suf-

fering and death and only those participated who formed the body of Christ, the baptized believers. Any real presence of Christ in and with the elements that both Luther and, to a large extent, Calvin affirmed, was rejected. When we hear that identification of the Lord with the elements in the Supper is only a figure of speech, we notice the influence of Zwingli's symbolic interpretation of the sacraments. Since the Eucharist was not seen primarily as God's action, the moral and ethical quality of the communicants had to be probed strenuously.[78]

Unlike Luther, according to whom a person was always unworthy of God's grace, the Anabaptists emphasized the worthiness of the communicant. Not unfrequently, Anabaptists abstained from communing, because they felt unworthy and they did not want to hurt themselves by partaking unworthily (cf. 1 Cor. 10:21). This practice indicates that the Anabaptists believed Christ was not absent from the celebration. Yet he was not understood to extend himself to the participants through the sacrament, but was present in the community of the believers. The community of the really faithful becomes his living temple in whom he dwells. The sacraments are then symbols of the relationship between the Lord and his church.

(4) Since the Christian community ought to be the visible presence of Christ, the fourth article on separation from the evil of the world follows naturally. It included renouncing the Roman Church, commerce with unbelievers, and frequenting taverns. The Anabaptists tried to follow the biblical advice on concern for each other's mutual aid and admonition, and separation from the world. Unlike the mainstream churches they did not seek to reform the world by infiltrating and transforming it, but through separation and exemplary life. Often the church was understood as a sharing brotherhood in which private property was no longer necessary.[79] The horizontal relationship became so important that one felt one should not come to God except together with one's brother.

(5) The communal view of the church excluded the possibility of seeing Peter as the foundation of the church. It also did not allow for a special clerical order, for fear that this might diminish the sovereignty of the community of believers. Yet it was commonly accepted that there were servants or shepherds who warned, taught, punished, and proclaimed within the community. They were to be examples of piety and dedication and were subject to the same reproach as other members. Though customs varied, usually their material necessities were taken care of by the congregation.

(6) When we come to the last two articles, on the sword and taking

oaths, the approach is almost predictable. The Anabaptists recognized that the political government has divine authority to punish the wicked with the sword as well as to protect good citizens. Christians, however, should be minded like Christ and reject their own use of the sword. As Christ had suffered, they should suffer too. The Anabaptists were not strict pacifists; they did not universally reject the use of arms. But they were concerned about themselves and their image as true followers of Christ and advocated among themselves defenselessness and passive obedience.[80] They also rejected for themselves any oath with the argument that the Bible wants the plain answer of yes or no and no one knows whether one can actually keep one's word even if one intends to.

The Anabaptists espoused a Bible-centered Christian life and attempted to realize the radical discipleship of Christ. They were the first advocates of a free church, acknowledging the existence of a (devilish) world around them. They also endeavored to convince others of the necessity of a Christlike life. That their idea of an "apostolic" Christian community proved attractive is shown by the rapid growth of Anabaptist communities in many parts of Europe. In spite of fierce persecutions, the Anabaptist movement was never completely extinguished. They lived on in the Mennonites and various nonconformist groups, and their influence can even be traced among the Baptists.

Their sense of mutual support and of proleptically anticipating the kingdom of God here on earth in their communal life deserves admiration. Their attempt to demonstrate that Christians live by different standards than the world should not be lightly classified as work righteousness. Yet if one really tries to take the New Testament as seriously and as obligatorily as the Anabaptists, how could one overlook that Jesus did not turn his back on the world? He lived and moved among sinners and tax collectors, among lepers and Roman soldiers. Jesus even restrained his zealous disciples: "Let both wheat and weeds grow together until harvest time" (Matt. 13:30). The world and the Christian community can never long exist separate from each other. Their respective communities always tend to permeate and penetrate each other. Thus the primacy of grace as demonstrated in infant baptism and the real presence of the Lord in the Eucharist dare not be neglected lest the church loses its transforming power.

When we now briefly attempt to describe the ecclesiastical concerns of the SPIRITUALISTS of the Reformation, such as Hans Denck, Caspar Schwenckfeld, or Sebastian Franck, we encounter at once an immense difficulty. Though the Spiritualists were sympathetic to each other they did not form a group in their own right. Unlike the Anabaptists, who emphasized the visible church, the Spiritualists were oblivious to exterior form. Important for them was the invisible church. For instance, Sebastian Franck asserted that "the church is today a purely spiritual thing" and "will remain scattered among the heathen until the end of the world." [81] He claimed that the outward church was destroyed right after the time of the apostles. Yet the outward arrangements and sacraments were not wiped out and "God through the Spirit in truth provided by means of his spiritual church all things which the signs and outward gifts are merely betokened."

Similarly we hear from Hans Denck that "outward baptism is not essential to salvation," but rather the proclamation of the gospel and the inward baptism through which "the Spirit of Christ reaches also and kindles the fire of love which fully consumes whatever is left of our infirmities."[82] He continues to assert that we can live without the visible bread and cup. But whoever drinks from "the invisible wine out of the invisible Cup, mixed by God from the beginning of time through his Son, the Word, will become drunk. He does not know anything about himself anymore, but becomes deified [*vergottet*] through the love of God while God becomes incarnate in him [*vermenscht*]." [83] We must distinguish here the inner, spiritual eating in faith from the external, sacramental eating.[84]

We notice in the position of the Spiritualists an affinity to the Eastern idea of deification through participation in the sacraments and also a distinct dualism between matter and Spirit. The latter is reinforced when we are admonished that we should not become so addicted to the letter of Scripture that we withdraw the heart from the teaching of the Spirit and drive out the Spirit itself.[85] The Spirit is important, not the Bible. We are even reminded that we "will surely let people go their own way" if we are disciples of God. What a contrast between this individualistic spiritualism and the community emphasis of the Anabaptists! Small wonder that we do not encounter congregations of Spiritualists. When a Spiritualist such as Caspar Schwenckfeld had a large following, his disciples were mainly literary followers. The Spiritualists have their roots in Greek dualism and medieval mysticism. They flourished through the decline of the Roman Church in the Reformation period and continued in groups such as the Quakers, Protestant Pietism, and in the rationalism of the Enlightenment.

Finally we must briefly deal with the ENTHUSIASTS of the Reformation.

They are chronologically earlier than the Anabaptists and are in several ways related to them. Through their attempt to establish the kingdom of God in Münster and their role in the Peasants' War, they often gained more attention than the two other groups of the left wing. Unfortunately, still today the undifferentiated 16th century terminology is often continued and everything outside the mainline Reformation movement is labeled with the term Enthusiasts or *Schwärmer*.

Even more than for the Spiritualists, Scripture for the Enthusiasts is no longer normative. For instance, Thomas Müntzer speaks of the gift of direct instruction from the Holy Spirit through visions, dreams, ecstatic utterances, or inspired exegesis.[86] Similar to the Anabaptists, the Enthusiasts regard the church as a pneumatic community of true believers. Yet unlike the Anabaptists, they consider themselves chosen instruments of God and his servants in the war against the godless at the dawn of the eschaton.

Most prominent of all Enthusiastic endeavors was the formation of the kingdom of God in Münster between February 1534 to June 1535. Here the attempt was made to reestablish the eschatological apostolic community with a group of people that had initially formed an Anabaptist group. The intention was to make visible the hidden reign of Christ in face of the end of the world expected for Easter, 1534. According to Old Testament ideas, a theonomous monarchy was established, private property was abolished and the Decalogue was enforced as the ethical political norm. There was no distinction made between political and spiritual order and any serious transgression resulted in capital punishment. To assure total equality within the community all privileges and debts were annulled. Extramarital relationships were punished by execution, but polygamy was introduced to enable each adult woman to be an equal member of the community. According to Old Testament thought as the Enthusisats interpreted it, only married and fertile women could be full members of a community. Jan van Leiden, the new David, perceived his Messianic leadership to be given directly from God. Yet the bishop of Münster, supported by Catholics and Protestants alike, captured the city and made an end to this premature and enthusiastic kingdom.[87]

The Enthusiasts had no lasting successes. Their revolutionary spirit was soon quenched by worldly authorities and their chiliastic ideas were being continuously revised by the progression of history. As we can see in Thomas Müntzer's glowing reference to Joachim of Fiore, they were influenced by the enthusiastic groupings of the Middle Ages. Yet for all their inadequacies, they rightly reminded the church of its essential eschatological component. They showed that a church cannot endure the injustices of the present with equanimity without betraying its mission.

3. The Reformation—a mixed blessing

Our brief review of the dominant currents of the Reformation shows us that it is difficult to endorse the Reformation with undifferentiated approval. The currents were too conflicting, diverse, and untested. Looking back at the Reformation from our perspective, we also realize that we cannot blame the Reformation for all the succeeding events in world history, such as the decrees of Trent, the abolition of God at the height of the French Revolution, and the plethora and rivalry of American denominationalism. It would also be wrong to credit solely the Reformation for the reform of the papacy and the rediscovery of the evangelical concern in Vatican II. The Reformation had its antecedents in movements and individuals prior to the 16th century and it had its successors in people and currents when the Reformers had died. But the Reformation was a turning point; it centered, focused, and intensified the issues at stake and the solutions applied to them. The Reformation opened bright prospects for the church's rediscovery of center and periphery, and it heralded the dangers of antagonistic entrenchment, and of individualism and secularism.

a. Rediscovery of center and periphery

The most significant achievement of the Reformation period was the rediscovery of the church's center and periphery. This might be surprising to those who assume that the big feat of the Reformation was the destruction of the Roman Church, the smashing of ecclesiastical authorities, of the pope and the church councils, and the rejection of tradition. Certainly, radical groups questioned the authority of Scripture. And Luther himself consigned to the flames the book of canon law and the papal bull which threatened him with excommunication.

We remember that in his tract *To the Christian Nobility* (1520), Luther attempted to tear down three walls which the Roman Church had built in its defense and from which the Christian church suffered: (1) He challenged the superiority of pope, bishops, priests, and monks over the laity on grounds that all Christians are priests by baptism. (2) He rejected the exclusive right of the pope to interpret Scripture on grounds that every true believer, being a priest, can discern what is right in matters of faith.

(3) He refuted the claim that only the pope could summon a council and confirm its acts on historical grounds and with explicit suggestions how to counter this claim. In his *Babylonian Captivity of the Church* of the same year, Luther attacked three other items through which Rome had made the church a captive: (1) The denial of the concept of the laity; (2) the doctrine of transubstantiation finally decided upon at the Fourth Lateran Council in 1215; and (3) the teaching that the Mass is a good work and a sacrifice, notions that made the people ever more dependent on the ordained priesthood.

With the exception of the Enthusiasts, who endowed new leadership authorities, Luther and the other Reformers emphasized the immediacy of God's redemptive word and deed so much that he could not see why it should be checked, channeled, and harnessed through all kinds of external authorities and intermediaries. God and his message is equally close to all people and he is active when and where it pleases him. Of course, these convictions implied a wholesale attack on the Roman Church structure and on the dogmas that upheld it by rendering the laity to docile immaturity. As the many developing church orders and church visitations show during the Reformation period, Luther did not intend to abolish the visible church or its unity. He did not spiritualize the church "in such a way that when one pursues these thoughts to their logical conclusion, it is eliminated as a formative energy of history." [88]

Neither Luther nor the other Reformers were Enthusiasts or Spiritualists. But for them the unity of the church consisted in conformity with Scripture. Whether Zwingli or Calvin, whether Luther or the Anabaptists, the Reformers insisted on the primacy of the Scriptures as the sole rule and norm for preaching and teaching. They did not always agree on what Scripture actually said, but in cutting through the layers of tradition and doctrine that obscured the church's origin, the Reformers discovered the essential difference between the center of the Christian faith, the Scripture as God's word, and the periphery, the reception of God's word through the centuries.

From the primacy of Scripture follows logically the primacy of Christ. The Reformers discovered that access to God is only possible through Christ. This move made them question the status of the saints, of the priests and church's hierarchy, and the merits of human activities. They saw that there are no intermediaries between God and humanity but God himself in Christ Jesus. Except for some of the radical groups in the Reformation who even preferred Arius over Athanasius and who denied Christ's divine status, there was this common consensus among the Reformers. Therefore the reception and adoption of the Christological and trinitarian dogmas becomes important for the course of the Reformation. In places where these dogmas were not affirmed, the sole sufficiency of God's self-disclosure as documented in Scripture was also not accepted.

The question soon arose whether the former intermediaries, such as saints, Mary, the priests, and good works should be totally rejected. Not every theologian was as open to the merits of the saints and of Mary as was Luther. He realized, however, that "no one possesses more grace than another even though he may indeed have more gifts and treasures." [89] He confessed that he could not "look upon the lowliest Christian with less regard than I do upon St. Peter and all the saints in heaven." The term saint should not be a tribute to the saints in heaven, Luther argued, but reclaimed for every Christian while he lives on earth.[90] We are holy not on account of our merits, but because Christ has made us holy. Yet we notice that the saints still occupied an important place for Luther when he said:

> Next to Holy Scripture there certainly is no more useful book for Christendom than that of the dear legends of the saints, especially when they are pure and righteous. For in them one is greatly pleased to find how sincerely they believed God's Word, proclaimed it with their lips, praised it by their works, and honored and confirmed it by their suffering and dying. All this immeasurably comforts and strengthens those weak in their faith and increases the courage and confidence of those who are already strong. When one teaches Scripture alone, without any examples and stories of the saints, though the Spirit performs his work abundantly within, it nonetheless helps very much to see or to hear the outward examples of others.[91]

The saints serve a very useful function by inspiring us to saintly life and by serving as examples of faith and courage. They do not stand between us and Christ, but next to us as our brothers and sisters in Christ and in faith.

Similarly, Luther remarked that Mary had been turned into an idol to whom people pray and whom they substitute for Christ.[92] But in his *Commentary on the Magnificat* (1521) Luther confesses that Mary is indeed the Mother of God. She has a unique place among us, with nobody being equal to her.[93] "No one can say anything greater of her or to her. . . . It needs to be pondered in the heart what it means to be the Mother of God." But then Luther cautions of any exuberance saying:

Her sole worthiness to become the Mother of God lay in her being fit and appointed for it, so that it might be pure grace and not a reward, that we might not take away from God's grace, worship, and honor by ascribing too great things to her. For it is better to take away too much from her than from the grace of God. . . . She gives nothing, God gives all.

She serves as an example of humility and obedience and demonstrates how God works among his people, in lowliness instead of pride, in hiddenness instead of splendor. Similar to the saints, she stands alongside us, but not between God and us, pointing to God in Christ whom she was allowed to bear.

The primacy of Christ cannot be severed from the benefits of Christ. Philip Melanchthon, Luther's coworker, rightly reminds us in his *Loci* that to know Christ is not to speculate about his nature and mode of incarnation but to know what he has done for us.[94] In adequately describing Christ's salvational benefits we must mention justification by grace appropriated by faith. That God justifies the unjust in unconditional grace was *the* experience of Luther that triggered the Reformation. Luther can state that on justification "rests all that we teach and practice," it is the main article of faith or the article by which the church stands or falls.[95] "The article of justification is the master and prince," Luther says, "the Lord, the ruler, and the judge over all kinds of doctrines; it preserves and governs all church doctrine and raises up our conscience before God. Without this article the world is in utter death and darkness."[96]

When the Augsburg Confession stated that we become "righteous before God by grace, for Christ's sake, through faith, when we believe that Christ suffered for us and that for his sake our sin is forgiven and righteousness and eternal life are given to us" (CA IV), it did not introduce anything new. At least since Augustine this had been the essential message of the Western Church. It had always asserted that God proclaims us justified if we accept what he has done for us through Jesus Christ. We are declared righteous, but do not ontologically change into a sinless state.

Yet over the centuries justification was perceived more and more as a human achievement. Though it never became the official position of the church, both the piety of the laity and the self-interest of the hierarchy furthered this self-redemptive attitude.[97] For instance, Mass was widely regarded as a priestly act on behalf of the believers; the veneration of saints and relics became stepping stones on the way to personal sanctification. The selling of indulgences to finance papal building projects and to obtain release from inconvenient church sanctions furthered the idea that we are justified by what we do. When he recognized the intrinsic sinfulness of humanity, Luther insisted on the opposite: Justification is not our doing. It has already been accomplished through Christ by God's grace and it cannot be appropriated through our own actions but only by trusting God or through faith.

Luther returned to the biblical notion of justification and made it the central theme of the church's proclamation. He emphasized the center of the Christian faith and weeded out things that obscured or distorted it. But he was not alone in his emphasis. Most of the Reformers found their major focus in the justification of the unjust. Some did not go far enough in distinguishing between center and periphery but in the face of a distorted church government insisted that church order should rank central. Others went almost too far in this newly found emphasis on the primacy of God's redemptive action when they questioned if an individual was worthy to accept such grace. Luther did not take church government lightly, nor the issue of cheap grace. He was adamant that the structure should further the proclamation of the gospel and not hinder it. He also insisted that grace, while freely given, cannot be cheap. It cost God the whole redemptive history and it costs us a totally new attitude towards life. But Luther recognized that this change in our way of living could not be a precondition for God's action. It is rather a result or consequence of God's grace. In emphasizing God's primacy in a way almost unheard of since Augustine, the Reformers could attempt to rebuild the church. They had discovered that which was central to its existence and purpose and that which was peripheral or even deleterious.

b. The danger of antagonistic entrenchment

When John F. Kennedy ran for the presidency of the United States in 1960, one of the important issues in the election campaign was whether one could trust a Roman Catholic president, since Washington might become a subsidiary of the Vatican. That such an issue could even emerge shows the deep-seated resentments that have existed, and perhaps still exist today, between the Roman Church and those who either voluntarily or by force were cut off from this church.

The Reformation movement set out to reform the church and, like some of the movements prior to the Reformation, ended up as an independent entity outside the Roman Church. Since he preferred to rule a confessionally unified empire, the emperor continued to hold to the idea of a reconciliation between the Roman Church and the Reformation movement. But the Roman Church insisted on drawing a strict line between the "heresy" of the Reformation and the "catholic" faith. When the Council of Trent convened in 1545 Emperor Charles V thought it could reform and unite the church. Once the Council had finished its task in 1563 it was clear that the Roman Catholic Church had managed to define itself largely in implicit contradistinction to the Augsburg Confession and other documents of the Reformation. The decisions against the Reformation were facilitated by the fact that the votes were taken according to the number of bishops present and not according to nations represented, as was done at the Council of Constance. This meant that the Italian bishops had a clear majority. There are three areas in which the decisions of Trent were especially noteworthy in their confrontation with the Reformation, (1) the area of Scripture and tradition, (2) the doctrine of justification, and (3) the sacramental practice.

(1) For the medieval church, Scripture had priority over tradition as we observe in Augustine and Thomas Aquinas. In the late Middle Ages, however, the protests against the church were often launched on the basis of Scripture as we have seen with Peter Waldo and Girolamo Savonarola. Unless they wanted to succumb to that criticism, church authorities had to resort more and more frequently to tradition in order to justify their teaching and practice. Many medieval theologians also had established long commentaries in which they adduced the opinion of one theologian after another to a particular issue or Scripture passage to give credence to their own interpretation.

When Luther brushed aside the tradition and emphasized the primacy of Scripture, the church had two possibilities, either to return with him to an earlier practice or to officially acknowledge the value of tradition. The majority of the bishops at Trent chose the latter declaring that the Synod

> following the examples of the orthodox Fathers, receives and holds in veneration with an equal affection of piety and reverence all the books both of the Old and of the New Testament, since one God is the author of both, and also the traditions themselves, those that appertain both to faith and to morals, as having been dictated either by Christ's own word of mouth or by the Holy Spirit, and preserved in the Catholic Church by a continuous succession.[98]

The tradition was accorded the same status as Scripture with the explanation that the Holy Spirit worked in the church, which in effect meant the church hierarchy. The results of the parity of Scripture and tradition can be seen in the 1950 declaration of the dogma of the bodily assumption of Mary into heaven. This dogma was declared on concurrence with ecclesiastical tradition and the sacred Scriptures.[99]

Another significant step was taken to solidify the Roman Catholic position on Scriptures and tradition. With the early church, Luther distinguished between the books of the Old and New Testament and the Apocrypha, judging the latter as not equal to the former but nevertheless as good and instructive books. The Council, however, refused such distinction and accorded all of them equal status. It even determined which version of Scripture should be regarded as normative when it declared that the "old Vulgate edition, which has been approved by the Church itself through long usage . . . be considered authentic." [100] This move looks again like a clear refutation of Luther who insisted to return to the original Hebrew and Greek to obtain the best possible text of the Bible. While such endeavor is not ruled out by the Council, its preference is clearly stated.

To safeguard the correct interpretation of Scripture and tradition the Council finally declared:

> In order to curb imprudent clever persons, the synod decrees that no one who relies on his own judgment in matters of faith and morals, which pertain to the building up of Christian doctrine, and that no one who distorts the Sacred Scripture according to his own opinions, shall dare to interpret the said Sacred Scripture contrary to that sense which is held by holy mother Church, whose duty it is to judge regarding the true sense and interpretation of holy Scriptures, or even contrary to the unanimous consent of the Fathers.[101]

It is now clearly stated that the church has the ultimate authority in matters of faith and morals. Contrary to Luther's assertion in the tract *To the Christian Nobility* the individual Christians cannot interpret the Scriptures validly on their own. The church can even contradict the joint judgment of the church fathers in asserting a doctrine. As the successor to Peter, the Roman pontiff holds the ultimate teaching office in the church. It was only logical then that at the Council of Vatican I in 1870 the Roman Catholic Church declared

that the Roman Pontiff, when he speaks *ex cathedra,* that is, when carrying out the duty of the pastor and the teacher of all Christians by virtue
of his supreme apostolic authority he defines a doctrine of faith **or morals**
to be held by the universal Church, through the divine assistance promised him in blessed Peter, possesses that infallibility with which the divine
Redeemer wished that his church be endowed in defining doctrine on
faith and morals.[102]

The only issue one might rightly wonder about is not why the Roman
Catholic Church declared papal infallibility, but why it declared it so
late. Since Trent, doctrines regarding faith and morals are to be safeguarded by the ultimate teaching authority of the church. It is not sufficient that they are contained in the living word of God that encounters
us in the Bible.

(2) The main project of the Council of Trent, the definitions regarding justification, is again slanted against what the fathers of the Council
understood Luther and other Reformers to have said. Though emphasizing original sin and human depravity, the Council does not affirm
total human depravity and total inability of exerting a free will toward
salvation. Instead, the Council declares that "the entire Adam was transformed in body and soul for the worse," but that the free will was not
extinguished, "however weakened and debased in its powers." [103] In
contrast, the Augsburg Confession had affirmed the free will in terms of
outward living, but declared that "without the grace, help, and activity
of the Holy Spirit man is not capable of making himself acceptable to
God, of fearing God and believing in God with his whole heart, or of
expelling inborn evil lusts from his heart" (CA 18).

When the Council affirmed the human involvement in the salvific
process, it endangered the primacy of God's activity and the certainty
of one's salvation. It described justification as an act of God in which
the Christians play a significant part. God gives them his predisposing
grace through which they are stimulated and assisted in converting
themselves

> to their own justification, by freely assenting to and cooperating with the
> same grace in such wise that, while God touches the heart of man through
> the illumination of the Holy Spirit, man himself receiving that inspiration
> does not do nothing at all inasmuch as he can indeed reject it.[104]

With God's help we must have the right disposition for justification to
be effective. Since the human element is involved here, we are not sur-

prised to hear that "no one can know with the certainty of faith . . . that he has obtained the grace of God." [105] Luther considered justification a fact, accomplished by God, that had to be appropriated daily. But Trent understood it as a lifelong process, since it did not distinguish it from sanctification. It admonished the Christians to keep the commandments and show forth good works as fruits of "justification." Yet it is clearly affirmed that no one "can be justified before God by his own works which are done either by his own natural powers, or through the teaching of the Law, and without divine grace through Christ Jesus." [106]

(3) When we come to the sacraments, it is significant to understand that they are introduced as means "through which all true justice either begins, or being begun is increased, or being lost is restored." [107] The sacraments are means of grace through which justification can be increased. Again we notice the cumulative understanding of justification, which almost necessarily leads to the question of what is "enough" justification.

In opposition to the Reformers, seven sacraments are reaffirmed— baptism, confirmation, Eucharist, penance, extreme unction, orders, and matrimony. They are also referred to as the sacraments of the new law which seems to imply a new legalism instead of emphasizing the primacy of grace. There also seems to be a certain automatism involved in administering them, since grace is conferred through their performing and not through the faith that appropriates them. [108] On the other hand it is important for their efficacy that a minister at least has the intention of obeying church doctrine when he administers them, though he might be a heretic. But the Lutheran idea that all Christians have in principle the privilege to administer the sacraments is rejected. The underlying notion of these statements seems to be that the efficacy of the sacraments as objective means of salvation depends on their lawful administration and not by faith of the recipient.

The significant definitions, concerning a specific sacrament, are reached in the considerations of the Eucharist. First the real presence of the Lord in the elements is asserted. [109] Then the transubstantiation is reaffirmed with the words that "by the consecration of the bread and wine a conversion takes place of the whole substance of bread into the substance of the body of Christ our Lord, and of the whole substance of the wine into the substance of his blood. This conversion is appropriately and properly called transubstantiation by the Catholic Church." [110] Especially against the Reformers, the Council reiterates that the sacrament should be worshiped, since it is the true God. [111] The ancient custom is reintroduced that with the elements consecrated in the Mass the sick can be communed in their homes. Finally we hear that the clerics who do not officiate in the Mass and the laity should not receive the Eucharist under both kinds, though communion under both kinds is not explicitly condemned.

In a special section the Mass is explained as a divine sacrifice representing "that bloody sacrifice once to be completed on the Cross" in an unbloody manner.[112]

> The fruits of that oblation (bloody, that is) are received most abundantly through this unbloody one. . . . Therefore, it is offered rightly according to the tradition of the apostles, not only for the sins of the faithful living, for their punishments and other necessities, but also for the dead in Christ not yet fully purged.

This understanding of the Mass comes close to one of a repetition of Christ's sacrifice, the benefits of which can be attributed both to the living and the dead. We also notice again the cumulative idea of justification, which never seems to allow for full assurance of salvation. It was exactly this approach that drove Luther into the monastery and prompted him to become a Reformer.

It would be wrong to see Trent only in a negative light. Certainly, it was a condemnation of what the Reformation stood for. But unintentionally the Reformation stimulated the Roman Catholic Church to formulate its own statement of faith. This resulted in the *Roman Catechism* (1566) that summed up the decisions of Trent for the laity. When we look at Trent we notice an amazing concentration of church doctrine on the essence of the Christian faith, on word and sacrament. Without the stimulus of the Reformation, the Roman Church would never have devoted the main portion of its deliberations in a council to justification. But its rejection of what it understood to be the position of the Reformers also meant that the Roman Church became the Roman Catholic Church in opposition and in contradistinction to the Lutheran Church, the Reformed Church and other groups of the Reformation.

That the split between Rome and these different movements could not be bridged in the 16th century was not only Rome's doing. The antagonistic entrenchment was reciprocal. For instance, in the second edition of the *Heidelberg Catechism* (1563), published one year after Trent's statements on Eucharist as sacrifice, we find a strong condemnation of the claim that the Mass can be offered for the remission of the sins of the living and the dead.[113]

On the Lutheran side, the teachings were solidified in the Formula of Concord which attempted to clarify and explain some articles of the Augsburg Confession. The Formula of Concord centers in on the issues and controversies that arose within the Lutheran camp and at the same time presents the Lutheran understanding of faith in opposition to other teachings. At the outset it declares that "the prophetic and apostolic writings of the Old and New Testaments are the only rule and norm according to which all doctrines and teachers alike must be appraised and judged." [114] Unlike the Council of Trent, the biblical books are not individually listed so that the canon remained open, for instance, for inclusion or exclusion of certain apocrypha. To demonstrate the continuity with the church universal, the three ecumenical creeds were affirmed, the Apostles' Creed, the Nicene Creed, and the Athanasian Creed, and the heresies and teachings were rejected that were contrary to them.

The Formula of Concord further affirms the exposition of the Christian faith in the Augsburg Confession, its Apology, the Smalcald Articles plus Melanchthon's Treatise on the Power and Primacy of the Pope, and Luther's Large and Small Catechism. All doctrines should conform to the standards set forth in them. Yet

> Holy Scripture remains the only judge, rule, and norm according to which as the only touchstone all doctrines should and must be understood and judged as good or evil, right or wrong. Other symbols and other writings are not judges like Holy Scripture, but merely witnesses and expositions of the faith, setting forth how at various times the Holy Scriptures were understood by contemporaries.[115]

Scripture is accorded absolute primacy while the ancient creeds and the above-mentioned writings of the Reformation enjoy elevated status, though clearly subordinate to Scripture.

In the first two articles of the Formula of Concord, original sin and free will are discussed. The slant against Trent becomes evident when we hear that "original sin is not a slight corruption of human nature, but that it is so deep a corruption that nothing sound or uncorrupted has survived in man's body or soul." [116] Though people are encouraged to hear God's word and not stop their ears, we are told that the Holy Spirit is present with this word and opens the hearts so that "they heed it and thus are converted solely through the grace and power of the Holy Spirit, for man's conversion is the Spirit's work alone. Without his grace our 'will and effort,' our planting, sowing, and watering are in vain unless he 'gives the growth.' " The emphasis is clearly on God's activity.

We should not be surprised, therefore, that Trent's formulation is expressly rejected that by our "own natural powers" human will is able to "help, to cooperate, or to prepare itself for grace, to dispose itself, to apprehend and accept it, and to believe in the Gospel." The Reformers rightly recognized that if justification, here described as conversion, is not totally God's doing, we will always be uncertain whether we have done enough to be justified by God. Their reason for insisting on God's sole activity was not so much that they mistrusted our abilities, but rather that they wanted to express as clearly as possible the assurance of God's grace and of our salvation.

Article four deals with good works, picking up the issue that we are certainly justified only through God's grace and not through good works, but reminding us that all people, and especially those "regenerated and renewed by the Holy Spirit, are obligated to do good works." [117] Articles five and six deal with law and gospel. Law is defined as a "divine doctrine which teaches what is right and God-pleasing and which condemns everything that is sinful and contrary to God's will," while gospel is the good news of redemption through Christ. The proclamation of God's word must always contain law and gospel in their proper distinction. Since the law is also that which is right and God-pleasing, it does not lose its validity for the justified. Yet it does no longer accuse the justified of his former sins, but serves as a guideline for Christian living.

Article seven deals with the Eucharist and affirms the real presence of Christ in the elements, even when received by sinners and unbelievers. Especially against the Reformed wing of the Reformation it emphasizes the reality of God's grace active in the sacrament.[118] Against Trent, the Formula rejects the idea of transubstantiation, the sacrifice of the Mass for the sins of the living and the dead, and the withholding of the cup from the laity.[119]

Article ten again is of interest for us, dealing with adiaphora or items peripheral to the faith. It affirms that the community of God has the authority to change ceremonies that are neither commanded nor forbidden in the word of God "according to circumstances, as it may be most profitable and edifying to the community of God." [120] But then it cautions that "in time of persecution, when a clear-cut confession of faith is demanded of us, we dare not yield to the enemies in such indifferent things." As soon as observance or abolition of these items is demanded, they cease to be adiaphora. Of course, it is a debatable point when such a state of confession is reached. For instance, if one group ordains women pastors and insists on continuing this practice, does this mean that an adiaphoron is made central? The issue of adiaphora has proved to be an occasional point of contention among Lutherans. This article unintentionally allowed for the possibility that peripheral points could become central and obscure the centrality of the gospel.

Together with other documents of the Lutheran Reformation that were included in the *Book of Concord,* the Formula of Concord provided the confessional basis for most Lutherans. It created a sense of confessional identity. Though the Lutherans' first statement of faith, the Augsburg Confession was designed to demonstrate their catholicity, the 16th century was the wrong time to make such an assertion if its main tenets stood in contrast to other prevailing traditions. Historical consciousness was not far enough developed to recognize that a tradition is not static but in flux and that it may indeed change with times as the Reformers had claimed.

The Lutheran Confessions are a unifying work, accepted by most Lutheran churches and supplemented by church orders or constitutions that provide the specific rules and regulations to worship, clergy, and local congregations. In the Reformed tradition, such a unifying body of documents is conspicuously absent. This does not mean that there are no Reformed Confessions. On the contrary, numerically they far exceed the Lutheran Confessions. But they apply to certain national bodies or certain regions. For instance, there is the Westminster Confession of 1647 for the English Presbyterians and the Church of Scotland, the Belgian Confession of 1564, the Confessio Helvetica Posterior of 1566, and many others.

The main reason for the limited range of the Reformed Confessions is the conviction of the Reformed that doctrine and order are of equal importance. Since it is difficult to settle church order on a universal scale and still make it effective for the local permeation of life, the conclusion was reached that both doctrine and order should be advanced together in regional confessions. The varying conditions of culture and language and the attitude of the respective governments could be more clearly discerned and made fruitful for the establishment of the Reformed churches.

In their main parts, the Reformed Confessions follow the great example of Calvin's *Institutes of the Christian Religion,* first published in 1536 and revised several times until 1559. Holy Scripture is introduced there as the fundamental law for Christian faith and teaching from which we should derive everything pertaining to faith, life, and church order. The continuous reference to the Bible meant that the distinction between Old and New Testament began to diminish. In most Confessions the biblical books are listed without the Apocrypha. Similar to Trent this meant that the canon had become fixed, but this time without the Apocrypha. Through basing their teachings on Scripture without much reference to the Confessions, the Reformed churches remained much more Bible conscious than other denominations. Yet their diminishing emphasis on the Confessions contained a grave danger. It could allow them to forget what the Confessions attempted to reintroduce with their emphasis on the Bible, the primacy of grace, of faith, and of Christ.

c. The danger of individualism and secularism

Contrary to popular opinion, the Reformation movement was not the beginning of the split in Western Christendom. It was the outward manifestation of a growing desire for (national) independence from a centralized church government. The Reformation movement certainly does not mark the first significant split in the church's unity. For instance, the Nestorian and Monophysite churches in the Near East split off from the main church in the fourth and fifth centuries during the time of the great christological controversies. In the Middle Ages we encounter the final separation between Eastern and Western Christendom.

The individualistic tendencies of many representatives of the left wing of the Reformation have their roots in medieval spiritualism and mysticism or, on the other hand, in the Renaissance movement of 14th and 15th century Italy. The attempt to escape from ecclesiastical domination altogether is again foreshadowed by Giordano Bruno and Machiavelli. The Reformation movement allowed these diverse elements to surface with renewed vigor though they were foreign to the major concerns of Reformers such as Calvin or Luther. Moreover, it provided the seedbed in which our modern emphasis on individualism and secularism could grow.

Luther himself asserted at the Diet of Worms that he would not recant one iota if he could not be persuaded on grounds of reason or Holy Scripture that he had taught something wrong. But this did not mean for Luther that reason had become the ultimate criterion for what he would believe. Such sentiment would not gain widespread acceptance until 250 years later during the Enlightenment. Luther did not appeal to autonomous reason, but to reason "guided by faith." This did not mean recourse to a neutral or skeptical reason but to one concomitant with logic and subjected to Scripture in the content of its logical assertions. Luther was much too aware of the dangers if "enlightened" reason would rule supreme that he would not allow reason to pursue an unrestricted course of action.

Yet Luther's "rebellion" in religious matters at Worms had consequences far beyond his own faith. Within one generation the relatively unified Christian West became divided into Roman Catholics on the one hand, and Lutherans, Calvinists, Anglicans, and Anabaptists on the other. In the eyes of the participants, this did not imply a relativizing of truth, since each group insisted vehemently and with utter self-confidence that it had the sole grasp of the Christian religion.[121] At the end of the Reformation period these diverse groups existed within their own territories quite often rather exclusively. But this did not continue for long. The first move toward ecclesiastical pluralism came at the Peace of Augsburg (1555) when those princes who adhered to the Augsburg Confession (Lutherans) were allowed to do so as long as princes who followed the "old religion" (Roman Catholicism) were not disturbed.

The compromise worked out at Augsburg did not yet tolerate other groups of the Reformation and only focused on the ruling authorities. People who did not want to follow the religious convictions of their political leaders had to sell their property and emigrate. While this arrangement assured uniformity in a given territory, it did so through the power of external authority. If the religious preference of the political leaders would change, for instance, through the efforts of the Counter-Reformation, the people living in a given territory had to change too or were forced to emigrate. Once this authority in religious matters was taken away from the political powers, as it happened deliberately in the Constitution of the United States, an unprecedented religious proliferation emerged. Everyone was now jealously safeguarding his or her own "true" religious insights with total disregard for the one, holy, catholic and apostolic church.

Regardless of their opposition to preventing church practice and teaching, the Reformers were still faithful to the notion of one church and were unwilling to establish breakaway churches. But their descendants no longer shared this desire for unity. For them the Christian faith had ceased to be a common and public affirmation but something that belonged to the liberty of the individual. Only in the state churches of Europe and their overseas descendants, or in the so-called *Volkskirche* (peoples' church) in Germany is there a sentiment that the church is basically one and has a public function. Yet centuries of religious authority exerted by the political powers have left an indelible imprint on the engagement of the most "faithful." They are part of the church, but the church has ceased to be part of them. It is something to be condoned and supported. Unlike in the free church milieu, it is not an existential ingredient of the private life of the individual. Unintentionally the Reformation paved the way for the privatization of the Christian faith in countries that are oriented toward separation of state and church. In countries with more state church flavor, the Reformation furthered the significance of the church as a public factor while at the same time eroding the commitment of the majority of the believers.

It would be shortsighted, however, to blame either the Reformers or the worldly authorities for the eventual outcome. For instance, the Augsburg Confession (1530) on the Lutheran side was a document clearly intended to demonstrate the catholicity of the (Lutheran) reform movement. In its main parts it attempted to show that the reform movement was deeply imbedded in the catholic tradition.[122] But eventually the same document served as the rallying point for a new branch of Christendom. Similarly, the Peace of Augsburg (1555) was intended as an interim agreement until the split within Christendom was resolved. Yet the split has continued until the present and the agreement has assumed permanent features. Thus the Reformation served more as a catalyst than as a source for the distinctly modern features of religious individualism. The actual roots go back much further, to some extent even into the Renaissance period or to pre-Reformation periods.

In addition to the modern emphasis on the individual pursuit of truth claims, there is another bothersome feature, unintentionally fostered by the Reformation movement—the emergence of a secular spirit. In a very manifest way this spirit surfaces in the secularization of church property. For instance, in Sweden King Gustavus Vasa deprived the church of all its landholdings and increased the land owned by the crown from 5.5 percent to 28 percent.[123] In other countries church property faced a similar secularization once the temporal authorities accepted the "new faith." That one could even dare to confiscate deserted ecclesiastical property or ask clerics to vacate monasteries and other establishments, indicates the immense change that had taken place since the struggle over the investiture of bishops.

Luther did not help the cause of the church either when he suggested that the princes could serve as emergency bishops. Similarly in Reformed territories, city councils were enlisted to uphold order in the church. This shows how far the churches of the Reformation had moved away from the medieval idea of clerical domination of the state. Once the church enlisted the services of the temporal authorities to maintain church order, they soon discovered this to be a convenient tool to further their own interests. Political domination of the church was especially easy in evangelical, i.e., protestant, lands. The church there had lost most of its land holdings and therewith its temporal power. Furthermore, the princes determined the kind of faith to be adhered to in a given territory. The church had become a territorial or at most a national church subject to the whims of the princes instead of the traditional Western Church under the rule of Rome.

But the emergence of territorial churches also had benevolent features. Now the church could much more easily adopt local features and further the interests of a certain geographical area. The church could come closer to the people, but it was also in danger of losing its transitional and universal character. For instance, the phenomenon of an "American civil religion" would be difficult to account for without the secularization and individualization of faith enabled by the Reformation. But nationalistic tendencies were already increasingly at work prior to the Reformation. As we have seen, the demise of John Hus at the Council of Constance was in large part due to the votes taken according to nationalities and not according to the number of delegates.

When the overarching arm of the Catholic Church had disappeared, it was only a question of time until the temporal authorities would extricate themselves altogether from the demands of the church. Furthermore, the continuing issue of minority religions, e.g., the Huguenots in France, the Lutherans in Austria, and the Reformed in the Netherlands, threatened more and more the possibility of truly homogeneous territories. Once a geographical region was no longer populated by one faith alone, the question had to be addressed how religious authority over different faiths could still be effectively administered by the same temporal power. Thus the diversity of religious persuasions engendered by the Reformation led eventually to religious toleration beyond the *cuius regio eius religio* to a secular state.

218 The Great Transformation

d. The phenomenon of free churches

While the term "free church" does not appear in the English language until the 19th century, the free church movement is in many ways a child of the Reformation. When the central church government collapsed in the 16th century, churchlike configurations often emerged which soon were placed under the authority of secular powers.[124] For instance, when we hear in CA 7 that "for the true unity of the church it is enough to agree concerning the teaching of the Gospel and the administration of the sacraments," we could almost consider this as a document of a free church. Constitutive for the church is word and sacrament but not hierarchy or territory. But the Lutheran Reformation was so quickly institutionalized that it did not provide an immediate stimulus for the free church movement.

When we consider the Reformed side of the Reformation of Zwingli and Calvin, we encounter a situation very different from the Lutheran stance. We remember Zwingli's Zurich gave rise to the Anabaptists (1525) when they attempted to radicalize Zwingli's reforms. The Anabaptist movement spread from there to the Netherlands and provided one source for the English free church movement in the Dissenters. Another source can be found in the Calvinist doctrine of the sovereignty of God and the double predestination of all people. If it is true that humanity consists of two kinds of people, those who are predestined to eternal bliss and those who will not reach salvation, then the church should not indiscriminately embrace all people. For England, a third source for the free church movement must be mentioned. It is not always discernible as a continuous well-stream, namely the influence of the pre-Reformation movement of the Lollards. There the emphasis is on personal piety, divine election, and studying the Bible. These doctrines were taught by laypeople whose precepts contradicted the teachings of the Roman Catholic Church, especially with regard to indulgence, celibacy, and papacy. In many ways they anticipated the English Reformation and eventually merged into the Congregationalists of the 17th century.

It would be wrong, however, to conclude that the free church movement is nothing more than a child of the Reformation. The roots go back much further. We should think here of the Hussites, the Waldensians, and even the Franciscan Spirituals under Joachim of Fiore. If we want to go back further, we could even mention the Montanists or the Albigenses. There have always been movements that blamed the institutionalized church for corruption and compromise with the world. They protested against the spiritual decay of their time and gathered their own groups. When they were labeled heretics, this may often have been justified given their tendency to apocalyptic enthusiasm and exclusion from the world. Yet even today heresy is a handy means to discredit a reform movement which emerges in protest against laxity of doctrine and action and in contradistinction to an established church.

The rise of the free church movement cannot be adequately accounted for without the unique configuration of the English state church. This church was a mixture of Roman Catholicism and Protestant reforms. Because of this inner contradiction, it broke up in the 17th century as an all-encompassing national church. Thus movements that were persecuted in the continental territorial churches could survive and grow in England. Most prominent are the Puritans and Separatists who adhered to a Calvinistic theology, emphasizing the sovereignty of God, keeping his commandments, and refusing to submit themselves to human authorities in religious matters. The name Puritans is derived from purifying and designated originally those who, according to biblical precepts, wanted to purify the church from rests of Catholicism. Their close ties to Calvinism show in the fact that initially whole congregations emigrated at least temporarily to the Calvinist Netherlands to escape persecution.

We must mention here especially Robert Browne who developed from a Presbyterian Puritan to a Separatist and who founded in 1581 together with his friend Robert Harrison an independent congregation in Norwich. After he had been imprisoned several times, he emigrated with most of his members to Middelburg in the Netherlands. There he published in 1582 a book containing three essays in which he characterized the true church as a voluntary assembly of believers. Christ is the head of the church. Each congregation administers its own affairs and, according to the New Testament, it has a pastor, teachers, elders, deacons, and widows. No congregation exercises authority over another congregation, though they help each other in brotherly love and support. Though we might recognize here Anabaptist tendencies, Browne had no connections to Anabaptists and affirmed infant baptism. Soon Browne returned to England and became a pastor in the Church of England. Other Separatists, however, were less open to compromise.

We should mention here John Smyth, a pastor of the Church of England, who adopted Separatistic principles and gathered his own congregation in Gainsborough. Again persecution led him and some of his followers into voluntary exile in Amsterdam and Leyden (1608). Studying the Bible, Smyth was convinced that the apostolic method for gaining new members was faith in Christ, repentance, and subsequent baptism. Attempting to follow biblical principles, he baptized himself and other members of his congregation by pouring water over himself and them. This act marks the beginning of the first English Baptist congregation, though on Dutch soil. Some of his followers joined the Dutch Mennonites, while others returned to England in 1612, the year Smyth had died. They founded the first permanent Baptist congregation in England.

Since the pressure of the state had become stronger and stronger on those who attempted to organize themselves on a Congregationalist basis, by 1640 more than 20,000 had emigrated to North America. They founded strong churches along the Massachusetts Bay with John Cotton in Boston and Richard Mather in Dorchester. In Connecticut there was Thomas Hooker in Hartford and John Davenport in New Haven. Since they were strong Puritans, the Bible was their norm for organizing congregational life. They could pursue what was not allowed to their non-separatistic brethren in the Old World, to establish a Congregational church order as the only officially established form guaranteed by the state. This means that even the Congregationalist free church in North America did not originate as a free church in the modern sense, i.e. without support and sanctioning by the state.

It was not until the Tolerance Act of 1689 that the Dissenters were granted religious freedom in England. Though they still were subject to many inconveniences, they were no longer persecuted. This was not yet true for the Roman Catholics and the anti-trinitarians for whom freedom came not until a century later. Similarly in North America, each colony usually had an established religion, such as the Church of England in Virginia, while other religious persuasions were at the most tolerated. The establishment of a colony on the principle of freedom of faith is connected with the arrival of Roger Williams in Boston in 1631. An Anglican by birth, he soon joined the Separatists and objected against church tax, restricting the right to vote to members of the established church, and the supervised attendance of church services. When he was finally banned, he and four others founded the Providence Colony on the basis of freedom of religion. Of course, Williams did not want to water down the faith, but he believed that if force is used in religious matters, persecution and religious wars would follow. Williams himself was not indifferent to religious matters and he tenaciously fought the Quakers with word and print.

When the North American colonies declared their independence and asserted in the Declaration of Rights in 1776 complete freedom in religious matters, they did not automatically disestablish the various churches. It was not until 1833 when the last state disestablished the church and changed its constitution accordingly (Massachusetts). Similarly on a federal level, the First Continental Congress of 1774 sent Christian missionaries to the Delaware Indians and sponsored the publication of an American Bible which was officially recognized by Congress. Even when it came to the First Amendment of 1789 which stated that "Congress shall make no law respecting an establishment of religion, or prohibiting the free exercise thereof," this would still allow individual states to have their own established church. Yet today, independence from the state in religious matters is jealously guarded by all denominations in the United States.

There is a period of about 150 years from the beginning of the Reformation to the inception of free churches. This shows how deeply ingrained the notion was that there should be a unity of political territory and a respective church. Since the free churches were not synonymous with a particular political territory, though they usually were more prominent in one area than another, they developed a missionary activity that went far beyond their original areas of influence. Many of the churches in younger nations would be unthinkable without the vigorous missionary effort of American and British denominations. They even penetrated the boundaries of state churches (Germany, Russia, Scandinavia) and established branches there, often in deliberate opposition to already established churches. While this missionary fervor is truly admirable, it often has shown a lack of awareness of ecclesiastical validity of other denominational bodies. At least in the past there were many cases of unhealthy rivalry and duplication both in overseas missions and on the home front. Only recently has there developed a growing awareness that the true church is not identical with a particular local manifestation to the exclusion of all others. Thus the rise of the free church movement is paralleled with a loss of oneness and often a helplessness of how to encounter the secular state that made possible this religious proliferation.

NOTES

1. According to Walter von Loewenich, *Die Geschichte der Kirche* (Witten-Ruhr: Luther-Verlag, 1957) 165.
2. *Lateran Council IV*, DS(E), pp. 169f. (430).

222 The Great Transformation

3. *Council of Lyons II*, DS(E), pp. 184f. (465).
4. Cf. Kurt-Victor Selge, *Die ersten Waldenser. Mit Edition des Liber Antiheresis des Durandus von Osca*. vol. 1: *Untersuchung und Darstellung* (Berlin: Walter de Gruyter, 1967) 22-26.
5. Cf. for the following ibid., 243 and 266f.
6. Ibid., 257.
7. Cf. for the following Leighton Pullan, *From Justinian to Luther*, 138.
8. So Roberto Ridolfi, *The Life of Girolamo Savonarola*, trans. C. Grayson (New York: Knopf, 1957) 4.
9. Cf. ibid., 11 and 29.
10. Ibid., 76.
11. Ibid., 160.
12. Ibid., 171.
13. Ibid., 198.
14. Ibid., 233.
15. Cf. John Wyclif, *De veritate sacrae scripturae* (6), ed. by Rudolf Buddensieg (London: Trübner, 1905), 1:135f.. vol. 18 of *Wyclif's Latin Works*.
16. John Wyclif, *Tractatus de civili dominio* (1.43), ed. by Reginald L. Poole (London: Trübner, 1885), 1:380, vol. 14 of *Wyclif's Latin Works*.
17. Ibid. (2.8), 2:77, vol. 15 of *Wyclif's Latin Works*.
18. Cf. for the following Wyclif, *De veritate sacrae scripturae* (27, 25, 25, 31, 25), 2:88ff., 16f., 21, 236, 23f., vol. 20 of *Wyclif's Latin Works*.
19. So rightly John Stacey, *John Wyclif and Reform* (London: Lutterworth, 1964), p. 152.
20. Wyclif, *Tractatus de civili dominio* (1.44), 1:415.
21. Cf. for the following ibid. (2.8), 2:77f.; and ibid. (1.43.43.44.43.37), 1:380, 384, 416, 390, 274f.; and ibid. (2.11), 2:123, vol. 15 of *Wyclif's Latin Works*.
22. Cf. for the following the perceptive evaluation in Heiko A. Oberman, ed. *Studies in the History of Christian Thought* (Leiden: Brill, 1974), Vol. 10: *John Wyclif as Legal Reformer*, by William Farr, esp. 170ff.
23. Stacey, 155.
24. Cf. for the following Matthew Spinka, *John Hus' Concept of the Church* (Princeton, NJ: Princeton University, 1966) 42, 45ff., and 59f.
25. Ibid., 83f.
26. Cf. ibid., 111. It must be said, however, that the bull makes the granting of indulgences contingent upon contrition and confession. Its real purpose, though, is to incite people to war, as Spinka rightly notes.
27. See ibid., 331ff., for details on this matter.
28. John Hus, *De Ecclesia. The Church,* trans. with notes and intr. D.S. Schaff (New York: Scribner's, 1915; reprint ed. Westport, CT: Greenwood, 1974), 27.
29. Ibid., 136.
30. For this and the following quote see ibid., 14 and 197.
31. Ibid., 205.
32. Martin Luther, *Letter No. 783,* WA.BR 3:359.
33. Cf. for the following Ruth Rouse and Stephen Ch. Neill, *A History of the Ecumenical Movement. 1517-1948,* 2nd rev. ed. (London: SPCK, 1967), 1:177f.
34. Martin Luther, *Large Catechism,* BC, 417, in his explanation of the third article of the Apostles' Creed.
35. Ibid., 415.
36. Martin Luther, *Smalcald Articles* (3/12: The Church), BC, 315.
37. Martin Luther, *Dictata super Psalterium.* (1513-16), WA 4:129.6-17.
38. So Martin Luther, *Answer to the Hyperchristian, Hyperspiritual, and Hyperlearned*

Book by Goat Emser in Leipzig—Including Some Thoughts Regarding His Companion, the Fool Murner. (1521), LW 39:218ff.

39. Cf. for the following Martin Luther, *A Sermon on the Ban* (1520), LW 39:7f.
40. Cf. for the following Martin Luther, WA 34/1:150.7-11, in a sermon of February 2, 1531; and Martin Luther, *Ad Librum Eximii Magistri Nostri Magistri Ambrosii Catharini* (1521), WA 7:720.32-38.
41. Cf. for the following Martin Luther, *Concerning the Ministry* (1523), LW 40:20f.
42. Martin Luther, *To the Christian Nobility of the German Nation Concerning the Reform of the Christian Estate* (1520), LW 44:129.
43. Cf. Bull *Exultate Deo* of 1439, DS(E), p. 221 (695).
44. Cf. for the following Martin Luther, *The Private Mass and the Consecration of Priests* (1533), LW 38:197; and *Lectures on Galatians* (1535), LW 26:17f.
45. Cf. for the following the enlightening comments by Paul Althaus, *The Theology of Martin Luther*, trans. R. C. Schultz (Philadelphia: Fortress, 1966) 314.
46. Cf. for the following Martin Luther, in a sermon of September 7, 1522, WA 10/3:309; *Concerning the Ministry* (1523), LW 40:21-32; and *That a Christian Assembly or Congregation Has the Right and Power to Judge All Teaching and to Call, Appoint, and Dismiss Teachers, Established and Proven by Scripture.* (1523), LW 39:309f.
47. For this and the following quote see Luther, *Lectures on Galatians* (1535), LW 26:18 and 17.
48. Martin Luther, *Infiltrating and Clandestine Preachers* (1532), LW 40:387f.
49. Martin Luther, *The Private Mass and the Consecration of Priests* (1533), LW 38:208f.
50. Martin Luther, *Against Hanswurst* (1541), LW 41:193f.
51. Martin Luther, *Praelectio in Psalmum 45* (1532), WA 40/2:546.13-15. Cf. also the interesting study by Wolfgang Höhne, *Luthers Anschauungen über die Kontinuität der Kirche* (Berlin: Lutherisches Verlagshaus, 1963), esp. 157-163, that rightly points out that Luther was very much concerned about the continuity of the church with its origin and early history, since it was now confronted with discontinuity and decay.
52. Cf. Reinhold Seeberg, *Lehrbuch der Dogmengeschichte*, 4/1:452 and n. 1.
53. Cf. for this Huldreich Zwingli, *Auslegen und Gründe der Schlussreden* (1523), CR 89:330f., in his explanation of article 39; and see for the quote Huldreich Zwingli, *Von göttlicher und menschlicher Gerechtigkeit* (1523), CR 89:521.
54. Huldreich Zwingli, *Epistola ad lectorem (Jeremia-Erklärungen)* (1531), CR 101:424.20ff.
55. For an excellent assessment of Zwingli cf. Robert C. Walton, *Zwingli's Theocracy* (Toronto: University of Toronto Press, 1967), esp. 225f.
56. Huldreich Zwingli, *Epistola ad lectorem*, CR 101:419.18f.
57. Cf. the excellent comments by Gottfried W. Locher, *Huldreich Zwingli in neuer Sicht, Zehn Beiträge zur Theologie der Zürcher Reformation* (Zürich: Zwingli Verlag, 1969) 15f.
58. John Baillie, John McNeill, and Henry Van Dusen, eds. *The Library of Christian Classics* (Philadelphia: Westminster, 1960), Vols. 20 & 21: *Institutes of the Christian Religion*, by John Calvin, ed. John T. McNeill, trans. F. L. Battles, (3.23.1) 947f.
59. John Calvin, *Catechism of the Church of Geneva*, in Thomas F. Torrance, ed., *The School of Faith. The Catechisms of the Reformed Church* (London: James Clarke, 1959) 19 (question 93).
60. Cf. for the following Calvin, *Institutes* (4.1.7 and 4.2.5), pp. 1021 and 1046f.
61. Cf. for the following ibid. (4.1.7), p. 1021.
62. Cf. for this and the following quote ibid. (4.1.10), p. 1024.
63. Cf. for the following ibid. (4.2.2 and 4.2.10), pp. 1042f. and 1050f.
64. Cf. for the following ibid., (4.3.1, 4.3.6-9, and 4.3.15), pp. 1053f., 1058-62, and 1065f.
65. Ibid. (4.3.6), p. 1059.

66. Cf. for the following ibid. (4.8.15 and 4.10.1), pp. 1164 and 1179f.
67. Cf. for the following the perspective comments by Reinhold Seeberg, *Lehrbuch der Dog-mengeschichte*, 4/2:615.
68. Cf. for the following Calvin, *Institutes* (2.8.33), p. 399; *Commentaries on the Four Last Books of Moses Arranged in the Form of a Harmony*, trans. Ch. W. Bingham (Grand Rapids, MI: Eerdmans, 1950), 1:263, in his comments on Ex. 15:20; and cf. Walter Blankenburg, "Johannes Calvin," in *Musik in Geschichte und Gegenwart*, 2:661f.
69. Calvin, *Institutes* (3.6.5), p. 689.
70. Ibid. (4.20.2), p. 1487.
71. Cf. Jasper Ridley, *John Knox* (Oxford: Clarendon Press, 1968), 171 and 529. Ridley may be right that Knox's doctrine of resistance was not basically the same as Calvin's. There certainly had been precedents for the idea of revolt against a government in the name of religion. Yet we must also note that Knox was confronted in Geneva with Calvin's liberal advocacy of the use of torture, execution, and banishment from the city in the name of true religion. Cf. Eustace Percy, *John Knox* (Richmond, VA: John Knox, 1965) 170f., for a lucid description of what Knox encountered in Geneva.
72. Cf. for the following the perceptive analysis by A. Mervyn Davies, *Foundation of American Freedom* (New York: Abingdon, 1955) 22f. and 156f.
73. So rightly Heiko A. Oberman, ed., *Studies in the History of Christian Thought* (Leiden: Brill, 1970), Vol. 5: *Calvin's Doctrine of the Church*, by Benjamin Ch. Milner, 195; for an excellent comparison between Luther and Calvin concerning their understanding of church and state see William A. Mueller, *Church and State in Luther and Calvin. A Comparative Study* (Nashville, TN: Broadman, 1954).
74. Cf. for a more extensive treatment the excellent comments by Franklin Littell, *The Origins of Sectarian Protestantism. A Study of the Anabaptist View of the Church* (New York: Macmillan,1964) 82ff.
75. For the text, see *The Schleitheim Confession*, trans. and ed. by John H. Yoder, intr. by L. Gross (Scottdale, PA: Herald, 1973). At least parenthetically we should mention here the Dordrecht Confession, which a century later 1632) presented a mature development of Anabaptist thought and is still valued today by Mennonite groups. For its text see John H. Leith, *Creeds of the Churches. A Reader in Christian Doctrine from the Bible to the Present*, rev. ed. (Atlanta: John Knox, 1977) 292-308.
76. So rightly Littell, 85.
77. Cf. for the following Robert Friedmann, *The Theology of Anabaptism. An Interpretation, Studies in Anabaptist and Mennonite History*, no. 15 (Scottdale, PA: Herald, 1973), 116ff.
78. Cf. Littell, 100.
79. Cf. for the following Friedmann, 123f.
80. Littell, 103.
81. For this and the following quotes see Sebastian Franck, "A Letter to John Campanus," in John Baillie; John McNeill; and Henry Van Dusen, eds., *The Library of Christian Classics* (Philadelphia: Westminster, 1957), Vol. 25: *Spiritual and Anabaptist Writers. Documents Illustrative of the Radical Reformation*, ed. George H. Williams, 150 and 152.
82. Hans Denck, "Confession Addressed to the City Council of Nürnberg" (1525), in *Selected Writings of Hans Denck*, from the text as established by Walter Fellmann, ed. and trans. E. J. Furcha and F. L. Battles (Pittsburgh, Pa: Pickwick, 1975) 19f.
83. Ibid., 21.
84. So Caspar Schwenckfeld, "An Answer to Luther's Malediction," in Williams, *Spiritual and Anabaptist Writers*, 167.
85. For this and the following quote see Franck, 159.

86. Cf. for the following the comprehensive volume on the left wing movements of the Reformation by George H. Williams, *The Radical Reformation* (Philadelphia: Westminster, 1962) 45-49.

87. For an excellent introduction of cf. Richard van Dülmen, ed., *Das Täuferreich zu Münster, 1534-1535. Berichte und Dokumente* (Munich: DTV, 1974).

88. Werner Elert, *The Structure of Lutheranism*. Vol. 1: *The Theology and Philosophy of Lutheranism Especially in the Sixteenth and Seventeenth Centuries,* trans. W. A. Hansen, foreword by Jaroslav Pelikan (St. Louis: Concordia, 1962) 258, is wrong when he makes this assertion in his otherwise instructive investigation.

89. For this and the following quotes see Martin Luther, *Über das erste Buch Mose. Predigten* (1527), WA 24:484.29-32.

90. Cf. for the following Martin Luther, *Sermons on the First Epistle of St. Peter* (1523), LW 30:7.

91. Martin Luther, *Vorrede zu Lazarus Spenglers Bekenntnis* (1535), WA 38:313.10-19.

92. Cf. Martin Luther, *Wochenpredigten über Joh. 16-20* (1528/9), WA 28:402.

93. For this and the following quotes see Martin Luther, *The Magnificat* (1521), LW 21:326ff.

94. Philipp Melanchthon, *The Loci Communes* (1521), trans. with a critical intr. Ch. L. Hill and a special intr. by E. E. Flack (Boston: Meador, 1944) 68.

95. Martin Luther, *Smalcald Articles* (2/1), BC, p. 292.

96. Martin Luther, *Die Promotionsdisputation von Palladius und Tilemann* (1537), WA 39/1:205.1-5.

97. Cf. the interesting conclusions in Harry J. McSorley, *Luther: Right or Wrong? An Ecumenical-Theological Study of Luther's Major Work, The Bondage of Will* (Minneapolis: Augsburg/New York: Newman, 1969) 368f.

98. *Council of Trent*, DS(E), p. 244 (783).

99. Apostolic Constitution *Munificentissimus Deus*, DS(E), p. 648 (2332). It is interesting that the paragraph containing this assertion is omitted in the most recent edition of Denzinger.

100. *Council of Trent*, DS(E), p. 245 (785).

101. Ibid., p. 245 (786).

102. *Vatican I*, DS(E), p. 457 (1839).

103. *Council of Trent*, DS(E), pp. 246 and 249 (788 and 793).

104. Ibid., p. 250 (797).

105. Ibid., p. 253 (802).

106. Ibid., p. 258 (811).

107. Ibid., p. 262 (843).

108. Cf. for the following ibid., p. 263 (851, 854).

109. Cf. ibid., p. 266 (874).

110. Ibid., pp. 267f. (877).

111. Cf. for the following ibid., pp. 268 and 286 (878 and 930).

112. For this quote and the following see ibid., pp. 288 and 289f. (938 and 940).

113. Cf. *The Heidelberg Catechism,* with commentary, trans. A. O. Miller and M. E. Osterhaven (Philadelphia: United Church Press, 1962) 136 (quest. 80).

114. *Formula of Concord,* BC, 464.

115. Ibid., 465.

116. For this and the following quotes see the *Formula of Concord* (1. Original Sin, 2. Free Will), BC, 467, 470, and 471.

117. For this and the following quotes see ibid. (4. Good Words, 5. Law and Gospel), 476 and 478.

118. Cf. *The Heidelberg Catechism* 130 and 132 (quest. 76 and 78).

119. Cf. *Formula of Concord* (7. Lord's Supper), BC, 484.

120. See for this and the following quotes, ibid. (10. Adiaphora) 493.
121. Cf. the comments on the consequences of the Reformation by Hans J. Hillerbrand, *Christendom Divided. The Protestant Reformation* (Philadelphia: Westminster, 1971) 289f.
122. Only recently has this original intention of the Augsburg Confession been rediscovered and officially recognized. Cf. the significant study by Heinrich Fries, et al., *Confessio Augustana. Hindernis oder Hilfe?* (Regensburg: Friedrich Pustet, 1979), which resulted from a colloquium on the Augsburg Confession in which Lutheran and Roman Catholic theologians and official representatives from both churches participated. For an earlier study that did not receive official sanctioning cf. Max Lackmann, *The Augsburg Confession and Catholic Unity*, trans. W. R. Bouman (New York: Herder and Herder, 1963).
123. According to A. G. Dickens, *Reformation and Society in Sixteenth Century Europe* (London: Thames and Hudson, 1966) 191.
124. For a more extensive treatment of the free churches see Hans Schwarz, *"Freikirche,"* in *Theologische Realenzyklopädie*.

PART III:

The Promise of the Future

A historical perspective can easily lead to a nostalgic view or to a defeatist attitude. This could also be true for perceiving the church in its historical context. Yet it is not a sign of realism to long for the days of old, nor is it justified to dwell only on the mistakes and defeats of the past. In its nearly two thousand years of existence the church has proved remarkably resilient. It did not just tumble from crisis to crisis but it has also grown in stature and maturity. It is conducting its mission on six continents and it lives on in viable indigenous communities in almost every country on the globe. The many blemishes notwithstanding, nowhere is genuine repentance and renewal more alive than in the church.

Yet the true power of the church for the future does not lie in its tenacity and will to improve. If the church is true to its calling, it is at its very best an interim church, foreshadowing the kingdom and actively waiting for the inauguration of the final victory of its Lord. The church keeps alive a hope for a new world and attempts to enflesh some of this hope, however incompletely, in its actions, its proclamation, and its corporate structure.

227

6

The Structural Elements of the Church

OUR LONG JOURNEY THROUGH THE AGES is far from complete. We have left out many important phenomena, such as the world mission movement or the rapid growth of ethnic churches. But it is time to turn our eyes to the present and the future. While in many ways our modern era grew out of the Enlightenment, culminating in the French Revolution, the most important decisions for the modern church were made much earlier. During the Reformation period and in the years immediately following, the destiny of the uniform Catholic West had been decided. The foundations were laid for the state churches and *Volkskirchen* in Europe and for our American denominational pluralism. But the old Catholic Church of the West did not simply die in the 16th or 17th century, nor did the Evangelical churches emerge through a *creatio ex nihilo*.

The intent of the Reformation was to reform the church completely. As the writings of the Reformers indicate, this did not mean a break with tradition. Rather, the intent of the Reformers was to return to that which gave rise to the tradition and to reject tradition unjustified in the light of (biblical) well-springs. Small wonder that initially the Humanists welcomed the Reformation, since Reformers and Humanists shared an emphasis on a return to the original sources. The results of the Council of Trent indicated that even the Roman Catholic Church could not escape asking itself the important question: How appropriate are the church's main tenets in the light of biblical (and extra-biblical) sources? But in the 16th and 17th centuries the wounds were too fresh and the battles too recent to discover that the common search for the appropriateness of the essential marks of the church would eventually lead to commonly accepted results. Today, we are closer than ever to this goal. The marks of the church are no longer considered the exclusive property of one denomination or of one church. We recognize more and more that the church, though still painfully divided and multi-faceted, is basically one. Thus in

229

talking about the structural elements of the church, we must first of all mention the amazing rediscovery of unity.

Excursus: The rediscovery of unity

The crisis of faith that grips many people is in many ways a crisis in ecclesiology. The diversity and near chaos in both Protestant and Catholic quarters concerning the content of the "true faith" is one of the main reasons why Christianity has lost its persuasive power. If the claims of the Christian faith were indeed true, Christians would express much more visibly the redemption in which they believe. That was the objection to Christianity by many of its prominent critics, such as Karl Marx or Friedrich Nietzsche. Yet an amazing thing has happened within our generation.

At the Second Vatican Council (1962-65) Protestant and Orthodox believers, formerly considered heretics and schismatics, were officially invited as guests and observers. In the first Constitution published by Vatican II (Constitution on the Sacred Liturgy), we read in the opening sentence: "It is the goal of this most sacred Council . . . to nurture whatever can contribute to the unity of all who believe in Christ." [1] In its Decree on Ecumenism the Council even declared: "Promoting the restoration of unity among all Christians is one of the Chief concerns of the Second Sacred Ecumenical Synod of the Vatican." [2] Now Roman Catholic scholars freely admit that historical circumstances forced the Church at Trent to take a clear and strong position against Protestant doctrinal "innovations," thereby minimizing the issues that the Reformers emphasized. This occurred even where they were in harmony with the Bible and the fathers. In turn Trent emphasized the issues the Reformers attacked. By the time of Trent the Reformers had rejected the visible, external, juridicial, institutional, and hierarchic church and emphasized the invisible, internal, and charismatic church. In turn the Roman Catholic Church decided to put almost exclusive emphasis on "the Church as a hierarchically organized society, directed from above by the bishop of Rome." [3] Now the tide had changed and many differences were discovered to be no longer of doctrinal nature, but largely stemming from historically conditioned antagonistic entrenchment.

Recent years have not only brought about the rediscovery of the already existing unity between the Roman Catholic Church and the Evangelical churches, but we have also seen an amazing awakening to the unity we share within the Protestant fold. At the Fifth Assembly of the World Council of Churches in Nairobi, 1975, the Assembly recommended that the churches "provide opportunities for a careful study and evaluation of the concept of conciliar fellowship as a way of describing the unity of the Church."[4] Similarly, the study document *One Baptism, One Eucharist and A Mutually Recognized Ministry* published in 1975 by the Commission on Faith and Order witnesses to the amazing unity that already exists within those churches represented in the Faith and Order Commission. To indicate at least in passing some of the many main facets of this newly discovered unity we should look at the documents of Vatican II and the results of the ecumenical dialogue among a multitude of different denominations.

a. The church of Vatican II

Ecclesiology has been one of the most important topics for Vatican II. The Dogmatic Constitution on the Church, the Constitution on the Sacred Liturgy, the Pastoral Constitution on the Church in the Modern World, the Decrees on Ecumenism, on Eastern Catholic Churches, on the Bishop's Pastoral Office in the Church, on the Apostolate of the Laity, on the Church's Missionary Activity, and the Declaration on the Relationship of the Church to Non-Christian Religions, are all in some way or other concerned about the structure and task of the church. Most other publications of the Council also deal with issues that affect the understanding of the church. Yet Vatican II was neither a repetition of Trent nor a continuation of the centralization process of Vatican I where papal infallibility was proclaimed.

The ecclesiology of Vatican II is ecumenical. This does not mean that the Roman Catholic Church suddenly rejected its past. For instance, in the Dogmatic Constitution on Divine Revelation we hear the affirmation of the equality of Scripture and tradition with nearly identical language as at Trent some 400 years ago.[5] Yet it was the great accomplishment of Vatican II that the Council placed the accents very differently. Vatican II did not say anything different from Trent, however, it said the same thing differently.

We hear now that the church has a hierarchic and a charismatic dimension and that the Holy Spirit with various gifts in both areas "adorns her with the fruits of His grace."[6] Since the christocentricity of the church gains renewed emphasis, the Council refers to the distinction between the visible (structural) church and the invisible church and admits that "many elements of sanctification and of truth can be found outside of her visible structure." In following Christ as its example the church emphasizes that it does not seek earthly glory, but proclaims humility and self-sacrifice, even by her own example. Of course, the church includes those who "are fully incorporated into the society of the Church who, possessing the Spirit of Christ, accept her entire system and all the means of salvation given to her, and through union with her visible structure are joined to Christ, who rules her through the Supreme Pontiff and the bishops." But the church recognizes "that in many ways she is linked with those who, being baptized, are honored with the name of Christian, though they do not profess the faith in its entirety or do not preserve unity of communion with the successor of Peter."

Vatican II reaffirms the decision of Vatican I to attribute to the Roman Pontiff, the Vicar of Christ, infallible teaching authority.[7] But the Council recognizes "that by divine institution bishops have succeeded to the place of the apostles as shepherds of the Church, and that he who hears them, hears Christ, while he who rejects them, rejects Christ and Him who sent Christ." While the Roman Pontiff stands in succession to Peter, the bishops are seen as the successors of the apostles. The college or body of bishops together with the Roman Pontiff, but not without him, exert supreme and full power over the universal church. Though the individual bishops do not enjoy the prerogative of infallibility, they can proclaim Christ's doctrine infallibly. But infallibility is not just reserved for the Roman Pontiff. The infallibility promised to the church resides also in the body of bishops when that body exercises supreme teaching authority together with the successor of Peter.

The laity are considerably upgraded as the ones who are "in their own way made sharers in the priestly, prophetic, and kingly functions of Christ. They carry out their own part in the mission of the whole Christian people with respect to the Church and the world."[8] Through baptism and confirmation the laity is commissioned to the apostolate by the Lord himself. Through the lay apostolate the faithful participate in the saving mission of the church. This means that while the functional and hierarchical differentiation between the Roman Pontiff, the bishops, and the laity is maintained all three enjoy equal participation in the work of the church.

Since Mariology was often considered a divisive point between Roman Catholics and Protestants, it is interesting how it is dealt with in Vatican II. First, the doctrine of the Assumption of Mary is reaffirmed, meaning that she was "taken up body and soul into heavenly glory upon the completion of her earthly sojourn." [9] We are even told that Mary has saving influence upon us. But then the christocentric emphasis comes through and we are assured that this does not obscure or diminish the unique mediation of Christ, but rather shows its power. Of course, we wonder to what extent this can be true if we hear at the same time that the Council "admonishes all the sons of the Church that the cult, especially the liturgical cult, of the Blessed Virgin, be generously fostered."

When one would ask how the Council arrived at its usually carefully balanced insights, we could give many answers. We could point to the growing awareness that a divided Christendom is a scandal to the unbeliever and the skeptic, or we could mention the increasing necessity of a joint witness against the onslaught of materialism and secularism. Next to these more external reasons is an important internal one, namely the rediscovery of the Bible. We do not mean to imply that the Roman Catholic Church ever forgot the Bible. On the contrary, it had always enjoyed almost unparalleled reverence. But the Bible was never the book of the laity. Now, however, the Council "earnestly and specifically urges all the Christian faithful, too, especially religious, to learn by frequent reading of the divine Scriptures the 'excelling knowledge of Jesus Christ' (Phil. 3:8). 'For ignorance of the Scriptures is ignorance of Christ.'" [10]

The church is concerned that suitable and correct translations are made from the original texts into the different languages. Thus the Vulgate is no longer considered the normative text of the Bible, as the Council of Trent once asserted. Believers should be able to read the Bible in their own language, as Luther had demanded. Encouragement is given, upon proper approval, to produce these translations "in cooperation with the separated brethren as well" so that everyone can use it. Careful exegesis of the Scriptures is encouraged so that one can determine the meaning the sacred writers intended, and what God wanted to manifest through their words. In the interpretation of Scripture attention should be given to the unity of Scripture and the living tradition of the whole church. Not every conceivable kind of exegesis suffices, but only exegesis that sees itself in harmony with the church and the Holy Spirit who is active in the church. Since the Council reaffirmed the equal emphasis on Scripture and tradition, we might wonder whether this does not put Scripture into the straightjacket of tradition. But our concerns are alleviated to a large extent.

With Trent the gospel is affirmed as the source of all saving truth and moral teaching. [11] Tradition is not seen as a human product, but coming from the apostles and developing in the church with the help of the Holy Spirit. Scripture and tradition exist in close connection and communication, "for both of them, flowing from the same divine wellspring, in a certain way merge into a unity and tend toward the same end." [12] The Council does not want to treat Scripture and tradition independently or separately; they must be taken together in a functional unity.

It is certainly true that the church always understands and interprets Scripture in the light of its continuous tradition. This even holds for the Evangelical churches as the bilateral talks between various denominations reveal. Exegetical studies too have posed the question whether one can as easily determine the point at which Scripture stops and tradition starts as one had once thought. It is now commonly accepted among biblical scholars that we have an oral tradition of various length behind the written documents of Scripture. [13] While the Council was unable to assign an unqualified priority to Scripture it made significant progress in that direction. But by insisting on the study of Scripture and making Scripture available to everyone, the Council insured that tradition would not grow into an independent authority. This rediscovery of the significance of the Bible led to many other shifts and emphases as we have seen.

Though the observers of the Council were consulted for opinion on the items discussed at the sessions, we should not make the mistake of regarding this Council as an actual Ecumenical Council. It was a Council of the Roman Catholic Church, but a Council that gave witness to a definite movement of renewal *within* that church. [14] Unity can only be brought about through renewal. Through the prominent presence of observers, many Council Fathers were confronted for the first time with the painful division among Christians. It brought them to realize that there are hundreds of millions of Christians, baptized and believers of Christ, who are separated from the Roman Catholic Church. [15] Small wonder that the Decree on Ecumenism starts with the statement: "Promoting the restoration of unity among all Christians is one of the Chief concerns of the Second Sacred Ecumenical Synod of the Vatican." [16]

Since the Council admitted that the current ecumenical movement came into existence by action of the Holy Spirit, it acknowledged that Catholics have a duty to take part in it. [17] At the same time it cautions that the ecumenical actions of Roman Catholics must be fully and sincerely Catholic, i.e., loyal to the truth received from the apostles and the fathers and in harmony with the faith that the Catholic Church has always professed. Such participation which would not deny the truth of their own heritage, must admit that ecclesial elements do exist among non-Catholic Christians and the Council exhorts that one should rejoice when such elements are discovered in other churches. To discover them, one must first of all come to know non-Catholic traditions and must also acquaint oneself better with the mentality of non-Catholic Christians. Such an attitude promulgated by the Council is very different from the triumphalist or introverted stance many Protestants associated with the Roman Catholic Church prior to Vatican II.

It is proper to conclude that Vatican II marked the end of the Counter-Reformation.[18] Doctrine is no longer defined in contrast to the tenets of the churches of the Reformation, even while intently listening to their concerns. The Council therefore marked the official entry of the Roman Catholic Church into the mainstream of the Ecumenical Movement.[19] Yet this does not make the search for unity easier. The presence of non-Catholic observers at the Council from widely different groups made painfully clear that the problem of division is not simply one between the Roman Catholic Church and the non-Roman community.[20] The search for unity is as much a task to be pursued between the Roman and non-Roman Catholic churches as among the churches of the Reformation themselves.

b. The churches in ecumenical dialogue

The most significant signs of an ongoing dialogue among the churches of the Reformation include the Faith and Order Movement, which held its first formal meeting in 1920, and the World Council of Churches, organized in Amsterdam in 1948. Other significant signs have been the close cooperation within confessional families, such as the Anglican Lambeth Conference first held in 1867, the World Alliance of Reformed Churches, founded in 1875, the World Methodist Council, organized in 1951 but going back to the 19th century, and the Lutheran World Federation, the largest of the confessional families, founded in 1947, and going back to the Lutheran World Convention that first met in 1923.[21] The national councils of churches established in many nations give ecumenical dialogue and cooperation added impetus. There are also many similar arrangements on state, regional, and metropolitan levels down to the local cluster of churches that sponsor joint programs, hire a joint staff, and engage in occasional exchange of representative members and pastors.

There are signs that amid all diversity and plurality more and more points of unity are being discovered. This becomes most noticeable in the so-called bilateral dialogues between representatives of different confessional families. For instance, in the United States the Lutherans, represented by The American Lutheran Church, the Lutheran Church in America, and The Lutheran Church—Missouri Synod, have engaged in dialogues with the Reformed Church, resulting after its first round in a book with the intriguing title, *Marburg Revisited: A Reexamination of Lutheran and Reformed Traditions*. In their final session the participants came to the following significant agreement:

> During these four meetings we have examined carefully the major issues which have aroused theological controversy between our traditions for generations past. At some points we have discovered that our respective views of each other have been inherited caricatures initially caused by misunderstanding or polemical zeal. In other instances it has become apparent that efforts to guard against possible distortions of truth have resulted in varying emphases in related doctrines which are not in themselves contradictory and in fact are complementary, and which are viewed in a more proper balance in our contemporary theological formulations.[22]

Such a statement is an important witness to the gradual overcoming of denominational entrenchment through which proper insights of one's own tradition were absolutized and therefore distorted. A similar tenor can be heard in the Leuenberg Agreement of 1973 between the Churches of the Reformation (Lutheran and Reformed) in Europe.[23]

Another very interesting series of dialogues has been taking place in the United States between the Roman Catholic Church and the Lutherans. The dialogue started with an issue on which there were apt to be minor differences, the status of the Nicene Creed as Dogma of the Church. The Lutheran-Catholic dialogue then investigated the significance of baptism and the Eucharist, and finally ventured to such potentially divisive issues as the infallibility and primacy of the papacy. An amazing consensus has so far been achieved, largely because of the kind of questions that have been asked. For instance, Lutherans always pride themselves in insisting on the real presence of Christ in the Lord's Supper. But, confronted with Roman Catholics, they suddenly are asked why it is that on the one hand they strongly affirm the real presence of Christ and then absolutely refuse on the other hand "to discuss theologically the nature of that presence or the manner in which a change is effected in the elements."[24] The tacit assumption behind this question is that perhaps Lutherans are not as far away from the Reformed symbolism as they themselves assume. The

Roman Catholics were surprised to learn that Lutherans believe as firmly in the real presence as do Catholics, but that they address the issue from a different tradition and a different concern.

Or let us take as another example the most recent discussions on infallibility. At first the Lutherans were convinced that the issue of papal infallibility was an inner-Catholic problem to which Lutherans had little to contribute. But soon they realized that the issues at stake in the general doctrine of infallibility are anything but a solely Roman Catholic problem. They involve the very nature and truth of the gospel and "the credibility of the Church's preaching and teaching Ministry."[25] There is no doubt that in some form or other many results of these dialogues filter down to the local level, whether in the form of educational materials or simply in the knowledge that the churches are growing closer together. One should remember also the numerous study documents released by interdenominational agencies. One of the most remarkable is a small booklet with the title *One Baptism, One Eucharist, and A Mutually Recognized Ministry*, issued by the Commission on Faith and Order of the World Council of Churches. The statement contained in the booklet resulted from several consultations of the Commission and was submitted to the member churches for consideration and comment. Since Vatican II Roman Catholic theologians have also been included in these discussions.[26]

The first two statements, on baptism and the Eucharist, present the summary of agreements reached by the Commission. The statement on ministry "is an attempt to survey the present ecumenical debate on the ordained ministry and to indicate the emerging common perspectives which may lead to the agreement required for the full mutual recognition of the ministries."[27] The statement on baptism is the briefest, perhaps because baptism is least controversial. Baptism is understood here as a sacrament that has at its center the participation in the death and resurrection of Christ. It is both God's gift and human commitment and looks towards its eschatological fulfillment. Both infant and adult baptism are allowed for. Potentially divisive questions, for instance, whether water baptism constitutes a complete sacrament or whether there is a separate sacramental act of laying on of hands at which the gift of the Spirit is given, are not evaded, but dealt with in a conciliatory manner, fully recognizing different traditions and different emphases.

About the Eucharist we hear that "Christ himself, with all He has accomplished for us and for all creation, is present in the Eucharist."[28] The eucharistic meal is the sacrament of the body and blood of Christ, the sacrament of his real presence. It is the great thanksgiving to the Father for everything he has done for us. Focusing on cross and resurrection, it is both representation of the whole of God's reconciling action in Christ, and anticipation of the future fulfillment of the kingdom. Following the discussion of the Eucharist we notice that rather diverse traditions have to be dealt with in the ecumenical dialogue. For instance, in one paragraph we are confronted with the *epiklesis,* in which the church in analogy to Eastern usage prays for the Spirit "in order that it may be sanctified and renewed" and, at the same time, evidently to accommodate Reformed thought, the Spirit is mentioned "who, in the Eucharist, makes Christ really present, and is given to us in the bread and wine, according to the words of institution."

The statement on the ministry starts from our commonly accepted notion of the church as the community of believers. It then proceeds to discuss the apostolicity of ministry. It concludes that ordained ministry cannot be understood or carried out in isolation from the general ministry of the people. But to the ordained there is a special, though not exclusive responsibility for proclaiming the message of reconciliation, establishing churches and building them up in apostolic faith. The first apostles were unique as Christ's immediate and personally chosen followers. Their task, however, must be continued by designated ministers. The diversity of the ordained ministry is bound up with the history and cultural particularity of the churches. Yet there is a unity in the diversity of the offices, ensuing in the episcopate, the presbyterate, and the diaconate.

One of the ways in which apostolicity of the church is expressed is. the succession of bishops. But the primary manifestation of an apostolic succession is to be found in the life of the church as a whole. "The act of ordination is at one and the same time: invocation of the Holy Spirit [*epiklesis*]; sacramental sign; acknowledgment of gifts and commitment." [29] We are assured that the setting apart is not to a superior level of discipleship, but to service within the church. "For the Church to be one the full mutual recognition of ministries is required . . . . [Therefore] it must be possible, at least in principle, that ministers be able to fulfill their ministry, upon invitation, in any church . . . . Unity requires that the calling to and the fruit of the ministry be recognized everywhere."

The statement on the ministry concludes by outlining different degrees of recognition and introducing proposals for advancing toward mutual recognition. We cannot but rejoice over the amazing degree of unity evidenced in this document. But there is still a long way to go before we have full and mutual recognition and complete unity. Yet important steps are taken toward that unity. Individual denominations and churches have discovered that they are not the only true church.[30] With this recognition the knowledge emerges that the way to unity is not one of victory but of prayer, humility, and repentance, imploring the Lord of the church that he may bring about this unity.[31]

The implicitly arrogant attitude in which we rejoice in self-righteousness when dialogue conclusions recognize the validity of our own doctrinal assertions can be an effective roadblock to unity. We must also become aware that "the message of reconciliation is scarcely believable to others when the people who bear the name of Christ are themselves at sharp odds with one another."[32] But the proclamation loses its force if we simply pretend that the still-existing differences, painful as they are, are totally irrelevant. Our understanding of the church must be necessarily confessional, though it dare not become sectarian. It must focus on the common source that enables the church's existence and the common goal that heightens and corrects our ecclesial vision. In talking in this way about the church we are confronted with the whole people of God, their proclamation of the Word of God, and their administration of and participation in the sacraments.

1. The whole people of God

When we talk about the church as the whole people of God we must avoid the twin dangers of inclusiveness and exclusivity.

(1) The exclusive error equates the institutional church with the whole people of God on the grounds that only those who belong to the body of Christ, i.e., the visible church, can be reckoned among the people of God. Yet how do we want to define church membership? Is it simply sufficient to belong to a denomination or should one at least minimally participate in the ongoing life of the church?

The membership in the German *Volkskirche,* for instance, is determined by not having officially renounced church membership and this means still paying church tax. In this way one could be a member "in good standing" without ever setting foot into a church sanctuary, except for one's own baptism. In contrast, many American denominations determine active church membership by communing at least once a year or by financially supporting the church at least once in the same period. After a certain time of inactive membership one is usually removed from the congregational roster unless the degree of participation improves. Such criteria hardly fit the description of the nascent church in Acts 2:42-46 where it states that day by day they attended the temple together and that they devoted themselves to the apostles' teaching and fellowship.

Regular attendance at worship and generous giving are not foolproof criteria by which we can determine who belongs to the whole people of God. Often these "positive" attitudes can be the result either of tradition followed without much reflection or of moralistic self-righteousness. Already Augustine equated the visible church with the institutional church, while he conceived of the invisible church as being in some contexts larger and in others narrower than the institutional church. Similarly, in one of the favorite motifs sculptured above church portals of medieval European churches, the scene of the last judgment, there are always some people on the side of the condemned that bear distinctive ecclesiastical attributes, such as the bishop's mitre. Again this indicates that medieval Christendom did not imply that church membership necessarily meant that one belonged to the whole people of God.

(2) Since the perimeters of the invisible can at times be more inclusive than the visible church, the suggestion has been made to include among the invisible church everyone, regardless of one's religious affiliation, or at least the most loyal members of all religions or pseudo-religious affiliations. Thus the transition between Christians and non-Christians, or between Christians and Christendom itself, is no longer expressed in terms of an absolute either/or, but in a gradual more or less.[33] Though it would be a confusion of terms and a potential act of Christian imperialism to call followers of non-Christian religions anonymous Christians, we must be aware that the whole people of God are not concomitant with the active or inactive membership of a denomination or of all the churches taken together.

Thus the term people of God does not refer to a church or denomination or to all of them, but it refers first of all to the one who gathers, sanctifies, and enlightens people of all nations and of all ethnic and religious origins. This means that at the beginning of any reflection about the whole people of God we must first reflect about the nature of the church as it expresses itself in the will of its founder, God in Christ through the power of the Spirit. This does not make irrelevant the institutional church. It is still the primary institution that treasures the Christian tradition and facilitates a Christian consciousness through its instructional media. Yet it must constantly be measured, criticized, and realigned by the will of its founder.

a. Christological character

The Christian church is not a club that was founded to serve the interests of its members, nor is it a social institution through which a group of people attempts to reform society. As the Apostles' Creed expresses, the church is holy catholic and a communion of saints. Similarly, in the Nicene Creed it is described as holy catholic and apostolic. The central determinant that these statements presuppose is Christ. The church is one not because it is undivided; it is in fact divided, but it is one because it is founded by one person, Jesus Christ. Thus the unity of the church is given through its origin and promised within its eschatological horizon. The eschaton will not be arranged according to confessional families or denominations. The church is not holy because of its members or its sacral buildings. It is one of the fundamental confessions of its members that they are sinful, and it is commonplace to point out the profane connotations in church architecture. The church, however, is holy because it is sanctified through its founder who is the source of all holiness.

When talking about the community of saints we arrive at similar conclusions. The members are not saints because of their conduct. In many ways their unsaintly behavior impedes the mission of the church. But they are saints because their founder has called, accepted, and sanctified them. Similarly, the community aspect of the church is not established through a common concern or a common goal. The concerns and aspirations of its members are as diverse as the membership itself. But through the founder of the church we find a common orientation and focal point.

It is relatively easy to assess that the central marks of the church are founded in Christ. But can we as easily assume that Jesus Christ founded the Christian church? While it cannot be established with certainty that Jesus of Nazareth did indeed found the church through Peter (Matt. 16:18), there can be no doubt that the followers of Jesus gathered in the name of Jesus Christ upon his death and resurrection. We also notice that the Eucharist was celebrated with reference to the express command of Christ: "Do this," and we hear that the Christians are baptized into the death of Christ (Rom. 6:4; 1 Cor. 11:25). Similarly, the public proclamation of the apostles is done in the name of Jesus and centers around Jesus Christ who was delivered to death by his enemies and who has been raised from the dead and now serves as a point of hope and encouragement (cf. Acts 4, esp. 2 and 18f.). Jesus Christ provides the source and the content of the Christian church: it is founded by him, proclaims redemption in his name, and celebrates the sacraments that he instituted.

Traditionally Pentecost is seen as the birthday of the church when the Holy Spirit was poured out on the followers of Christ. Since the "miracle of Pentecost" is also the instance at which the language barrier separating different nationalities was overcome, the pouring out of the Spirit is often understood as the provision of ecstasy. Yet the Spirit of God should not be understood primarily as providing otherwise inaccessible knowledge or experience, but as the foundation of life.[34] For instance, according to the Old Testament, the Spirit created the cosmos (Gen. 1:2) and all life within it (Psalm 33:6). The Spirit of God is the active principle which gives physical life and from which everything living derives its dynamic power.[35] If God withdraws his Spirit, our flesh must die. Thus Job confesses: "The Spirit of God has made me, and the breath of the Almighty gives me life" (Job 33:4).

The Spirit is not only the life-giving and sustaining power, but he will bring about the eschatological fulfillment. For instance, we hear Yahweh promise to Israel: "I will give them one heart, and put a new spirit within them; I will take the stony heart out of their flesh and give them a heart of flesh, that they may walk in my statutes and keep my ordinances and obey them; and they shall be my people, and I will be their God (Ezek. 11:19f.). Similarly, the Psalmist prays: "Create in me a clean heart, O God, and put a new and right spirit within me" (Ps. 51:10). Of course, the Spirit of God also provides ecstasy, excitement, and dynamic drive. Yet its main intention is life-creating, life-preserving, and life-fulfilling.

The miracle of understanding at Pentecost stands in antithesis to the dispersion of humanity (Gen. 11:7f.). The birthdate of the church and the outpouring of the Holy Spirit coincide with the rediscovery of human unity that transcends ethnic and national diversity. The power of the Spirit enables humanity to rediscover its original unity. The outpouring of the Spirit and the birth date of the church are therefore a sign of God through which he brings together humanity in unity and community. Since human beings are rational beings, unable to exist for long periods in isolation, the Spirit brings to fulfillment the intended communal structure in exemplary fashion in and with the church. Human community is now possible beyond the arbitrary or intentional confines of political configurations. The church foreshadows the eschatological phenomenon of human solidarity and practices it in the midst of today's life. At Pentecost was begun the creation of a new humanity as an inclusive community of people. Yet almost immediately there were again dissensions.

Human sinfulness still attempts to assert the individual self to the exclusion of others in the face of the common ground and destiny. Only the power of the Spirit enables the church to be community. The church owes its unity to its founding in the Spirit, but not to its structure or its practice. This fact is illustrated many times in the New Testament when we are reminded that there is no unity apart from the unity in Christ. For instance, according to the Gospel of John, Jesus reminds his disciples: "I am the vine, you are the branches. He who abides in me and I in him, he it is that bears much fruit, for apart from me you can do nothing" (John 15:5). This means that the community is only community while it is in communion with its Lord.[36]

Another image for the church, that of the body, is often used by Paul. To free ourselves from the possible misunderstanding of the church as a corporation we must first note that the term body is also an integral part of the eucharistic vocabulary. For instance, Paul asks rhetorically: "The bread which we break, is it not a participation in the body of Christ?" and then he continues: "Because there is one bread, we who are many are one body, for we all partake of the one bread" (1 Cor. 10:16f.). The presence of the body of Christ is perceived in two ways: It is the blessing of liberation which is made available in the Eucharist, and it is the power that unites the believers with Christ. But the community does not simply participate in the body of Christ. Paul reminds us that we are the body of Christ and individually members of it (1 Cor. 12:27). We gain access to Christ's body in baptism (1 Cor. 12:13). The image of the body of Christ emphasizes our unity as individuals by reminding us that the members of a body have different functions but are of equal status (cf. 1 Cor. 12:14-26).[37]

While the term "people of God" is also used by Paul to connect the church with the history of salvation, the body image is more spatially oriented. Some New Testament writers recognized the danger that could ensue from a narrow identification of the church with Christ or his body. Therefore the church is related to Christ's cosmic dominion. For instance, in Colossians, Christ is understood as the head of the whole world. Yet only the church is his body and his power permeates it to assure its steadfastness and growth (Col. 2:19).[38] The church is not identical with Christ, but closely related to him. This gives it a special place in history and carries an exceptional obligation, to be true to its source of power.

In the Letter to the Ephesians the cosmic aspect of the church receives renewed attention. Christ is designated the head of the church in which the fullness of Christ dwells (Eph. 1:23). As Christ's body, the church can even be the bearer of the Christian message to demonic powers (Eph. 3:10). We also notice that the writer draws an analogy between the relationship of husband and wife and that of Christ and the church (Eph. 5:22-33). Though this passage serves primarily as instruction to the married, indirectly we obtain the writer's insight into the relationship between Christ and the church.[39] We hear that the church is subject to Christ (Eph. 5:24) and is to be obedient to him. But significantly, in comparing husband and wife with Christ and the church, the writer does not reflect upon the copulative act, as could be expected in the context of mystery religions. Rather, the sacrificial love stands in the forefront and reveals itself in Christ's sacrificial death (Eph. 5:25). This passage would refute the allegation that Christ preached the coming of the kingdom of God, but the church emerged instead of the kingdom. This passage clearly indicates that with the church, God and Christ are also present. The church is the new community made possible through Christ's redemptive act.

In talking about Christ as the head of the church, we must again define what we mean by church. Here the New Testament offers valuable help. In the New Testament the term church means first the local church, such as the church at Cenchreae (Rom. 16:1) or the church at Corinth (1 Cor. 1:2 and 2 Cor. 1:1). This might convey the impression that church is simply the local congregation. But in looking more closely at the Greek text we notice that "the church at" really means "the church as it is at." [40] The church is not produced by adding up all the local churches, nor is it the local church by itself. Each Christian community, however small, represents the whole church. Whether there are problems of injustice (1 Cor. 6:4) or of tradition (1 Tim. 5:16), issues and problems in the church are never a matter of strictly local dimensions, but they affect the whole church.

Church is wherever the Christian community is in union with its founder and head, Jesus Christ. While we do not want to leave the impression that the ecumenical movement serves no useful purpose, even the most vigorous ecumenical movement cannot produce or further the unity of the church by deciding or implementing new plans or models for unity. It can only appeal to the local manifestations of the church, assisting them to live up to the intentions that Jesus Christ has for his church. Through discovering the common ground in Christ the unity is then furthered and strengthened. Only a christocentric concern at the very roots of the church, at its local level, can help the cause of unity.

The church is founded by Christ and finds its unity in and with him. But it also represents Christ. It is the visible expression of his lordship. As Matt. 16:18 clearly indicates, this does not imply any kind of tri- umphalistic attitude. Only through Christ will the gates of Hades not prevail against the church. Only through the wisdom of God in Christ can the church withstand the evil powers and proclaim the good news (Eph. 3:10). Therefore Paul can exclaim in joy: "For I am sure that neither death, nor life, nor angels, nor principalities, nor things present, nor things to come, nor powers, nor height, nor depth, nor anything else in all creation, will be able to separate us from the love of God in Christ Jesus our Lord" (Rom. 8:38f.).

Christ has charged the church with the privilege of representing him. Of course, this implies that the church is endowed with saving power. It is the agency which treasures and administers word and sacrament, and it is under the great commission to go into all the world to baptize and to preach. But the great commission includes the reminder "teach- ing them all that I have commanded you" (Matt. 28:20). This means two things: (1) The church is placed under the same word that it proclaims and (2) the church does not proclaim its own word but that of its Lord. The church, therefore, is the mediator of Christ and his gospel. Small wonder that already in the early church Cyprian declared that "there is no salvation out[side] of the Church." [41] That he meant here more than the church as an institution becomes obvious when he states at another occasion: "He can no longer have God for his Father, who has not the Church for his mother."

The Roman Catholic Church especially has adhered until the present to the notion of being Christ's representative. Yet until Vatican II rep- resentation was understood in strictly institutional terms. The church meant the Roman Catholic Church and to be cut off from it through excommunication meant to be cut off from the gospel of Christ. While it is certainly true that the church is the body of Christ and it manifests him in this world, this prerogative is not confined to one or several of its ecclesiastical manifestations. Yet Christ can only be known through the body of Christ which treasures his memory and celebrates his pres- ence, and which instructs the people in this living tradition. [42] Without the churches the knowledge of Christ would diminish rapidly among humanity. Moreover, the Christian faith needs a living context in which to express itself. Even Count Zinzendorf, who established his own (separate) Christian community, claimed emphatically that without community he would not accept one as a Christian.[43]

The church is indeed Christ's representative, mediating his message, issuing the offer of salvation, and providing the content for Christian nurture. Yet in this context it is presumptuous to confine the notion of church to one or the sum total of the established churches or to a certain denomination. The church is where community is assembled to direct its life according to the word of its founder and to spread the good news of Christ. Without such a church, wherever it may manifest itself, we have at most a religious relationship to God, adhering to some general moral and religious principles, but we miss God's living word, because we miss Christ.

b. Priesthood of all believers

The common priesthood of all who form the people of God is one of the rediscoveries of the Reformation. Since the term laity is derived from the Greek *laos,* meaning people, we are not surprised that the grassroots movement of the Reformation facilitated this rediscovery. Originally *laos* meant, as the Septuagint usage shows, the people of God or Israel. Besides this, of course, the term could also refer simply to the people or the crowd. This is also true for the New Testament. But soon it denoted the Christian community. For instance, Paul writes in quoting Hosea: "Those who were not my people I will call 'my people,' and her who was not beloved I will call 'my beloved' " (Rom. 9:25). This usage is also continued into the early church.

In the early church, however, *laos* came more and more to stand for the Christian community in distinction from its leaders, especially as they conducted the worship.[44] This was not an innovation, because we find this distinction already mentioned in the New Testament with reference to the synagogue practice (Acts 13:15). The laity was now no longer seen as comprising the whole people of God, but only the people apart from its leaders.

Another significant shift that occurs in the transition from Judaism to Christianity is that the opposition between *laos,* meaning the Jewish people, and Gentiles is no longer seen as an exclusive one. Now we hear that "God first visited the Gentiles, to take out of them a people for his name" (Acts 15:14). The new people of God, then, is no longer confined to any ethnic or national group.

Today the laity is seldom regarded as the people of God. In everyday language, the opposite of lay is not leader, but expert. Whether within the church or in other fields of knowledge, to be a layperson is to be considered inferior and ignorant. We might want to defend this state of affairs. We can point out that in theology, as in other fields, the knowledge to be mastered has increased to such an extent that it can only be handled by experts. But the dilemma of such a distinction becomes evident when we remember that the people of God are also referred to as the community of saints. Is it really permissible, we must ask, to distinguish between a large body of saints and a few especially equipped super saints? The conclusion would be that if we want to preserve the unity of the people of God, we are not allowed to distinguish in rank between the laity and its leaders, and this would also apply ontologically, but only with regard to their respective function.

Contrary to the frequent assumption, the laity dare not be relegated to passivity, with only leaders the expert and active. Laity means neither inferior in rank, nor in expertise, nor activity. It simply means that quite often the means with which to carry out the lay tasks are very different from the way the leadership functions. The differentiation between clerics and laity, but also their basic unity, is well captured in the Roman Catholic canon law: "There is by divine ordinance a distinction between the *clergy* and the *laity* . . . on the other hand, both clerics and laymen can be *religious* [i.e., members of religious orders]." [45] Yet we also notice here an appeal to a divinely instituted distinction between lay and clergy.

While the people of God never existed without a special leadership, the question must be raised concerning what this divinely instituted division implies. Perhaps Vatican II shed some light on the issue when it declared: "Though they differ from one another in essence and not only in degree, the common priesthood of the faithful and the ministerial or hierarchical priesthood are nonetheless interrelated. Each of them in its own special way is a participation in the one priesthood of Christ." [46] Again the question is left open of the meaning of a difference "in essence and not only in degree." Should we conclude that the clergy are by nature different from the laity? Perhaps we can only pursue this question further once we investigate the Roman Catholic understanding of the ministerial office.

According to Roman Catholic understanding, the laity shares uniquely in the one priesthood of Christ. This means two things. (1) The priesthood of Christ is not divided into a priesthood that the clerics hold and an inferior priesthood for the laity. There is only one common priesthood in which all Christians participate. (2) Christ is the only source of the church's apostolate.[47] The lay apostolate is founded in the living union with Christ and not in special gifts of an individual. The documents of Vatican II also affirm that "the laity, too, share in the priestly, prophetic and royal office of Christ, and therefore have their own role to play in the mission of the whole People of God in the Church and in the world." [48] The ministry of the laity is not a truncated or additional ministry of the church. Through their relation to Christ the laity share in their own way fully in the church's ministry.

The ordained ministry cannot be understood or carried out in isolation from the general ministry of the whole people of God. This caution is not only directed against an understanding of the pastoral ministry in which the pastor is so elevated that he does not seem to need the laity, but also against a totally people-oriented ministry. In this type of ministry certain individuals become oblivious to the Christian community, since they perceive themselves as God's direct gift to this world. The ordained ministry needs the laity as its support and as the arena in whose midst the ordained can minister.

The Roman Catholic Church has rediscovered the necessity of the laity for the carrying out of the mission and the work of the church. Since it clearly distinguishes between laity and clerics, it realizes that the laity occupies a unique position. The laity belongs both to the world and to the church in a way that is true neither of the clergy nor of the monks.[49] In this dual position the laity are the proper and irreplaceable agents through whom the mission and work of the church in relation to the world is fully accomplished. If we would obliterate the distinction between clergy and laity and assume that the clergy can fulfill the witnessing function as well as the laity, we would endanger the effectiveness of the Christian ministry to the world. The validity of this distinction is shown more and more by the effectiveness of lay people as they witness to the community in which they live and work.

Frederick K. Wentz, in his interesting study *The Layman's Role Today,* sees a fourfold role of the laity's ministry in today's world.[50] The laity are called to be servants, charged to be the light, empowered to be the salt, and encouraged to be soldiers. The laity carry on a full and responsible mission in serving others in the midst of egocentricity; they add flavor in the midst of blandness; they enlighten the darkness of the world with the word of God; they take a militant stand against all injustice, and a conciliatory posture amidst strife and dissension. Their tasks show paradigmatically that the church exists for the world and not for itself. The church therefore should not bask in the glory of Christ, but, in a missionary move, dispense this glory and permeate the world with it. Since the laity live in both dimensions, the church and the world, they remind the church of its essential world-relatedness and of its missionary task.[51] Since the church is related to the world, it can only give credible witness if it approaches the world in unity. Thus the rediscovery of the missionary dimension of the church, the awakening of the ecumenical movement, and the rediscovery of the laity go hand in hand.[52]

Another factor that led to the rediscovery of the laity was the renewed emphasis on the Bible as it emerged in the ecumenical movement. Suddenly what should have always been clear became evident, namely, that before Christ and God all Christians are of equal status. Paul, for instance, emphasizes that "there is no distinction between Jew and Greek; the same Lord is Lord of all and bestows his riches upon all who call upon him" (Rom. 10:12). This does not just imply that the former distinctions in rank have lost their separating power but that there is an immediacy to Christ involved in the Christian faith. Before Christ all are equal and nobody can interfere or intercede on someone else's behalf. No one enjoys a preferred status in acquiring or dispensing of salvation.

Baptism now takes on new significance as the sacrament that confers upon all of us equal status with regard to Christ. For instance, Paul reminds us: "For as many of you as were baptized into Christ have put on Christ. There is neither Jew nor Greek, there is neither slave nor free, there is neither male nor female; for you all are one in Christ Jesus" (Gal. 3:27f.). Baptism is incorporation in Christ and therewith into the Christian community. We are initiated into fellowship with Christ and with our fellow Christians. Baptism can be understood as the basic ordination of each Christian, commissioning him/her to be part of the church and of the witnessing community.[53] As a sign and seal of this ordination the minister lays the hand on each baptized and the baptized receives the Holy Spirit. Incorporation into the church means total devotion and service in and with the community of believers.

Ordination for the "ordained clergy" is not an additional or separate rite, but something that must be seen in analogy to the commissioning for special tasks that arise within the Christian community. It is as dangerous to divide Christians into ordained and unordained as it is to assume that there are full-time Christians and part-time Christians, or trained and untrained ones. All Christians are ordained to full-time service and must be trained in one way or another. It is relatively unimportant whether this means special instruction prior to adult baptism or following infant baptism and resulting in confirmation. But one cannot be a Christian in the full sense without the basic knowledge of what this privilege of being a Christian means in general and also in specific situations.

Laity cannot be defined over against clergy or vice versa. Paul makes this abundantly clear with his imagery of the body. For instance, he states: "For just as the body is one and has many members, and all the members of the body, though many, are one body, so it is with Christ" (1 Cor. 12:12). At another occasion he claims:

> For as in one body we have many members, and all the members do not have the same function, so we, though many, are one body in Christ, and individually members one of another. Having gifts that differ according to the grace given to us, let us use them: if prophecy, in proportion to our faith; if service, in our serving; he who teaches, in his teaching; he who exhorts, in his exhortation; he who contributes, in liberality; he who gives aid, with zeal; he who does acts of mercy, with cheerfulness (Rom. 12:4-8).

Several items are evident from Paul's statement. Since all Christians are joined together, the individual Christian, a congregation, or even a denomination cannot act in whatever manner it pleases without potentially behaving destructively. An individual member can as easily bring discredit to the Christian faith as can an individual congregation, or a denomination. Many people are only waiting for a signal to put the blame for all kinds of evils indiscriminately on all Christians. When one Lutheran church body, for example, is torn by internal strife, this does not only grieve all Lutherans, but many people do not differentiate and blame all Lutherans for this sign of disunity. This is similar with other denominations as recent history has testified. Only in mutual consultation and respect can action be taken that is appropriate with representing Christ. Doing one's own thing is more often the sign of the sectarian than of the righteous. As the body imagery indicates, unity does not mean synonymity or uniformity. Each will act according to the individual gifts and the action required in a specific situation. Such coordination requires discipline and sensitivity, but it will not mean relinquishing one's individuality.

Similar to the clerics being commissioned to the exclusive service of furthering the kingdom, the lay members are also commissioned for the same purpose to fulfill individual tasks within their competency. Their pursuit of a secular profession does not mitigate against this, but will enhance their work, since it will specify and diversify their particular competency. Confronted with the world, they will share the general missionary and pastoral functions with their fellow Christians as the situation requires. They will proclaim the gospel in word and deed to non-Christians, they will teach as parents, administer the sacraments if necessary, listen to the confession of their fellow workers, and give exhortation and absolution. In their work within the church, however, the laity will contribute the skills they exhibit in the secular world, e.g. teachers as Sunday school teachers, banking personnel as financial secretaries, construction workers in building projects, etc. But they will also continue their general Christian duties within the church as the need arises, e.g., evangelism and stewardship projects, adult education, pre-school programs, etc. Beyond this there are special needs peculiar to every congregation, such as serving as ushers, acolytes, lectors, and perhaps preachers.

The laity does not compete with the clergy nor is it their back-up and support system. Laity and clergy cooperate and support each other. What should be remembered, however, is that the laity usually pursue secular professions and have not an extended formal theological education. Therefore their resources and theological expertise are usually limited. It is unrealistic and ill-advised to burden them with demands that require full-time or even part-time personnel or extensive theological training. The laity are not lesser clerics; they are Christians charged with the responsibility of witnessing in an alien world.

c. The called leaders

The ministers or priests are neither at the disposal of a certain congregation for tasks nobody else wants to tackle, nor are they professional Christians who get paid for what they believe. Usually ministers are paid by the congregation in whose midst and for whom they serve.

It is questionable whether a totally subsidized ministry should always be the rule. Especially in developing countries, a fully paid clergy, as a rule, does one of two things. It either imposes an exorbitant financial strain on the local congregations or it means keeping the salaries at such a low level that the pastor (and the pastor's family), though expected to devote full-time to the ministry, can hardly exist on the salary provided. As a consequence, there are only a few full-time and theologically trained pastors who supervise 15 to 30 Bible teachers or evangelists. This means, however, that the least theologically educated persons, the teachers and evangelists, have the primary teaching responsibility, while the better trained theologians perform most of the ritual and administrative functions. Of course, in most churches and denominations only ordained pastors are allowed to administer the sacraments, while everybody seems to be allowed to teach. This is especially prevalent in the American Sunday school system.

Yet such an assumption is not well-founded. For instance, the Augsburg Confession states that without being properly called nobody should teach publicly in the church (the public teaching is contrasted here against the teaching in the home which at the time of the Reformation was thought to be the prime duty of the father) or administer the sacraments (CA 14). Properly called was not understood to be confined to the call for an ordained priesthood. This becomes clear when we hear how important the call to the doctorate was for Luther amidst his temptations.[54] Luther also argued that those who are baptized are certainly entitled to be priests and bishops, though nobody should execute the functions going with these offices unless chosen and certified to do this by the Christian community.[55] This means that one cannot fulfill priestly functions indiscriminately wherever one wants. It was especially important to emphasize this over against the Enthusiasts who exercised their "priestly" functions wherever they felt the Spirit led them.

In this context it is also important that the Constitution on the Church of Vatican II declared: "Among the principal duties of bishop, the preaching of the gospel occupies an eminent place. For bishops are preachers of the faith who lead new disciples to Christ. They are authentic teachers, that is, teachers endowed with the authority of Christ."[56] The Roman Catholic Church puts the teaching function first and not the administrative or the ritual functions. Yet the Protestant churches usually claim to be the church of the word, i.e., teaching and preaching church. One must wonder, however, why in reality they value the teaching function so little, while the priestly function for which the words and motions are usually fairly well prescribed can only be exercised by those with the highest theological training.

We should also remember the early Christian custom according to which the deacons were allowed to administer the Communion to the shut-ins. Perhaps where circumstances do not allow for a sufficient number of well-trained pastors, but for a large number of enthusiastic and nearly unpaid evangelists, one might at least consider assigning to them functions for which fairly well-prescribed (liturgical) texts exist. The actual teaching function should then be reserved for pastors with sufficient theological training. This would alleviate the problem that due to the lack of "qualified" pastors in many developing countries, congregations are unable to participate in the sacraments on a frequent and regular basis.

Encountering the differentiation between the teaching, administrative, and cultic roles, we have already noticed that there is a graduation among the called leaders. This is true for any denominational organization, regardless of how high or low it views the role of the clergy. Whether one talks about the hierarchy of ministers, elders, and moderators, or one mentions the congregations, societies, conventions, and general councils, or one moves in a more traditional fashion between deacons, priests, bishops, and archbishops, we notice a hierarchy of jurisdiction and often also one of ordination.[57] In the Reformed and Roman Catholic traditions, the church structure and corresponding offices and clergy are derived from divine law as given in the biblical tradition. The free churches and the Lutherans, however, claim that the hierarchies are designed to facilitate cooperation among local churches.

While we can certainly claim divine institution for the existence of the leadership function in the Christian community, we have noticed that the New Testament does not present a clear order as to hierarchy or polity. It is not clearly spelled out who should preside over the administration of the sacraments or the proclamation of the word. But Paul especially reminds us repeatedly to do everything in orderly fashion and according to the tradition (received from the Lord). Within that directive of freedom it follows that the called leaders act in a truly leading way for whatever function they are called. Though usually only qualified persons are called to a certain office their authority is not derived from their qualifications. A leadership position should never result in the glorification of the leader, but in the leader's service to glorify Christ. The authority for any ecclesiastical office ultimately rests in Christ in whose name the office is administered. Therefore an office is never the office of a person, but of Christ whom a person serves in a certain capacity. For instance, we hear that Christ "gave us the ministry of reconciliation" (2 Cor. 5:18).

Since the officebearer serves and represents Christ, we could even speak of an identification of the called leader with Christ. According to Luke, Jesus told the disciples: "He who hears you hears me, and he who rejects you rejects me, and he who rejects me rejects him who sent me" (Luke 10:16). It would be wrong to infer from such a statement a special quality of the officebearer. Yet if someone wants to be true to one's calling one cannot but identify with that for which one stands. This means that one does not administer one's own church or one's own proclamation, but Christ's church and his proclamation. This also is the deeper meaning of liturgical vestments and of the habit of monks and nuns. They diminish as much as possible the emphasis on the individuals and make them as much as possible transparent for Christ in whose service these people function.

The called leaders administer Christ's gospel in his name and foster participation in and spreading of the redemptive news. The material limits of this function are given through the content of the gospel and not through one's own desires or opinions or through those to whom one ministers. The formal limits are defined through the specific location in which the ministry takes place. Since the call is always extended through a community of believers, one will always be sensitive to their needs and desires. But they always extend the call for Christ's sake and not on their own behalf. Their needs and desires must continuously be judged by the demands of the gospel. Thus a called leader of a certain Christian community can never let his/her calling be degraded to the point that he/she becomes an employer of that community. Of course, a call can be revoked when a certain situation no longer demands a called leader. A congregation can merge with another congregation and thereby a surplus of called leaders could ensue, or a called person through his/her conduct could act contrary to the exemplary lifestyle demanded in leadership positions.

Yet a call cannot be revoked just because the word of God preached by the leader is offensive to the church by all its implications. The question, however, must be asked whether it would not even be wise for a faithful servant to seek a call from a different location if the congregation now being served is no longer receptive to unbiased proclamation of the word of God. Perhaps a different leader would encounter less bias and could work more effectively. This does not imply a compromise of the office, but an exchange of the bearers of the office to insure continued faithfulness. The so-called leaders are much more interchangeable than the function or the office in which they serve.

The office and its function: It should be self-evident that the offices in the church should enhance and not detract from that which is the church. If the church is the body of Christ, a metaphor that Paul occasionally uses, or the community of saints, or the faithful who listen to the word of their Lord, as Luther mentioned in the Smalcald Articles, then the offices must be designed to enhance these basic characteristics. For instance, the Augsburg Confession asserts that to obtain such faith (that lives from the grace of God) God has instituted the office of teaching the gospel and administering the sacraments (CA 5). In the Lutheran tradition the office is basically considered as one which should not be divided into one office for preaching and teaching and another one for administering the sacraments.[58] The one office in turn has often been identified with the office and role of the pastor. The notion of the common priesthood of all believers notwithstanding, the laity often felt that it did not participate in this office except as a subject of ministry. That led to a deplorable inactivity of the laity in the traditionally Lutheran countries of Scandinavia and Germany.

The office finds its unity in Christ who is present in his church through word and sacrament. Christ's presence cannot be divided by claiming that the teaching aspect would be valued higher than the sacramental or vice versa. Both are manifestations of Christ and of God's grace. But the function of the office, even when it is united in one pastor as officebearer, does not exhaust itself with the narrowly conceived teaching and sacerdotal functions. One of the frequent observations of a conscientious pastor is that the multitude of demands on the office are much greater than the time available to exercise them properly. This means that the office, while in itself one, entails many different functions, since it represents Christ to the Christian community and to all humanity. To facilitate the greatest possible effectiveness of the office, certain functions are often specialized and staffed with specially qualified people.

Increasingly popular are the so-called multiple staff ministries in which one pastor is mainly responsible for the teaching function, another for worship and preaching, while a third concentrates on the counseling aspect of the ministry. This does not imply that there are three different offices, but the one office is in itself differentiated to maximize its proper functioning. Whether and how such specialization takes place is contingent upon the local needs and should not be determined in advance. The idea that certain specializations are divinely decreed, for instance, the distinction between the priestly office and the diaconate, does not always corroborate with the needs in a given area. For instance, the diaconate in the Roman Catholic Church assumes more and more functions of the priestly office, while still seen in a subservient role. The issue is compounded by a notable shortage of priests. While people often are deprived of the presence of a priest, the deacon is still not allowed to administer his place. Yet we should assert that all Christians participate in the one office through which faith in God's love is acquired. On the other side, the Protestant emphasis on the full-time, ordained ministerial office quite often did away with a gradation of service, such as deacons and deaconesses, subdeacons, etc. To be actively involved in the affairs of the church, one often has no other choice but to aspire the ordained ministry.

It is the special function of the laity to witness in the name of Christ wherever they live. Through their baptism they are authorized to share Christ with their families and neighbors through word and deed. Yet such witness remains individual and private unless they are properly set apart to full-time or even part-time evangelistic witness or a teaching ministry (e.g., Sunday School). A called leader is not exempt from this private role either as a father or mother. Yet due to the call to a particular office, the leader assumes a public witnessing function through word, action, and administration of the sacraments. The reason why the administration of the sacraments is, with the exception of emergency cases, reserved for called leaders is not that these are holy functions and can only be performed by holy people.[59] Yet such ideas are still advocated, for instance, when in some churches women are not ordained or are excluded from administering the Lord's Supper.

We remember, that similar to baptism, the Lord's Supper and, in the Roman Catholic tradition the other sacraments too, have a public aspect. We do not celebrate the Lord's Supper when we witness to our neighbors or when we conduct family devotions. Called leaders are the public representatives of the congregation beyond individual and internal matters. To emphasize the church's oneness, its corporate nature, and its joint witness to the world, the representative teaching and sacerdotal office dare not be taken lightly. Wherever this priestly office was downplayed, as in American denominationalism and in certain segments of the so-called Free Church Movement, the unity of the church suffered at the expense of sectarian individualism, and often self-serving idiosyncrasies emerged. Yet the teaching and sacerdotal office dare not be divorced from the common priesthood of all believers. When this happened, as for instance in the Roman Catholic Church or in segments of the so-called state churches, the church became synonymous with its leaders and therefore void of active and meaningful lay participation. In order to clarify the function and status of the so-called leaders, we will now briefly investigate the call to the office.

Character of the call to the office: The call to the office is always a mediated one, extended on behalf of the Lord of the church, but actualized through representatives of the institutional church. The subjective moment, which the one who is called by God feels, is clearly secondary to the fact that one is called by the church on behalf of Christ. Similarly, the laity is called to its apostolate through the visible sign of baptism. Being called by the visible church ensures that one stands in the context of the church and in the living tradition.

Since the called leaders are called on behalf of Christ, the notion of an apostolic succession as prevalent in the Roman Catholic Church and in the Anglican tradition can be misleading. We have seen that the apostles exercised a unique and vital role in the first Christian communities. They preserved the living memory of the early Jesus, a role which could not be handed on. But insofar as they were sharers in the responsibility—next to the leaders—of proclaiming the message of reconciliation, "establishing churches and building them up in the apostolic faith, their ministry had to be continued." [60] Thus our ministry must be seen in succession to the apostolic ministry, but not to the singular status of the apostles. It would therefore be better to talk about a material or doctrinal succession, in the sense of the truthfulness of the church, instead of a formal or historical succession depicting an unbroken line of tradition.

The setting apart for the called leaders is already practiced in Old Testament times. According to Numbers 11:16f. Moses is commanded by Yahweh to choose among the elders of Israel seventy people who are to share with him the burden of guiding Israel. Consequently they received the Lord's Spirit that rested upon Moses and they assumed leadership and prophesied. Similarly, we hear in Deuteronomy 34:9 that Joshua "was full of the spirit of wisdom, for Moses had laid his hands upon him; so the people of Israel obeyed him and did as the Lord had commanded Moses." Rabbinic Judaism saw in the installation of Joshua through Moses the paradigm for the relationship between teacher and disciple.[61] In Jewish understanding there existed an uninterrupted chain of the spirit of wisdom which had been handed on from Moses to later scribes.

In pre-Christian Judaism a scribe ordained a disciple publicly to the duties and privileges of a rabbi. Prerequisite was the knowledge of exegesis and the understanding and application of tradition. Ordination was a juridicial act, and a handing on of wisdom. It also was a singular act and could not be repeated. Once ordained, the title *rabbi* could be used and binding decisions could be made concerning the teaching of the law. Especially from the end of the second century A.D. onward the Sanhedrin made the selection from among the candidates and the patriarch conducted the ordination. This move was intended to eliminate unqualified students who would explain the law incorrectly. But in the fifth century, ordinations ceased completely, perhaps because the practice had now been adopted by Christianity.[62] The ordained scribes were the bearers of tradition which was handed on from generation to generation.

Though there is no specific Greek equivalent to the term "ordination" we have a few cases of the laying on of hands in the New Testament that are analogous to Jewish ordination. They are different from other cases of laying on of hands in the New Testament, for instance to heal, to bless, or to hand on the spirit. In Mark 7:32 Jesus was asked to lay his hand upon someone who was deaf and had a speech impediment. In Mark 10:16 we read that Jesus laid his hands upon the children and blessed them. And in Acts 19:6 Paul laid his hands upon the disciples of John and they received the Holy Spirit. While the sending of Barnabas and Saul can still be understood in analogy to the Jewish custom of sending out apostles (Acts 13:1-13), we are fairly safe in assuming that the appointment of the seven (deacons) resembles an ordination ceremony (Acts 6:1-6).[63]

In contrast to Jewish practice, the early Christian ordination is accompanied by prayers (Acts 6:6).[64] It is significant that in Acts 6 the congregation chose the ones to be ordained while the apostles ordained them and laid on them their hands. Another case of ordination is presented in the pastoral epistles with reference to Timothy. Though it is not clear whether he is ordained by presbyters or apostles, we read that he is selected through prophetic voices.[65] In front of many witnesses he receives a brief summary of apostolic teaching and he is instructed to faithful service under a solemn confession.[66] Through the laying on of hands by the apostles or presbyters, or perhaps by both, he is ordained. He is also empowered by God with the gifts commensurate with his task. Timothy's work points in the direction of congregational leadership (1 Tim. 1:3), to ordain other leaders (1 Tim. 5:22), to guard the truth entrusted to him (2 Tim. 1:14), lead the worship service (1 Tim. 4:13), and enforce the discipline in the congregation (1 Tim. 5:1f.).

The basic structure of ordination has not changed since the New Testament times, nor the basic demands on the called leadership. Ordination is done under the laying on of hands by leaders who are themselves ordained. Scripture readings and prayers assume an important place in the rite. The service is always public, with the participation of the assembled congregation. One is also never ordained per se but is ordained only for a specific call and service. Ordination is a liturgical act by which one is incorporated into a certain office and enabled to obtain the juridicial and spiritual power that allows one to administer the rites and duties connected with the office. Often there are certain hierarchical levels of ordination, as in the Roman Catholic Church where one is ordained subdeacon, deacon, or priest, to name just a few of its hierarchical levels.

The Roman Catholic Church at the Council of Trent even speaks of ordination as having a spiritual and indelible character.[67] Yet the Roman Catholic Church saw this sign only pertaining to this life, but not as having eternal significance. The idea behind the elevated status of the priest is the fear that the Reformers had obliterated the distinction between priesthood and laity. But at Vatican II the Roman Catholic Church rediscovered that though the ordained is set apart from the congregation, he is not separated from them who still remain his brothers and sisters.[68] Yet ordination is still considered a unique event, and a priest is not ordained twice.

A certain openness toward a more functional and role-oriented aspect emerges. We are told that "there is nothing to prevent the Church freeing a priest temporarily or permanently from the obligations of his ordination to return him to the condition and life of the laity."[69] The indelible character seems to last only as long as the priest fulfills his priestly position. The priestly character is indelible in the sense that he is a priest not only when he performs a certain ceremony, but is also a priest when he is on vacation. Yet once the priestly call is discontinued, the character no longer adheres. Thus we cannot speak of a strictly ontological but rather a functional understanding of ordination. This is reinforced by the understanding that ordination to the priesthood is a sacrament. However, that sacramental grace conveyed is identical to the fundamental grace of justification. The grace conveyed through ordination is understood as a

> deepening and a re-orientation of baptismal grace in view of the specific mission and service of the priest. It thus allows for the development of a truly priestly spirituality, fundamentally identical with that of the rest of the faithful in the brotherhood of the same faith. This grace also unites the priest to the other members of his order in the brotherhood of their common mission.[70]

One cannot but notice the implicit tension contained in this statement, while it asserts the fundamental unity of all faithful and it insists on a special "truly priestly spirituality."

We find the same tension in the Lutheran position. On the one hand, the emphasis is on the priesthood of all believers. Yet then we hear that in ordination a special blessing, the gift of the Holy Spirit, is imparted to the ordinand.[71] The Reformed tradition is perhaps the most informal, since it conceives of a plurality of offices which can be conferred on someone and can also be taken away. Therefore the Reformed do not regard ordination as conferring a habitual status, but it simply designates someone to a functional role. The Anglican communion surpasses the Lutheran on the other side. Importance is given there to apostolic succession where one is ordained through a bishop who is in that succession. In recent years this formalistic continuity has received more positive attention by the Roman Catholic Church. Most members of the Orthodox community and the Old Catholic Church even accept the Anglican ordination and ministry as valid.[72]

The most hopeful sign amid the still existing differences as to the ministerial office is not found in comparing traditions, but in returning to the biblical documents that engender this ministry. We might realize which emphases find support in Scripture and where we have gone astray, inventing a tradition of our own liking. We have noticed to our surprise that the New Testament witness is far from unanimous when it comes to church order and organization. Also very little is said in the New Testament as to how the leaders were appointed and what the requirements were for presiding over the Eucharist. The various lines of succession claimed by the early church are more necessary to combat heretics than to reflect historic realities. Thus there is a growing tendency to interpret the episcopal succession as an effective means, but not a guarantee, of the continuity of the church in apostolic faith and mission.[73]

The continuity in faith, mission, and ministry is being recognized in churches which have not retained the historic episcopacy. Even Roman Catholics suggest today that "treatment of the apostolic succession of the whole community should be given precedence over treatment of hierarchical succession."[74] The formal matter of a strictly apostolic succession is more and more seen as secondary to the apostolicity of doctrine in a given church. Once the apostolicity of doctrine is established, it also makes sense to look at the apostolicity of ministry.[75]

Significance of Ordination: When we finally consider the significance of ordination we must remember that, like any other ritual in the church, ordination is an act conducted on behalf of Christ. Since ordination is Christ-centered, there is a unity of call, blessing, and sending. Christ causes readiness for ordination, he calls to ordination through the Spirit, and he blesses the ordained. Since the Holy Spirit is already received through baptism it seems redundant to expect that the Spirit is received again in ordination. Yet it is good to reaffirm the presence of the Spirit in the ordained.

Since the Spirit is undivided, it is unthinkable that a special spirit of the office would be conveyed. Since Christ places the ordained into a special leadership service, we should rather assume that the grace to meet the demands of this office is asked for at ordination. Since the leadership office is a necessary one, we could expect that Christ gives us this grace. But we meet the demand in free responsibility and not as puppets. The history of the church has shown us that ordination does not guarantee proper fulfillment of the functions of the office. Occasionally people may be ordained who are unfit or become unfit for exercising the ministerial office. To minimize this danger and to take ordination seriously, and not to regard it as an automatic qualification ritual, the church has always insisted on adequate preparation of the ordained on a spiritual, intellectual, and practical level. This implies adequate physical and mental health, and an adequate reputation. The person who is ordained should be of such quality that the church can expect that his/her ordination will further the spreading of the gospel and not impede it or leave it at a standstill.

These considerations are of prime importance for the ordination of women. With reference to 1 Cor. 14:34 ("The women should keep silence in the churches"), Luther remarked that one should certainly obey this teaching of Paul. "If, however, only women were present and no men, as in nunneries, then one of the women might be authorized to preach."[76] Since some Roman Catholic scholars now even admit that "exegetically there is no compelling argument for the exclusion of woman from office", the ordination of women need no longer be a theological issue that divides us, but primarily a practical and ethical point of concern.[77] If the ordination of women does not hinder or slow down the spreading of the gospel and the recognition of Christian unity, such a move is certainly in accordance with Scripture.

We have noticed that Luther followed the reasoning of Paul, insisting that women should not assume public teaching office (in the church). Yet he allowed for exceptions from this rule, if they would enhance the effectiveness of the pastoral office. Analogous reasoning seems appropriate in our deliberations of the ordination of women. Prime concern should not be given to the sociological shift from a patriarchal to a more egalitarian society, or to the public acceptance of women in a variety of "nontraditional" roles. Also the arguments from a "natural" law basis that women are not fitting for the pastoral office since Jesus was male, are not convincing. The new creation that Christian baptism promises applies to both men and women, and even to children. The argument in favor of the ordination of women by claiming that the ministerial office needs female ministers to be whole and complete again misses the point that this office must be seen in functional basis, and not as being endowed with an ontological quality. The office is whole and complete by its very institution. Whether the administrators of this office are equally whole and balanced is a different question. Yet we must also remember that the efficacy of the functions does not depend on the worthiness of the administrator.

The question that must be addressed here is primarily a functional one: Does the ordination of women enhance the effectiveness of the pastoral office? Though an answer to this question can hardly be given in advance, it is too early to answer it from a wide variety of data. Apart from the full and equal involvement of women in ministry, there are some areas, however, in which ordained women might provide a decided complement to an all male ministry, e.g., ministering to women and to single parents, and certain institutional functions. In many Protestant denominations the problem of an exclusively male clergy is compounded by the fact that there are no intermediate ranks (deacon, monastic orders, etc.). If one wants to be significantly involved in the affairs of the church, one has then no choice but to seek the ordained ministry.

Ordination is always an act of the worshiping community on behalf of its Lord. This means that ordination cannot occur in secret but must have the approval of the worshiping community which extends the call. The church therefore stands behind the ordained in its support and encouragement. The ordained is entrusted with the gospel and is in succession of the Christian tradition as represented in the church. By ordaining someone, the community sets apart that person to the office of acting on behalf of God. It is not an office that includes certain privileges and liberties, but that carries the duty of continuing Christ's mission to lead and care for his people. While ordination is conditional upon certain prerequisites, it does not depend upon one's own worthiness. It is ultimately the will of God that is expressed in the ordination.

Finally ordination is closely connected with installation, i.e., the designation to a certain task. In contrast to ordination, the installation is repeated with each new task and is usually of limited duration, occasionally even for a period specified in advance (especially administrative offices). An installation recognizes the specific place within the ministerial office that is to be served. It presupposes an agreement on the specific function, place, range of duties, and remuneration, if any, that the particular call involves. It is performed publicly with participation of the congregation in whose midst the services will be performed. Installation, however, is not primarily for ordained ministers, but also for lay workers, such as Sunday School teachers, acolytes, ushers, and altar guild, choir members, and for many other officers. By subsuming laity and clergy under the aspect of installation we notice again that the service aspect of the Christian life is not fundamentally different for the laity or the professional leadership. The call to serve is different in range and in authority, but not in quality.

After our brief survey of the whole people of God in their community and leadership aspects, we must now turn to that which is of ultimate concern and centrality to the life of the people of God, namely the pronouncement of law and gospel and the administration of the sacraments.

2. The pronouncement of law and gospel

One may wonder why such a Lutheran term as law and gospel should be introduced here as being central to the Christian community.[78] The word of God which is preserved in the Christian community, and which encounters us in the church's doctrine and proclamation basically assumes one of three functions. It either judges and condemns us, or it frees and affirms us, or it guides us. The first of these three forms can easily be classified as law, the second as gospel, and the third can be associated with either one of the two. The distinction between law and gospel is not synonymous with the distinction between the Old Testament law and the gospel of Jesus Christ. The distinction between law and gospel is founded in a diametrically opposed perception and reaction to the word of God. Therefore we see a basic unity in the opposition between law and gospel.

a. Basic unity and opposition between law and gospel

The law has basically a two-fold function within humanity, a civil and a theological function. According to the civil function, God preserves his creation and prevents its decay and universal chaos. This implies that the law is universally known to all people. This view has been held in the natural law tradition and has recently received renewed attention by behavioral scientists who argue that the basic norms of moral behavior are common to all societies, human and even nonhuman.[79]

For the law to preserve public peace according to the civil use, it must be known by Christians, Jews, and pagans alike. Such common knowledge is indeed the stance that seems to be advocated by the New Testament. For instance, Paul mentions that

> When Gentiles who have not the law do by nature what the law requires, they are a law to themselves, even though they do not have the law. They show that what the law requires is written on their hearts, while their conscience also bears witness and their conflicting thoughts accuse or perhaps excuse them on that day when, according to my gospel, God judges the secrets of men by Christ Jesus (Rom. 2:14f.).

Paul does not say here that the pagans know the law which was given to the Jews. While they do not have the law, given to the Jews at Mount Sinai, they have something analogous to it and must be as responsive and responsible to this as the Jews are to Torah.[80] The pagans do not know the divine will from the Torah, but from that which is inscribed in their hearts.

Luther especially claims on the basis of Romans 2:14 that if God had never given the written law through Moses, our human spirit would still know by nature that we should worship God and love our neighbor.[81] From the beginning of the world, Luther argues in his disputes with the antinomians, the decalogue has been inscribed in the mind of humanity.[82]

> Therefore there is one law which runs through all ages, is known to all men, is written in the hearts of all people, and leaves no one from beginning to end with an excuse, although for the Jews ceremonies were added and the other nations had their own laws, which were not binding upon the whole world, but only this one, which the Holy Spirit dictates unceasingly in the hearts of all.[83]

The natural law which is largely concomitant with the law of Moses is distinguished from the positive law of the country and the Jewish ceremonial law. Luther does not admit full equality between the law of Moses and the natural law which prevails in other places. Moses, though not originator of the natural law, interprets and clarifies it. Luther therefore states that "it is clearly and well summarized at Mount Sinai and in a better way than by the philosophers." [84]

According to Luther and his interpretation of the New Testament tradition, the law inscribed in the hearts of all people is not just synonymous with the first, the civil use of the law. Since the law is expressive of God's will and since all people are in some way or other religious beings, the presence of the law as attested by Romans 2:15f., also fulfills a theological function. As the eternal expression of God's will, the law is present in the human conscience, and serves as a reminder of his will. It reminds us of our alienation from God and shows us that we do not live as we ought. Through alienation from God this second, theological or convicting, use of the law is often not clearly expressed outside the Judeo-Christian tradition. Since everyone can at least in part know God's will, there is no excuse for not living up to the law.

Paul tells us that the "Law came in, to increase the trespass" (Rom. 5:20). Such an assertion sounds strange! Would God give the law in this second (theological) sense in order to evoke sin and to let it develop all its power? There certainly was sin before one was explicitly confronted with the law. But, as Jesus shows in the Sermon on the Mount, quite often the transgressions against the law were made unconsciously. Thus sin lay dormant. Yet God wants sin exposed through the law and perceived for what it really is, revolt against God.[85] In this sense sin is increased and sharpened. The more conscientiously we attempt to fulfill the will of God, the more we realize our shortcomings and discover our immense sinfulness. That which was originally designed as a sign of God's love and care, his will, becomes a sign of our despair and of God's wrath.

The law sharpens our conscience and shows us that we are in a hopeless predicament. For instance, Paul admits in despair: "For I know that

nothing good dwells within me, that is, in my flesh. I can will what is
right, but I cannot do it. For I do not do the good I want, but the evil
I do not want is what I do" (Rom. 7:18f.). Luther rightly recognized
that the law constantly accuses us; it delivers us to God's wrath, to judgment, and eternal death.[86] The exclusive emphasis on the law leads to
condemnation instead of salvation. Yet Luther also emphasized that whoever does not wish the law to be preached refuses to hear the truth of God.
While the law accuses us, the law also moves us to seek grace. Supported
by Augustine, and similar to Luther, Calvin argues in his *Institutes* that
the accusing law makes us ask for God's grace.[87] Grace encounters us in
God's redemptive work in Christ.

Paul continues the statement that law came in to increase the trespass
by saying: "But where sin increased, grace abounded all the more, so that,
as sin reigned in death, grace also might reign through righteousness to
eternal life through Jesus Christ our Lord" (Rom. 5:20f.). In his letter
to the Galatians, Paul even states that "Christ redeemed us from the curse
of the law, having become a curse for us" (Gal. 3:13). The law leads and
urges us towards Christ. The same is expressed when Paul calls the law
"our custodian until Christ came" (Gal. 3:24). The law as tutor or governor, as the term custodian can also be translated, kept us under tutelage
and the yoke until we were released into freedom through Christ.[88]
Through Christ we recognize that the law is not God's entire word and
the whole content of the Christian proclamation. The gospel stands alongside the law.

Both law and gospel have very different functions. The law meets us
in God's place, demanding that something be done and forbidding the
doing of something else. It accuses and condemns us because we have
failed to live up to God's will. The gospel, however, proclaims that God's
will has been met in Christ. It shows us the God who meets us in Christ
and tells us that he is a gracious God who has forgiven us our sins. Paul
expresses this eloquently when he says: "But now the righteousness of
God has been manifested apart from law, although the law and the
prophets bear witness to it" (Rom. 3:21). God's righteousness has been
manifested through the historical occurrence of Jesus Christ. God can
now be perceived as wanting the redemption of his people and not their
destruction.

The gospel of redemption is not confined to the Christ event though it
best comes to expression there. Paul reminds us that "the law and the
prophets bear witness to it." This means that the Old Testament already

testifies to the gracious love of God which culminates in the life and destiny of Christ.[89] Karl Barth seems to have perceived this insight in his famous 1935 paper, "Gospel and Law." Barth assures us that he does not intend to reverse the traditional order of law and gospel, but by changing the sequence, he hopes to demonstrate that "the law is in the Gospel, comes from the Gospel and is directed to the Gospel." [90] If we are going to find out what the law is, we must first of all know about the gospel, and not vice versa.

According to Barth, God's word contains both law and gospel. Since the law is God's manifest will, we have access to it only where it comes loudly and audibly to us, in Jesus Christ.[91] "When we see here the will of God being done, when, that is, we see his grace in action, the law is manifested to us." When we perceive God's grace, we realize what the law actually demands. "The law, then, is in the Gospel as the tables of Sinai were in the ark of the covenant." [92] Barth can even say that "the law is nothing else than the necessary form of the Gospel, whose content is grace." This reminds us somewhat of Augustine when he defined evil as both a deficiency of the good and a necessary ingredient that helps us to perceive the good ever more clearly. But Barth reverses the process, now the goodness of the gospel makes us realize our depravity and sinfulness so that we cling to the gospel. Barth even defines the law as the form of the gospel, since it bears witness to the gospel.[93] He claims that the sequence of law and then gospel is only legitimate if we would first look at Christ who reveals himself through the law as our Savior. Knowing that Christ affirms God's valid but misused law, we perceive our shortcoming and flee to God's grace revealed in Christ who fulfills the demands of the law.[94] For Barth the proper order actually is gospel-law-gospel instead of law-gospel.

Barth has recognized that we only gain a clear vision of the law if we preach the word of God as law and gospel which both Old and New Testament contain. While the order of law-gospel may leave the impression that it is synonymous with the succession of Old and New Testament, the order gospel-law-gospel is even more misleading. It obscures the fact that law and gospel are the same word of God. One cannot divide God's word in statements that contain law and others that contain gospel. The law or gospel character of God's word depends on how it meets us, as condemnation or confirmation. If we would envelop God's demand in his grace, the word would lose its seriousness and we would be in danger of offering cheap grace. Luther was right when he said that the proclamation of the law is the indispensable and necessary presupposition for the preaching of the gospel.[95] Without the law we do not recognize our own deficiency and remain secure and proud of our moral capacity. In this way the law is God's alien work that opens for us the necessity and appreciation of the gospel as God's proper work. Though certainly opposite in their functions, law and gospel are the same word of God.

The term law, as used in the distinction between law and gospel, is not identical with the Law, meaning the Pentateuch, or with the Old Testament. The term gospel in the same distinction is also not synonymous with the proclamation of Jesus or the New Testament kerygma. Law and gospel are two different functions of the same word of God, the accusing and the liberating one.

b. The significance of the law for the Christian

At Jesus' time many people had turned the word of God into a series of human regulations to assure that they were righteous before God and his law. This was the situation that Jesus addressed in the Sermon on the Mount and at many other occasions. The same attitude is prevalent today with many people who are only nominally in contact with the Christian gospel. They lead ethically virtuous lives, assuming that this life-style, though short of perfection, will ultimately be met with divine approval. The German poet Johann Wolfgang von Goethe summed up well this sentiment when he declared in his dramatic poem, *Faust*: "Who e'er aspiring, struggles on, for him there is salvation."[96] This understanding of the law portrayed here, will ultimately enslave people, since it suggests that they are righteous, though they are not. People become enslaved to ethical principles, such as the greatest good for the greatest number of people, or freedom and equality for the underprivileged, instead of responding to the personal will of God. Often these self-righteous attempts lead to the establishing of new barriers of injustice and inequality. Law divorced from the gospel can easily turn into a self-serving and self-justifying philosophy.

Since people sin by focusing their attention on the law instead of on God himself, should we then follow Barth's advice and call for repentance by referring to Christ, the Son of God incarnate? Here Luther reminds us that repentance can be induced by preaching Christ's cross as well as Moses' Law.[97] We are brought to repentance when God's word encounters us as his law and not as our self-designed plan. It leads us to repentance by meeting us as a demand and making us recognize our shortcomings.

According to Luther, one of the places where God's demanding word can meet us is in the Lord's Prayer. Each of the petitions is perceived as a demand that reminds us of our imperfection. But the same word of God can also encounter us as gospel. For example, Luther assures us that there is much gospel contained in the first commandment, since God there promises us his faithfulness. We are reminded here that the Old Testament law also originally served as gospel, as the pledge of God's faithfulness to which the Israelites were asked to respond.

The same word of God can meet us as law or gospel, as demand or as promise. There is, however, an irreversible movement from law to gospel. If we grasp the gospel in faith we are convinced and know God's acceptance. The condemnation and the accusing function of the law have vanished. The law is replaced by the gospel and we recognize that God has assumed entirely different features. He is no longer the righteous God who demands compliance with his will, but a gracious God who for Christ's sake forgives us our noncompliance. His alien work in the accusing function of the law has been changed to his proper work, the liberating power of the gospel. Such understanding, of course, leads to the question whether the law still has any significance for the Christian.

If Christ is the end of the law, as Paul claims, then the law is abrogated for the justified insofar as it makes demands on them, or accuses and condemns them. Christ, however, did not abolish the law but fulfilled it. Through Christ God's will for us has been accomplished vicariously. But the law has not lost its validity for us as God's will. If it had, we would no longer be sinners but justified only.

Calvin claims that there is a third use of the law. "The third and principal use, which pertains more closely to the proper purpose of the law, finds its place among believers in whose hearts the Spirit of God already lives and reigns."[98] This was also the line of thinking which was taken by Melanchthon, the Lutheran Book of Concord, and the theologians of Lutheran Orthodoxy. In backing this third use of the law (for the regenerate) with quotations from the Bible, Calvin adduces primarily texts from the Old Testament. For instance, he quotes the Psalmist saying: "Thy word is a lamp to my feet and a light to my path" (Ps. 119:105). Or at another place: "The law of the Lord is perfect, reviving the soul" (Ps. 19:7).

Certainly the lives of Christians need moral directives and guidelines; Christians need to hear God's will to order their lives. Yet once we are confronted with the gospel, once we understand the full implications of

God's gracious will, our response does not come from pressure and coax-
ing; instead Christians conform freely to God's will. Christians live up
to the law, not because it is demanded but because they love God and
appreciate his righteousness.[99] This means that not even the Old Testament Law can be labeled appropriately as law. For instance, the Ten
Commandments are introduced not by claiming: This is what God
demands, but: This is what God has done for you. They begin with the
reminder of what God has done for Israel: "I am the Lord your God, who
brought you out of the land of Egypt, out of the house of bondage" (Exod.
20:2). The commandment to love one's neighbor is introduced in a similar
way when we hear: You shall love your neighbor as yourself: I am the
Lord" (Lev. 19:18). Because God is so gracious, we are responding by
transferring his love to our neighbor. This shows that even in the Old Testament God's word was originally intended as gospel. It illustrates what
kind of God we have and evokes our response, a response freely given.

    The justified seek and do the will of God. This means we must acknowl-
edge the existence of commandments in the Bible that serve as guiding
moral directives.[100] It would be potentially misleading, however, to regard
them as law. They do not depict the legal and accusing use of the law,
but its evangelical use of the divine command.[101] They do not originate
from the demand "you shall in order to . . . ," but from the offer "you may
because . . ." They are guidelines to meet the will of God and not a set
of legal devices to assure a righteous life.

    In contrast to the law-oriented existence of many people, the Christian
life is an oscillating existence. Christians do not suddenly find themselves
beyond the possibility of sinning in the state of the redeemed. Paul indicates with his frequent use of imperatives, that the redeemed Christian
existence remains marked by sin. The Christian existence has often been
described as one of sinner and justified at the same time.[102] Being a Christian is not a matter of possession, but of continuous struggle. Justification
before God does not induce an ontological change. Justification is rather
indicative of our relationship to God which, of course, is subject to change.
This does not mean that Christians are sitting on the edge of a sword
always in danger of falling off the thin edge. Christians can and do lapse
into sin. God's word then again becomes law, driving them back to the
gospel. This is one of the reasons why even in the Christian community
the proclamation of the gospel alone does not suffice. As justified, Christians live without the law, but as sinners they live under the law. The law
drives the sinner back to a gracious God who forgives and encourages.

The cutting of our relationship with God is never a bilateral action. God never severs the ties to his people. We stay and remain Christians, even as lapsed ones. The promise of the gospel does not become void—like the threat of the law—once we turn our back on it. God's gracious word always stands. As Christians we do not live under God's thumb. We are called to freedom as sons and daughters of God. This freedom is not unlimited. However, its limits are not in demands that are beyond fulfillment but rather in orders and guidelines that allow us to live in a "responsive responsibility." Walter Kaspar recaptured well Luther's insistence on the distinction between law and gospel when he said: Law and gospel "is regarded as the distinctive feature of the Chritsian faith as contrasted not only with Judaism but also with all pagan religions, with philosophy, ethics, and the like." [103]

c. Pronouncement of absolution

The pronouncement of law and gospel assumes a peculiar form in the office of the keys, also known as confession and absolution. While the Roman Catholic tradition considers penance a sacrament which includes the office of the keys and the action of confession and absolution, Lutherans see it closely associated with a sacrament but do not actually consider it as one. For instance, in the Augsburg Confession, penitence is located after baptism and Holy Communion. In Luther's Small Catechism penitence is placed after baptism and before the Lord's Supper, indicating a close connection between it and the two sacraments without admitting that it is an actual sacrament. Melanchthon in his Apology of the Augsburg Confession states that penitence is one of three sacraments. [104] In the Calvinist tradition, however, confession and absolution is not considered a sacrament. [105]

While we do not want to pursue at this point what constitutes a sacrament it is evident that confession and absolution are intimately connected with the proclamation of law and gospel as the one word of God. The main passages in the New Testament that undergird the function and office of the keys are in the Gospel according to Matthew. For instance, in connection with the word to Peter that on this rock Jesus will build his church, we hear: "I will give you the keys of the kingdom of heaven, and whatever you bind on earth shall be bound in heaven, and whatever you loose on earth shall be loosed in heaven" (Matt. 16:19). Binding and loosing on earth means here exclusion from and acceptance into the Christian community. In the Gospel of John this function is no longer restricted to Peter and is also understood more theologically as remission of sins. So we hear Jesus say to his disciples: "Receive the Holy Spirit. If you forgive the sins of any, they are forgiven; if you retain the sins of any, they are retained" (John 20:22f.).[106] That the Christian community, or at least the twelve, understood themselves to succeed Peter in the office of the keys is obvious from Matthew 18:18 where the function of the office is extended to a wider circle. Now Jesus is referred to as saying to his disciples: "Truly, I say to you, whatever you bind on earth shall be bound in heaven, and whatever you loose on earth shall be loosed in heaven."

The so-called office of the keys is intimately connected with the proclamation of the word of God. This is indicated by the parallel between the consequences of not listening to God's word and of not receiving forgiveness of sins. When Jesus sent out the disciples he admonished them: "And if any one will not receive you or listen to your words, shake off the dust from your feet as you leave that house or town. Truly, I say to you, it shall be more tolerable on the day of judgment for the land of Sodom and Gomorrah than for that town" (Matt. 10:14f.). Thus the proclamation determines life or death, and those who are charged with proclamation shall symbolize this by shaking off the dust from their feet as the sign that they have separated themselves from those who rejected God's word. The proclamation of God's word has eternal significance and those entrusted with it should make that known to their listeners. The office of the keys then results from the pronouncement of the one word of God, law and gospel. Response to God's word has eternal importance. Those who administer the keys are empowered to make these consequences known, by absolving the listeners or leaving them in their sins. Consequently God's word is experienced as condemning or liberating.

Since penance is inextricably connected with the word of God, those who handle the word's public proclamation should also handle the use of penance. This logic is especially well followed in the Roman Catholic Church. Similar to the hierarchical teaching order, we encounter there a hierarchical order for administering varying degrees of penance. Yet the office of the keys should never be considered a purely juridicial matter, but exercised on behalf of God who issues the word that gives life or death. Contrary to past use, the office of the keys is not a convenient means to enforce ecclesial decisions. It is handled representatively in the exclusive authority of the Lord of the church, but not in the name of the leaders he appointed.

Since proclamation and penitence go hand in hand, the church soon realized that the one-time forgiving of sins in baptism was not sufficient. There is a necessity for continuous forgiving of sins. This is most clearly expressed in the explanation of baptism in the Small Catechism where Luther says: "The old Adam in us, together with all sins and evil lusts, should be drowned by daily sorrow and repentance and be put to death, and that the new man shall come forth daily and rise up, cleansed and righteous, to live forever in God's presence." [107] Confession and absolution must be a daily process, not confined to special occasions when one has committed especially grave sins. This is apparent from the first of Luther's Ninety-five Theses: "When our Lord and Master Jesus Christ said, 'Repent' (Matt. 4:17), he willed the entire life of believers be one of repentance." [108]

As with the third use of the law a similar question emerges with penitence. Is it proper to distinguish three parts in the confessional process, contrition, confession, and satisfaction, as the Roman Catholic tradition teaches, or shall we side with the Lutheran tradition that sees contrition and confession as sufficient (CA 11 and 12)? [109] It is significant that Luther rejects in his Ninety-five Theses only the clergy-imposed satisfaction, while insisting that "inner repentance is worthless unless it produces various outward mortifications of the flesh." [110] There is certainly no law that can spell out in each case what kind of restitution must be made. Since we are unable to reverse history, a sinful act can never be completely undone. Only God who set history into motion and has it under his control can effect restitution in the true sense. There is no doubt, however, that the one who receives forgiveness needs ethical guidance, showing how to respond properly to the grace freely received. Satisfaction should never become a new law or a demand, but an opportunity to restore that part of God's creation which we willfully impaired in our sinful activities.[111] Where this opportunity is not grasped, Luther is right that even the most convincing "inner repentance is worthless."

Even as a freeing word, God's word cannot be taken lightly. God's word asks for our response as new beings, a response expressive of our newly found union with God. That the word of God is not automatically a liberating word underscores the utmost seriousness of the penitential process. It might even be necessary that so-called church sanctions be imposed on the unrepentant sinner. Yet such sanctions, such as exclusion from certain offices or activities of the Christian community, should always be administered to benefit the punished. The movement from law to grace should be at the core of such a sanction. Though they should never be administered too quickly, sanctions dare not be considered relics of medieval authoritarianism. Ultimately they are an offer of the gospel through the administration of the law. God is a God of grace, who does not let the sinners run into their self-inflicted punishment, but he punishes sinners, that they may amend their ways and be saved.

3. Administration of the sacraments

The sacraments are an essential part of the church. The Augsburg Confession, for instance, states that the church "is the assembly of all believers among whom the Gospel is preached in its purity and the holy sacraments are administered according to the Gospel" (CA 7).

a. Nature of sacraments and their relation to God's word

There seems to be wide disagreement on what a sacrament is or even the number of sacraments. The Heidelberg Catechism states that sacraments "are visible, holy signs and seals instituted by God in order that by their use he may the more fully disclose and seal to us the promise of the gospel" (Ques. 66). When we ask how many sacraments there are, the commentary to the answer declares: "The Reformed Church recognizes only two sacraments: Baptism and the Lord's Supper, those which have been instituted by Jesus Christ" (Ques. 68). The decisive point from which to approach the two sacraments is not the institution by God, as Question 66 makes us believe, but by Jesus Christ. Similarly, we hear in the Augsburg Confession that "the sacraments were instituted not only to be signs by which people might be identified outwardly as Christians, but that they are signs and testimonies of God's will toward us for the purpose of awakening and strengthening of our faith" (CA 13). When only two sacraments are introduced, Luther too refers to them as "instituted by Christ." [112] When Melanchthon, however, defines sacraments as "rites which have the command of God and to which the promise of grace has been added," he arrives at three sacraments, baptism, the Lord's Supper, and absolution. [113]

It is interesting that Vatican II does not provide a strict definition of a sacrament, but instead asserts that "the purpose of the sacraments is to sanctify men, to build up the body of Christ, and finally, to give worship to God." [114] Similarly, we read in *Sacramentum Mundi* that the sacraments, "as defined in the theology of the Church, are the seven vital actions of Church in its liturgy which are efficacious for salvation." [115]

Thus the sacraments are seen more as actions of the church than as actions on behalf of Christ. Karl Rahner may have sensed this shortcoming when he declared that since "the Church is of itself the final, irrevocable, eschatologically permanent word of salvation to the world," it is also "the primary sacrament." [116] Since Christ instituted the church, he also instituted the sacraments even though they are not attested to by any express texts of Scripture. Of course, Christ instituted the sacraments mentioned in Scripture as part of the establishment of the church. While this mediated origin of the sacraments (through the church by Christ) would relieve us from the task of ascertaining that all the sacraments were actually instituted by Jesus (Eucharist) or at least by the risen Christ (baptism), it would leave open room for more or fewer than the seven sacraments specified at Trent.

Perhaps we get a more tenable approach to the sacraments if we investigate their historical origin. In Latin, the term sacrament had initially two meanings that had nothing to do with what we today understand by a sacrament. The word could denote a sum of money which two parties to a legal suit deposited in escrow pending the decision of the court. The sum contributed by the losing party was then used for religious purposes. The word sacrament could also mean a military oath of allegiance.[117] The latter use seemed to give rise to the Western theological use of the term. The transition from the military to the theological use is clearly seen in Tertullian. He refers to the baptismal vows of the Christians, and states: "We were called to the service in the army of the living God in the very moment when we gave response to the words of the sacramental oath." [118] Tertullian also mentions by name the sacrament of the Eucharist and the sacrament of "water." [119] There is no doubt for Tertullian that in performing these sacraments we follow the command of the Lord. It is God who calls us, asking for our response to his promise of the sacrament. Thus God binds himself in the sacrament and in turn induces an obligation and response from us.

The Eastern Churches preserved for sacraments the New Testament term *mystery*. Their administration of the sacraments (baptism, chrism/confirmation, penance, Eucharist, priesthood, marriage, and anointing of the sick) were declared valid by Vatican II.[120] These mysteries, of which baptism and Eucharist have prime importance, are perceived as having their source in Christ.[121] In the New Testament, however, the term mysteries is not used to denote the sacraments, but primarily the secret (mystery) of the kingdom of God (Mark 4:11f.) and/or the mystery (secret) of Christ (1 Cor. 2:7f.), meaning Christ crucified.

The notion of mysteries in analogy to ancient mystery cults could not be excluded from Eastern piety. The sacraments can be seen as cultic rites in which the destiny of the deity is portrayed by sacred action before the devotees in such a way as to give them a part in the destiny of the deity.[122] Mysteries therefore promise salvation and allow their devotees participation in the suffering of the deity. The church fathers were not unaware of these analogies. Justin Martyr, for instance, claims that "the wicked devils have imitated in the mysteries of Mithras" the celebration of the Eucharist, "commanding the same thing to be done." [123] Similarly, Tertullian remarks that the devil "by the mystic rites of his idols, vies even with the essential portions of the sacraments of God." [124] It may be understandable that the church in the West attempted to avoid the dangerously loaded term mystery by using the term sacrament. In so doing, the West took over the freight of the military and juridicial connotations, a move which led to a rather one-sided ethical emphasis on the response to God's grace.

In the East, the term mystery allowed more for perceiving the ontological reality of the life to which the sacraments initiated. This may also be underscored by the so-called secret discipline, especially prevalent in the Eastern church between the end of the second and the end of the fifth century. The idea was to keep secret the administration of baptism and Eucharist and the related doctrines and rites from all except the baptized. For instance, John Chrysostom, referring to the Eucharist, says: "Those who partake of the mysteries understand what I say." [125] The emphasis on initiation implies not just a response to God's grace, but indicates a different state of being. The West, less interested in divinization as the goal of salvation, preserved the ontological component of the sacraments only in the insistence on Christ's real presence in the Lord's Supper and through the emphasis on the incorporation of the Christian into the redemptive drama through baptism.

Since the sacraments point to the redemptive event encountered in Christ, baptism and Eucharist occupy by necessity central character. The other five sacraments can at the most assume peripheral standing, since they are certainly not all necessary for salvation (cf. priesthood or matrimony). While it is impossible to admit their truly sacramental character —even Rahner's thoughtful construct is of no help here—the redemptive or preserving activity of God addressed in them should not be taken lightly. At the height of scholastic theology Hugo of St. Victor stated in his *De sacramentis christianae fidei* that some sacraments are necessary for salvation while others, while not necessary for salvation, advance sanctification.[126] Unintentionally Hugo distinguished between sacraments in the proper sense, baptism and Eucharist, and what the Roman Catholic Church calls sacramentals, namely rites or items that in imitation of the sacraments attempt to produce certain effects. Augustine's definition, for instance, that sacraments "contain the announcement that He [Christ] has been born, has suffered, has risen" could hardly be used to substantiate all seven sacraments.[127]

Augustine could use the term sacrament more loosely than we do today. For instance, he talked about the "sacrament of Christ's body . . . the sacrament of Christ's blood" and "the sacrament of faith."[128] But he leaves no doubt that a sacrament is intimately connected with the pronouncement of the gospel of Christ. He even called it the visible word, saying: "The word is added to the element, and there results the Sacrament, as if itself also a kind of visible word."[129] Luther declared in his Small Catechism: "It is not the water that produces these effects, but the Word of God connected with the water, and our faith which relies on the Word of God connected with the water." Augustine had anticipated this insight a thousand years earlier when he stated: "Take away the word, and the water is neither more nor less than water."[130] Sacraments are the visible side of the pronouncement of God's redemptive word. But the sign that signifies the sacrament should not be taken lightly as Augustine assures us saying: "For if sacraments had not some points of real resemblance to the things of which they are sacraments, they would be no sacraments at all. In most cases, moreover, they do in virtue of this likeness bear the names of the realities which they resemble."[131] The sacraments are not only visible signs of an invisible grace announced in and with their administration; they also depict that grace which is announced in them, e.g., Jesus' cross and resurrection.

b. The efficacy of the sacraments

Since the sacraments are the visible side of God's redemptive word, their efficacy should be analogous to the word. The Augsburg Confession points this out very eloquently: "For through the Word and the sacraments, as through instruments, the Holy Spirit is given, and the Holy Spirit produces faith, where and when it pleases God, in those who hear the Gospel" (CA 5). The sacraments are powerful instruments of God's grace and should not be administered casually but "in accordance with the divine Word" (CA 7). Their efficacy, however, does not depend on the righteousness of those who administer them. Those to whom they are administered usually do not have a sufficient knowledge of the spiritual life of their ministers to judge their worthiness. Thus the effectiveness of the sacraments and the assurance of God's gifts would always be in jeopardy if their efficacy were contingent on the worthiness of the ministers. To alleviate such fears the Augsburg Confession rightly declares: "Both the sacraments and the Word are effectual by reason of the institution and commandment of Christ even if they are administered by evil men" (CA 8). Sacraments administered by heretics can be accepted as valid. For instance, rebaptisms are the exception rather than the norm, even in cases where denominations have no mutual recognition. The church will always see to it that their ministers are examples of faith and conduct, not only to assure right proclamation and administration of the sacraments, but to inspire the faithful through the example of their leadership.

If the sacraments can be effective without being administered by worthy celebrants, the question must also be asked whether there is a precondition on the side of the recipient to assure efficacy. Here especially two assertions of the Council of Trent have caused much dissatisfaction among Protestants. The Council declared that the sacraments confer grace "on those who do not place an obstacle in the way," implying the notion of cooperation toward salvation.[132] Yet the Council then stated that in the sacraments grace is "conferred from the work which has been worked," saying in effect that it is not faith that grasps the gift offered in the sacraments but that the gift is automatically conferred through that which has been accomplished. But Catholic scholars caution us not to interpret this in a crassly mechanistic way. For instance, we hear that "the *opus operatum* does not mean that the sacraments produce their proper effects in an automatic and mechanical way, or by some sort of magic."[133] By the phrase, "from the work which has been worked [*ex opere operato*]" we should rather be assured that grace is not mediated in the sacrament by virtue of the personal merits of the minister or the recipient. On the contrary, Rahner affirms: "The *opus operatum* is the eschatologically efficacious word of God."[134] God's work will not return empty but deliver the promises contained in it.

The question still must be asked how the phrase of Trent "those who do not place an obstacle in the way" is to be interpreted. Again we are assured that "the mediation of grace, both in its actual occurrence and in its 'measure' is essentially dependent on the disposition of the recipient (which is a condition, not a cause)." [135] We recall that the Augsburg Confession does not totally exclude reflection on the condition of the recipient when it says that the Holy Spirit produces faith "in those who hear the Gospel" (CA 5). Luther even seems to go one step further when he states in the Small Catechism that "the Word of God connected with the water, and our faith which relies on the Word of God connected with the water" produces these great saving effects. [136] It is, however, another step further when we hear on the Roman Catholic side that the mediation of grace "depends on the faith of the recipient as he lays himself open and surrenders to the sacramental grace, as also on the intention of the recipient." [137] The reflection on the recipients and their disposition is certainly necessary to avoid the idea of a mechanistic and impersonal mediation of grace. But a stronger emphasis on the primacy of grace would assure the certainty of salvation.

With his forceful renunciation of infant baptism, Karl Barth seems to embark on an even stronger cooperative emphasis than the Roman Catholic Church. He admits that baptism without willingness and readiness of the baptized is true, effectual, and effective baptism. While it must and ought not to be repeated, it is however, not correct usage. "It is not done in obedience, it is not administered according to proper order, and therefore it is necessarily clouded baptism." [138] Barth sees in the attempts of Luther and Calvin to justify infant baptism unconvincing arguments that cannot suffice without exegetical and practical "artifices and sophisms." He wonders whether the real reason for infant baptism operative in the Reformers and in the theologians today is the fear that without infant baptism the Constantinian majority church would collapse. Even Luther, he says, once confessed that "there would not be too many people baptized, if, instead of being brought to baptism, they had to come of their own accord." Barth in turn does not want these politico-practical questions to decide the issue. Since baptism always demands a response on the part of the baptized, he simply wants "instead of the present infant-baptism, a baptism which on the part of the baptized is a responsible act."

The Reformers, indeed, devised all kinds of theories to justify infant baptism, as we can see in Luther's case. [139] Yet none of these sufficed. At the end, it is very clear for Luther that bapitsm is totally God's gift. It summons us to faith and its reality and validity do not depend on our faith. Luther sees the same as true for adult baptism. [140] On similar grounds

Oscar Cullmann declares both infant and adult baptism as equally biblical.[141]

Yet Barth has touched on a significant point. Our response to the grace offered in baptism is important. Without this, baptism is incomplete unless we grant a mechanistic view of infusion of grace through infant baptism. It is therefore very thoughtful when Vatican II decrees: "The rite for the baptism of infants is to be revised, and should be adapted to the circumstances that those to be baptized are, in fact, infants. The roles of parents and godparents, and also their duties, should be brought out more sharply in the rite itself." [142] This means that no sacrament, not even infant baptism, should be administered lightly. If there is no reasonable assurance of facilitating a response of faith (through Christian upbringing), it would be frivolous to administer infant baptism. Similarly, adult baptism should never become just a traditional act, but a reasonable assurance of an adequate response should be secured. Even in the case of the Eucharist, an adequate notion and acceptance of the grace offered are minimal expectations for admission to this sacrament.

Where these safeguards to insure proper administration cannot be given, as in the case of so-called "emergency" infant baptism, we would accept the dictum of Barth that "the power of Jesus Christ . . . is not dependent upon the carrying out of baptism" and would not insist on baptism.[143] Emergency baptism is much more a pastoral case, for the sake of a good conscience of the next of kin, than a theological case, for the sake of salvation. Yet the argument would be ill-founded that (infant) baptism is not necessary for salvation. Since baptism, however, means incorporation into the visible body of Christ, this incorporation would be of such short duration in case of emergency baptism, that it would lose its meaning.

In question 74, the Heidelberg Catechism deals explicitly with the issue, "Are infants also to be baptized?", and affirms without reservation that infants should be included in the new covenant. Yet under the influence of Barth, the contemporary commentary comes to the conclusion that the danger of making people indifferent to a confessional stand is greater with infant baptism than with adult baptism.[144] There is no clear theological preference possible for infant baptism over adult baptism or vice versa. If adult baptism, however, is exclusively based on the immediate response to God's grace, then the danger is evident that God's word does no longer have the primacy, but that such is accorded to our own action. The proper place for adult baptism is the mission field and not the confessional situation. This becomes especially clear in some socialist countries in which infant baptism and subsequent confirmation deprives the children of many educational and professional opportunities while adult baptism would escape such "confessional" consequences. Yet in such situations, adult baptism may be the wiser decision to circumvent the desired oppression of believers by an officially atheistic government.

In recent years, the issue of infant communion has stirred up controversy in some Lutheran circles and has often been treated in a more emotional than theological fashion. Richard John Neuhaus put the issue in the proper light when he confessed: "I believe the communing of infants is permissible (to deny that would be to hereticize the Eastern churches). I am persuaded it is not mandatory and am not persuaded it is desirable —for reasons theological, pastoral, liturgical, ecumenical, and psychological." [145] The argument for infant communion is usually advanced that "if Baptism is the full initiation into the Church, then Communion could follow immediately." [146] According to Lutheran understanding this is certainly true. The same could also be argued for other "sacraments," such as ordination, marriage, extreme unction, etc. We remember that Luther insisted that through baptism one is already a priest, a bishop, and a pope. Nevertheless he demanded proper education, and a call to qualify for exercising the priestly office. So the full initiation does not imply that one should also assume immediately all the privileges of full citizenship in the visible church. For instance, one does not allow infants to vote at congregational meetings, though theologically we could hardly bar them from exercising this right.

One might be tempted to argue against infant communion on the basis that this practice was not mentioned until about 251 when Cyprian wrote of it in *De lapsis*.[147] Yet the argument of a fairly late date could then also be used against infant baptism, since this was not explicitly mentioned either until about A.D. 180 when Irenaeus referred to it. The rejection of infant communion as a later innovation could easily necessitate the rejection of infant baptism with the same argument, a move that not many are willing to make who argue against infant communion. Also the rejection of infant communion with the argument that its rise stems from the emergence of the prevalent practice of infant baptism is unconvincing, since the Western church finally abandoned the former while it maintained the latter.

One might not be wrong to assume that the reason infant communion is practiced now almost exclusively in Eastern Orthodox churches is that there the participation in commuion is understood as a means toward divinization, the desired goal of salvation in Eastern piety. Thus one should not wait with communion until adulthood, but start as soon as possible. As the juridicial understanding of justification gained more and more importance in the West, there was less and less need felt for infant communion. It was finally dropped completely in the late Middle Ages. In some ways that may seem regrettable. But the Eastern churches are not very consistent in their practice. If communion is indeed so vital that there should be a natural move from the baptismal font to the altar, why is there not more urgency for infants to commune as often as do adults? Perhaps divinization for infants is more symbolic than real (as many parents painfully notice).

Though a recovery of the Eastern notion of divinization would be good for the West to balance its exaggerated (juridicial) emphasis on justification, infant communion might be the wrong move in this direction. Even for Christians, as they progress in maturity and age, certain rites of passage, such as the sacraments, are helpful aids toward the goal of sanctification. Thus we should not exclude Christian children on theological principles from communion, ordination, or any other grades of participation among the faithful, but on pedagogical grounds. The introduction of a flexible communion age seems a step in the right direction, removing a barrier and establishing guidelines for Christian life and growth.

Another issue that arises in connection with the efficacy of the sacraments is whether they have only symbolic or also realistic character. The two poles here are the extreme symbolism of Zwingli and the idea of transubstantiation in the Roman Catholic teaching, with the Lutheran real presence holding a middle position. As the Leuenberg Agreement of the European Churches of the Reformation of 1973 confesses, many of the old stereotypes no longer hold as one reconsiders and reinterprets one's own history and the history of other denominations, and as biblical exegesis leads to deeper insight.[148] It further states that "in the Lord's Supper the resurrected Christ gives himself to us through his promising Word with bread and wine in his body and blood given for all."

The Reformed tradition emphasizes that "although he [Christ] is in heaven and we are on earth, we are nevertheless flesh of his flesh and bone of his bone, always living and being governed by one Spirit, as the members of our bodies are governed by one soul." [149] Though this statement allows for a kind of "sacramental realism," we should not forget that Christ remains in heaven. This means that communion with him is possible only through the Holy Spirit. This does not mean that Christ is present only symbolically in and with the elements. The Reformed theologians do assert that we "eat the crucified body of Christ" and we drink "his shed blood." [150] The Lutheran side also emphasizes very much Christ's real presence, saying, for instance, in the Augsburg Confession that "the true body and blood of Christ are really present in the Supper of our Lord under the form of bread and wine and are there distributed and received" (CA 10). Similarly, Luther says in the Small Catechism that the Lord's Supper "is the true body and blood of our Lord Jesus Christ, under the bread and wine, given to us Christians to eat and to drink." [151]

Unlike the Reformed tradition, the Lutheran emphasis on the real presence is not coupled with an equal emphasis on the circumstances of his presence. There is no reflection on the Holy Spirit as the mediator of the real presence or on the difference between the presence in heaven and in the Lord's Supper. Lutherans insist that, similarly to God, Christ can be present wherever he wants, and that he can be present everywhere, even at the same time.[152] Lutheran official documents, however, show a remarkable restraint in pointing out the mode of the Lord's presence.

Through the centuries the Roman Catholic Church became more and more specific about the mode of this real presence. At Trent it picked up the notion of transubstantiation, first declared at the Fourth Lateran Council (1215), and finally stated:

> By the consecration of the bread and wine a conversion takes place of the whole substance of bread into the substance of the body of Christ our Lord, and of the whole substance of wine into the substance of His blood. This conversion is appropriately and properly called transubstantiation by the Catholic Church.[153]

Christ's presence is somehow "produced" through the words of institution. Especially in ecumenical dialogues the question has been repeatedly raised what such transubstantiation actually means. It is evident that it opposes a strictly symbolic understanding of the Lord's presence. Yet it does not imply the transformation of substance (matter) as we would assume according to today's terminology.[154] Substance would mean here either substance in contrast to outward appearance, or substance in opposition to that which is accidental, or substance as that being which underlies any other feature that is added to it. Thus one could come to the conclusion that "a symbolism and transignification" that maintains the realism of Christ's presence is within the limits that the doctrine of transubstantiation describes.

Each of these diverse interpretations shows that transubstantiation emphasizes that God acts in the Eucharist, effecting a change in the elements. But it is not a rationalistic attempt to explain the mystery of Christ's presence in the elements.[155] Similar to the Reformed and the Lutheran assertions concerning the real presence, it shows the limits of our theological efforts to explore the mystery of Christ's presence. The same is true for the Orthodox tradition. There too the terms "change, transubstantiation, and re-creation" indicate that the elements of bread and wine are inseparably united with the body and blood of Christ.[156] It becomes clear that with different conceptual tools the presence of Christ in his sacrament is asserted, similarly as we asserted Christ's presence in his word of law and grace.

Yet the Eucharist also has a symbolic function, reminding us and God of Christ's sacrifice on Good Friday. Since Christ's presence is celebrated, it also foreshadows his Parousia. Without the real presence, the efficacy would be limited to psychological or group dynamic results. But without the symbolism of cross and Parousia the sacrament would be robbed of its dynamic structure of memory and hope.

In exploring the efficacy of the sacraments we must finally mention their unifying character. If God in Christ encounters us in the sacraments, he is the prime actor. This has become most evident in baptism. Christ calls, Christ incorporates us into his body, and we respond to the grace extended to us. Thus the unity of the church is built through Christ in baptism. But we do not discover and affirm our unity and then baptize.

Similarly, Christ meets us in the Eucharist. Christ's presence is experienced by us, and Christ sanctifies us through his presence. The Eucharist always has a cleansing effect, being administered for the forgiveness of sins. However, those who reject God's grace, Christ's sacrifice on our behalf, experience judgment. Since the Eucharist is the most intense and intimate communion with the resurrected Lord, it is the expression and symbol of existing unity of the church as Christ's body. Fellowship at the altar and fellowship in the pulpit—proclaiming the same word of God— signifies the ultimate union among Christians.

When Paul says about the Eucharist: "Because there is one bread, we who are many are one body, for we all partake of the one bread" (1 Cor. 10:17), he does not, however, simply mean that the Eucharist is a confirmation of our unity in Christ. Since Christ is the main actor and the gift, we should also expect something, namely that "the sacramental participation in Christ's body makes us into the body of Christ." [157] Wolfhart Pannenberg comments very appropriately that the Eucharist is

> the source and root from which the unity of the Christians lives and is continuously renewed. This corresponds with the idea that fellowship in the Lord's Supper need not stand at the end of the process of church union, but it can also be already the present power of Christ on the way towards this goal.[158]

It is as wrong to expect that communion fellowship magically or automatically creates church union as to assume that eucharistic fellowship is only permissible if this union has already been achieved. If there is power in the Eucharist through Christ's presence which implies forgiveness of sins, we should also expect that it can forgive the sins of separating and dividing the body of Christ. Otherwise the efficacy of the sacrament is neglected. It becomes more a symbol of what we do or have done than it is expressive of God's own activity. The expectation of God's power is implied in the understanding that the Eucharist, and analogically baptism, is not simply an act of remembrance, reminding us of Christ's death. It is as powerfully an act of anticipation, foreshadowing the return of the glorified Christ and the celebration of the celestial banquet in union with Christ and all the faithful. The sacraments are not only expressive of the union already existing. Because of Christ's presence in them, they have unifying character and can properly be celebrated together on the way toward union.

NOTES

1. DVC, 137 (1).
2. Ibid., 341 (1).
3. Bonaventure Kloppenburg, *The Ecclesiology of Vatican II*, trans. by M. J. O'Connell (Chicago: Franciscan Herald Press, 1974) 3, gives an excellent description of the shift in emphasis and the reproachment following Vatican II.
4. *Breaking Barriers. Nairobi 1975*. The Official Report of the Fifth Assembly of the World Council of Churches, Nairobi, 23 November—10 December, 1975, ed. by David M. Paton (Grand Rapids: Eerdmans, 1976) 69.
5. DVC, 117 (9).
6. For this and the following, including the quotes, see DVC, 17 (4), 18 (6), 23 (8), 33 (14), and 33f. (15).
7. For this and the following, including the quotes, see ibid., 38 (18), 43 (22), 40 (20), 48f. (25), and 49 (25).
8. For this quote and the following see ibid., 57 (31) and 59 (33).
9. For this quote and the following see ibid., 90 (59), 90 (60), and 94 (67).

10. For this quote and the following see *Dogmatic Constitution on Divine Revelation*, DVC, 127 (25), 125f. (22), and 120 (12).

11. Cf. *Council of Trent*, DS(E), 244 (783); and DVC, 115 (7).

12. *Dogmatic Constitution on Divine Revelation* , DVC, 117 (9).

13. Oscar Cullmann, *Vatican Council II. The New Directions*. Essays, selected and arranged by J. D. Hester (New York: Harper, 1968) 47, rightly claims that Protestants could admit equality with Scripture for the apostolic tradition, since it was eventually accepted into the canon, but not so for the post-apostolic tradition.

14. So rightly Karl Barth, Ad *Limina Apostolorum. An Appraisal of Vatican II*, trans. K. R. Crim (Richmond, VA: John Knox, 1968) 66f. and 72.

15. Augustine Cardinal Bea, *The Way to Unity After the Council* (New York: Herder and Herder, 1967) 9f., also emphasizes the impact of the observers on the ecumenical discussion of the Council.

16. DVC, 341 (1).

17. Cf. for the following the perceptive comments by Kloppenburg, 352-358.

18. So rightly George H. Tavard in his excellent book *The Church Tomorrow* (New York: Herder, 1965) 24f.

19. Hermann Dietzfelbinger, "Postscript," in Warren A. Quanbeck, ed., *Challenge . . . and Response. A Protestant Perspective of the Vatican Council*, trans. E. H. Gordon, D. J. S. Lee, R. C. Schultz, W. G. Tillmanns (Minneapolis: Augsburg, 1966), 220f., rightly poses the question whether the churches of the Reformation, and here especially the Lutheran churches, are willing to accept this challenge.

20. Cf. the perceptive remarks by Gerrit C. Berkouwer, *The Second Vatican Council and the New Catholicism*, trans. L. B. Smedes (Grand Rapids, MI: Eerdmans, 1965) 254.

21. For a brief history of the Faith and Order Movement cf. John E. Skoglund and J. Robert Nelson, *Fifty Years of Faith and Order. An Interpretation of the Faith and Order Movement* (New York: Interseminary Movement, 1963); cf. for the wider scope of the ecumenical movement, Harold E. Fey "Confessional Families and the Ecumenical Movement," Harold E. Fey, ed., *The Ecumenical Advance. A History of the Ecumenical Movement, Vol. 2: 1948-1968* (London: SPCK, 1970) 117-142.

22. *Marburg Revisited. A Reexamination of Lutheran and Reformed Traditions*, ed. Paul C. Empie and James I. McCord (Minneapolis: Augsburg, 1966), (Preface).

23. Cf. *Konkordie reformatorischer Kirchen in Europa (Leuenburger Konkordie, 16. März 1973)*; and Warren A. Quanbeck, *Search for Understanding. Lutheran Conversations with Reformed, Anglican, and Roman Catholic Churches* (Minneapolis: Augsburg, 1972), esp. 119ff., where he assesses the impact of various dialogues on the future of these denominations.

24. So Thomas E. Ambrogi, "Contemporary Roman Catholic Theology of the Eucharistic Sacrifice," in *Lutherans and Catholics in Dialogue*, vol. 3: *The Eucharist as Sacrifice* (New York: USA National Committee for Lutheran World Federation, 1967) 162.

25. Paul C. Empie, T. Austin Murphy, and Joseph Burgess, eds., *Lutherans and Catholics in Dialogue*, vol. 6: *Teaching Authority and Infallibility in the Church* (Minneapolis: Augsburg, 1980) 60, in the "Lutheran Reflections."

26. For details of the process cf. *One Baptism, One Eucharist, and a Mutually Recognized Ministry*, Faith and Order Paper No. 73 (Geneva: World Council of Churches, 1975) 58-61.

27. Ibid., 60.

28. For this quote and the following see ibid., 18 (1) and 21 (14).

29. For this quote and the following see ibid., 41 (44) and 53 (88).

30. Cf. the consequences for Vatican II after the discovery of the existence of other churches see Gregory Baum, "The Ecclesial Reality of the Other Churches," in Gregory Baum, ed., *Ecumenical Theology No. 2* (New York: Paulist, 1967) 154ff.

31. Cf. George Tavard, *Protestant Hopes and the Catholic Responsibility* (Notre Dame, IN: Fides, 1960) 59.
32. So rightly J. Robert Nelson, "Signs of Mankind's Solidarity," in J. Robert Nelson, ed., *No Man Is Alien. Essays on the Unity of Mankind* (Leiden: Brill, 1971) 14.
33. Cf. for a more extensive treatment of the term anonymous Christian, Hans Schwarz, *The Search for God* (Minneapolis: Augsburg, 1975) 142ff.
34. So rightly Wolfhart Pannenberg, *Thesen zur Theologie der Kirche* (Munich: Claudius, 1970) 23.
35. Cf. for the following the thorough collection of material by Friedrich Baumgärtel, *"Pneuma:* Spirit in the OT," TDNT, esp. 6:362-367.
36. This notion is intensified by the eucharistic tone that this verse carries. Cf. Raymond E. Brown, *The Gospel according to John (XIII-XXI)* (Garden City, NY: Doubleday, 1970) 672f., in his comments on John 15:1-6.
37. Cf. Eduard Schweizer, soma, TDNT 7:1068-1073, for a perceptive treatment of the community as the body of Christ.
38. Cf. ibid., 7:1077, esp. n. 491.
39. So rightly Franz Mussner, *Christus, das All und die Kirche. Studien zur Theologie des Epheserbriefes,* 2nd ed. (Trier: Paulinus, 1968) 147f.
40. Cf. for the following Karl Ludwig Schmidt, *ekklesia,* TDNT 3:504f.
41. For this quote and the next see Cyprian, *Epistle 72* (21), ANFa 5:384; and *On the Unity of the Church* (6), ibid., 5:423.
42. Cf. for the following Wolfhart Pannenberg: *"Christsein ohne Kirche," Ethik und Ekklesiologie. Gesammelte Aufsätze* (Göttingen: Vandenhoeck & Ruprecht, 1977) 190 and 192.
43. According to A. J. Lewis, *Zinzendorf. The Ecumenical Pioneer. A Study in the Moravian Contribution to Christian Mission and Unity* (Philadelphia: Westminster, 1962) 67, Zinzendorf states in a conversation of 1736: "I acknowledge no Christianity without fellowship."
44. Cf. Justin Martyr, *The First Apology* (67), ANFa 1:186, where he says: "And the people |*laos*| assent, saying Amen." Cf. also for the following Hermann Strathmann, *laos,* TDNT 4:57.
45. John A. Abbo and Jerome D. Hannan, *The Sacred Canons. A Concise Presentation of the Current Disciplinary Norms of the Church* (St. Louis, MO: Herder, 1952), 1:157 (can. 107).
46. *Dogmatic Constitution on the Church,* DVC, 27 (10).
47. *Decree on the Apostolate of the Laity,* DVC, 493f.(4).
48. Ibid., 491 (2).
49. So rightly Yves M. J. Congar, *Lay People in the Church. A Study for a Theology of the Laity,* trans. D. Attwater (Westminster, MD: Newman, 1959) 432.
50. Frederick K. Wentz, *The Layman's Role Today* (Garden City, NY: Doubleday, 1963) 69-158.
51. Cf. Hendrik Kraemer, *A Theology of the Laity* (Philadelphia: Westminster, 1958) 127-135.
52. Cf. Hans-Ruedi Weber, "The Rediscovery of the Laity in the Ecumenical Movement," in the highly informative volume by Stephen Neill, and Hans Ruedi-Weber, eds., *The Layman in Christian History* (Philadelphia: Westminster, 1963) 377-394.
53. Cf. Hans-Ruedi Weber, *The Militant Ministry. People and Pastors of the Early Church and Today. The Knubel-Miller Lectures for 1963* (Philadelphia: Fortress, 1963), esp. 14-19.
54. Cf. *Augsburg Confession* (14) in *Die Bekenntnisschriften der evangelisch-lutherischen Kirche,* 5th rev. ed. (Göttingen: Vandenhoeck & Ruprecht, 1963) 69 n. 1, with reference to Luther's doctorate.

55. For this and the following cf. Martin Luther, *To the Christian Nobility of the German Nation Concerning the Reform of the Christian Estate* (1520), LW 44:129; and WA. TR 1:34.18-24 (90).

56. *Constitution on the Church*, DVC, 47 (25).

57. Cf. for instance the interesting study by Paul M. Harrison, *Authority and Power in the Free Church Tradition. A Social Case Study of the American Baptist Convention* (Princeton, NJ: Princeton University, 1959).

58. Cf. the illuminating comments by Joachim Heubach, *Die Ordination zum Amte der Kirche* (Berlin: Lutherisches Verlagshaus, 1956) 152ff.

59. It is surprising that Paul Althaus, *Die christliche Wahrheit. Lehrbuch der Dogmatik*, 5th ed. (Gütersloh: Gerd Mohn, 1959) 508, in his otherwise very careful and persuasive analysis of the relationship between the common priesthood and the pastoral office claims that this office originated from the communal aspect of the eucharistic celebration.

60. *One Baptism, One Eucharist, and A Mutually Recognized Ministry*, 33 (13).

61. Cf. for the following the instructive study by Eduard Lohse, *Die Ordination im Spätjudentum und im Neuen Testament* (Göttingen: Vandenhoeck & Ruprecht, 1951), here esp. 27.

62. Ibid., 40, and J. Z. Lauterbach, "Ordination," in *The Jewish Encyclopedia* (1905), 9:429.

63. Lohse, 74.

64. Ibid., 77.

65. Cf. Martin Dibelius and Hans Conzelmann, *A Commentary on the Pastoral Epistles*, ed. Helmut Koester, trans. P. Buttolph and A. Yarbro (Philadelphia: Fortress, 1972) 70f., in his exegesis of 1 Tim. 4:14.

66. Cf. for details Lohse, 86f.

67. DS(E), 294 (960).

68. *Decree on the Ministry and Life of Priests*, DVC, 536f. (3).

69. Piet Fransen, "Orders and Ordination," SM(E) 4:325.

70. Ibid

71. Heubach, 101.

72. Cf. Edward P. Echlin, *The Story of Anglican Ministry* (Slough, England: St. Paul Publications, 1974) 146f.

73. Cf. for the following *One Baptism, One Eucharist, and a Mutually Recognized Ministry*, 37f, (34).

74. Johannes Remmers, "Apostolic Succession: An Attribute of the Whole Church," trans. J. Drury, in Conc(USA), vol. 34: *Apostolic Succession. Rethinking a Barrier to Unity*, ed. by Hans Küng (New York: Paulist, 1968), 34:51.

75. So Maurice Villain, "Can There Be Apostolic Succession Outside the Chain of Imposition of Hands?" trans. Th. L. Westow, in *Apostolic Succession*, 96.

76. Martin Luther, *Sermons on the First Epistle of St. Peter* (1523), LW 30:55, in his comments on 1 Pet. 2:5.

77. Jan Peters, "Is There Room for Women in the Functions of the Church?" trans. Th. L. Westow, in *Apostolic Succession*, 134. A very useful book concerning the ordination of women and their contribution to the life of the church is that by Georgia Harkness, *Women in Church and Society. A Historical and Theological Inquiry* (Nashville, TN: Abingdon, 1972) 205-227.

78. It is not without significance that in the index to Gordon D. Kaufman, *Systematic Theology. A Historicist Perspective* (New York: Scribner's, 1968), neither the terms "law" nor "gospel" appear, but only "word of God."

79. Cf. Wolfgang Wickler, *The Biology of the Ten Commandments*, trans. D. Smith (New York: McGraw-Hill, 1972), esp. 75-164.

80. So rightly Ernst Käsemann, *An die Römer* (Tübingen: J. C. B. Mohr, 1973) 59, in his exegesis of this passage.
81. Martin Luther, *Die erste Disputation gegen die Antinomer* (1537), WA 39/1:402. 15ff. For the understanding of the relationship between law and gospel in Luther cf. the extensive and excellent remarks in Althaus, *The Theology of Martin Luther*, 251-273.
82. Luther, *Die erste Disputation gegen die Antinomer* (1537), WA 39/1:478.15-18.
83. Martin Luther, *Lectures on Galatians* (1519), LW 27:355, in his exegesis of Gal. 5:14.
84. Martin Luther, *Predigten des Jahres 1540*, WA 49:2.1f., in a sermon on January 1, 1540.
85. Cf. Anders Nygren, *Commentary on Romans*, trans. C. C. Rasmussen (Philadelphia: Muhlenberg, 1949) 225f., in his explanation of Rom. 5:12-21.
86. For this and the following cf. Martin Luther, *Die erste Disputation gegen die Antinomer*, WA 39/1:412.2ff.; and *Die Thesen gegen die Antinomer* (27ff.), WA 39/1:349.
87. John Calvin, *Institutes of the Christian Religion* (2.7.9), 1:357.
88. Cf. the perceptive comments by Herman N. Ridderbos, *The Epistle of Paul to the Churches in Galatia*, trans. H. Zylstra (Grand Rapids, MI: Eerdmans, 1953) 145f., in his exegesis of Gal. 3:24.
89. Otto Michel, *Der Brief an die Römer*, 90, in his exegesis of Rom. 3:21, rightly mentions that the righteousness of God has its pre-history in the law and the prophets. Thus God's righteousness is certainly not foreign to the Old Testament.
90. Karl Barth, "Gospel and Law," in *God, Grace and Gospel*, Scottish Journal of Theology Occasional Papers, no. 8, trans. J. S. McNab (Edinburgh: Oliver and Boyd, 1959) 3.
91. For this and the following quote see ibid., 8.
92. For this and the following quote see ibid., 10.
93. Cf. ibid., 11.
94. Cf. ibid., 24.
95. Cf. Martin Luther, *Against Latomus* (1521), LW 32:226f., and Althaus, *The Theology of Martin Luther*, 258.
96. Robert M. Hutchins, ed., *Great Books of the Western World*, Vol. 47: *Faust*, by Johann Wolfgang von Goethe, parts one and two, trans. G. M. Priest (Chicago: Encyclopaedia Britannica, 1952), 290 (11936f.).
97. Cf. for this and the following Martin Luther, *Die erste Disputation gegen die Antinomer*, WA 39/1:405.7-11; and *Die Thesen gegen die Antinomer* (27), WA 39/1:351.
98. John Calvin, *Institutes of the Christian Religion* (2.7.12), 1:360.
99. Cf. Martin Luther, *Ad librum eximii Magistri Nostri Ambrosii Catharini* (1521), WA 7:760.6-9.
100. So Paul Althaus, *The Divine Command. A New Perspective on Law and Gospel*, Social Ethics Series, no. 9, trans. F. Sherman, intr. W. H. Lazareth (Philadelphia: Fortress, Facet Books, 1966) 45, who introduces the term "command" for these imperatives to distinguish them from the law.
101. This helpful distinction between the *usus legalis* and *usus evangelicus* of the divine command is introduced by Wilfried Joest, *Gesetz und Freiheit. Das Problem des Tertius usus legis bei Luther und die neutestamentlichen Parainese*, 2nd ed. (Göttingen: Vandenhoeck & Ruprecht, 1956) 200.
102. So Luther, *Lectures on Galatians* (1519), LW 27:230, in his exegesis of Gal. 2:18.
103. Walter Kaspar, "Law and Gospel," SM(E) 3:297.
104. *Apology of the Augsburg Confession* (art. 13), BC, 211.
105. *The Heidelberg Catechism*, 117f. (ques. 68).

106. Cf. to both passages Walter Grundmann, *Das Evangelium nach Mätthaus*, 2nd ed. (Berlin: Evangelische Verlagsanstalt, 1971) 391f., in his exegesis of Matt. 16:19.
107. "The Sacrament of Holy Baptism" in Luther's *Small Catechism*, BC, 349.
108. Luther's *Ninety-five Theses* of October 31, 1517, LW 31:25.
109. Cf. also Luther, *The Small Catechism* (Confession and Absolution), BC, 349f.
110. *The Ninety-five Theses* LW 31:25 (thesis 3).
111. This also seems to be the tenor of Rahner's reflections in his article on penance when he ponders a "theology of satisfaction." Cf. Karl Rahner, "Penance," in SM(E) 4:399.
112. Luther, *The Large Catechism* (Baptism), BC 436.
113. *The Apology of the Augsburg Confession* (art. 13), BC, 211.
114. *Constitution of the Sacred Liturgy* (59), DVC, 158.
115. Raphael Schulte, "Sacraments," SM(E) 5:378.
116. For this and the following cf. Karl Rahner, "The Word and the Eucharist," in *Theological Investigations*, vol. 4: *More Recent Writings*, trans. K. Smyth (Baltimore: Helicon, 1966) 274.
117. For further information on the original meaning of the term sacrament see Klingen-müller, "Sacramentum," PRE 1A 2:1667-1674.
118. Tertullian, *To the Martyrs* (3.1), FaCh 40:22.
119. Tertullian, *De Corona* (3) and *On Baptism* (1), ANFa 3:94 and 669.
120. *Decree on Eastern Catholic Churches* (27ff.), DVC, 384f.
121. John Chrysostom, *Homily 85 on John 19:16-20:9*, FaCh 41:435.
122. Cf. for the definition of mysteries and for the following Günther Bornkamm, *"mys-terion,"* in TDNT 4:803 and 805.
123. Justin Martyr, *The First Apology* (66), ANFa 1:185.
124. Tertullian, *On Prescription against Heretics* (40), ANFa 3:262. It is not without sig-nificance that he too refers to the Mithras cult, perhaps implying the threatening nature of this cult for the Christian notion of the sacraments, and the affinity of their rituals.
125. John Chrysostom, *Homily 15 on John 1:18*, FaCh 33:150.
126. Cf. Hugo of St. Victor as quoted in Jaroslav Pelikan, *The Christian Tradition*, vol. 3: *The Growth of Medieval Theology (600-1300)* (Chicago: University of Chicago Press, 1978), 207.
127. Augustine, *Reply to Faustus the Manichaean* (19.16), NPNF(FS) 4:245.
128. Augustine, *Letters* (98.9) NPNF, First Series, 1:410.
129. Augustine, *On the Gospel of St. John* (80.3), NPNF(FS) 7:344, in his exegesis of John 15:1-3.
130. BC, 349, in Luther's explanation of "The Sacrament of Holy Baptism;" and Augustine, *On the Gospel of St. John* (80.3), NPNF(FS) 7:344, in his exegesis of John 15:1-3.
131. Augustine, *Letters* (98.9), NPNF(FS) 1:410.
132. For this and the following quote see DS(E), 262f. (849 and 851).
133. Raphael Schulte, "Sacraments," SM(E) 5:380.
134. Karl Rahner, "The Word and the Eucharist," 4:274.
135. Schulte, 5:380.
136. BC, 349, in Luther's explanation of "The Sacrament of Holy Baptism."
137. Schulte, 5:380.
138. For this and the following quotes see Karl Barth, *The Teaching of the Church Re-garding Baptism*, trans. by E. A. Payne (London: SCM, 1948) 40, 49, 52, 53, and 54.
139. For details cf. Althaus, *The Theology of Martin Luther*, 364-370.
140. According to ibid., 369.
141. Oscar Cullmann, *Baptism in the New Testament*, trans. J. K. S. Reid (London: SCM. 1950) 70.
142. *Constitution on the Sacred Liturgy* (67), DVC, 160.

143. Barth, 23.
144. See *The Heidelberg Catechism*, 122 and 127.
145. Richard John Neuhaus, *Forum Letter* (March 21, 1980) 5.
146. So Eric W. Gritsch, "Infant Communion: Old Bone in New Contention," *Lutheran Forum*, vol. 13 (Lent 1979) 6.
147. Cyprian, *De Lapsis and De Ecclesiae Catholicae Unitate*, text and trans. M. Bévenot (Oxford: Clarendon, 1971) 15, 37f. (9 and 25), for more historical information cf. also Roger T. Beckwith, "The Age of Admission to the Lord's Supper," *Westminster Theological Journal*, vol. 38 (Winter 1976), esp. 125ff.; and Eugene L. Brand, "Baptism and Communion of Infants: A Lutheran View," *Worship*, vol. 50 (January 1976) 36ff.
148. For this and the following quote see *Leuenberger Konkordie*, 3 and 5.
149. *The Heidelberg Catechism*, 129, in the explanation of question 76. The term "sacramental realism" is used by the commentator on the question (cf. 130).
150. Ibid., 130.
151. BC, 351, in Luther's explanation of "The Sacrament of the Altar."
152. Cf. Albrecht Peters, *Realpräsenz. Luthers Zeugnis von Christi Gegenwart im Abendmahl* (Berlin: Lutherisches Verlagshaus, 1960) 78ff.
153. DS(E), 267f. (877) and cf. DS(E), 169 (430).
154. Cf. for the following the illuminating deliberations by Piet Schoonenberg, "Transubstantiation: How Far Is This Doctrine Historically Determined?", trans. Th. L. Westow, in Conc(USA), vol. 24: *The Sacraments. An Ecumenical Dilemma*, ed. by Hans Küng (New York: Paulist, 1967) 80f. and 91.
155. So rightly in the conclusion of the Lutheran-Roman Catholic Dialogue on Eucharist as sacrifice, in *Lutherans and Catholics in Dialogue* 3:195f.
156. Cf. the theses in *Die Eucharistie. Das Sagorsker Gespräch über das hl. Abendmahl zwischen Vertretern der Evangelischen Kirche in Deutschland und der Russischen Orthodoxen Kirche* (Bielefeld: Luther-Verlag, 1974) 23f. (esp. thesis 4).
157. So Hans Conzelmann, *1 Corinthians*, 172, in his exegesis of 1 Cor. 10:17.
158. Wolfhart Pannenberg, "*Das Abendmahl—Sakrament der Einheit*," in *Ethik und Ekklesiologie*, 287.

7

The Church as Memory, Anticipation, and Hope

OUR DESCRIPTION OF THE CHURCH WOULD BE INCOMPLETE if we would only consider bare ecclesiastical structures. Necessary as structures are, they only enable an organization to fulfill the task to which it has been assigned. In this final chapter we must describe this task. In our attempt to sketch out the development of the church into its present form, we have realized that, without losing itself, the church cannot be separated from its foundation. Therefore the church serves as the collective memory of that which gave rise to its existence. Yet the church does not simply focus on the past. As history has shown, the church is keenly involved in the affairs of the day. While it has often been in danger of losing itself in contemporary affairs, the church serves as a living reminder of the roots and destiny of the present, by providing direction and encouragement for bringing about the present. Yet in so doing the church dare not become oblivious to the future, both in its ultimate and penultimate sense. If apocalyptic is the seedbed of the Christian faith, the Christian church must always be mindful of the future, as a challenge toward which to strive and a restraint that reminds us that the future is a gift and not an accomplished fact.

1. The guardian of the past

The church must be conservative in the true sense of the word, preserving the past, in harmony with what gave rise to the church. The church dare not automatically sanction everything which in the past has received approval, but it must continuously discern between what should be discarded and what should be preserved. The reason for being a guardian of the past is not that the church has a history of nearly 2,000 years. Rather, the church is the past's guardian because its sources lie in the past and its present direction must be measured by the extent to which it is true to its sources.

The New Testament is not a monument carved out of one or several rocks, but rather reflects the growth of a tradition which was solidified in the biblical manuscripts. Consequently, the source of the church by which its validity can be measured is not simply the New Testament Scripture itself. There were external forces at work that shaped the New Testament. Surprising as it may sound, if we encounter different traditions in the New Testament, then the affirmation of the Reformation insight, Scripture alone, necessitates a doctrine of tradition. The content of the tradition that is to be handed on is not a doctrinal statement in terms of the peculiar tradition, but, "the very Person of Jesus himself as the incarnate Word of God, giving its authority to the Gospel and to the event of the authoritative Word of faith." [1] All other traditions must be judged by the gospel of Jesus Christ and the tradition that he engendered. Without that tradition, nobody would have preserved the gospel for us. Tradition is a necessity of the Christian faith.

Yet the church is the guardian of the past in still another respect. Since the church also includes members who are no longer living, the reality of the communion of saints necessitates that we devote ourselves also to our common past.

a. The necessity of tradition

God's word comes to us only through the medium of tradition. Tradition is vital for a church that wants to adhere to God's word. Scripture itself is the result of a traditioning process, as it freely admits (Luke 1:1-4 and John 20:30f.). Furthermore, Scripture is always encountered within a particular tradition, such as the Roman Catholic tradition, the Reformed tradition, etc. Ecumenical dialogue shows increasingly that even cultural traditions within the same confessional family color certain strands of the gospel tradition (e.g., the rise of liberation theology in predominantly Catholic Latin America). There is a difference if a Roman Catholic appeals to Scripture or if a Lutheran appeals to it, and there is also a difference if the appeal is made by a Roman Catholic in Italy or one living in Latin America. Our varying traditions necessarily influence our perception of the gospel. For instance, a liberation theologian would give more emphasis to the prophetic writings of the Old Testament, a Lutheran would focus on the Gospel of John and Paul's Letter to the Romans, while a more traditional Roman Catholic might emphasize the Gospel of Luke and the Epistle of James.

The historical conditioning of our understanding of the gospel is both a promise and a danger. It is promising insofar as it shows that God's word does not speak in opaque neutrality but it is a word in and for a particular situation. The danger lies in the individualization of the historical particularity, suggesting that since truth is relational it is also relative. To combat this potential misunderstanding we must remember that the historical appropriation of the gospel in the particular tradition is nourished by the fact that we are all living in a tradition that goes back to our Lord and has its roots in the Old Testament. We exist as Christians because of the handing on (tradition) of the gospel testified to in Scripture, as transmitted in and by the church through the power of the Holy Spirit.[2] Without the handing on of the gospel tradition and its living presence today, there would be no church and no Christian faith. In this respect the dictum of Cyprian is certainly correct that outside the church there is no salvation.

Each theological discussion and ecumenical encounter makes us painfully aware that the Christian tradition is not equally present in every Christian group or individual. For the church to become one, it is certainly not necessary to agree on each minute detail concerning worship or church structure. But we notice that not even the gospel tradition is equally present among us. Yet there are already different emphases in the New Testament. There is Peter next to Paul, and John next to the synoptics. While these different emphases found their way into the New Testament, we also discover warnings there against false teachings and deviations from the truth of the gospel, evidently implying that there are traditions outside Scripture that contain distortions. To safeguard the gospel tradition against false interpretations, the canon of biblical writings evolved, and with it the creeds and the apostolic teaching office. Since the teaching office could not rely on a literary tradition except for creed and canon, a history of doctrines evolved in distinguishing right interpretations of the gospel from incorrect ones. At the same time the question again arose by what criterion one could determine genuine tradition.

The key for deciding between valid and invalid tradition is even more necessary, since the Reformers brought forth the charge that the teaching office had inadequately interpreted the tradition. It is significant, however, that Luther made this charge not by referring to the Scripture as a whole, but by using as a hermeneutical key the Pauline insight of justification. Other Reformers used similar hermeneutical keys, such as the individual conscience under the guidance of the Holy Spirit (Enthusiasts) or the glory and kingdom of God (Calvin). The Reformation emphasis on the Bible alone is to be understood more in a polemical sense, directed against the teaching office, than in a purist sense by eliminating all other criteria.

One encounters the gospel contained in Scripture always from a particular perspective which to some extent predetermines our possibility of understanding the gospel. But such discovery cannot be made as long as one is in a position of isolation or antagonistic entrenchment. The experience of an ecumenical encounter does not only sharpen our eyes for better perceiving our own hermeneutical key to the gospel tradition, it also makes us aware that other keys open up insights that are inaccessible from our own perspective. A careful analysis of different traditions will not result in the naive euphemism that they are all equally valid. We will notice, however, that all of them, including our own, contain peculiar virtues and shortcomings. We will also find that with some traditions that are very close to our own we usually have strong ecclesiastical ties, while with those who are very much unlike our own, we usually have little fellowship. Since the life of the Christian Church is lived in a continuous recalling, appropriation, and transmission of the gospel tradition, our listening to each other will enhance and enrich this process, while ecumenical isolation leads to increasing onesidedness and eventual distortion of the gospel. "So the attempt must always be made to transmit the Tradition in its fulness and to remain within the community of the whole of God's people, and the temptation must be avoided of overemphasizing those elements which are especially congenial to a particular culture." [3]

Catholicity is not a possession of one particular configuration of the church. Similar to the wholeness of the body of Christ, catholicity is a gift of God's grace and results in the task of its continuous appropriation. Contrary to Vincent of Lerins, catholic is not that which has been believed always, everywhere, and by everyone. Such a notion would lead to a static concept of tradition. It would not do justice to the dynamism of the living tradition operating by the power of the Spirit throughout the church. Catholic is rather the gospel tradition which always, everywhere, and by everyone is attested to in a variety of ways. If one closes oneself off to the living tradition, assuming in exalting self-righteousness that one has the sole and complete grasp of that tradition, sectarianism or even heresy arises. It was crucial that the proponents of divergent streams in the early church did not pursue their own way in splendid isolation, but that they talked to each other, attempting to maintain the wholeness of the body of Christ and a joint witness to the world (1 Cor. 1:13, 12:12).

b. Between heresy and truth

There were primarily three occasions when the church was tempted with a sectarian or heretical posture. In its first centuries, in the wake of the christological controversies, the Nestorian and Monophysite churches were excluded from the mainstream of Christendom. In the Middle Ages, the rift between the Eastern and Western church occurred, and at the beginning of modernity as the Western church disintegrated into the churches of the Reformation and the Roman Catholic Church sectarian positions again appeared in Christianity. A belated consequence of this latter schism can also be seen in the phenomenon of American denominationalism. To assess correctly what happened in each instance with regard to the tradition of the gospel, we must first recognize that the church is always endangered by heresy. Heresy is not a threat from outside, as the impact of world religion is, or of secularism. Rather heresy is a threat from within, of no longer listening to one another and, as the terms heresy and sectarianism indicate, attacking each other and cutting the ties with each other. The emergence of sects and heretics is therefore an assault on the unity of the tradition.

Since a heretical or sectarian group usually continues its existence within one strand of tradition by absolutizing its position, there is always an element of truth contained in any heresy.[4] Certainly, a heresy is a deviation from the truth that the church cherishes as its own tradition. But looking back at movements that were declared heretical, we notice two characteristics. (1) Heretical movements that persist for any length of time are never completely void of truth. Even in their distorted ways they acknowledge the gospel tradition. (2) Heretical movements concentrate more or less exclusively on one or a few parts of the tradition which have usually been neglected by the church. While the church will perhaps never find it possible to give as much attention to these specific issues as heretics do, the origin of a heretical movement should challenge the church to reexamine its own understanding of the tradition and to decide whether the neglect was a necessity or an oversight.

If the church wants to preserve the whole truth of the tradition, it dare not neglect the truth contained in the distorted statements of the heretic. Simple exclusion of heretics does not lead the church to a deeper appropriation of the truth. Exclusiveness leads instead to impoverishment. Thus the Reformation led not only to antagonistic retrenchment on the side of the Roman Catholic Church, it led also—though perhaps not clearly perceived at that time—toward greater orthodoxy. As Augustine observed, a heretic must always be taken seriously, since heresies cannot "be produced through any little souls. None save great men have been the authors of heresies." [5] Heretics are not liars or dishonest people but fellow searchers for the truth who appropriate the gospel tradition in an overly slanted and therefore heterodox way.

The attitude toward a heretic should be one of dialogue, of conversation in love, and only as a last, but painful resort, one of exclusion. The church cannot accept heretical views without abandoning its own position as the guardian of the tradition. But the relationship with a heretic can never be settled once and for all. The ecumenical dialogue has taught us that views once considered divisive, through more intensive study of the common tradition and of each other's tradition, have more than once been interpreted only as different aspects of the same concern. Thus the discovery of a heresy challenges the church to strive for new unity and deepening of insight.

Confronted with the religious plurality of American denominationalism the church serves a particularly important function as the guardian of the one tradition. When we first glance at the immensely diverse pluralism of American denominations, we might be tempted to regard denominations primarily as sects. Yet following the distinction between church and sect introduced by Ernst Troeltsch, we immediately realize that denominations are sectarian only in a very limited sense. Troeltsch suggested that the church, basically conservative, accepts to a certain extent the secular order. It wants to dominate the masses and desires to cover the whole of humanity. [6] The sects, on the other hand, are relatively small groups that aspire to personal inward perfection and aim for direct personal fellowship among the members of the group. They have no interest in dominating the world and are either indifferent, tolerant, or hostile toward the world, the state, and society without much desire of controlling or incorporating these forms of social life. Though sects do not seek dialogue with other religious or secular institutions, they usually do not live completely by themselves. In pronounced opposition to the church they claim to preserve the truth of the gospel tradition which the church has neglected or suppressed.

While the sect is a kind of voluntary protest organization, it usually retains its status for only one generation. [7] With the next generation, a sect must institute educational and disciplinary policies. As the social status of its members improves, it must also come to terms with its relationship to the world, i.e., make the transition from indifference, isolation, or hostility to that of compromise. In other words, eventually a sect will either become extinct or assume many of the features of the church. As the ongoing divisions on the American denominational scene indicate, denominations are not sects, but give rise to them. Denominations are told by opposing and separating groups that they have betrayed the gospel tradition.

The common spiritual heritage of any denomination usually centers in the Bible. Whether Baptist or Lutheran, Quaker or Presbyterian, Anglican or Congregational, the Bible is the center and symbol of the common Christian tradition and the highest authority to which they appeal. Each defends its idiosyncrasies by this common authority, attempting to show that its denominational teaching and way most closely conform to the biblical pattern.[8] As Thomas Jefferson confessed: "As to tradition, if we are Protestants we reject all tradition, and rely on the scripture alone, for that is the essence and common principle of all the protestant churches."[9] This sentiment is shared by many Protestants. But it does not imply, as we might assume, a joint appeal to the common tradition. On the contrary, freed from the tutelage of European state churches, each denomination feels free to appeal to the common tradition with the result of justifying its own peculiar position and proving its superiority over others. Indicative of this mood is the amazing competition that has been waged between different denominations until very recently.

While denominations preserved much of the heritage of their European parent churches, they became voluntary associations "of like-hearted and like-minded individuals, who are united on the basis of common beliefs for the purpose of accomplishing tangible and defined objectives."[10] These aims include religious objectives as well as cultural and educational ones. Denominations initially helped to mold and shape the life of the immigrants in the United States by keeping alive deep emotions of kinship and belonging.[11] Yet ethnic lines are not sufficient to explain that multiplicity of denominationalism. The denominations also portrayed a kind of socioeconomic caste system which still today distinguishes the lower class denominations from the ones of the middle and upper middle class. The denominations became "the mouthpieces of the economic and sectional groups they represented."[12] Denominations divided and emerged along the lines of geography and color of skin as well as along ethnic and religious allegiance, and along the lines of income, or even adaptation to the English language as the many First English churches or even English synods indicate.

By appeal to the common biblical tradition the churches represented and perpetuated the ethics of class and nation rather than the common ethic of the gospel. While denominations still provide a haven for those who refuse to accept the ideology of the melting pot, they have largely succumbed to the compromise between the gospel tradition and the secular world which has its own tradition of religious autonomy. Only in recent years are the denominations beginning to learn that their common Christian heritage requires a joint recapturing and reliance on the Christian tradition and a joint witness to the world. American Protestants are beginning to learn that one cannot naively reject all traditions, and at the same time attempt to retain the biblical tradition, without ending in separatistic self-righteousness. We can only hope to uncover in our own denomination the common tradition that binds all Christians together as the body of Christ and present to the world a joint witness of that common heritage.

c. The community of saints

One might at first wonder whether the community of saints is properly located under the aspect of the church as the guardian of the past. Indeed the community of saints has a present and a future dimension. Yet we get a glimpse of what should be expressed at this point when we read in the Great Thanksgiving of the *Lutheran Book of Worship* that we "join our prayers with those of your servants of every time and place, and unite them with the ceaseless petitions of our great high priest until he comes as victorious Lord of all." [13] The church is a community of people that transcends the visible boundaries of an institution and of space and time.

It is vital for the church to remember that it participates in the community of saints. This combats the errant notion, often prominent in denominationalism, that the church is a gathering of like-minded people. The church cannot be derived from the desires of individuals. Bonhoeffer aptly reminds us that "the church does not come into being through people coming together (genetic sociology). But it is in being through the Spirit which is effective in the community." [14] It is a wrong notion that one can "attend the church of one's choice." The church is a given which we cannot choose, but through which God has chosen to accept us sinners. The church is not just an eschatological community which receives its peculiar shape from the future. The church is founded on that which God has done for us.[15]

Belonging to the church means that we belong to the Lord who has been active in the past, who is active in the present, and who will be active in the future. We are not the first Christians, but as a community of saints we are one with those with whom God has worked in the past. In its liturgical calendar the church rightly remembers the saints who have participated in the visible community. It does not adore them but it praises God for the good he has done through and with them. A church without saints is not a church in the strict sense, because it is oblivious to God's past activity. It also deprives itself of the stimulus which the community of saints exerts on our present lives.

Where the saints are not explicitly recognized as being part of the Christian community—presumably out of fear of being crypto-Roman Catholic—they are usually accepted implicitly. We preserve and use their songbook, the Old Testament Psalter, and the many hymns that have come to us through the centuries. Some of these were written by Augustine, Ambrose, Francis of Assisi, Martin Luther, Paul Gerhardt, and Charles Wesley. For instance, Paul makes clear his dependence on the saints when he calls Abraham "the father of all who believe" (Rom. 4:11). This is the same Paul who claimed that the Jewish law was abolished through the coming of Christ. Yet he did not feel that this meant that God had not been active in humanity. His fervent struggle in Romans 9-11 clearly indicates that Paul was well aware that the Christian community of saints did not originate out of thin air. We stand in succession of an earlier community, the Israelites, through and in whom God worked.

New Testament research has clearly shown that we cannot sufficiently understand the roots of our faith and therefore our tradition, unless we perceive them as coming out of the Israelite faith. The acceptance of the Jewish Scriptures as our Old Testament is an acknowledgment of the community of saints that comprises more than just the Christian community. It is a witness to God's larger saving activity. When Rudolf Bultmann claimed that the Old Testament Jewish history is a history of failure and because of this failure it finds its fulfillment in the New Testament, he shortchanges us of this very important part of God's salvation history.[16]

The Old Testament is very much our history and, as Luther picturesquely claimed, it is "the swaddling cloths and the manger in which Christ lies, and to which the angel points the shepherds." [17] The Old Testament, therefore, is important for Christians in its own right and also because the New Testament would make little sense without it. [18] Thus we stand in true succession to the history it portrays. In this way the Old Testament is part of our own history and we can say with Luther and in contrast to Bultmann that "all the fathers in the Old Testament, together with all the holy prophets, had the same faith and Gospel as we have." [19] The Old Testament is more than a negative backdrop against which the Christian faith looms in new light. [20] Its people are part of the community of saints and they are in every respect our spiritual ancestors.

The Christian community, while guarding the past, is also directed toward the present. From the hope that the past engenders, both as the reminder of God's activity and as an acknowledgement that this activity is unfinished, we are summoned to inaugurate this hope in the present.

2. The heart of the present

A sociological survey might question that the church plays a significant role in today's society. In most countries the effect that it exerts on the social and political life of the community and the private life of the individual is waning. Even where it is still effective, it is often claimed that its impact is minimal. [21] Yet in most Western countries the majority of the people claim to be Christian and in many younger nations the number of Christians is rapidly increasing. In most predominantly Christian countries, Sunday after Sunday more people turn out for worship than for any other single event, including soccer and football. Yet we do not simply record what the church is presently doing. Having traced the major steps of the church in the past, we want to ask theologically what the place of the church should be. We do not see our primary task in describing phenomenologically what place it presently occupies. Similar to the heart in a human being, the church pumps lifeblood into a cold society, it activates complacent people to thought and action, and amid self-perpetuating routine, it provides the impulse for new direction. Among the church's many different responsibilities that should be mentioned, three seem to be most important: The church is the conscience of society, it is the haven of the neglected, and it is the anticipation of the heavenly city.

a. The conscience of society [22]

While in the Israelite theocracy the worshiping community was identical with the political community, the story is different in Christendom. Ever since the church first emerged, the question was debated how the church should be related to society. Initially it was clear that the church, as a relatively small community, had to preserve its identity to survive. Its members conducted their lives according to their own agreed rules without rejecting that which they found acceptable in the rest of society. Once the church had gained majority status, the notion in the East developed that the church was the extended arm of the state with the emperor assuming the role of *Pontifex Maximus*. In the West, due to the absence of the emperor from the cradle of Latin Christianity, the church assumed many functions of the state, becoming the guardian of the emperor and in many instances his opponent. The price the church paid was heavy for this status in the West. To a large degree the Western Church exchanged its spiritual role for a political one, a role severely challenged by the Reformation. Yet the Reformers were by no means unanimous in their understanding of how to relate church and society. In the Geneva of Calvin the attempt was made to establish a theocracy with the church becoming synonymous with the state. This idea was also propagated by the Enthusiasts (Thomas Müntzer), and later by some English reformers and by the Puritans. On the Lutheran side, we notice an insistence on the distinction between church and state, though actually the princes never granted the church fully independent status. In the Anglican tradition we have the wedding of state and church, very much along the line of the Eastern Christendom.

The real challenge to the relationship of church and society has come during the last 200 years in the separation of church and state in almost all countries. Now the question had to be addressed anew how the church should be related to a society that by and large felt it had no need for religious guidance. Through the separation of state and church the typological distinction between church and sect, set forth by Ernst Troeltsch, was no longer adequate to describe the task of the church in relation to society. It would have been utopian to assume with Troeltsch that the church is an institution that wants to include all of humanity. On the other hand, the arrangement of the sect that Troeltsch contrasts with the church also is not adequate to describe the task of the church. A sect, he feels, can only exist in confrontation with the church, and furthermore within a few generations it will assume church-like features.

A more realistic possibility would be to perceive the function of today's church in analogy to that of a club. Those who still share religious feelings met at specified times and places to cultivate their own interests. To a large extent this is the official status allowed to the church in Marxist societies. Any functions beyond conducting religious rites and ceremonies for its own members are severely restricted for the church. Though the voluntary nature of the church would be a tacit admission of its alleged club status, Christians assert that the church is not simply constituted by its members but by God. Further, in contrast to a club, the church encourages infant membership. And finally, the church does not seek those that already have "a religious antenna," but it searches for those that do not seem to care about the church, the sinners and outcasts.[23]

Another possibility would be to conceive of the church as an institution through which we receive certain benefits if we also make our own contribution.[24] For instance, we could perceive the church in analogy to the institution of the family or the state. We might say that we participate in the rituals of the church and support it financially and receive eternal salvation as a compensation. Indeed the church has distinct institutional features, asking for contributions and involvement of its members, electing leaders, instituting rules of conduct to assure good standing, and granting the promise of certain blessings.

Yet the church as an institution does not exist apart from the people that constitute it. (1) The church does not exist for the people but people themselves form the institutional church. By contrast, form of government, for the people, by the people, of the people, is institutionalized in the United States in such a way that the institutional government operates largely independent from the people. Even frequent elections do not change this, as we become painfully aware when we elect a different government. (2) Any benefit derived from the church as an institution is not in response to our participation, but, conversely, our participation in the church is in response to the promises derived from the church. Even in its darkest moments, the church never forgot completely that it could be the institution of salvation only because of what God has promised to his church, not because of what we might bring to it.

Since the church has many institutional features, it must be an institution of a very special kind. To explain this special status we must remember that the church's reason for existence is the fact that Christ is risen from the dead and that he is both the head of the church and the redeemer of the world.[25] Since the risen Lord is the head of the church, we should not only expect to foreshadow the new creation and the glory of the risen Lord, but it is its mark of truthfulness to do so. In many ways the path of the church may resemble the *via dolorosa* (path of sorrows). Nevertheless, the church is called to foreshadow the glorified Christ and to announce his dominion over all the world. Since the risen Lord is also the redeemer of the world, the church cannot be silent in the face of a secular world. It is called to announce Christ's ultimate victory over the world and to symbolize his already commenced presence within it.

As H. Richard Niebuhr so admirably pointed out in his lucid study, *Christ and Culture,* the relationship between Christ and culture, or between Christ and society, can assume five positions: The church can stand against society, the church can affirm society, the church can come to stand above society, church and society can hold each other in tension, and finally the church can transform society. Niebuhr attempts to attribute to each of these types certain dominant streams in the history of the church. He sees Culture-Protestantism of 19th century Germany as the church affirmation of culture, or Luther's attitude toward church and state as expressive of a tension between church and culture. But Niebuhr realizes that such typology "is always something of a construct . . . no person or group ever conforms completely to a type. Each historical figure will show characteristics that are more reminiscent of some other family than the one by whose name he has been called, or traits will appear that seem wholly unique and individual.[26] Yet he asserts that such typology has the advantage of calling to attention the continuity and significance of the great motifs that appear and reappear in the long history of the church and in wrestling with its problems.

Niebuhr admits that none of these types appears in its true form and that all of them have their advantages and shortcomings. Therefore it seems much more logical to us that they should not be separated and attributed to distinct streams if we want to discuss the task of the church in today's society. On the contrary, by learning from their individual shortcomings we should take them together and carefully balance them against each other. Then we might arrive at an adequate framework within which we could describe the function of the church in today's society. We might also assume that the reason for the nonexistence of pure types is not only that they are not viable, but that they provide more a caricature of the church than its proper description.[27]

1. The church in its opposition to society: If the church does not want to lose itself it must first of all stand in opposition to society. This does not mean that the church is opposed to society. Yet from the very beginning there was a fundamental tension between church and the world and, simultaneously, one of intense relevance.[28] For instance, the Son of man came into the world to save it; the Christian dies to the sinful world to rise as a new creature; the world is ruled by the prince of the world who is already judged. Each of these assertions reflect the immense opposition of church and society. Yet the church does not abandon society. To fulfill its task, the church must be itself, true to its own calling, not of the world but in the world.

The church must be an institution, insisting strongly on the continuity with its origins. Amidst a situation of unrest and instability it provides a haven of rest and stability, the tranquil eye at the center of a stormy world. Amid the world's emphasis on transitoriness and change the church provides a strong sense of corporate identity. It knows what it stands for, it knows its Lord and what he has in store. It is not swayed by steadily varying trends and fads. As a beacon of heavenly guidance the church cherishes the gospel tradition and the administration of the sacraments. In other words, the church has what the world cannot give, an ultimate reference point for life and living and the living presence of the power of the resurrection that protects it from ultimate destruction. The church lives by the standard of grace and forgiveness which entitles it to ever new beginnings. It does not live by the law of achievement and the selective pressure that is derived from a finite creation and therefore bears the sting of death in itself.

Tempting as it may be, the church's otherness dare not lead it to isolation or withdrawal. It is significant that the stepping stones of the church out of Jerusalem were not the secluded desert sites of Pella and Qumran, but the bustling cities of Ephesus, Corinth, and Rome. Steering its own course, the church ventured into a foreign world, challenging what it found and calling this same world to a higher and more durable allegiance. Opposition to the world is always characterized by a momentum for mission.

It is not mere accident that in the United States at the present time the mainline churches are barely holding their own while the conservative churches are still growing amid a slightly expanding population. The acknowledgment that the world is corrupted by sin, that the world endangers our humanity, that earthly treasures are eaten up by moth and rust, leads to the realization that the world needs to be saved.

Christians, of course, are reminded not to love the world or the things that are of the world. They are strangers and pilgrims in this world. Yet the biblical witnesses assure us that Christ came into the world to save it and not to condemn it. As God has sent me, so do I send you, Jesus reminds us according to the Johannine witness. Similarly we hear Paul saying that God was in Christ reconciling the world unto himself. Therefore Luther could claim: "A mighty fortress is our God, a bulwark never failing." In the same vein we sing today: "Onward Christian soldiers, marching as to war." The opposition to the world is opposition to the belief in self-righteousness, in humanity's inherent natural goodness and moral perfectability.

By exposing the world as corrupt, as being under the dominion of the seductive and anti-Godly powers, the church does not confine itself to redeeming individual souls.[29] The church dare not neglect the individual and the spiritual side of its message. But its effectiveness is severely hampered, if not brought to naught, unless it also addresses itself to the bodily and material dimensions. This means that the church's opposition to society and its subsequent redemptive onslaught must be directed to the whole of society, both to body and spirit, both to corporate structure and individual human beings. Yet any missionary approach toward society would be futile or, at most, would result in an exchange of respective positions, unless the church were convinced that it comes to stand above society.

2. *The church in its stand above society:* At the height of the Middle Ages Pope Innocent III asserted that the relationship between church and state compared to that between sun and moon, i.e., that the moon receives its splendor from the sun. Though we might find such statement ill-fitting for a church that imitates the servant role of its Lord, there is some truth contained in this assessment of the relationship between church and society. Without the influence of the church—or a comparable religious organization—society does not gain a complete understanding of humanity. For instance, in a society in which so-called human rights are violated, usually the church does not have freedom of expression either.

The church, however, defending the human within a society, does not rival the task of the state. When in its socialization process the state assumes many of the traditional functions of the church, such as the care for the poor, the sick, and the old, and the education of the young, the church will not be edged out of its decisive role in the world. Other neglected areas will demand its attention, such as humanization of technology, labor and management relationship, and sensitizing affluent societies to the needs of developing countries. By claiming as its own new areas of responsibility, the church is not pushed from one corner into another. Rather the opposite is true. Through its involvement in areas neglected by society it examines and sharpens society's understanding of humanity. It makes society aware of what it neglects and encourages society to accord justice to everyone.

In the process of adequately defending the human in society, the church needs and will demand a somewhat preferred or exceptional position in society. Most countries recognize this by providing certain privileges for the church, such as subsidy for operating expenses, the privilege of collecting church tax from its members, exemption from real estate tax, etc. While these prerogatives may vary considerably from country to country, it is fair to say that "the churches have as their primary exception from the state a freedom to practice and propagate their faith. The state on the other hand has as its primary expectation the formulation by the churches of virtuous and patriotic citizens." [30]

Often the idea is advanced that in fulfilling its function as the conscience of society, the church does not expect to receive anything from the state nor does it give anything away. Similarly, the sentiment is strong that the state as the guardian of the temporal order acts autonomously in its own sphere without expecting any aid from the church. Yet being the guardian of the temporal order, the state realizes that this order is not simply given, but must be continuously shaped and maintained. Such order, however, cannot be safeguarded without the implicit or explicit consent of society. It is especially in this regard that the government has a fundamental expectation of the church, namely that it forms in society virtuous and patriotic citizens.

But how can the church educate Christians who function as virtuous and patriotic citizens if the dimension of religious freedom and therefore of religious influence never reaches beyond the completely private life of a Christian? [31] Moreover, how can society expect ultimate sanctioning of any virtue or of patriotism if the church is excluded from the public sector? A truly secular state that by its definition eliminates (metaphysical) ultimacy from its public horizon, relativizes itself and the values it espouses so much that in the long run it is doomed to failure. For instance, what would be the bond that binds public servants to their duty?

The only alternative is a state ideology, as it is advocated in the frequent singing of the national anthem and the pledge of allegiance to the flag. But the ideas of freedom, liberty, and concern for the well-being of the community, that are commonly associated with such state ideologies, are by no means secular insights. Historically they are grounded in deep religious commitments, and this means for us in the West as well as many developing countries, the Judeo-Christian tradition.[32] One might argue that the case is different in Marxist countries. Contrary to Friedrich Engels, the most revolutionary insights of Marxism—the concern for the oppressed and the outcast, the anticipation of the kingdom, the equality of all people—do not only *show* a similarity to those of the early Christian tradition, but in an intrinsic sense these *are* insights that stem directly from the gospel tradition.[33] Yet in separating them from the liberating power of that tradition they became truncated and, in many instances, their application led to renewed bondage and new enslavement instead of freedom and greater equality.

Society cannot dissociate or even emancipate itself from the church, unless it wants eventually to abrogate its task of maintaining temporal order and upholding virtue and patriotism. That most of our societies, influenced by the West, are still functioning relatively well is not the result of the separation of church and state or due to the fact that these societies are secular. The reason is rather that there is still so much Western, and this means Judeo-Christian sediment present in our societies that helps to form a bond of unity and advances self-respect and mutual concern. Yet the more this Judeo-Christian sediment becomes obliterated or attenuated the more it becomes necessary for the church to act as the guardian of society, to function as the state's reminder of the eternal value and responsibility of each human being. However, any attempt of the church to rise above our sinful society, to act as a beacon and reminder of a common metaphysical obligation, will arouse the suspicion of some people. They will question whether such a position is too presumptuous or unnecessary. Therefore the tension between church and society becomes unavoidable.

3. *Church and society in tension:* As long as the church exists it will live in tension with society. Even in the United States, a country that prides itself on its clear separation of state and church, the state is always in danger of becoming a church, with an official faith or ideology, called civil religion, and the White House serving as the focal point of that ideology. Is it really by mere accident that in the United States most state capitols and the national capitol bear so much resemblance to St. Peter's basilica in Rome, the heart of the Roman Catholic Church? Is it

only by accident that occasionally some U.S. presidents have asked pastors
to conduct worship services in the White House with invited guests as
worshipers? Yet the temptation for the church to become a state is
equally tempting. More than once the church has attempted to legislate
its own rules of conduct for everyone.

To avoid the twin dangers of clerical domination or of a civil religion,
some theologians introduced the distinction between two kingdoms of
God, the kingdom to the left (the world) and the kingdom to the right
(the church). Picking up the biblical notion of a distinction between the
world and the kingdom of God, Augustine outlined the progress of the
city of God over the city of the world, intending to show the spiritual
superiority of the former. While such a view left no doubt as to the abiding necessity of the church for society, it also furthered the clerical domination over the world instead of holding it in check. It was not until
Luther that a doctrine of the two kingdoms evolved that avoided the
danger inherent in Augustine's system without abolishing the tension
between church and state.[34]

It is unfortunate that H. Richard Niebuhr labels as dualistic the tension between church and culture that results from the doctrine of the two
kingdoms. Though Niebuhr immediately qualifies his typological assessment, it certainly colors his description and evaluation as to the relationship between church and society.[35] Niebuhr, however, recognizes that
Luther does not compartmentalize the world into church and state, but
that he strictly distinguishes between the kingdom on the left or the
earthly kingdom, and the kingdom on the right or the heavenly kingdom.
We will also agree with Niebuhr that, though Luther's approach brought
about valuable social change, it was basically conservative, more apt to
preserve the world than to change it.[36]

Unlike Augustine, Luther did not identify the kingdom of God with
the kingdom on the right, and the kingdom of the devil with the kingdom
on the left. Though Luther distinguishes between the kingdom of Christ
and the kingdom of the world, the latter means for him the totality of all
orders of God, the orders of nature as well as civil justice. The line of
scrimmage between God and the anti-Godly powers goes through both
kingdoms and Satan attempts to turn both into an anti-Godly chaos.[37]
Their purpose as bulwarks of God against the destructive assaults of the
devil testifies to their inner unity. Luther says:

> For God has established two kinds of government among men. The one
> is spiritual; it has no sword, but it has the word, by means of which men

are to become good and righteous, so that with this righteousness they may attain eternal life. He administers this righteousness through the word, which he has committed to the preachers. The other kind of worldly government, which works through the sword so that those who do not want to be good and righteous to eternal life may be forced to become good and righteous in the eyes of the world. He administers this righteousness through the sword. And although God will not reward this kind of righteousness with eternal life, nonetheless, he still wishes peace to be maintained among men and rewards them with temporal blessings.[38]

This passage from 1526 shows very clearly that the same God stands behind both kingdoms and is actively present in them, but in different ways. While God works in both kingdoms according to his goodness and love, one kingdom is concerned with faith and eternal salvation, the other with outward peace and prevention of evil.[39] The secular kingdom serves the earthly life and is temporal like our life on earth, while the spiritual kingdom serves for eternal life, the actual goal of God's work.[40] Luther observes very properly that even Christians cannot escape the secular kingdom and its distinctions: "We are all included in them; indeed, we were born into them even before we became Christians. Therefore we must also remain in them as long as we are on earth, but only according to our outward life and our physical existence." [41] We are citizens of the secular kingdom according to our secular needs, while we are citizens of the spiritual kingdom according to our spiritual existence. This shows that all of their differences notwithstanding there is an organic interdependence between the two kingdoms.[42]

This interdependence becomes especially evident when Luther observes that the spiritual kingdom needs peace and order in this world—results of the secular kingdom—so that word and sacrament can be .effectively administered. Another point where this interdependence is found is in the inclusive character of the secular kingdom. The secular or temporal kingdom does not just comprise authority, government, and the orders of nature, but all means of earthly sustenance of life, such as matrimony, family, property, economy, and all professions.[43] These human enterprises are exercised according to the law, or what is synonymous for Luther, according to the sword. But how does one know about the law if one is not a Christian? Luther recognizes that the rules and regulations of and in this world are not given through Christ, but they are given as a natural law.

While the knowledge of God's will is often distorted and obliterated
in this world, Luther is convinced that the law of the country sufficiently
answers the questions what a father, a mother, a prince, or a judge must
do in a particular situation. Of course, these laws are historically conditioned and changeable. Luther demands that we must use reason to
investigate expression of the natural law they ought to represent. But he
is rather optimistic about the value of the positive law of a country. He
is convinced that there is always a hidden order behind the world's
obvious order, or disorder. In the long run, no power can exist without
God's hidden order. We see, Luther contends, that according to this
hidden order God allows one state to grow and thrive, but he also
dissolves it.

The natural order is expressed, for instance, in the Magnificat.[44] The
rational order of the world is God's order without his actual presence.
But how can we penetrate to the natural law and judge whether these
orders are still God's orders and in accordance with the natural law?
Luther points here to the golden rule and responds: "For nature teaches
—as does love—that I should do as I would be done by." [45] Luther refers
here to the same maxim that was used more than two centuries later
by Immanuel Kant in his *Groundwork of the Metaphysics of Morals*.
Luther mentions nature and love in one breath. He is convinced that
though the secular kingdom is governed by power, this does not exclude
love. This is especially important for Christians, since they, being led by
love, must by necessity live in the secular kingdom which is governed
by power.

Thus Luther can encourage Christians to assume secular office. He
says if there is need of judges, lords, and princes, and if you think you
are qualified for it, you should apply for such offices, otherwise the necessary authority is held in contempt and becomes weakened.[46] Whereas
he admonishes neither to exert power too freely nor too sparsely, he concedes: "To err in this direction, however, and punish too little is more tolerable, for it is always better to let a scoundrel live than to put a godly
man to death." [47] How far Luther is from the idea of a power-centered
secular order can be seen when he advises Christians in secular authority
to imitate Christ.[48] Since Christ, as supreme prince, came and served us
without seeking his own power and honor, so Christians in authority
shall not look out for their own but serve those under them so that they
will protect and defend them.

While Luther's distinction between the two kingdoms certainly provides no panacea of how to relate church and society, it makes one point unmistakably clear: No sphere of our life can be excluded from Christ's lordship.[49] His lordship, extending over all of life, proceeds in different forms and with different methods. If the distinction becomes blurred between the different forms and methods according to which the two kingdoms conduct their affairs, either clerical triumphalism or secular utopianism results. The church must remind society under whose dominion society stands and under whose ultimate authority it conducts its business. Conversely, society serves as a reminder for the church that this world, though urging and longing for wholeness and redemption, is still broken.

Luther realistically discerned that the same forces of darkness are at work in both church and society. In the church the lust for power, the execution of injustice, and the disregard for love are present to threaten the very credibility of the gospel. The church is always called to repentance not only for the sins of society but also for its very own sins. As a community of people the church cannot escape the necessity for law and order. Its structures cannot be maintained with love, but they must be upheld with power in the name of love. However, the necessity for a hierarchical order in the church and the call to obedience that this order implies dare not be mixed with or misunderstood as the call to obey the gospel tradition. Even in its own house the church must distinguish between the kingdom on the left and the kingdom on the right or it preaches law in the name of the gospel.

That Christ is the Lord of the whole world and not only of the interior life of the Christian has been rediscovered by many who do not necessarily claim the name of Luther in their heritage. For instance, in *The Chicago Declaration of Evangelicals* we read that "we affirm that God lays total claim upon the lives of his people. We cannot, therefore, separate our lives in Christ from the situation in which God has placed us."[50] This sentiment is compounded by the growing number of people who having set their heart primarily on social causes now realize that their gains do not compare to the time, capital, and energy that they have invested. Therefore, there is an increased readiness to accept "a balanced biblical concern for both social restructuring and individual conversion." This insight gains new vigor when "conservatives" discover also to what extent governments who espouse law and order are morally corrupt. Thus evangelism and social concern not only are considered as very important, but we increasingly realize that they are inseparable. Ronald Sider addresses the issue very appropriately when he claims:

> Evangelistic proclamation is fully biblical only when it calls for repentance from all types of sins [i.e., not just private ones] and urges a biblical discipleship in which all relationships, both personal and societal, are transformed. And prophetic social criticism is fully biblical only when it announces both that participation in structural evil is a damnable sin against God Almighty and also that divine forgiveness is bestowed on those who repent and turn from all their sins.

Sherwood Wirt comes at the issue of relating church and society from a slightly different angle. Acknowledging that social problems exist wherever humans exist, he is still hesitant to address social issues on a large scale. He distinguishes appropriately between evangelism and social action, defining evangelism as "presenting Christ to men in the power of the Holy Spirit," while social action is seen as "an effort to apply Christ in finding solutions to human problems." [51] But he wonders whether one really can or should convert power structures, since it is always individuals who make up these structures.[52] It might be much better to address the individuals within the structures so that the structures would change with them. Wirt also questions whether the church should act as a pressure group and engage in political lobbying. Yet he recognizes that the church has a biblical mandate to be alert to its social responsibility. But corporate church pronouncements on social matters "should deal with the heart of the moral issue and where possible should be couched in general rather than specific terms." [53]

As Sherwood Wirt paradigmatically demonstrates there is still a frequent tendency within the church to shy away from specific corporate pronouncements concerning significant issues in society. The reason for this hesitancy is not a lack of courage—evangelism requires courage too—but a wrong notion of society, namely that it is seen as the enemy of the church, instead of as an additional element of God's presence in the world. To overcome this inadequacy, the church must affirm society and dialogue with it.

4. *The church's affirmation of society:* Immanuel Kant's *Religion within the Limits of Reason Alone,* Friedrich Schleiermacher's *On Religion. Speeches to Its Cultured Despisers,* and finally Adolf von Harnack's famous literary exchange with Karl Barth, had convinced many that the affirmation of society had gone too far. It became labeled Culture-Protes-

tantism and therefore received an unsavory reputation. We certainly
cannot advocate that God is synonymous with humanity's own possibilities. But Harnack was rightly worried when he asked Karl Barth:

> If religious experience is contrary to or disparate from all other experi-
> ence, how can the necessity of a radical flight from the world be avoided
> . . . ? If God and world (life in God and worldly life) are absolute con-
> trasts, how are we to understand the close connection, even equating,
> of love for God and love for one's neighbor which constitutes the heart
> of the Gospel? . . . If God and world (life in God and worldly life) are
> absolute contrasts, how can we lead people to God, that is, to what is
> good? [54]

Barth's answer was not very comforting when he asserted that "the
faith which is awakened by God will never be able fully to avoid the necessity of a more or less 'radical' protest against *this* world, inasmuch as it is a
hope for that which is promised but unseen." [55]

Barth's attitude of a protesting disassociation from the world was well
taken in confrontation with the Nazi tyranny of the 1930s and 40s. But if
Barth had remembered Luther's insight that a tyrant is against God's will
and will be toppled by another tyrant, his unqualified acceptance of Stalin-
ist Communism would have been more discerning. Furthermore, if we
claim the lordship of God as christocentrically as does Barth, how can we
convincingly assert that God is also present and active in the whole world
and not just in the church? If we would follow Barth, the church could
not even meaningfully criticize society, since society would have no God-
given antenna to understand this criticism and respond with positive
action. But what positive force could be present in the world that would
allow for such response unless it were God himself to whom all people
witness (Rom. 1:19)? Knowing about human sinfulness, the church
cannot assume that God's presence in the world is self-evident to everyone. The church must therefore act as the conscience of society, acting in
solidarity with it, and at the same time sharpen society's own conscience
for the demands of God.

It is very unlikely that in secular society the church will get a hearing,
except among its own members, if it cannot appeal to insights that are
accessible to everyone in church and society. Thus we must look for a
common ethical sphere, and set common ethical goals for Christians and
non-Christians in society.[56] Such "Christian humanism" would take
seriously that all of humanity, not only that part which associates with
the church, is created and sustained by God.

But where do we perceive such common meeting ground? Today a metaphysically grounded natural law has fallen in disrepute. Yet Luther's emphasis on the common knowledge of the natural law, in his attempt to relate church and society, may contain more insight than we are willing to attribute to him. For instance, Emil Brunner warned that if there is nothing universally valid and no justice beyond ourselves that meets all of us as an undeniable demand, then there is no actual justice, only organized power play.[57] The alarming frequency with which totalitarian systems have emerged during the last one hundred years should make us wonder whether our own humanity is a sufficient foundation to ensure the survival of human existence. Even during the reign of absolutism the kings and princes understood that they enjoyed their rule through the grace of God. But today's dictators exercise their rule in their own name. They no longer feel themselves subjected to higher powers. The individual human being has become his own ultimate measure for right and wrong.

But we should also remember Charles Darwin's assertion that human moral and mental faculties differ in degree rather than in kind from the capacities of animals. If there is indeed a moral continuity between animals and humans, there should be even more ground to assume such continuity between one human being and another. Perhaps the reason why we tend to deny the basic unity of the human moral process lies in the fact of our sinful estrangement from each other. We are so far apart from each other that we tend to forget our common destiny. Ethological research has adduced more and more evidence that indeed there are some basic norms of human behavior. Arnold W. Ravin expressed this very appropriately when he said:

> Every culture has a concept of murder, that is a specification of conditions under which homicide is unjustifiable. Every culture has a taboo upon incest and usually other regulations upon sexual behavior. Similarly, all cultures hold untruth to be abhorrent, at least under most conditions. Finally, all have a notion of reciprocal obligation between parents and their children. These universal or near-universal ethics . . . indicate some profound and fundamental needs in all men to behave within certain limits or ethical boundaries.[58]

This tells us that by nature the behavior of society is not as free and unspecified as we might initially assume. To be a human being means to act according to certain norms that enable us to live together and further our own species. The explicit forms which these norms assume, however, depend upon the environment in which the social behavior takes place.

These insights and conclusions give new significance to the traditional theology of orders. Since the moral norms, in principle, at least, accessible to everyone, are goal-oriented, intended to preserve the species rather than to constitute it, it might be good to follow the suggestion of Walter Künneth and perceive moral norms as orders of preservation instead of orders of creation. Künneth does not intend to diminish the creational character of these orders, but he denounces a static interpretation of these orders and maintains that the creation must be perceived under the aspect of God's conserving activity.[59] This is even more necessary, since we know God's creation only in its fallen condition, under the aspect of preservation. According to Künneth the orders of preservation counteract the tendencies of the destructive anti-Godly powers. They are a sign that God does not want to destroy the world but instead conserves it for Christ's sake and toward Christ. The orders of preservation therefore have eschatological character, for they urge on toward eschatological fulfillment in the new creation.

Since these orders are no longer evident in their original divine creational intention, they assume the character of a law. But as law they enable and facilitate the living together of people. They express a mutual obligation and therefore have a basically diaconal character. Yet they are also susceptible to sinful distortion and can be misused to perpetuate injustice and inequality. Therefore, it is necessary never to divorce them from God as the originator and granter of these orders. This does not mean, however, that we should go as far as Karl Barth does when he claims that through its sinful existence humanity is in such a depravity that it has no possibility of knowing about these fundamental moral laws of nature. Barth therefore insists that these orders cannot be found anywhere; they are disclosed to us through Jesus Christ in God's word.[60] But such an exclusively christocentric approach to these orders—whether we accept their foundation in Christ or not—obscures the fact that the acknowledgment of certain moral norms is a necessary condition for human existence as such.[61]

Atheists can recognize these norms of moral behavior as partly inborn and partly handed on by tradition. In the light of God's self-disclosure in Jesus Christ, however, Christians perceive in these norms God's preserving activity. They realize that through the evolving moral process God is present in the human community, preserving it against self-destruction and against the destructive and seductive tendencies of the anti-Godly powers. Luther has expressed this once very picturesquely when he said: "If God would withdraw his protective hand you would become blind, or an adulterer and murderer like David, you would fall and break your leg and drown." [62]

Through God's self-disclosure in Jesus Christ we are reminded of God's presence in society, and of society's transitory character. Society will find its fulfillment and completion in the eschatological new creation, when God's orders will be unimpaired and self-evident and when God will dwell in the midst of his people. It would be short-sighted and a neglect of our responsibility as people of God, if we would simply sit back and wait for that eschatological goal of perfection to arrive. Once we have discovered our common meeting point and affirmed God's preserving presence in society, we should witness to God's presence in the midst of his fallen world. This means that we attempt to transform the world so that it may bear more resemblance to the new creation toward which it is designed.

5. *The task of the church to transform society:* The abiding presence of the anti-Godly destructive powers in this world makes the task of the church to transform society a continuous and perennial one. Any millennial or utopian ideas that advocate an evolutionary convergence of church and society neglect the reality and radicality of evil in this world and forget the eschatological proviso that limits all human endeavors. Yet shy of establishing the kingdom of God, which by its very nature is an eschatological event, the church would betray its own reason for being if it would not press on to transform society.

The transformation process, however, must go in two directions. There is a need for a continuous transformation of that part of society which is the church so that it may become a better example of the new community and the beacon of hope in the face of oppression and injustice. There is also a continuous need for a transformation of that part of society which is outside the church. The truth that God is active in the world must come to ever clearer expression. Sinful humanity and the structures it designed to perpetuate its sinfulness must be converted to become expressive of the will of the Lord. The process of such conversion would foreshadow God's eschatological goal of salvation envisioned for all people. This pressing on for the enchantment of humanity would include on the social level: economic justice in the face of the exploitation of people by others, human dignity in the face of political oppression of human beings by other human beings, human solidarity in the face of alienation of person from person, and hope in the face of despair in personal life.[63]

Some rightly ask whether the theologies of liberation, revolution, hope, and even of rebellion are not just transitory fads that seek to ride the bandwagon of global social upheavals which mark the collapse of the European colonial powers. Though there may be some truth to this, the attempt of the church to transform the world is as old as the church itself. While the church has compromised this missionary goal many times, Friedrich Engels made a significant observation when he said: "In the popular risings of the Christian West . . . the religious disguise is only a flag and a mask for attacks on an economic order which is becoming antiquated. This is finally overthrown, a new one arises and the world progresses." [64] Engels recognized that in the name of the Judeo-Christian tradition actual societal changes take place, whereas in other societies reform movements "are clothed in religion but they have their source in economic causes; and yet, even when they are victorious, they allow the old economic conditions to persist untouched."

We must now ask what allows for and engenders this transformation of society in the "Christian West." What was it that drew millions of people to emigrate to the "New World" and what stimulated them to turn into a beacon of hope for many others living under oppression and poverty? What was it that has lured at least one third of the world's population to embrace Marxist doctrines, a teaching that still serves as a sign of freedom from domination and slavery in many younger nations? Though economic reasons are a powerful stimulus, they fail to explain the whole picture, because often the affluent intellectuals of a nation are especially attracted to Marxist doctrines.

Of course, we could say that the endeavor to transform society results from the peculiarly human phenomenon of pressing on to ever new horizons, of being open to the world and searching for constantly new experiences. Again this answer fails to account for the fact that primarily the "Christian West" served as the starting point for societal transformations. Perhaps the religious component cannot just be understood with Engels as a disguise, but as the propelling and driving force for the creation of a new society. The Judeo-Christian hope for a new world order and for a new humanity served as the stimulus for the Marxist vision of a "socialized humanity." [65] The Judeo-Christian faith also stood behind the assertion in The Declaration of Independence "that all men are created equal, that they are endowed by their Creator with certain inalienable rights, that among these are life, liberty, and the pursuit of happiness."

But we recognize at the same time that the Marxist vision is tarnished by countless acts of new oppression. The Declaration of Independence also significantly qualified the insight of equality within the human family when it called the American Indians "merciless savages" who attack the white immigrants. Regardless of these frequent lapses the search for a responsible world society continues. This search involves not just rudiments of the Judeo-Christian tradition as in the Marxist vision or in the American Declaration of Independence but Christians themselves of many nationalities and confessions are active in it. Inspired by the hope that is within them they are willing to give account for it (1 Peter 3:15) and contribute through a common effort to a deeper unity and deeper insight. For Christians humanity is not a fact that can be taken for granted, but it is understood as a process, constantly being created and recreating itself.[66]

The Christian vision of a new world order gains constantly new hope and refinement through its connection with Jesus Christ as the originator and source of the hope for a new humanity.[67] Consequently it is distinguished from all ideologies and movements it engendered, through its intensity and clarity. The living dialog of summons and response between Christ and his followers ensures that the hope for a new humanity, though not without a material basis, is different from what can be expected through genetic input and environmental conditioning alone. It will result in a truly human creation of a loving process.[68] This dialog will also assure that we are not taking the future in our own hands by replacing the old tyrannies of oppression with new tyrannies of liberation.

We must caution here that the abolition of laws and orders of oppression does not necessarily imply freedom and justice. History has shown that, for instance, the transformation of the bourgeois capitalist societies into socialist ones has often not yielded the desired results, but the emerging new power structures have again become instruments of oppression.[69] The church must be discerning and cautious in its inclination to support any and every so-called revolution. Not only can it come under the control of extremists, but a revolution can never be an end in itself, or be identified with ushering in the kingdom. "Revolution should not be regarded as a normal remedy, as a beneficial panacea, but as a last desperate operation and it carries with it certain serious risks."[70]

Once the careful and deliberate conclusion is reached that the evil and risks of a revolution outweigh by far the injustice and cruelty of the present system one should always keep in mind that "there is no basis in the New Testament for identifying the Kingdom with a new social order and there is no basis in our experience for doing so either." [71] At the most, we can attain a partial embodiment of the kingdom of God in society. This means that revolution, whether peaceful or not, falls shy of its goal, to bring about true justice, and therefore stands under the judgment of God who calls it to repentance and renewed transformation. Consequently God "has chosen to create human beings as makers of their own history with full freedom inherent in their individual and collective destinies." [72] We must understand ourselves as the hands and arms of God, molding ourselves and others and being molded into a foretaste of the eschatological kingdom.

The representatives of liberation theology rightly remind us that, as ambassadors of God's redemptive news, we are accountable to the global human family and must become living witnesses to the coming of the kingdom. If we take seriously God's covenant extended to us in Christ, the eschatological vision of a renewed humanity is not just otherworldly. Paul's insight reinforces this when he claims: "And we all, with unveiled face, beholding the glory of the Lord, are being changed into his likeness from one degree of glory to another" (2 Cor. 3:18).

We can argue that the prospect of sanctification, the progressive transformation into God's true representatives, is too costly. If this were our response we would not exert any inspiring and corrective influence on the global human family. We would rather tacitly condone present turmoil, violence, and oppression. Any vision of a new humanity, whether utopian or ideological, would be superior to such a negative stand and offer at least a semblance of hope. On the other hand, we can participate in God's covenant community and become beacons of hope for a new humanity. Such a venture, however, will not be convenient. As the frequent imperatives in the Pauline letters indicate, it will mean a continuous battle against our sinful desire to join the mainstream of society. We will also become offensive to those who want to perpetuate traditional patterns of oppression, injustice, and exploitation, and who mistakenly look for Christians to uphold the status quo. But by pressing on in patient hope for signs of the new creation we will take seriously our charge to be the conscience of society. We will make people more sensitive to each other's needs and we will become living witnesses of the good news of God's new creation.

b. The haven of the neglected

If the church assumes the role of the conscience in society, it cannot in triumphalist fashion do this without betraying its own objective. The church must rather assume a servant model, working on the fringes of society on behalf of those who are neglected and outcast. The church is certainly never free of arrogance and self-aggrandizement especially when it speaks out against social inequality in a faraway country, or supports the politically oppressed or economically exploited in a distant land or in a different economic system. Yet the actual reason for such involvement is usually an expression of global solidarity in the attempt to eliminate unnecessary pain and hurt.

In an age in which millions of people travel to different countries every year and in which global communication has become nearly instantaneous, no situation of any magnitude remains hidden before the eyes of the world community. But the speck in the brother's eye should never deserve priority over the log in our own eye (Matt. 7:3) lest our concern be turned into hypocrisy. The church's most convincing stand for the disinherited in a different societal context must be accompanied by a similar attitude on the home front. The church also must realize that siding with those without material and political power is not something to be desired. But by so doing the church follows the example of its Lord of whom Scripture says that he "came not to be served but to serve, and to give his life as a ransom for many" (Matt. 20:28). The Gospel of John even reminds us that "greater love has no man than this, that a man lay down his life for his friends" (John 15:13).

The notion of a servant church was vigorously expressed in the Vatican II statement "On the Church in the Modern World." Since this pastoral constitution was published, the concept of the church as servant has been restated in many other official documents of the churches.[73] Yet this emphasis on the imitation of Christ as one who lays down his life for others had been advocated earlier in this century by Dietrich Bonhoeffer in his *Letters and Papers from Prison*. Bonhoeffer wrote:

> The Church is the Church only when it exists for others. To make a start, it should give away all its property to those in need. The clergy must live solely on the freewill offerings of their congregations, or possibly engage in some secular calling. The Church must share in the secular problems of ordinary human life, not dominating, but helping and serving. It must tell men of every calling what it means to live in Christ, to exist for others. In particular, our Church will have to take the field

against the vices of *hubris,* power-worship, envy, and humbug, as the roots of all evil. It will have to speak of moderation, purity, trust, loyalty, constancy, patience, discipline, humility, contentment, and modesty.[74]

Bonhoeffer gains these insights from the example that Jesus set and with which Paul confronts us when he mentions the cross as the decisive event in Jesus' life.

Others have picked up this emphasis. For instance, Harvey Cox claims: "The church's task in the secular city is to be the *diakonos* of the city, the servant who bends himself to struggle for its wholeness and health."[75] Two years before Harvey Cox, Gibson Winter entitled a whole chapter of a book "The Servant Church in a Secularized World" and stated: "In the servant Church, ministry is servanthood within the world. Ministry is discerning the promise of the saving history in the historical decisions of public responsibility; ministry is also discerning the truly human in the spheres of personal association and family life."[76]

While the servant role portrayed by Cox and Winter was a rather confident one, convinced that this involvement would lead to a brighter future, more recent writings have gone back to Bonhoeffer's original observation which showed more genuine suffering and self-giving. For instance, we hear from Dorothee Sölle that "we can change the social conditions under which people experience suffering. . . ." But there are also "brutalization, insensibility, mutilation and injury that no longer can be reversed."[77] Sölle discovered correctly that "the difficulty and the future task of a political theology consists in speaking appropriately of the gospel. . . . What is involved is giving credibility to the possibility of liberation from oppressive structures; what is involved is the inducement-model for becoming truly human."[78] We realize more and more the depth and complexity of injustice and suffering and the limited resources that the church has to alleviate them. Even the giving away of the church's riches would not go far in the face of worldwide famine, fully one-fourth of the world's population going to sleep hungry every night.

The awareness that our own resources and powers will not noticeably change the human predicament dare not serve as an excuse for conducting business as usual. Bonhoeffer was certainly right when he reminded us that we should not underestimate the importance of examples.[79] The greatest handicaps for the church are usually not its limited resources but its own posture. The power struggle within many church bureaucracies, the want of thrift and exemplary life-style of both leaders and followers, and the discrepancy between creed and action are greater liabilities than the lack of skill or workers. When the spirit of self-giving love prevails, it can often be the leaven which makes change and renewal both possible and endurable.[80]

We should remember that the church has always seen the servant role as a characteristic ingredient of being in the world. Following the example of its Lord, it has been willing to serve even to the point of self-sacrifice (Mark 10:45). The church knows that service to the least in this world is service to its Lord, and we are reminded: "As you did it to one of the least of these my brethren, you did it to me" (Matt. 25:40). In a similar vein Paul encourages us when he says: "Do not use your freedom as an opportunity for the flesh, but through love be servants of one another (Gal. 5:13). From the very beginning the church realized that service includes those who are in need within the church as well as those on the outside. For instance, Paul collected for the suffering in Jerusalem. Especially in the first centuries of the Christian faith, it was a "trademark" of a Christian to care for the less fortunate people. Lactantius admonishes the Christians that God teaches us never to do evil and always to do good. This means for him "to give assistance to the depressed and those laboring, to furnish food to those who have it not." [81] Similarly, Bishop Ambrose of Milan asserted: "Your office will shine gloriously, if the oppression of widows and orphans attempted by the powerful, should be hindered by the servants of the Church, if you show that the command of the Lord is more to you than the favour of the rich." [82]

Being a servant does not mean simply giving from one's surplus; it also means standing up for the underprivileged and taking the risk of becoming one of them. In other words, servanthood is solidarity with the suffering. The servant character pertains to the individual who does duties of charity, as well as to the whole church. If one is elected to public office one's conduct must still be measured with the same criteria. It is significant that the public servant role of the Christians was emphasized very early in the history of the church. As soon as the Christian faith had become the majority religion, the Council of Arles (A.D. 314) stated that since the Christian faith has now become a recognized religion, the bishop in the area in which a governor resides should watch over him and assist the governor with advice that he might commit no injustice in his office.[83] If he violated Christian principles and did not heed the advice of his bishop, he was to be excluded from the congregation. The same was true for municipal authorities. Living a Christian life means doing what is right, even if it excludes that which is popular. Gerhard Uhlhorn summed up well the servant function of the early church:

> It was when misery became greater and greater in the perishing world, when the arm of the state was more and more paralyzed, when the authorities no longer offered assistance to the poor and the oppressed, nay, themselves took a part in oppressing and exhausting them, that the Church became on a grand scale the refuge of all the oppressed and suffering.[84]

The servant role of the church did not go unnoticed in the world. Often worldly authorities took advantage of the church's servant role, installing bishops to fulfill temporal functions and endowing them with lands and valuables as compensation. Consequently, the church often and involuntarily exchanged its servant role for one of domination and support of the oppressors. We remember that the Reformation was due in part to the church's having become primarily a pursuer of worldly goals. Yet the servant role had never died out completely. As the examples of Savonarola and St. Francis of Assisi show, it was continued at least in some circles, such as in certain (reform) monasteries. Today the servant role has again assumed a very significant function. The modern economic industrialization has brought undreamed of blessings for many, but in its wake have emerged new forms of injustice and widespread poverty. Thus we have witnessed the rise of the church's social mission, exemplified by people such as Bodelschwingh in Bethel, Germany, Wichern in Hamburg, Germany, and Rauschenbusch in New York. Today there are attempts to give a technological world a more human face and more the resemblance of human solidarity and care for each other through programs such as Church World Service, Caritas, Miserior, and Bread for the World.

c. The anticipation of the heavenly city

Confronted with the huge problems of today and the limited resources that the church has, one is tempted to conclude that the church's servant role will not significantly alter the face of this world. At first sight this might be true. But we must remember that the church does not gain its strength from the imitation of Jesus or from his cross. Quite the opposite, it knows that its Lord could not be contained by cross and tomb. The symbols of apparent defeat were turned into signs of triumph over the powers of destruction. Where Christians are living out their allegiance to the Lord, the cross of Christ takes on new meaning. It becomes the rallying point for the oppressed and the powerless and a sign of inspiration that in this sign we will win over all adversity and be able to participate in a new heavenly community. In the face of a torn and divided world, in the face of the rift between east and west and south and north, the church anticipates proleptically this new community now on a local and also on a global scale.

When we talk here about proleptic anticipation, three potential misunderstandings must be averted:

(1) Anticipation of the heavenly city does not mean that we attempt to institute now what is promised to us as an eschatological, i.e., heavenly, reality. As Dietrich Bonhoeffer in his seminal book, *Life Together,* has pointed out:

> So between the death of Christ and the Last Day it is only by a gracious anticipation of the last things that Christians are privileged to live in visible fellowship with other Christians. It is by the grace of God that a congregation is permitted to gather visibly in this world to share God's Word and sacrament.[85]

The church is only an interim institution between Pentecost and Parousia, waiting and hoping for replacement by the heavenly community of all the saints. A utopian attempt to bring about in totality that toward which the church now lives would destroy the condition which makes such existence possible. It is, for instance, one of the strange paradoxes of Marxism that it lives and strives for the anticipation of the heavenly community in a Marxist classless society. By refusing, however, to admit that its attempts and programs are only provisional, Marxism destroys that which engendered and encouraged its hopes, the God-provided eschatological perfection. Moreover, since perfection must now be attained in this world, utopian systems behave intolerantly and dictatorially, and diminish even more the ideal vision for which they stand.

(2) Anticipation of the heavenly city is a divine gift and not a human accomplishment. Community is not something we accomplish, but something which is given and which we discover. In our anticipatory endeavors we do not attempt to fulfill a dream or a utopian vision, but we live according to the presence of God through his Spirit. Whenever the church loses its spiritual dimensions it is reduced to the status of a club in which its members seek to pursue their own interests. The theocentric structure of the Christian community reminds us of God, our ultimate allegiance and authority. All dreams and visions will be destroyed by the cross of

Christ, the living reminder that we live under the realities of this world but are not sustained by them.

There have been many visionary Christian communities, the Oneida community in New York, the Franciscan Spiritualists under Joachim of Fiore, and the Enthusiasts under Thomas Müntzer. Though assuming they lived from the power of the Spirit, they lived according to their dreams and hopes, neglecting the reality of the cross. After the initial excitement had waned, their attempts were doomed to failure. Bonhoeffer rightly reminds us here that "God hates visionary dreaming; it makes the dreamer proud and pretentious." [86] Living under the new life means for the Christian community to live under the world of forgiveness, the source of new life, and under God's word which is extended to us through others. Since the extension of the forgiving and encouraging word of God is always mediated through the community in which we live, we must mention a third misunderstanding.

(3) Anticipation of the heavenly city is not a purely spiritual reality, but is enfleshed in everyday life. While we distinguish between body and spirit, we realize that physical limitations can and are transcended by a spiritual unity bridging space and time. But we dare not restrict the anticipation of the heavenly city to the spiritual, unless we would encourage the strange notion that the Christian community does not transform lives and conditions but only spirits. Bonhoeffer rightly observes that "a purely spiritual relationship is not only dangerous but also an altogether abnormal thing." [87] There must also be a physical interaction between members of any spiritual community to which we are a part. Process thought has perhaps best captured this notion when it talks about the close interaction between God and the world. For instance, according to Alfred North Whitehead there exists a reciprocal relation between God and the world. "What is done in the world is transformed into a reality in heaven, and the reality in heaven passes back into the world." [88] Similarly, Paul depicts with the image of the body of Christ an intense interaction between the Lord and his church. The body of Christ is mirrored in the Christian community and its individual members who form this body.

Throughout the centuries the anticipation of the heavenly city has perhaps best been enfleshed in the monastic ideal. Monastic groups were usually started to strengthen people's spiritual life. They thereby disciplined their daily lives and transformed the surroundings in which they lived, working through education, buildings and art, and community projects of charity. Similarly, the Protestant counterparts, such as the

Oxford group of Frank Buchman or the Herrnhut Brethren of Count Zinzendorf, had a profound impact not only on their own adherents but on the communities in which they lived and worked. Of course, the same is expected of the local worshiping community. The Christian faith is not only a Sunday morning affair. It lays claim on the total lives of the members of the local congregation and exerts an impact on the community in which a congregation is located. As anticipation of the heavenly city the church on the local level becomes a visible reality, a beacon of hope and a bastion of a new humanity within a fallen and hurting world. Yet the vision of the church is always larger than the local church. J. Robert Nelson rightly pointed out that "the primary task of the church in history is to be the bearer of that reconciling work in every generation."[89] To make credible such reconciling message and action at least two criteria must be met:

(1) The church would contradict its message as a beacon of hope if it were torn by strife and rivalry. The church needs to give witness to the unity to which it points. This does not mean that suddenly all diversity and plurality should disappear either in favor of a relativistic concept of truth or in favor of a monolithic authoritarian faith structure.[90] Even when the church looked like a uniform edifice, as for instance in the Middle Ages, the diversity of its theological production bore witness to a considerable plurality. Since the gospel comes to us always through other Christians, we must realize that we do not own the truth or the gospel. It opens itself to us only if we listen to it as it is offered to us. We also notice that other Christians are not always from our own tradition. We must acknowledge that our grasp of the gospel tradition, accurate as it may be, does not have an original claim on the whole truth, but grasps it only from a certain perspective. It is in constant need of correction and upbuilding, lest it become exclusive and distorted. Unity means realizing and making manifest our interdependence as heirs of the kingdom, celebrating the unity we seek, and amalgamating the pieces thereof which we have already discovered. With its many bilateral talks the ecumenical movement is a serious first step in this direction. It shows that our respective insights gain new clarity and correction from joint listening to the gospel tradition.

(2) Our credibility as bearers of the message of reconciliation only holds up if we venture beyond the local situation. Friedrich Nietzsche rightly reminded us that Christians should not just express love toward our neighbor, but toward those who are most distant from us.[91] As bearers

of the message of Christ we cannot stop at our own city walls, we must go beyond our local communities to the ends of the earth. The mission of the church goes hand in hand with discovering the church's unity, since only a reunited Christian church can become the symbol and the instrument of the unity of humanity.[92] The pursuit of Christian unity and the concern for human solidarity are closely related among different churches, and come most eloquently to surface in the World Council of Churches.

Foreshadowing the heavenly city which is neither torn by rivalry, strife, nor injustice, the church seeks to manifest the criteria of a new humanity in its global structure. Also through its global witness, the church serves as a powerful stimulus to induce signs of the eschaton among the whole humanity. Without the church's presence, life in the twentieth century would grow colder and more merciless. Serving as the conscience of society, as the haven of the neglected, and as the anticipation of the heavenly city, the church is the symbol of human solidarity, expressing in its internal relationship and in its outward actions God's love for the world, God's cherishing of each human being, and his desire that none be lost. The church is a manifestation and reminder of God's love amid a world in turmoil. The reason for the church's functioning in this direction cannot be derived from the dedication of its members, though that should not be underestimated. The reason for the church being the heart of the present can also not be delineated from its strong ties to the past, though they serve as a strong reminder to live up to the ideals of its founder, Jesus of Nazareth.

The reason for the church to continue its task in the face of all defeat and misery can only come from a power which at least in principle is stronger than all distortions, injustice, and self-centeredness. This power has shown that it can and will destroy all darkness, nay it has destroyed it already. The power of the church is not its own, but that of its Lord. As Paul asserted, he has shown in his resurrection that the ultimate victory is his. Since we have such a Lord, Paul can admonish us: "Be steadfast, immovable, always abounding in the work of the Lord, knowing that in the Lord your labor is not in vain" (1 Cor. 15:58). With such confidence the church cannot just be the heart of the present. It will gladly become the reminder of the future, of the new world to come.

3. The reminder of the future

The church in this world is always in danger of becoming a stumbling block. The church does not fit into a world that assumes that the course of its history is predictable, being determined by humanity's own efforts and the available resources. The church, however, knows and confesses that "did we in our own strength confide, our striving would be losing." In a secular and self-relying culture, the church is not only essentially countercultural, it also gives witness to a future provided by God and not by humanity.

a. The symbol of the future

The involvement of the church in the affairs of the world, in the struggle for justice, human rights, and the provision of life's necessities serves a dual purpose. (1) The church indeed wants to serve those who are in need. (2) Yet being aware that all of its efforts are at best patchwork, Band-Aids on the wounds of a hurting world, the church points with its actions to a world which will no longer be torn apart. Similar to the miracles of our Lord having not only the function of helping people in need, but being signs of a new creation, the church in its actions is a symbol of the future.

The eschatological symbol of the new creation becomes visible not just in social involvement, but in every activity of the church. Each absolution is a reminder of the love of God that one day will find its completion. Each Eucharist is a reminder of the celestial banquet. The twofold phrase in the words of institution of the Lord's Supper, "This do in remembrance of me," does not just imply that we should remember Christ's sacrifice. It also means that God should remember the sacrifice of his Son and speed up the coming and completion of the kingdom. At every celebration of the Eucharist the church proclaims the beginning of the time of salvation and waits for the inception of the consummation.[93] The community is reminded to celebrate the Eucharist until he comes, again a vivid pointer toward the eschatological consummation.

In the context of the Lord's Supper we must also remember the Aramaic term *maranatha,* occurring in 1 Cor. 16:22, Didache 10:6, and perhaps in translated form in Rev. 22:20. Though it can not be clearly decided whether the term means "our Lord is present" or "Lord, come," it is clear that this formula had common liturgical usage.[94] If *maranatha* means "our Lord is present" then it is a phrase that asserts the Lord's presence in the Eucharist, but also presses for the final public disclosure of his presence. If, however, it can be translated "Lord, come," then we again encounter the eschatological waiting and longing of the community for his coming in glory.

The Christian community understands itself as the symbol of a future which has already commenced. This is also emphasized in the Lord's Prayer. As a constitutent part of the communion liturgy, the Lord's Prayer belonged, in the early church, to that part of the service in which only those who were baptized were permitted to participate.[95] Both thou-petitions, "hallowed be thy name," and "thy kingdom come" are in content closely related to the expectant cry "Come, Lord."[96] They are seeking the point at which God's profaned and misused name will be glorified and the reign of his kingdom be revealed. In a world enslaved by evil, distress, and conflict, the Christian community looks forward to the revelation of God's glory. These petitions are filled with confidence and are not wishful thoughts. In the face of an evil world surrounding and encroaching upon the church, the faithful take seriously God's promise and address him in the utmost confidence with "Our Father." Since his Son taught the disciples this prayer they are absolutely certain that God will redeem his promises as he spoke according to Ezekiel: "I will vindicate the holiness of my great name, which has been profaned among the nations, and which you have profaned among them; and the nations will know that I am the Lord, says the Lord God, when through you I vindicate my holiness before their eyes" (Ezek. 36:23).

The other phrases in the Lord's Prayer witness also to the yearning for and expectation of the eschaton. For instance, in the petition for bread and forgiveness, the church asks that God might grant today, in this place the bread of life and the blotting out of sins. The praying church here becomes a beacon of hope in the darkness of this world. Amid failure, apostasy, and denial, God's kingly rule over the lives of his people is being realized. Though still a symbol of the future, the bread of life and God's endless mercy are present already, indicators of his almighty glory and the coming of the kingdom.

When we briefly look at baptism we immediately perceive that the prevalent practice of infant baptism would be utterly ridiculous, if we regard baptism simply as incorporation into the visible, institutional church. The notion of dying and rising with Christ, or of being incorporated into his body, certainly envisions more than just institutional membership. It also means more than being converted to Christ and becoming a confessing Christian. When Paul mentions that we should walk in newness of life since we have become a new creation, he admits two things: (1) We are still in a state of transition, from this aeon to the future aeon. While it cannot hold us completely, the world still ensnares us. Luther was right when he called for drowning of the old Adam through daily repentance. (2) Yet we must recognize a second moment. A Christian's existence is dynamic and not static. Together with the whole creation we are yearning and longing for the revelation of the sons of God and the manifestation of the kingdom.

Dying and rising with Christ makes sense only when it means breaking out of the natural cycle of birth and death from which the image is borrowed. There must be a time when death will no longer score a victory and we can forever walk in newness of life. Similarly, becoming part of the body of Christ only makes sense when at one point our sinful alienation and spatio-temporal separation from Christ is overcome. We must be able to celebrate with him the proverbial celestial banquet and enjoy him forever. In other words, baptism remains an empty shell unless it is verified through the coming of the kingdom. But baptism is also a sign and symbol of that future verification and it is administered in trust and hope. The same is true for the Eucharist. It is intrinsically eschatological, foreshadowing and hoping for the eschatological realization.

It has become clear that in its actions, in its liturgical celebrations, and in its prayer life the church is a symbol of the future, in part foreshadowing the things to come, and in part patiently but intensely hoping and trusting for their ultimate verification. Yet the church would be a strange community if it could bring about these things by its own power. The power and the encouragement for both anticipation and expectation is derived from the experience of Christ. Through the presence of Christ and the power of the Spirit the church realizes that the life and destiny of Jesus the Christ are the prime examples of its own life and destiny. It knows beyond doubt that ultimately all history will serve to make his kingdom triumph. We can be confident that God "will vindicate his people, and have compassion on his servants" (Psalm 135:14), so that this hope which he inspired will not be in vain.

b. The whole people of God

Intrinsic to the Christian hope is a common destiny for all humanity. It expresses itself in the hope for the unity of the whole church and for the unity of all people under the dominion of God. Friedrich Schleiermacher certainly had a point when he argued that "there are great difficulties in thinking that the finite issue of redemption is such that some thereby obtain the highest bliss, while others (on the ordinary view, indeed, the majority of the human race) are lost in irrevocable misery."[97]

The church cannot stand in judgment of the unbelievers, but must be the vivid and living reminder that God wants all people to be saved. But the church would rob itself of its reason for being if it would assert with Schleiermacher that "through the power of redemption there will one day be a universal restoration of all souls."

The church's reason for being is to represent Christ to the world and to bring it the gospel. It is dangerous to assume that we have to revise our hopes about converting the world to Christ, with the argument that it is no longer plausible to believe that the church will score big victories on secular or religious fronts.[98] If success were our criterion for engagement we would also give up the hope of making this world a better place in which to live. Yet despite continuous setbacks, those who have given up converting the world in the traditional sense, often continue their crusade with ever increasing vigor to make our world more human. A church that rallies around the crucified and risen Lord cannot take success or plausibility as its prime criterion. It cannot even make its work easier or its failures less painful by attributing to all "good" and "faithful" non-Christian believers the honorary title anonymous Christians.[99] If the church wants to be the reminder of the future, it dare not leave humanity as it is, in its dispersion, antagonism, and self-destruction. The faithful proclamation of the gospel tradition must be a challenge to every status quo whether it be Muslim or Buddhist, Marxist or Capitalist.

The acknowledgment and proclamation of Christ as Lord of the whole world will not simply bring Christ to the world, it must also ask how Christ is "present and operative in the faith of the individual non-Christian."[100] Since Christ is present and operative in and through his Spirit in non-Christian believers and their religions, we can affirm what is good and wholesome in them. Conversely, we should expect that they also recognize good and wholesome features in the gospel tradition. It would be utopian, however, to demand that in every dialogue commonality would triumph over diversity and contradictions. Yet a dialogue might foster understanding fellowship and unity among people of different religions.[101] We might begin to understand that all people form a single community, springing from God as their origin and moving toward him as their goal. There is a positive point of contact, however hidden, in every religious expression, something worthy of cultivation, augmentation, and enlargement. But we dare not close our eyes to that which is wrong and misapprehended, that which needs true supplanting and conversion.

Since the church is never identical with Christ, it also stands under affirmation and judgment as do the non-Christian believers. Only the Lord and his gospel are the criteria for discovering what is good and true and what is in error and misconceived. The dialogue with all people brings us closer together, since it places all of us under the judging and liberating word of our Lord. Though we hope that his word will make a difference in this world, creating increasing solidarity among all people, we are not sure that all people will eventually listen to him. Our most sincere proclamation of the gospel tradition in word and deed, for the soul and the body, and through words of grace and acts of mercy, can never assume that a universal homecoming of all people will result. The realization of our common destiny as the whole people of God can only be a most daring eschatological hope and the content of fervent prayers. By sharing Christ even at the most remote places of the earth, we are reminded that in one way or other, whether with everyone's approval or without, our Lord will one day be acknowledged as the Lord so that he may be everything to every one (1 Cor. 15:28).

It would be totally irresponsible if the church would bring the gospel to non-Christians, calling for solidarity and jointly listening to the Lord of the world, without being utterly disturbed about its own divided house. The division into different churches and denominations is not just the fault of others. Every Christian is responsible for this disunion. While the church must be Greek to the Greeks and American to the Americans, its necessary culturalization and diversity does not justify the present divisiveness. Immense progress toward representing the whole people of God has been made through the World Council of Churches, the various world federations of confessional families, the national councils, and the many bilateral dialogues. But institutional inertia and egoistic pride are still the two greatest obstacles to actual unity. Movements toward unity, such as the Consultation on Church Union in the United States, progress much more slowly than originally envisioned and with less tangible results. The sentiment for institutional self-preservation looms high even in ecumenically-minded circles. Yet every day we discover more how much we actually share. The division in different denominations and churches seems in many cases at least, anachronistic and therefore sinful. In the last fifty years approximately sixty church unions have taken place, resulting in churches such as the Church of South India and the United Church of Christ in the United States. Today in about thirty countries negotiations towards church union are being conducted.

The Fifth Assembly of the World Council of Churches in Nairobi (1975) again instructed its member churches to "provide opportunities for a careful study and evaluation of the concept of conciliar fellowship as a way of describing the unity of the Church." [102] Conciliarity is not the same as the medieval call for conciliarism, meaning the shift of power from a central authority (the pope) to the councils. Conciliarity is also not the result of reconciled diversity. Rather conciliarity means that the churches no longer exclude and fight each other, but instead realize each other's validity while they preserve at the same time their own integrity and structure. Conciliarity recognizes the fact that the church always needs assemblies to represent it. As history shows, councils are convened by churches that enjoy a unity of faith and that faith expresses itself prominently in eucharistic fellowship. Yet the frequent assemblies of churches that do not enjoy full eucharistic fellowship, while they are not councils in the strict sense, can decisively advance unity and in fact have done so. We could even say that the ecumenical movement is working toward that point at which a true ecumenical council can become a reality. Conciliarity therefore does not exclude organic union, nor does it merely encourage organic church union but instead it requires it.

The vision of organic union should not be misunderstood as moving toward a centralized super-church. Such structure would neither do justice to the local necessities nor would it be an effective instrument in witnessing to the world. Conciliarity is not reserved for a superstructure but belongs to all levels, the congregational, national, regional, and worldwide. The reason why union must be expressed on every level is grounded in the biblical concept that at each point at which the church exists, the whole church comes to expression. Knowing the local or regional church means knowing the whole church, and knowing the worldwide church means knowing its local manifestation. There is an intrinsic connection between the local and the universal life of the church. For instance, if the local church is not mission-minded, the mission-mindedness of the church headquarters does not compensate for this lack of vision. On the other hand, if the church as a synod or convention is hopelessly entrenched in parochialism, the local congregation can only venture so far without alienating itself too much from the rest of the church.

The Salamanca Consultation (1973) of the Faith and Order Commission put our dilemma, our task, and our hopes very succinctly: *Jesus Christ founded one Church. Today we live in diverse churches divided from one another. Yet our vision of the future is that we shall once again*

live as brothers and sisters in one undivided Church.[103] A divided church
is an offense to its Lord, an offense to the gospel, and an impediment to
mission. Divided Christendom is a reminder of our sinfulness and of the
task still ahead of us. But it also reminds us of the eschatological future,
when our human divisiveness can no longer intrude on the manifestation
of the whole people of God. Therefore intermediate steps toward union,
such as involvement in joint mission projects, shared worship, public
declaration of our common intention on all levels, common theological
education, training of laity, Christian education and literature, and joint
evaluation of priorities and use of funds, are not only a sign of repentance
of our sins of the past and of overcoming them. They are also indications
that the power of the Spirit is at work in his people and that the people
are willing to anticipate something of the great celestial council when all
will share the same table and the same food.

Even at the risk of being redundant we must again mention here that
the vision of the whole people of God includes church and synagogue,
Jew and Gentile. It should at least make us wonder why a people without
a homeland for nearly 2,000 years, a people who suffered the most cruel
and systematic persecution ever staged, a people dispersed throughout the
world, why such a people did not abandon its faith in God. The Jewish
people are surely an enigma. But they are also a source of inspiration and
hope. God may lead his people through valleys of shadow and death, but
he does not abandon them. He sustains, calls, and nourishes them.

The Jewish people are more than a symbol of survival, they are a symbol of insight. As the sculpture on medieval churches of the blindfolded
synagogue indicates, Jews may have been tolerated, but Christians have
never accepted them as equals. Yet Jews consider us and all other peoples
as equals. They perceive all of humanity "as the descendants of one father
and the creatures of one Creator" and similarly cherish "a complementary
vision of a reunited mankind under God at the end of time." [104] In the
face of its own adverse history, Israel has not given up this hope for one
humanity reunited under God. The Jewish people have even "recognized
access to God and saving virtue outside of Judaism, since its own covenant
with God bound the covenant-community only." [105] The church, therefore, must take the great commission seriously and go into all the world,
proclaim the good news, and baptize those who are still without a covenant
relationship with God.

Instead of aiming at victories for our Lord, we should acknowledge
that the victory has already been won and that his love is greater than

our accomplishments. The hope kept alive among Jewish people serves as a timely reminder that the wholeness of God's people does not depend on our actions, though it can be considerably enhanced by them. The oneness of the human family rests on God's promises which will not return empty.

c. "And God will dwell in their midst"

A theology of glory is not the proper topic to conclude a study on ecclesiology. Even the Roman Catholic Church, with which the notion of a theology of glory has often been associated, is rediscovering the role of servanthood and suffering. But persecution and suffering are not necessarily the signs of the true church either.[106] God distributes suffering and pain indiscriminately among believers and unbelievers, among Christians and non-Christians. But if the church is a historical agency "through which God is remaking the human world," [107] and if it is the living organism that connects the historical acts of God through which he overcame our sinfulness with the future acts of the establishment of the new Jerusalem, then it would be anachronistic to contemplate only suffering and pain. Even servants need moments of festivity and celebration to make their servanthood livable and meaningful.

Festivity and celebration are not moments of rest in a troubled world, but the point from which we look forward to an eternal Sabbath, a time of pure joy and rejoicing. In remembering Christ as both crucified and resurrected, we faithfully celebrate our liberation and freedom as children of God though knowing that we are still entangled in a troubled world. The church would betray its own source of strength and hope if it would see its function exhausted in rendering assistance to a troubled world. The church also serves as a beacon of hope, demonstrating the Christ-won freedom in its own life and manifesting its rejoicing in that freedom.[108] A theology of glory need not be a betrayal of the gospel tradition if it means glorying in what God has done in and through the church, what he is doing, and what he will do. Anticipation of the heavenly glory, both in remembering God's past acts and in looking forward and hoping for the eschatological perfection, is as important for the church as realizing that it still lives in a valley of death and injustice.

Especially in worship, proclamation, and ecclesiastical arts the church must express something of the anticipated glory. It is a misunderstood sense of the servant role when the church opts only for multipurpose buildings and folding chairs. Certainly the lush carpeting of the sanctuary can stand in the way of spreading the gospel and serving the world. Yet a world characterized by efficiency and the increase of the capital of its investors needs to be reminded that we do not live by bread alone. A God who produces so much splendor in nature deserves praise and adoration through all the media. His eschatological perfection though depicted with restraint is never painted in drab and efficient colors, but with vivid and splendid images of pearly gates and celestial choirs. The last judgment painted by Michelangelo in the Sistine Chapel in Rome, the majestic oratorios of the Messiah by George Frederick Handel, the chorale preludes by Johann Sebastian Bach, and the spires of the Cathedral in Chartres are just a few examples of praise to God for his past actions and his future promises. A church that no longer uses art as a form of remembering and anticipating God's promises has a truncated understanding of the magnitude of the gospel tradition. It also underestimates the expected response to God with our whole being. If we refrain from giving glory to God with all our senses and all means of expression, we fail to recognize that participation in this glory is more than verbal or literary assent.

It is significant that in the wake of liturgical experimentation and renewal the Roman Catholic Church is moving away from a one-sided display of splendor, rediscovering the necessity for proclamation, while many Protestant denominations now detect that worship is more than listening to a sermon and singing a few hymns. It is dramatizing God's saving acts in Christ and a celebration of the future glory of all the saints. Liturgical gowns, processions, chanted liturgy, and even occasionally incense, remind us that we do not just celebrate God with our ears, but with our whole being and with all our senses. Similarly, in proclamation we notice a more balanced expression of the whole gospel tradition, that gives adequate focus on Christ's death and resurrection and no longer dwells almost exclusively on the cross. We remember with sorrow that our world did not accept its Lord and rejected him through the cross. But we must also triumph in the glory of the resurrected and the promise that his resurrection contains. There is also emerging a more inclusive understanding of the gospel tradition that includes the Hebrew Scriptures as part of this tradition which should be proclaimed in sermons as our Old Testament. We remember with thanksgiving that God has acted in this world throughout the centuries, even before the incarnation of our Lord and that he continues to act in his world. We expect and hope that he will complete his actions so that finally he will dwell in the midst of his people.

It is unfortunate that the expectation of the heavenly future has never been a strong point of the church. Sectarian groups always had to remind the church of the necessity and centrality of this part of the gospel from which we derive our power and vision. Theology has recaptured in this century the significance of an eschatological perspective. With the same token the rediscovery of the so-called last things still remains to be done. Perhaps the church rightly feels that it is a rather threatening vision that the seer of the Book of Revelation expresses:

> I saw no temple in the city, for its temple is the Lord God the Almighty and the Lamb. And the city has no need of sun or moon to shine upon, it, for the glory of God is its light, and its lamp is the Lamb. By its light shall the nations walk; and the kings of the earth shall bring their glory into it, and its gates shall never be shut by day—and there shall be no night there. (Rev. 21:22-25.)

In the midst of a cruel, unjust, and divided earth, such eschatological harmony among people and nations seems unreal. We might also feel that we are too solidly grounded in our own achievements on this earth to abandon it in favor of God's complete dominion in a heavenly city. Staunch church members and ecclesiastical administrators may feel uneasy over the vision of a city in which the presence of God will replace all temples. How dearly do we love our church structures and ecclesiastical empires which we erect and safeguard?

Indeed, the vision shared by the Book of Revelation sounds unreal. It is something out of a different world that threatens the status quo and our self-established security. But was not the same already true for the coming of the Lord? Does not the Gospel of Matthew tell us that Herod slaughtered all the innocent infants in Bethlehem because he felt the birth of the Messiah threatened his security? God's saving activity always threatens our security. Yet how reliable is our security? In the last fifty years we have staggered from one crisis to another. The Great Depression, World War II, the Korean War, the numerous Middle East Crises, the Vietnam War, and the Energy Crisis are just a few reminders that our security is more a wishful dream than a reality. Perhaps the Psalmist was much more realistic in assessing our situation when he said that our years contain "but toil and trouble; they are soon gone, and we fly away" (Ps. 90:10).

As we discover more and more the fleetingness of time and our dwindling natural resources, the vision of eschatological perfection gains new credibility and urgency. The church does a disservice to its members and to a world in trouble and turmoil when it neglects announcing the eschatological future when God will dwell in the midst of his people. Yet such a message proclaimed with vigor and confident hope must not induce a relinquishing of our responsibility. It must not be used as a heavenly escape valve as Karl Marx predicted. As Walbert Bühlmann recognized:

> The orientation towards God as our absolute future does not remove our responsibility for this world but makes it more radical. He who knows that God will one day wipe away all tears will not resign himself to letting the tortured go on suffering . . . . Either hope with anticipatory realization now in this world created and loved by God, or no hope at all!" [109]

Our hope encourages us to take the parable of the faithful steward seriously, because we know that our Lord and the Lord of all the world is coming. Only when we become oblivious to the coming of our Lord will we be tempted to shed our responsibility and set ourselves up as masters and oppressors (Luke 12:45), even in the name of freedom and liberation. A church that remains faithful to its calling of announcing the glad news that God will dwell in our midst, will instill hope, courage, and a sense of direction in a confused world. It will remain and become a beacon and a rallying point for the future. Although it is a stumbling block for some, it is a firm foundation for many. The church is a symbol of Christ's promise that the gates of hell shall not prevail.

NOTES

1. Cf. for this and the following Gerhard Ebeling, *The Word of God and Tradition. Historical Studies Interpreting the Divisions of Christianity*, trans. S. H. Hooke (Philadelphia: Fortress, 1968) 146.
2. Cf. "Scripture, Tradition and Traditions," in P. C. Rodger and Lukas Vischer, eds., *The Fourth World Conference on Faith and Order. Montreal 1963* (New York: Association, 1964) 51f.
3. Ibid., 59.
4. Cf. for the following the excellent remarks by Hans Küng, *The Church*, trans. R. and R. Ockenden (New York: Sheed and Ward, 1967) 241-260.
5. Augustine, *On the Psalms* 5, NPNF(FS) 8:601, in his comments on Ps. 125.
6. Cf. for the following Ernst Troeltsch, *The Social Teaching of the Christian Churches*, trans. O. Wyon, introduction by Charles Gore (New York: Macmillan, 1931), 1:331ff.
7. Cf. for the following the perceptive remarks by H. Richard Niebuhr, *The Social Sources of Denominationalism* (Hamden, CT: Shoe String Press, 1929) 19ff.
8. Cf. Sidney E. Mead, "Denominationalism: The Shape of Protestantism in America," *Church History* 23 (December 1954) 296.

9. According to Sidney E. Mead, ibid., 293.
10. Ibid., 291.
11. So rightly Timothy L. Smith, "Religious Denominations as Ethnic Communities: A Regional Case Study," *Church History* 35 (June 1966) 225, in a case study of a mining region in Northern Minnesota.
12. Niebuhr, *Social Sources*, 24.
13. *Lutheran Book of Worship* (Minneapolis: Augsburg, 1978) 70f.
14. Dietrich Bonhoeffer, *The Communion of Saints. A Dogmatic Inquiry into the Sociology of the Church*, trans. R. G. Smith (New York: Harper, 1963) 116.
15. So rightly Carl Heinz Ratschow, "Die Lehre von der Kirche. Eine trinitarisch aufgebaute dogmatische Skizze," in Werner Danielsmeyer and Carl Heinz Ratschow, eds., *Kirche und Gemeinde. Präses D. Dr. Hans Thimme zum 65. Geburtstag.* (Witten: Luther-Verlag, 1974) 206.
16. Cf. Rudolf Bultmann, "Prophecy and Fulfillment," *Essays. Philosophical and Theological*, trans. J. C. G. Greig (New York: Macmillan, 1955) 205ff. The term *"scheitern"* is translated here somewhat inappropriately as "miscarriage." We prefer to translate it as "failure."
17. Martin Luther, *Das Alte Testament* (1545) *Luthers Vorrede*, WA.DB 8:13.6f.
18. Martin Luther, *Der Prophet Habakuk ausgelegt* (1526), WA 19:351.3ff.
19. Martin Luther, *The Magnificat* (1521), LW 21:354, with reference to 1 Cor. 10:1-4.
20. This reservation against Bultmann is rightly expressed by Jürgen Moltmann, *The Church in the Power of the Spirit*, 140f.
21. Cf. the insights gathered by Merton P. Strommen, *et al.*, *A Study of Generations. Report of a Two-Year Study of 5,000 Lutherans between the Age of 15-65: Their Beliefs, Values, Attitudes, Behavior* (Minneapolis: Augsburg, 1972).
22. For an abbreviated version of the following cf. my inaugural lecture as Edward C. Fendt Professor of Systematic Theology, "The Church as the Conscience of Society," *The Seminary Bulletin* (Lutheran Theological Seminary, Columbus, OH) 12 (Summer 1978) 4-14.
23. Cf. Bonhoeffer, *The Communion of Saints*, 176, on the comparison between the church and an association.
24. Cf. for the following the perceptive comments by Dietrich Bonhoeffer, ibid., pp. 176ff. Cf. also Avery Dulles, *Models of the Church* (Garden City, NY: Doubleday, 1974), 31-42.
25. Cf. the concluding remarks in the incisive book by H. Richard Niebuhr, *Christ and Culture* (New York: Harper, 1951; Colophon Books, 1975) 256.
26. Ibid. 43f.
27. It is noteworthy that Avery Dulles, 185, comes to the conclusion that his task is "to harmonize the models in such a way that their differences become complementary rather than mutually repugnant." He outlines five models, the church as institution, mystical communion, sacrament, herald, and servant. The first and the last two in part overlap with what we must mention in connection with the church as the conscience of society.
28. Cf. Langdon Gilkey, *How the Church Can Minister to the World Without Losing Itself* (New York: Harper, 1964) 1f.
29. Cf. the justified reservations against this approach in Willem A. Visser 't Hooft and Joseph H. Oldham, *The Church and Its Function in Society* (Chicago: Willet, Clark, 1937) 122ff.
30. So Robert F. Drinan, *Religion, the Courts, and Public Policy* (New York: McGraw-Hill, 1963) 219. Though Drinan calls this an oversimplified generalization, it presents a fairly correct summary.
31. Cf. the dilemma pointed out by Robert Drinan, pp. 50-55, with regard to the Jewish

opposition to any religious intervention in the public sector of society. Of course, these fears are historically founded in the political pressure that Christians brought to bear on the Jewish community.

32. Cf. ibid., p. 220.

33. Cf. Friedrich Engels, "On the History of Early Christianity" (1894/5), in Karl Marx and Friedrich Engels, *On Religion*, introduction by Reinhold Niebuhr (New York: Schocken, 1964) 316f.

34. For the history and development of the doctrine of the two kingdoms cf. *Two Kingdoms and One World. A Sourcebook in Christian Social Ethics*, ed. Karl H. Hertz (Minneapolis: Augsburg, 1976).

35. For this and the following cf. H. Richard Niebuhr, *Christ and Culture*, 149f. and 171f.

36. Ibid., 187f. That Luther's doctrine of the two kingdoms can be a helpful tool to introduce social change I have stated elsewhere. Cf. Hans Schwarz, "The Two Kingdoms—Tool of Shibboleth (in reply to Karl Hertz)," *Lutheran Quarterly* 27 (August 1975) 257-59.

37. So Paul Althaus, *The Ethics of Martin Luther*, trans. with a foreword by Robert C. Schultz (Philadelphia: Fortress, 1972) 81.

38. Martin Luther, *Whether Soldiers, Too, Can Be Saved* (1526), LW 46:99f.

39. Martin Luther, *Temporal Authority: To What Extent It Should Be Obeyed* (1523), LW 45:92.

40. Cf. for the following Althaus, *The Ethics of Martin Luther*, 62, and "Luthers Lehre von den beiden Reichen im Feuer der Kritik," in Heinz-Horst Schrey, ed., *Reich Gottes und Welt. Die Lehre Luthers von den zwei Reichen* (Darmstadt: Wissenschaftliche Buchgesellschaft, 1969) 108.

41. Martin Luther, *The Sermon on the Mount* (1530/2), LW 21:109, in his comments on Matt. 5:38-42.

42. Cf. Althaus, *The Ethics of Martin Luther*, 66f.

43. Cf. ibid., pp. 52f.

44. Martin Luther, WA.TR 2:209.11-13, and cf. for this and the following Franz Lau, *"Äusserlich Ordnung" und "Weltlich Ding" in Luthers Theologie* (Göttingen: Vandenhoeck & Ruprecht, 1933) 11B and 59.

45. Martin Luther, *Temporal Authority*, LW 45:128.

46. Ibid., LW 45:95.

47. Ibid., 45:10f.

48. Cf. for the following ibid., 45:120.

49. Cf. also the significant comments by Ivar Asheim, "Humanity and Christian Responsibility," in Ivar Asheim, ed., *Christ and Humanity* (Philadelphia: Fortress, 1970) 11. For a valid contemporary approach to relating the church and the world from a Lutheran perspective, cf. Richard J. Neuhaus, *Christian Faith and Public Policy* (Minneapolis: Augsburg, 1977).

50. For this and the next two quotes see Ronald Sider, ed., *The Chicago Declaration of Evangelicals* (Carol Stream, IL: Creation House, 1974), from "A Declaration of Evangelical Social Concern" (front cover); and Ronald Sider, "An Historic Moment for Biblical Social Concern," ibid., 17 and 30, text in brackets added by the author.

51. Sherwood E. Wirt, *The Social Conscience of the Evangelical* (New York: Harper, 1968) 129.

52. Cf. for the following ibid., 131ff.

53. Ibid., 134.

54. Adolf Harnack, "Fifteen Questions to Those among the Theologians Who Are Contemptuous of the Scientific Theology" (1923), in *The Beginnings of Dialectic Theology,*

ed. James M. Robinson, trans. K. R. Crim, and L. D. Grazia (Richmond: John Knox, 1962) 165.

55. Karl Barth, "Fifteen Answers to Professor von Harnack," in James M. Robinson, ed., ibid., 168 (answer # 4).

56. Cf. Guyla Nagy, "Christlicher Humanismus und soziale Diakonie in einer nicht-christlichen Gesellschaft," *Humane Gesellschaft. Beiträge zu ihrer sozialen Gestaltung,* ed. Trutz Rendtorff and Arthur Rich (Hamburg: Furche, 1970) 167, in the English summary.

57. Cf. the eloquent argument in Emil Brunner, *Justice and the Social Order,* trans. M. Hottinger (New York: Harper, 1945) 8.

58. Cf. the excellent article by Arnold W. Ravin, "Science, Values, and Human Evolution," *Zygon* 11 (June 1976) 138-154, esp. 151. For a more extensive discussion of inborn norms cf. Hans Schwarz, *Our Cosmic Journey* (Minneapolis: Augsburg, 1977) 238ff.

59. Cf. for the following Walter Künneth, *Politik zwischen Dämon und Gott. Eine christliche Ethik des Politischen.* (Berlin: Lutherisches Verlagshaus, 1954) 139f. Cf. in contrast Werner Elert, *The Christian Ethos,* trans. C. J. Schindler (Philadelphia: Muhlenberg, 1957) 77f., who opts for an order of creation and therewith introduces more static features into the consideration of natural orders.

60. Karl Barth, *Church Dogmatics,* vol. 3: *The Doctrine of Creation,* part 4, trans. A. T. Mackay *et al.* (Edinburgh: T. & T. Clark, 1961) 45.

61. Immanuel Kant, *Foundations of the Metaphysics of Morals,* in *Foundations of the Metaphysics of Morals and What Is Enlightenment?,* trans. with an intr. Lewis W. Beck (New York: Bobbs-Merrill, 1959), esp. 38ff., argues on the basis of "pure reason" that there are certain moral norms that, when universalized, will support human existence, while others, when universalized, will impede it.

62. Martin Luther, *Predigten des Jahres 1531,* WA 34/2:237.3f., in a sermon on the eve of the festival of St. Michael's.

63. Cf. Bangkok: Salvation Today Conference, 1973, Section III: "Salvation in Four Dimensions" (excerpt), in George H. Anderson and Thomas F. Stransky, ed., *Mission Trends No. 2: Evangelization* (New York: Paulist, 1975) 237.

64. For this quotation and the following see Friedrich Engels, "On the History of Early Christianity" (1894/95), in Karl Marx and Friedrich Engels, *On Religion,* 317f., in a footnote by Engels.

65. Cf. Karl Marx, "Thesis on Feuerbach," (1845), in *On Religion.* 72, where he talks about a new society as a "human society, or socialized humanity." Cf. also the important study by Norman Cohn, *The Pursuit of the Millennium. Revolutionary Messianism in Medieval and Reformation Europe and Its Bearings on Modern Totalitarian Movements.* 2nd ed. (New York: Harper Torchbook, 1961), in which he convincingly shows that many modern totalitarian movements, such as Marxism and Leninism, have their roots in medieval millennial movements.

66. Philip Hefner, in his thoughtful essay, "Toward a New Doctrine of Man: The Relationship of Man and Nature," in *Zygon* 2 (June 1967) 145, appropriately reminds us that humanity is not a solid, given entity, but "a bundle of energy, organized in a certain manner, proceeding in a certain direction."

67. Cf. the instructive book by Paul Bock, *In Search of a Responsible World Society. The Social Teachings of the World Council of Churches* (Philadelphia: Westminster, 1974), esp. 226; Wolfhart Pannenberg, "Man—the Image of God?" in *Faith and Reality,* trans. J. Maxwell (Philadelphia: Westminster, 1977) 45, rightly states that we are destined to realize our true humanity in communion with God. Since our humanizing as the goal of history has already become visible in Jesus, the process of becoming fully

human has become the theme for all subsequent history: All people shall participate in the true humanity as it appeared in Jesus Christ.

68. Cf. the interesting remarks by Hugo Assmann, *Theology for a Nomad Church*, trans. P. Burns, introduction by Frederick Herzog (Maryknoll, NY: Orbis, 1976) 141, where he says: "If the formative content of material structures is not joined by the loving process of call and response, the result is a simple product of the environment and not of the new man."

69. Cf. the illustrative examples by J. G. Davies, *Christians, Politics, and Violent Revolution* (Maryknoll, NY: Orbis, 1976) 78.

70. Ibid., 112.

71. So rightly John C. Bennett, *Christians and the State* (New York: Chas. Scribner's, 1958), p. 203, who concedes, however, that the kingdom can be partially embodied in a society.

72. Dennis Goulet, *A New Moral Order. Studies in Development Ethics and Liberation Theology*, foreword by Paulo Freire (Maryknoll, NY: Orbis, 1974) 130. It is significant for the interdependence between evolutionary advancement and the striving for a new humanity that Goulet finds in Teilhard the main advocate for the eschatological vision of a new humanity.

73. DVC, esp. 200f. (3), and 230f. (32). Cf. Avery Dulles, *Models of the Church*, 87, for a list of some of the statements.

74. Dietrich Bonhoeffer, *Letters and Papers from Prison*, rev. ed., ed. Eberhard Bethge, trans. R. Fuller (New York: Macmillan, 1967) 211.

75. Harvey Cox, *The Secular City. Secularization and Urbanization in Theological Perspective*, rev. ed. (New York: Macmillan, [1965] 1968) 116.

76. Gibson Winter, *The New Creation as Metropolis* (New York: Macmillan, 1963) 59.

77. Dorothee Sölle, *Suffering*, trans. E. R. Kallin (Philadelphia: Fortress, 1975), 178.

78. Dorothee Sölle, *Political Theology*, trans. with an introduction by J. Shelley (Philadelphia: Fortress, 1974) 106.

79. *Letters and Papers from Prison*, 211.

80. So rightly George D. Younger, *The Church and Urban Renewal* (Philadelphia: Lippincott, 1965) 171, with regard to the church's servant role in urban renewal.

81. Lactantius, *The Divine Institutes* 6.10, FaCh 49:418.

82. Ambrose, *De officiis* 2.29, according to Gerhard Uhlhorn, *Christian Charity in the Ancient Church* (New York: Scribner's, 1883) 361.

83. Karl Hefele, *History of Councils*, 1:187f., in his comments on canon 7.

84. Uhlhorn, 362.

85. Dietrich Bonhoeffer, *Life Together*, trans. with an introduction by John W. Doberstein (New York: Harper, 1954) 18.

86. Ibid., 27.

87. Ibid., 38.

88. Alfred North Whitehead, *Process and Reality. An Essay in Cosmology* (New York: Macmillan, 1929) 532.

89. J. Robert Nelson, "Signs of Mankind's Solidarity," in J. Robert Nelson, ed., *No Man Is Alien*, 14.

90. Cf. for the following the insightful comments by Wolfhart Pannenberg, "Einheit der Kirche und Einheit der Menschheit," *Ethik und Ekklesiologie*, 321.

91. Friedrich Nietzsche, *Thus Spoke Zarathustra* 1, in *The Portable Nietzsche*, sel. and trans. with intro., pref., and notes by Walter Kaufmann (New York: Viking, 1954) 174 (On Love of Thy Neighbor).

92. Cf. Pannenberg, 322.

93. Joachim Jeremias, *The Eucharistic Words of Jesus*, trans. N. Perrin, 3rd ed. (Philadelphia: Fortress, 1977) 254.

94. For details of the argument see Kurt Georg Kuhn, *maranatha*, TDNT, 4:471f.
95. So Joachim Jeremias, *The Lord's Prayer*, Biblical Series no. 8 trans. by J. Reumann (Philadelphia: Fortress Facet Books, 1964) 2.
96. Ibid., 22.
97. See for this and the following quote Friedrich Schleiermacher, *The Christian Faith*, ed. H. R. Mackintosh and J. S. Stewart, trans. D. M. Baillie, *et al.* (Edinburgh: T. & T. Clark, 1928) 722 (par. 163, appendix).
98. So unfortunately Carl H. Braaten, *The Flaming Center. A Theology of the Christian Mission* (Philadelphia: Fortress, 1977) 116, in his otherwise highly commendable and forthright book.
99. Cf. for details Hans Schwarz, *The Search for God*, 142ff.; and Braaten, 93-119, where he discusses perceptively the main representatives of the inclusionist and exclusionist approaches to mission. Karl Rahner seems to have abandoned the misleading term "anonymous Christians" when he now speaks of the presence of Christ through the Spirit among non-Christian believers. Cf. Karl Rahner, *Foundations of Christian Faith. An Introduction to the Idea of Christianity*, trans. W. V. Dych (New York: Seabury, 1978) 315-321.
100. Rahner, 315, still seems to underestimate the necessity for proclaiming Christ to non-Christians.
101. Cf. for the following *Declaration on the Relationship of the Church to Non-Christian Religions*, DVC, 660f.
102. "Recommendations of Section 2: What Unity Requires," in *Breaking Barriers. Nairobi 1975*, 69.
103. "The Unity of the Church—Next Steps," *Report of the Salamanca Consultation*, reprinted in *Ecumenical Review* 26 (April 1974) 293.
104. So Moshe Greenberg, "Mankind, Israel and the Nations in the Hebraic Heritage," in J. Robert Nelson, ed., *No Man Is Alien*, 35.
105. Ibid., 37.
106. So rightly Paul Althaus, *Die christliche Wahrheit*, 503, in his insightful and differentiating comments.
107. So rightly Gordon D. Kaufman, *Systematic Theology*, 482.
108. Cf. Jürgen Moltmann, *Theology of Play*, trans. R. Ulrich (New York: Harper, 1972) 71f.; cf. also Jürgen Moltmann, *The Church in the Power of the Spirit*, 261f., unfortunately Moltmann does not sufficiently balance in his ecclesiology the strong call for involvement with the need for rejoicing and festivity.
109. Walbert Bühlmann, *The Coming of the Third Church. An Analysis of the Present and Future of the Church* English translation ed. Ralph Woodhall, and A. N. Other. (Maryknoll, NY: Orbis, 1977) 397f.

BIBLIOGRAPHY

(For further bibliographic information, particularly of primary sources, consult the footnotes.)

1. GENERAL WORKS

Gerrish, Brian A. *The Faith of Christendom. A Source Book of Creeds and Confessions.* Cleveland: World, 1963.

González, Justo L. *A History of Christian Thought.* 3 vols. Nashville: Abingdon, 1970-75.

Harnack, Adolf von. *History of Dogma.* 7 vols. Edited by A. B. Bruce. Translated by N. Buchanan, J. Millar, E. B. Speirs, and W. M'Gilchrist. London: Williams and Norgate, 1894-99.

Hefele, Karl J. von. *A History of the Councils of the Church. From the Original Documents.* 5 vols. Edited and translated by W. R. Clark. Edinburgh: Clark, 1883-96.

Jay, Eric G. *The Church. Its Changing Image Through Twenty Centuries.* Atlanta: John Knox, 1980.

Lietzmann, Hans. *A History of the Early Church.* 4 vols. Translated by B. L. Woolf. New York: Scribner's, 1937; London: Lutterworth, 1950-51. Also in a paperback edition, Cleveland: World, 1961 (4 vols. in 2).

Pelikan, Jaroslav. *The Christian Tradition.* 5 vols. Chicago: University of Chicago, 1971.

Piepkorn, Arthur C. *Profiles in Belief. The Religious Bodies of the United States and Canada.* 7 vols. Edited by John Tietjen. New York: Harper, 1977-.

Schaff, Philip. *The Creeds of Christendom with a History and Critical Notes.* 3 vols. Grand Rapids: Baker (1877) 1977.

2. THE FORMATIVE ERA

A. The Roots

Jesus, the Disciples, and the Church:

Bornkamm, Günther. *Jesus of Nazareth.* Translated by I. and F. McLuskey with J. M. Robinson. New York: Harper, 1960.

Brown, Raymond E.; Donfried, Karl P.; and Reumann, John, eds. *Peter in the New Testament. A Collaborative Assessment by Protestant and Roman Catholic Scholars.* Minneapolis: Augsburg, 1973.

Clower, Joseph B. Jr. *The Church in the Thought of Jesus.* Richmond: John Knox, 1959.

Connick, C. Milo. *Jesus. The Man, the Mission, and the Message.* 2nd ed. Englewood Cliffs, NJ: Prentice-Hall, 1974.

Cullmann, Oscar. *Peter. Disciple, Apostle, Martyr. A Historical and Theological Study.* 2nd ed. revised and expanded. Translated by F. V. Filson. Philadelphia: Westminster, 1962.

Dodd, Charles H. *The Founder of Christianity.* New York: Macmillan, 1970.

Flew, R. Newton. *Jesus and His Church. A Study of the Idea of the Ecclesia in the New Testament.* London: Epworth, 1960.

Jeremias, Joachim. *New Testament Theology.* Vol. 1: *The Proclamation of Jesus.* Translated by J. Bowden. New York: Scribner's, 1971.

Karrer, Otto. *Peter and the Church. An Examination of Cullmann's Thesis.* Translated
by R. Walls. London: Nelson, 1963.
Scobie, Charles H. H. *John the Baptist.* Philadelphia: Fortress, 1964.

The Church in the New Testament:
Conzelmann, Hans. *History of Primitive Christianity.* Translated by J. E. Steely. Nash-
ville: Abingdon, 1973.
Davies, John G. *The Early Christian Church.* London: Weidenfeld and Nicolson, 1965.
————. *The Making of the Church.* London: Skeffington, 1960.
Dunn, James D. G. *Unity and Diversity in the New Testament. An Inquiry Into the Char-
acter of Earliest Christianity.* Philadelphia: Westminster, 1977.
Enslin, Morton S. *From Jesus to Christianity.* Boston: Beacon, 1964.
Gager, John G. *Kingdom and Community. The Social World of Early Christianity.* Engle-
wood Cliffs, NJ: Prentice-Hall, 1975.
Goguel, Maurice. *The Birth of Christianity.* Translated by H. C. Snape. New York: Mac-
millan, 1954.
————. *The Primitive Church.* Translated by H. C. Snape. New York: Macmillan, 1964.
Goppelt, Leonhard. *Apostolic and Post-Apostolic Times.* Translated by R. A. Guelich. Lon-
don: Black, 1970.
Grant, Robert M. *Early Christanity and Society. Seven Studies.* New York: Harper, 1977.
Haenchen, Ernst. *The Acts of the Apostles. A Commentary.* Translated by B. Noble and
G. Shinn with H. Anderson and R. McL. Wilson. Philadelphia: Westminster, 1971.
Hahn, Ferdinand; Strobel, August; and Schweizer, Eduard. *The Beginnings of the Church
in the New Testament.* Preface by Paul Rieger. Translated by I. and U. Nicol. Minne-
apolis: Augsburg, 1970.
Hengel, Martin. *Acts and the History of Earliest Christianity.* Translated by J. Bowden.
Philadelphia: Fortress, 1979.
Hyde, Walter W. *Paganism to Christianity in the Roman Empire.* New York: Octagon,
1970.
Moule, Charles F. D. *Worship in the New Testament.* Richmond: John Knox, 1961.
Schnackenburg, Rudolf. *The Church in the New Testament.* Translated by W. J. O'Hara.
New York: Herder, 1966.

The Church and Judaism:
Davies, William D. *Christian Origins and Judaism.* London: Darton, Longman, and Todd,
1962.
Finkel, Asher. *The Pharisees and the Teacher of Nazareth. A Study of Their Background,
Their Halachic and Midrashic Teachings, the Similarities and Differences.* Leiden: Brill,
1964.
Goppelt, Leonhard. *Jesus, Paul, and Judaism. An Introduction to New Testament The-
ology.* English ed. translated and edited by E. Schroeder. New York: Nelson, 1964.
Grant, Frederick C. *Ancient Judaism and the New Testament.* New York: Macmillan,
1959.
Klausner, Jospeh. *The Messianic Idea in Israel from Its Beginning to the Completion of
the Mishnah.* Translated by W. F. Stinespring. New York: Macmillan, 1955.
Parkes, James. *The Foundations of Judaism and Christianity.* London: Vallentine, Mitchell
and Co., 1960.
Richardson, Peter. *Israel in the Apostolic Church.* Society for New Testament Studies
Monograph Series, no. 10. Cambridge: Cambridge University, 1969.
Sandmel, Samuel. *Judaism and Christian Beginnings.* New York: Oxford University, 1978.
Strack, Herman L., and Billerbeck, Paul, eds. *Kommentar zum Neuen Testament aus
Talmud und Midrasch.* 6 vols. Munich: Beck, 1922-61.

Baptism and Eucharist in the New Testament:

Beasley-Murray, George R. *Baptism in the New Testament*. London: Macmillan, 1962.

Clark, Neville. *An Approach to the Theology of the Sacraments*. Studies in Biblical Theology, no. 17. Chicago: Allenson, 1956.

Cullman, Oscar. *Baptism in the New Testament*. Translated by J. K. S. Reid. London: SCM, 1950.

Flemington, W. F. *The New Testament Doctrine of Baptism*. London: SPCK, 1957.

George, Augustin; Delorme, J.; Mollat, D.; Guillet, J.; Boismard, M. E.; Duplacy, J.; Giblet, J.; and Tremel, Y. B. *Baptism in the New Testament. A Symposium*. Translated by D. Askew. Baltimore: Helicon, 1964.

Hook, Norman. *The Eucharist in the New Testament*. London: Epworth, 1964.

Jeremias, Joachim. *The Eucharistic Words of Jesus*. Translated by N. Perrin. Philadelphia: Fortress (1966), 1977.

Schnackenburg, Rudolf. *Baptism in the Thought of St. Paul. A Study in Pauline Theology*. Translated by G. R. Beasley-Murray. Oxford: Blackwell, 1964.

Schweizer, Eduard. *The Lord's Supper According to the New Testament*. Biblical Stories, no. 18. Philadelphia: Fortress, Facet Books, 1967.

B. The Worship

Worship in the Early Church:

Cullmann, Oscar. *Early Christian Worship*. 2nd ed. Studies in Biblical Theology, no. 10. Translated by A. S. Todd and J. B. Torrance. London: SCM, 1953.

Deiss, Lucien. *Springtime of the Liturgy. Liturgical Texts of the First Four Centuries*. Translated by M. J. O'Connell. Collegeville, MN: Liturgical Press, 1979.

Delling, Gerhard. *Worship in the New Testament*. Translated by P. Scott. London: Darton, Longman, and Todd, 1962.

Dugmore, Clifford. *The Influence of the Synagogue Upon the Divine Office*. Oxford: University Press, 1964.

Hahn, Ferdinand. *The Worship of the Early Church*. Edited with an introduction by J. Reumann. Transalted by D. E. Green. Philadelphia: Fortress, 1973.

Jungmann, Josef A. *The Early Liturgy. To the Time of Gregory the Great*. Translated by F. A. Brunner. Notre Dame, IN: University of Notre Dame, 1959.

Martin, Ralph P. *Worship in the Early Church*. London: Marshall, Morgan, and Scott, 1964.

Shepherd, Massey H. Jr., ed. *Worship in Structure and Tradition*. New York: Oxford University, 1963.

Simpson, Robert L. *The Interpretation of Prayer in the Early Church*. Philadelphia: Westminster, 1965.

Baptism in the First Four Centuries:

Aland, Kurt. *Did the Early Church Baptize Infants?* Translated with an introduction by G. R. Beasley-Murray. Preface by John F. Jansen. Philadelphia: Westminster, 1963.

Gilmore, A., ed. *Christian Baptism. A Fresh Attempt to Understand the Rite in Terms of Scripture, History and Theology*. Chicago: Judson, 1959.

Jeremias, Joachim. *Infant Baptism in the First Four Centuries*. Translated by D. Cairns. London: SCM, 1960.

———. *The Origins of Infant Baptism. A Further Study in Reply to Kurt Aland*. Translated by D. M. Barton. London: SCM, 1963.

Lampe, Geoffrey W. H. *The Seal of the Spirit. A Study in the Doctrine of Baptism and Confirmation in the New Testament and the Fathers*. 2nd ed. with corrections, new introduction, and bibliography. London: SPCK, 1967.

Neunheuser, Burkhard. *Baptism and Confirmation.* Translated by J. J. Hughes. New York: Herder, 1964.

Eucharist and Sacraments in the Early Church:

Cullmann, Oscar, and Leenhardt, Franz J. *Essays on the Lord's Supper.* Ecumenical Studies in Worship, no. 1. Translated by J. G. Davies. Richmond: John Knox, 1958.
Elert, Werner. *Eucharist and Church Fellowship in the First Four Centuries.* Translated by N. E. Nagel. St. Louis: Concordia, 1966.
Hein, Kenneth. *Eucharist and Excommunication. A Study in Early Christian Doctrine and Discipline.* Bern, Switz.: Lang, 1973.
Kilmartin, Edward J. *The Eucharist in the Primitive Church.* Englewood Cliffs, NJ: Prentice-Hall, 1965.
Marxsen, Willi. *The Lord's Supper as a Christological Problem.* Translated by L. Nieting. Philadelphia: Fortress, 1970.

C. The Faith

Origin and Development of the Creeds:

Barr, O. Sydney. *From the Apostles' Faith to the Apostles' Creed.* New York: Oxford University, 1964.
Burnaby, John. *The Belief of Christendom. A Commentary on the Nicene Creed.* London: SPCK, 1959.
Cullmann, Oscar. *The Earliest Christian Confessions.* Translated by J. K. S. Reid. London: Lutterworth, 1949.
Kelly, J. N. D. *The Athanasian Creed.* New York: Harper, 1964.
————. *Early Christian Creeds.* 3rd ed. London: Longman, 1972.
Neufeld, Vernon H. *The Earliest Christian Confessions.* Grand Rapids: Eerdmans, 1963.
Pannenberg, Wolfhart. *The Apostles' Creed in Light of Today's Questions.* Translated by M. Kohl. Philadelphia: Westminster, 1972.
Wood, Edward. *Whosoever Will. Quicunque Vult.* London: Faith Press, 1961.

Origin and Development of the Canon:

Aland, Kurt. *The Problem of the New Testament Canon.* London: Mowbray, 1962.
Campenhausen, Hans von. *The Formation of the Christian Bible.* Translated by J. A. Baker. Philadelphia: Fortress, 1972.
Filson, Floyd V. *Which Books Belong in the Bible? A Study of the Canon.* Philadelphia: Westminster, 1957.
Grant, Robert M. *The Formation of the New Testament.* New York: Harper, 1965.
Moule, C. F. D. *The Birth of the New Testament,* 3rd ed. New York: Harper, 1982.
Sundberg, Albert C. Jr. *The Old Testament of the Early Church.* Harvard Theological Studies, no. 20. Cambridge, MA: Harvard University, 1964.

Development of the Christological Dogma in the Early Church:

Cullman, Oscar. *The Christology of the New Testament.* Rev. ed. Translated by S. C. Guthrie and C. A. M. Hall. Philadelphia: Westminster, 1963.
Dahl, Nils A. *Jesus in the Memory of the Early Church.* Minneapolis: Augsburg, 1976.
Fuller, Reginald H. *The Foundations of New Testament Christology.* London: Lutterworth, 1965.
Grillmeier, Aloys. *Christ in Christian Tradition.* Vol. 1: *From the Apostolic Age to Chalcedon (451).* 2nd rev. ed. Translated by J. Bowden. Atlanta: John Knox, 1975.
Longenecker, Richard N. *The Christology of Early Jewish Christianity.* Studies in Biblical Theology, Second Series, no. 17. Naperville, IL: Allenson, 1970.

Marxsen, Willi. *The Beginnings of Christology. A Study in Its Problems.* Biblical Series, no. 22. Translated by P. J. Achtemeier. Philadelphia: Fortress, Facet Books, 1969.

Margull, Hans J., ed. *The Councils of the Church. History and Analysis.* Translated by W. F. Bense. Philadelphia: Fortress, 1966.

Palmer, Paul, gen. ed. *Sources of Christian Theology.* Westminster, MD: Newman, 1966. Volume 3: *Christ and His Mission. Christology and Soteriology.* Edited with commentary by James M. Carmody and Thomas E. Clarke.

Pollard, T. E. *Johannine Christology and the Early Church.* Society for New Testament Studies Monograph Series, no. 13. Cambridge: Cambridge University, 1970.

Stevenson, James, ed. *Creeds, Councils, and Controversies. Documents Illustrative of the History of the Church A.D. 337-461.* London: SPCK, 1966.

Werner, Martin. *The Formation of Christian Dogma. An Historical Study of Its Problem.* Translated with an introduction by S. G. F. Brandon. New York: Harper, 1957.

Development of the Trinitarian Dogma in the Early Church:

Fortman, Edmund J. *The Triune God. A Historical Study of the Doctrine of the Trinity.* Philadelphia: Westminster, 1972.

Grant, Robert M. *The Early Christian Doctrine of God.* Charlottesville, VA: University Press of Virginia, 1966.

Haugh, Richard. *Photius and the Carolingians. The Trinitarian Controversy.* Belmont, MA: Nordland, 1975.

Lonergan, Bernard. *The Way to Nicea. The Dialectical Development of Trinitarian Theology.* Philadelphia: Westminster, 1976.

Moule, C. F. D. *The Holy Spirit.* Grand Rapids: Eerdmans, 1978.

Pelikan, Jaroslav. *Development of Christian Doctrine. Some Historical Prolegomena.* New Haven: Yale University, 1969.

Ramsey, Arthur M. *Holy Spirit. A Biblical Study.* Grand Rapids: Eerdmans, 1977.

D. The Structure

Office and Structure in the Early Church:

Campenhausen, Hans von. *Ecclesiastical Authority and Spiritual Power in the Church of the First Three Centuries.* Translated by J. A. Baker. London: Black, 1969.

———. *Tradition and Life in the Church. Essays and Lectures in Church History.* Translated by A. V. Littledale. Philadelphia: Fortress, 1968.

Chadwick, Henry, and Campenhausen, Hans von. *Jerusalem and Rome. The Problem of Authority in the Early Church.* Historical Series, no. 4. Philadelphia: Fortress, Facet Books, 1966.

Schmithals, Walter. *The Office of Apostle in the Early Church.* Translated by J. E. Steely. Nashville: Abingdon, 1969.

Schweizer, Eduard. *Church Order in the New Testament.* Studies in Biblical Theology, no. 32. Translated by F. Clarke. London: SCM, 1961.

Telfer, W. *The Office of a Bishop.* London: Darton, Longman, and Todd, 1962.

Church and State Up to the Fifth Century:

Bowder, Diana. *The Age of Constantine and Julian.* London: Elek, 1978.

Brown, Peter. *Religion and Society in the Age of Saint Augustine.* New York: Harper, 1972.

Coleman-Norton, Paul R. *Roman State and Christian Church. A Collection of Legal Documents to A.D. 535.* 3 vols. London: SPCK, 1966.

Dörries, Hermann. *Constantine and Religious Liberty.* Translated by R. H. Bainton. New Haven: Yale University, 1960.

————. *Constantine the Great*. Translated by R. H. Bainton. New York: Harper, 1972.

Frend, W. H. C. *The Early Church*. London: Hodder and Stoughton, 1965.

Grant, Robert M. *Augustus to Constantine*. New York: Harper, 1970.

————. *The Sword and the Cross*. New York: Macmillan, 1955.

Gunterman, Simeon L. *Religious Toleration and Persecution in Ancient Rome*. Westport, CT: Greenwood, 1951.

King, Noel Q. *The Emperor Theodosius and the Establishment of Christianity*. Philadelphia: Westminster, 1960.

MacMullen, Ramsey. *Constantine*. New York: Dial, 1969.

Norris, Richard A. Jr. *God and World in Early Christian Theology. A Study in Justin Martyr, Irenaeus, Tertullian, and Origen*. New York: Seabury, 1965.

3. THE GREAT TRANSFORMATION

A. The Development of the Eastern Orthodox Church

The Theology:

Le Guillou, M. J. *The Spirit of Eastern Orthodoxy*. Translated by D. Attwater. New York: Hawthorn, 1962.

Losskey, Vladimir. *In the Image and Likeness of God*. Edited by J. H. Erikson and T. E. Bird with an introduction by J. Meyendorff. Crestwood, NY: St. Vladimir's Seminary, 1974.

Maloney, George. *A History of Orthodox Theology Since 1453*. Belmont, MA: Nordland, 1976.

Meyendorff, John. *Byzantine Theology. Historical Trends and Doctrinal Themes*. New York: Fordham University, 1974.

————. *Christ in Eastern Christian Thought*. Washington, DC: Corpus, 1969.

Meyendorff, John; Schmemann, Alexander; Afanassieff, N.; and Koulomzine, N. *The Primacy of Peter*. 2nd ed. Library of Orthodox Thought, no. 1. Translated by K. Farrar. Bedfordshire, England: Faith Press, 1973.

Schmemann, Alexander. *The World as Sacrament*. London: Darton, Longman, and Todd, 1966.

The Piety and Worship:

Barrois, Georges. *Scripture Readings in Orthodox Worship*. Crestwood, NY: St. Vladimir's Seminary, 1977.

Daniel-Rops, Henry, ed. *The Twentieth Century Encyclopedia of Catholicism*. New York: Hawthorn, 1960. Vol. 112: *Eastern Liturgies*, by Irenee-Henri Dalmais. Translated by D. Attwater.

Englert, Clement C. *An Appreciation of Eastern Christianity*. Liguori, MO: Liguori Publications, 1972.

Liesel, Nikolaus. *The Eastern Catholic Liturgies. A Study in Words and Pictures*. Foreword by D. Attwater. Westminster, MD: Newman, 1960.

A Monk of the Eastern Church. *Orthodox Spirituality. An Outline of the Orthodox Ascetical and Mystical Tradition*. London: SPCK, 1961.

Ouspensky, Leonid. *Theology of the Icon*. Translated by E. Meyendorff. Crestwood, NY: St. Vladimir's Seminary, 1978.

Schmemann, Alexander. *Introduction to Liturgical Theology*. Translated by A. E. Moorhouse. Portland, ME: American Orthodox Press, 1966.

Verghese, Paul. *The Joy of Freedom. Eastern Worship and Modern Man*. Richmond: John Knox, 1967.

Its Outlook and Its Major Contemporary Theologians:

Benz, Ernst. *The Eastern Orthodox Church. Its Thought and Life.* Translated by C. and R. Winston. Chicago: Aldine, 1963.

Bulgakov, Sergius. *A Bulgakov Anthology.* Edited by J. Pain and N. Zernov. Philadelphia: Westminster, 1976.

Calian, Carnegie S. *Icon and Pulpit. The Protestant-Orthodox Encounter.* Philadelphia: Westminster, 1968.

Florovsky, Georges. *The Collected Works of Georges Florovsky.* 4 vols. Belmont, MA: Nordland, 1972-75.

Meyendorff, John. *Living Tradition. Orthodox Witness in the Contemporary World.* Crestwood, NY: St. Vladimir's Seminary, 1978.

————. *The Orthodox Church. Its Past and Its Role in the World Today.* Translated by J. Chapin. New York: Pantheon, 1962.

Rinvolucri, Mario. *Anatomy of a Church. Greek Orthodoxy Today.* Bronx, NY: Fordham University, 1966.

Runciman, Steven. *The Byzantine Theocracy.* Cambridge: Cambridge University, 1977.

Waddams, Herbert. *Meeting the Orthodox Churches.* London: SCM, 1965.

World Council of Churches; Sub-Unit on Women in Church and Society. *Orthodox Women. Their Role and Participation in the Orthodox Church.* Edited by C. J. Tarasar and I. Kirilbra. Geneva: World Council of Churches, 1977.

Other Eastern Churches:

Attwater, Donald. *Eastern Catholic Worship.* New York: Devin-Adair, 1945.

Brown, Leslie W. *The Indian Christians of St. Thomas. An Account of the Ancient Syrian Church of Malabar.* Cambridge: Cambridge University, 1956.

Butler, Alfred J. *The Ancient Coptic Churches of Egypt.* With a new appendix. 2 vols. Oxford: Clarendon, 1970 (1884).

Coptic Orthodox Patriarchate. *St. Mark and the Coptic Church.* Cairo: 1968.

Day, Peter. *Eastern Christian Liturgies. The Armenian, Coptic, Ethiopian, and Syrian Rites. Eucharistic Rites with Introductory Notes and Rubrical Instructions.* Shannon, Ireland: Irish University, 1972.

Meinardus, Otto F. A. *Christian Egypt. Faith and Life.* Cairo: American University in Cairo, 1970.

Pothan, S. G. *The Syrian Christians of Kerala.* New York: Asia Publishing House, 1963.

B. Leading Up to the Reformation

Church and State in the Middle Ages:

Brooke, Christopher. *Medieval Church and Society.* London: Sidgwick and Jackson, 1971.

Cannon, William R. *History of Christianity in the Middle Ages. From the Fall of Rome to the Fall of Constantinople.* Nashville: Abingdon, 1960.

Gilchrist, John. *The Church and Economic Activity in the Middle Ages.* New York: St. Martin's, 1969.

Hill, Bennett D., ed. *Church and State in the Middle Ages.* New York: Wiley and Sons, 1970.

Mayer, Hans E. *The Crusades.* Translated by J. Gillingham. London: Oxford University, 1972.

Southern, Richard W. *Western Society and the Church in the Middle Ages.* Baltimore: Penguin, 1970.

Tierney, Brian. *The Crisis of Church and State 1050-1300. With Selected Documents.* Englewood Cliffs, NJ: Prentice-Hall, 1964.

Watt, John A. *The Theory of Papal Monarchy in the Thirteenth Century. The Contribution of the Canonists.* London: Burns and Oates, 1965.

Development of the Papacy Prior to the Reformation:

Barraclough, Geoffrey. *The Medieval Papacy.* New York: Harcourt, Brace, and World, 1968.

Gontard, Friedrich. *The Chair of Peter. A History of the Papacy.* Translated by A. J. and E. F. Peeler. New York: Holt, Rinehart, and Winston, 1959.

Partner, Peter. *The Lands of St. Peter. The Papal State in the Middle Ages and Early Renaissance.* Berkeley: University of California, 1972.

Renouard, Yves. *The Avignon Papacy 1305-1403.* Translated by D. Bethell. London: Faber and Faber, 1970.

Runciman, Steven. *The Eastern Schism. A Study of the Papacy and the Eastern Churches During the XIth and XIIth Centuries.* Oxford: Clarendon, 1955.

Setton, Kenneth M. *The Papacy and the Levant.* Vol. 1: *The Thirteenth and Fourteenth Centuries.* Philadelphia: American Philosophical Society, 1976.

Schmandt, Raymond, gen. ed. *The Popes Through History.* New York: Newman, 1968. Vol. 3: *Alexander III and the Twelfth Century,* by Marshall W. Baldwin.

Tierney, Brian. *Origins of Papal Infallibility 1150-1350. A Study of the Concept of Infallibility, Sovereignty and Tradition in the Middle Ages.* Leiden: Brill, 1972.

Ullman, Walter. *The Growth of Papal Government in the Middle Ages. A Study in the Ideological Relation of Clerical to Lay Power.* New York: Barnes and Noble, 1953.

————. *A Short History of the Papacy in the Middle Ages.* London: Methuen, 1972.

Reform Movements Prior to the Reformation:

Baillie, John; McNeill, John; and Van Dusen, Henry, gen. eds. *The Library of Christian Classics.* Philadelphia: Westminster, 1953. Vol. 14: *Advocates of Reform. From Wyclif to Erasmus,* edited by Matthew Spinka.

Cowdrey, Herbert E. J. *The Cluniacs and the Gregorian Reform.* Oxford: Clarendon, 1970.

Hinnebusch, William A. *The History of the Dominican Order.* 2 vols. New York: Alba, 1973.

Kaminsky, Howard A. *History of the Hussite Revolution.* Berkeley: University of California, 1967.

Moorman, John. *A History of the Franciscan Order from Its Origin to the Year 1517.* Oxford: Clarendon, 1968.

Morrall, John. *Gerson and the Great Schism.* Manchester: Manchester University, 1960.

Oberman, Heiko A. *Forerunners of the Reformation. The Shape of Late Medieval Thought.* Translations by P. L. Nyhus. New York: Holt, Rinehart and Winston, 1966.

Parker, Geoffrey H. W. *The Morning Star. Wycliffe and the Dawn of the Reformation.* Grand Rapids: Eerdmans, 1965.

Pascoe, Louis B. *Jean Gerson. Principles of Church Reform.* Leiden: Brill, 1973.

Spinka, Matthew. *John Hus. A Biography.* Princeton: Princeton University, 1968.

————. *John Hus' Concept of the Church.* Princeton: Princeton University, 1966.

Stacey, John. *John Wyclif and Reform.* London: Lutterworth, 1964.

Underhill, Evelyn. *The Mystics of the Church.* New York: Schocken, 1964.

C. The Main Stream of the Reformation

Martin Luther and the Lutheran Reformation:

Aland, Kurt. *Four Reformers: Luther, Melanchthon, Calvin, Zwingli.* Translated by J. L. Schaaf. Minneapolis: Augsburg, 1979.

————, ed. *Martin Luther's 95 Theses with Pertinent Documents from the History of the Reformation.* St. Louis, MO: Concordia, 1967.

Althaus, Paul. *The Ethics of Martin Luther.* Translated with an introduction by R. C. Schultz. Philadelphia: Fortress, 1972.

———. *The Theology of Martin Luther.* Translated by R. C. Schultz. Philadelphia: Fortress, 1966.

Aulen, Gustaf. *Reformation and Catholicity.* Translated by E. H. Wahlstrom. Philadelphia: Muhlenberg, 1961.

Bainton, Roland H. *Here I Stand. A Life of Martin Luther.* New York: Abingdon, 1950.

Daniel-Rops, Henry. *The Protestant Reformation.* Translated by A. Butler. New York: Dutton, 1961.

Dickens, Arthur G. *Reformation and Society.* London: Thames and Hudson, 1966.

Edward, Mark Jr. *Luther and the False Brethren.* Stanford: Stanford University, 1975.

Friedenthal, Richard. *Luther. His Life and Times.* Translated by J. Nowell. New York: Harcourt, Brace, Jovanovich, 1970.

Grimm, Harold J. *The Reformation Era. 1500-1650.* 2nd ed. New York: Macmillan, 1973.

Hillerbrand, Hans J. *Christendom Divided. The Protestant Reformation.* New York: Corpus, 1971.

———, ed. *The Reformation. A Narrative History Related by Contemporary Observers and Participants.* New York: Harper, 1964.

———. *The World of Reformation.* New York: Scribner's, 1973.

Lilje, Hanns. *Luther and the Reformation. An Illustrated Review.* Edited and translated by M. O. Dietrich. Philadelphia: Fortress, 1967.

Manschreck, Clyde L. *Melanchthon. The Quiet Reformer.* New York: Abingdon, 1958.

Siggins, Ian D. K., ed. *Luther.* Edinburgh: Oliver and Boyd, 1972.

Tavard, George. *Protestantism.* Translated by R. Attwater. New York: Hawthorn, 1959.

Thulin, Oskar, ed. *A Life of Luther, Told in Pictures and Narrative by the Reformer and His Contemporaries.* Translated by M. O. Dietrich. Philadelphia: Fortress, 1966.

John Calvin and the Calvinistic Reformation:

Courvoisier, Jacques. *Zwingli. A Reformation Theologian.* Richmond: John Knox, 1963.

McNeill, John T. *The History and Character of Calvinism.* New York: Oxford, 1954; Galaxy Books, 1967.

Niesel, Wilhelm. *The Theology of Calvin.* Translated by Harold Knight. Philadelphia: Westminster, 1956.

Oberman, Heiko A., ed. *Studies in the History of Christian Thought.* Leiden: Brill, 1970. Vol. 5: *Calvin's Doctrine of the Church,* by Benjamin Charles Milner Jr.

Parker, Thomas H. L. *John Calvin. A Biography.* Philadelphia: Westminster, 1975.

Potter, George R. *Huldrych Zwingli.* New York: St. Martin's, 1977.

Walton, Robert C. *Zwingli's Theocracy.* Toronto: University of Toronto, 1967.

Wendel, François. *Calvin. The Origins and Development of His Religious Thought.* Translated by P. Mairet. New York: Harper, 1960.

Calvinistic Reform in England:

Dickens, Arthur G. *The English Reformation.* London: Batsford, 1965.

Donaldson, Gordon. *The Scottish Reformation.* Cambridge: Cambridge University, 1960.

Elton, Geoffrey R. *Reform and Reformation. England 1509-1558.* Cambridge, MA: Harvard University, 1977.

George, Charles H., and Katherine. *The Protestant Mind of the English Reformation 1570-1640.* Princeton: Princeton University, 1961.

Hughes, Philip E. *Theology of the English Reformers.* London: Hodder and Stoughton, 1965.

Parker, Thomas M. *The English Reformation to 1558.* 2nd ed. London: Oxford University, 1966.

Percy, Lord Eustace. *John Knox*. Foreword by the Duke of Hamilton. Richmond, VA: John Knox, 1965.

Pill, David. *The English Reformation. 1529-58*. Totowa, NJ: Rowman and Littlefield, 1973.

Ridley, Jasper. *John Knox*. Oxford: Clarendon, 1968.

The Left Wing of the Reformation:

Baillie, John; McNeill, John T.; and Van Dusen, Henry, gen. eds. *The Library of Christian Classics*. Philadelphia: Westminster, 1957. Vol. 25: *Spiritual and Anabaptist Writers. Documents Illustrative of the Radical Reformation,* edited by George H. Williams.

Bainton, Roland H. *Hunted Heretic. The Life and Death of Michael Servetus 1511-1553*. Boston: Beacon, 1953.

Beachy, Alvin J. *The Concept of Grace in the Radical Reformation*. Nieuwkoop, Netherlands: De Graaf, 1977.

Clasen, Claus-Peter. *Anabaptism. A Social History, 1525-1618. Switzerland, Austria, Moravia, South and Central Germany*. Ithaca, NY: Cornell University, 1972.

Davis, Kenneth B. *Anabaptism and Asceticism. A Study in Intellectual Origins*. Studies in Anabaptist and Mennonite History, no. 16. Scottdale, PA: Herald, 1964.

Friedmann, Robert. *The Theology of Anabaptism. An Interpretation*. Scottdale, PA: Herald, 1973.

Gritsch, Eric W. *Reformer without a Church. The Life and Thought of Thomas Müntzer 1488(?)-1525*. Philadelphia: Fortress, 1967.

Horst, Irvin. *The Radical Brethren. Anabaptism and the English Reformation to 1558*. Nieuwkoop, Netherlands: De Graaf, 1972.

Krahn, Cornelius. *Dutch Anabaptism*. The Hague: Nijhoff, 1968.

Littell, Franklin H. *The Origins of Sectarian Protestantism. A Study of the Anabaptist View of the Church*. New York: Macmillan, 1964.

Oyer, John S. *Lutheran Reformers against Anabaptists. Luther, Melanchthon, and Menius against Anabaptists of Central Germany*. The Hague: Nijhoff, 1964.

Steinmetz, David C. *Reformers in the Wings*. Philadelphia: Fortress, 1971.

Williams, George H. *The Radical Reformation*. Philadelphia: Westminster, 1962.

Reformation and Humanism:

Bainton, Roland H. *Erasmus of Christendom*. New York: Scribner's, 1969.

Blayney, Ida Walz. *The Age of Luther. The Spirit of Renaissance-Humanism and the Reformation*. New York: Vantage, 1957.

Bouyer, Louis. *Erasmus and His Times*. Translated by F. X. Murphy. Westminster, MD: Newman, 1959.

DeMolen, Richard L., ed. *The Meaning of the Renaissance and Reformation*. Boston: Houghton Mifflin, 1974.

Dickens,, Arthur G. *The Age of Humanism and Reformation. Europe in the Fourteenth, Fifteenth, and Sixteenth Centuries*. Englewood Cliffs, NJ: Prentice-Hall, 1972.

Faludy, George. *Erasmus*. New York: Stein and Day, 1970.

Gelder, H. A. Enno van. *The Two Reformations of the Sixteenth Century. A Study of the Religious Aspects and Consequences of Renaissance and Humanism*. The Hague: Nijhoff, 1961.

Huizinga, Johan. *Erasmus and the Age of Reformation*. Translated by F. Hopman with a selection from the letters of Erasmus translated by B. Flower. New York: Harper, 1957.

Kingdon, Robert M., ed. *Transition and Revolution. Problems and Issues of European Renaissance and Reformation History*. Minneapolis: Burgess, 1974.

Olin, John C.; Smart, James D.; and McNally, Robert E., eds. *Luther, Erasmus, and the Reformation. A Catholic-Protestant Reappraisal.* New York: Fordham, 1969.

Spitz, Lewis W. *The Religious Renaissance of the German Humanists.* Cambridge, MA: Harvard University, 1963.

D. The Impact of the Reformation

The Confessional Writings of the Reformation:

Allbeck, Willard D. *Studies in the Lutheran Confessions.* Rev. ed. Philadelphia: Fortress, 1968.

Anderson, Charles S. *Faith and Freedom. The Christian Faith According to the Lutheran Confession.* Minneapolis: Augsburg, 1977.

Cochrane, Arthur C., ed. *Reformed Confessions of the 16th Century. With Historical Introductions.* Philadelphia: Westminster, 1966.

Fagerberg, Holsten. *A New Look at the Lutheran Confessions (1529-1537).* Translated by G. J. Lund. St. Louis, MO: Concordia, 1972.

Gritsch, Eric W., and Jenson, Robert W. *Lutheranism. The Theological Movement and Its Confessional Writings.* Philadelphia: Fortress, 1976.

Kimme, August. *Theology of the Augsburg Confession. Makumira Lectures.* Berlin: Lutherisches Verlagshaus, 1968.

Leith, John H. *Assembly at Westminster. Reformed Theology in the Making.* Richmond: John Knox, 1973.

Schlink, Edmund. *Theology of the Lutheran Confessions.* Translated by P. F. Koehneke and H. J. A. Bouman. Philadelphia: Muhlenberg, 1961.

Vajta, Vilmos, and Weissgerber, Hans, eds. *The Church and the Confessions. The Role of the Confessions in the Life and Doctrine of the Lutheran Churches.* Philadelphia: Fortress, 1963.

The Catholic Response (Trent):

Daniel-Rops, Henry. *History of the Church of Christ.* Vol. 5: *The Catholic Reformation.* Translated by J. Warrington. New York: Dutton, 1962.

Dickens, Arthur G. *The Counter Reformation.* New York: Harcourt, Brace and World, 1969.

Hughes, Philip. *The Church in Crisis. A History of the General Councils. 325-1870.* Garden City, NY: Hanover House, 1961.

Jedin, Hubert. *A History of the Council of Trent.* 2 vols. Translated by E. Graf. London: Nelson, 1961.

O'Connell, Marvin R. *The Counter Reformation. 1559-1680.* New York: Harper, 1974.

Searle, Graham W. *The Counter Reformation.* London: University of London, 1973.

Reformation and Modernity:

Holl, Karl. *The Cultural Significance of the Reformation.* Translated by K. and B. Hertz, and J. H. Lichtblau. New York: Meridian, 1959.

———. *The Reconstruction of Morality.* Edited by James Luther Adams, and Walter F. Bense. Translated by Fred W. Meuser and Walter R. Wietzke. Minneapolis: Augsburg, 1979.

Lortz, Joseph. *The Reformation. A Problem for Today.* Translated by J. C. Dwyer. Westminster, MD: Newman, 1964.

McLelland, Joseph C. *The Reformation and Its Significance Today.* Philadelphia: Westminster, 1962.

Pelikan, Jaroslav. *Historical Theology. Continuity and Change in Christian Doctrine.* New York: Corpus, 1971.

Routley, Erik. *Creeds and Confessions. The Reformation and Its Modern Ecumenical Implications.* London: Duckworth, 1962.

Rupp, Ernest G. *The Old Reformation and the New.* London: Epworth, 1967.

Transition to the Modern Age (17th-19th Centuries):

Butler, Cuthbert. *The Vatican Council. 1869-1870. Based on Bishop Ullathorne's Letters.* Edited by Christopher Butler. Westminster, MD: Newman, 1962.

Cragg, Gerald R. *The Church and the Age of Reason. 1648-1789.* New York: Atheneum, 1961.

Daniel-Rops, Henry. *History of the Church of Christ.* Vol. 7: *The Church in the Eighteenth Century.* Translated by J. Warrington. New York: Dutton, 1964.

Gay, Peter. *The Enlightenment. An Interpretation.* Vol. 1: *The Rise of Modern Paganism.* New York: Knopf, 1967.

Goldmann, Lucien. *The Philosophy of the Enlightenment. The Christian Burgess and the Enlightenment.* Translated by H. Maas. Cambridge, MA: MIT Press, 1973.

Knox, Ronald. *Enthusiasm. A Chapter in the History of Religion. With Special Reference to the XVII and XVIII Centuries.* New York: Oxford University, 1950.

Stoeffler, F. Ernest. *The Rise of Evangelical Pietism.* Studies in the History of Religion, no. 9. Leiden: Brill, 1965.

4. FACING THE MODERN AGE

A. The Emergence of Modern Catholicism

Catholicism in the 20th Century:

Hales, Edward E. Y. *Pope John and His Revolution.* London: Eyre and Spottiswoode, 1965.

Küng, Hans. *Infallible? An Inquiry.* Translated by E. Quinn. Garden City, NY: Doubleday, 1971.

――――. *Structures of the Church.* Translated by S. Attanasio. New York: Nelson, 1964.

Loewenich, Walther von. *Modern Catholicism.* Translated by R. H. Fuller. New York: St. Martin's, 1959.

McKenzie, John L. *The Roman Catholic Church.* New York: Holt, Rinehart, and Winston, 1969.

O'Dea, Thomas F. *American Catholic Dilemma. An Inquiry into the Intellectual Life.* New York: Sheed and Ward, 1958.

Roche, Douglas J. *The Catholic Revolution.* New York: David McKay, 1968.

Schoof, T. Mark. *A Survey of Catholic Theology. 1800-1970.* Introduction by E. Schillebeeckx. Translated by N. D. Smith. New York: Paulist, 1970.

Mary and the Saints:

Attwater, Donald. *Saints of the East.* London: Harvill, 1963.

Bouyer, Louis. *Woman and Man with God.* Translated by A. V. Littledale. London: Darton, Longman, and Todd, 1960.

Brown, Raymond; Donfried, Karl; Fitzmyer, Joseph; and Reumann, John, eds. *Mary in the New Testament. A Collaborative Assessment by Protestant and Roman Catholic Scholars.* Philadelphia: Fortress, 1978.

Graef, Hilda. *Mary. A History of Doctrine and Devotion.* 2 vols. New York: Sheed and Ward, 1963-65.

Laurentin, Rene. *Mary's Place in the Church.* Foreword by Hilda Graef. Translated by I. G. Pidoux. London: Burns and Oates, 1965.

Mascall, Eric L., and Box, Hubert S., eds. *The Blessed Virgin Mary. Essays by Anglican Writers.* London: Darton, Longman, and Todd, 1963.

Rahner, Hugo. *Our Lady and the Church.* Translated by S. Bullough. Chicago: Regnery, 1965.

Thurian, Max. *Mary, Mother of the Lord, Figure of the Church.* Translated by N. B. Cryer. London: Faith Press, 1963.

Vatican II:

Cullmann, Oscar. *Vatican Council II. The New Direction.* Essays selected and arranged by J. D. Hester. Translated by F. Burgess, C. Schneider, J. Hester, and R. Holland. New York: Harper, 1968.

Küng, Hans. *The Council in Action. Theological Reflections on the Second Vatican Council.* Translated by C. Hasting. New York: Sheed and Ward, 1963.

Küng, Hans; Congar, Yves; and O'Hanlon, Daniel, eds. *Council Speeches of Vatican II.* London: Sheed and Ward, 1964.

MacEoin, Gary. *What Happened at Rome? The Council and Its Implications for the Modern World.* Introduction by J. Cogley. New York: Holt, Rinehart, and Winston, 1966.

Miller, John H., ed. *Vatican II. An Interfaith Appraisal.* Notre Dame, IN: University of Notre Dame, 1966.

Schillebeeckx, Edward. *Vatican II. The Real Achievement.* Translated by H. J. J. Vaughan. London: Sheed and Ward, 1967.

Schlink, Edmund. *After the Council.* Translated by H. J. A. Bouman. Philadelphia: Westminster, 1968.

Yzermans, Vincent A., ed. *American Participation in the Second Vatican Council.* New York: Sheed and Ward, 1967.

Roman Catholicism in Ecumenical Dialogue:

Baum, Gregory. *Progress and Perspectives. The Catholic Quest for Christian Unity.* New York: Sheed and Ward, 1962.

Bea, Augustin. *The Way to Unity after the Council.* New York: Herder, 1967.

Delaney, John J., gen. ed. *Catholic Perspectives.* New York: Hawthorn, 1966. *Christian Reunion. The Ecumenical Movement and American Catholics,* by John B. Sheerin.

Kloppenburg, Bonaventure. *The Ecclesiology of Vatican II.* Translated by M. J. O'Connell. Chicago: Franciscan Herald, 1974.

Lambert, Bernard. *Ecumenism. Theology and History.* Translated by L. C. Sheppard. New York: Herder, 1967.

Leeming, Bernard. *The Vatican Council and Christian Unity. A Commentary on the Decree of Ecumenism of the Second Vatican Council, Together with a Translation of the Text.* New York: Harper, 1966.

Minus, Paul M., Jr. *The Catholic Rediscovery of Protestantism. A History of Roman Catholic Ecumenical Pioneering.* New York: Paulist, 1976.

Molnar, Thomas. *Ecumenism or New Reformation?* New York: Funk and Wagnalls, 1968.

O'Neill, Charles, Jr., ed. *Ecumenism and Vatican II.* Foreword by Vincent O'Keefe. Milwaukee: Bruce, 1964.

B. The Church as the Ferment in Society

Church and State:

Hertz, Karl H., ed. *Two Kingdoms and One World.* Minneapolis: Augsburg, 1976.

Huegli, Albert G., ed., *Church and State under God.* St. Louis, MO: Concordia, 1964.

Lazareth, William H., ed. *The Left Hand of God.* Philadelphia: Fortress, 1976.

Meinhold, Peter. *Caesar's or God's? The Conflict of Church and State in Modern Society.* Translated by W. G. Tillmanns. Minneapolis: Augsburg, 1962.

Mueller, William. *Church and State in Luther and Calvin. A Comparative Study.* Nashville: Broadman, 1954.

Parker, Thomas M. *Christianity and the State in the Light of History.* New York: Harper, 1955.

Smith, Elwyn A. *Religious Liberty in the United States. The Development of Church-State Thought Since the Revolutionary Era.* Philadelphia: Fortress, 1972.

Williamson, Rene de Visme. *Politics and Protestant Theology. An Interpretation of Tillich, Barth, Bonhoeffer, and Brunner.* Baton Rouge: Louisiana State University, 1976.

World Council of Churches. *Church and State. Opening a New Ecumenical Discussion.* Faith and Order Paper, no. 85. Geneva: World Council of Churches, 1978.

*Church and Social Issues*s

Abell, Aaron I. *American Catholicism and Social Action. A Search for Social Justice 1865-1950.* Notre Dame, IN: University of Notre Dame, 1960.

Bainton, Roland H. *Christian Attitudes Toward War and Peace. A Historical Survey and Critical Re-evaluation.* New York: Abingdon, 1960.

Berger, Peter L. *The Precarious Vision. A Socialist Looks at Social Fictions and Christian Faith.* Garden City, NY: Doubleday, 1961.

Bock, Paul. *In Search of a Responsible World Society. The Social Teachings of the World Council of Churches.* Philadelphia: Westminster, 1974.

Calvez, Jean-Yves, and Perrin, Jacques, eds. *The Church and Social Justice. The Social Teachings of the Popes from Leo XIII to Pius XII* (1878-1958). Translated by J. R. Kirwan. Chicago: Regnery, 1961.

Forell, George, ed. *Christian Social Teachings. A Reader in Christian Social Ethics from the Bible to the Present.* Minneapolis: Augsburg, 1971.

Forell, George, and Lazareth, William, eds. *Human Rights. Rhetoric or Reality.* Philadelphia: Fortress, 1978.

Fremantle, Anne, ed. *Social Teachings of the Church.* New York: New American Library, 1963.

Ramsey, Paul. *War and the Christian Conscience. How Shall Modern War Be Conducted Justly?* Durham, NC: Duke University, 1961.

Robinson, John A. T. *On Being the Church in the World.* Philadelphia: Westminster, 1960.

Schillebeeckx, Edward. *World and Church.* Translated by N. D. Smith. New York: Sheed and Ward, 1971.

Seven Great Encyclicals. Labor, Education, Marriage, Reconstructing the Social Order, Atheistic Communism, World Social Problems, World Peace. Glen Rock, NJ: Paulist, 1963.

Sider, Ronald, ed. *The Chicago Declaration of Evangelicals.* Carol Stream, IL: Creation House, 1974.

The Church in Socialist Countries:

Beeson, Trevor. *Discretion and Valour. Religious Conditions in Russia and Eastern Europe.* Foreword by Sir John Lawrence. Glasgow: Collins, 1974.

Fletcher, William C. *The Russian Orthodox Church Underground. 1917-1970.* London: Oxford University, 1971.

Hayward, Max, and Fletcher, William, eds. *Religion and the Soviet State. A Dilemma of Power.* London: Pall Mall, 1969.

Lochman, Jan Milic. *Encountering Marx. Bonds and Barriers between Christians and Marxists.* Translated by E. H. Robertson. Philadelphia: Fortress, 1977.

Marshall, Richard H., Jr. *Aspects of Religion in the Soviet Union. 1917-1967.* Chicago: University of Chicago, 1971.

Metz, Johann-Baptist, and Jossua, Jean-Pierre. *Christianity and Socialism.* New York: Seabury, 1977.

Mojzes, Paul. *Christian-Marxist Dialogue in Eastern Europe.* Minneapolis: Augsburg, 1981.

Ostreicher, Paul. *The Christian Marxist Dialogue. An International Symposium.* New York: Macmillan, 1969.

Simon, Gerhard. *Church, State and Opposition in the U.S.S.R.* Translated by K. Matchett. Berkeley: University of California, 1974.

Struve, Nikita. *Christians in Contemporary Russia.* Translated by L. Sheppard and A. Manson. New York: Scribner's, 1967.

Weingartner, Erich, ed. *Church within Socialism. Church and State in East European Socialist Republics.* Based on the Work of Giovanni Barbarini. Rome: IDOC, 1976.

C. The Church Universal

The Ecumenical Movement:

Brown, Robert McAfee. *The Ecumenical Revolution. An Interpretation of the Catholic-Protestant Dialogue.* Garden City, NY: Doubleday, 1967.

Fey, Harold E. *The Ecumenical Advance. A History of the Ecumenical Movement. Volume 2. 1948-1968.* London: SPCK, 1970.

Küng, Hans, ed. *Ecumenical Theology. The Church and Ecumenism.* Conc(USA) 4. New York: Paulist, 1965.

Lange, Ernst. *And Yet It Moves. Dream and Reality in the Ecumenical Movement.* Grand Rapids: Eerdmans, 1979.

Mudge, Lewis S. *One Church. Catholic and Reformed. Toward a Theology for Ecumenical Decision.* Philadelphia: Westminster, 1963.

Piper, Otto A. *Protestantism in an Ecumenical Age. Its Root, Its Right, Its Task.* Philadelphia: Fortress, 1965.

Rouse, Ruth, and Neill, Stephen C., eds. *A History of the Ecumenical Movement 1517-1948.* 2nd ed. Philadelphia: Westminster, 1967.

Sartory, Thomas. *The Oecumenical Movement and the Unity of the Church.* Translated by H. C. Graef. Oxford: Blackwell, 1963.

Villain, Maurice. *Unity. A History and Some Reflection.* Translated by J. R. Foster. Baltimore: Helicon, 1963.

Rediscovering the Church Universal:

Bea, Augustin. *Unity in Freedom. Reflections on the Human Family.* New York: Harper, 1964.

Covert, Samuel McC. *On the Road to Christian Unity. An Appraisal of the Ecumenical Movement.* New York: Harper, 1961.

Gerard, François. *The Future of the Church. The Theology of Renewal of Willem Adolf Visser't Hooft.* Pittsburgh Theological Monograph Series, no. 2. Pittsburgh: Pickwick, 1974.

Lee, Robert. *The Social Sources of Christian Unity. An Interpretation of Unitive Movements in American Protestantism.* New York: Abingdon, 1960.

Mackie, Robert C., and West, Charles C., eds. *The Sufficiency of God. Essays on the Ecumenical Hope in Honor of W. A. Visser't Hooft.* London: SCM, 1963.

One Baptism, One Eucharist, and a Mutually Recognized Ministry. Faith and Order Papers, No. 73. Geneva: World Council of Churches, 1975.

Protestant Churches in Dialogue:

Bridston, Keith R., and Wagoner, Walter D. *Unity in Mid-Career. An Ecumenical Critique.* New York: Macmillan, 1963.

Good, James. *The Church of England and the Ecumenical Movement.* London: Cork University, 1961.

Holt, Ivan L., and Clark, Elmer T. *The World Methodist Movement.* Nashville: Upper Room, 1956.

Kean, Charles D. *The Road to Reunion.* Greenwich, CT: Seabury, 1958.

Kik, J. Marcellus. *Ecumenism and the Evangelical.* Philadelphia: Presbyterian and Reformed, 1958.

Newbigin, James E. L. *That All May Be One. A South India Diary. The Story of an Experiment in Christian Unity.* New York: Association, 1952.

D. The Church and Its Worship

The Priestly Office and the Priesthood of All Believers:

Brunner, Peter. *The Ministry and the Ministry of Women.* St. Louis, MO: Concordia, 1971.

Congar, Yves. *Lay People in the Church. A Study for a Theology of the Laity.* Translated by D. Attwater. Westminster, MD: Newman, 1957.

Cooke, Bernard. *Ministry to Word and Sacraments. History and Theology.* Philadelphia: Fortress, 1976.

Eastwood, Cyril. *The Priesthood of All Believers. An Examination of the Doctrine from the Reform to the Present Day.* Minneapolis: Augsburg, 1962.

————. *The Royal Priesthood of the Faithful. An Investigation of the Doctrine from Biblical Times to the Reformation.* Minneapolis: Augsburg, 1963.

Feuillet, Andre. *The Priesthood of Christ and His Ministers.* Translated by M. J. O'Connell. Garden City, NY: Doubleday, 1975.

Iersel, Bas van, and Murphy, Roland, eds. *Office and Ministry in the Church.* Conc(USA) 80. New York: Herder, 1972.

Lutheran Council in the United States of America, Division of Theological Studies. *The Ordination of Women.* Condensed by Raymond Tiemeyer. Minneapolis: Augsburg, 1970.

Rahner, Karl, ed. *The Identity of the Priest.* Conc(USA) 43. New York: Paulist, 1969.

Thrall, Margaret E. *The Ordination of Women to the Priesthood.* London: SCM, 1958.

World Council of Churches. *Concerning the Ordination of Women.* World Council Studies, no. 1. Geneva: World Council of Churches, 1964.

The Sacraments:

Barclay, William. *The Lord's Supper.* London: SCM, 1967.

Beasley-Murray, George R. *Baptism Today and Tomorrow.* New York: St. Martin's, 1966.

Berkouwer, Gerrit C. *The Sacraments.* Translated by H. Bekker. Grand Rapids: Eerdmans, 1969.

Bouyer, Louis. *Eucharist. Theology and Spirituality of the Eucharistic Prayer.* Translated by C. U. Quinn. Notre Dame, IN: University of Notre Dame, 1968.

Cochrane, Arthur C. *Eating and Drinking with Jesus. An Ethical and Biblical Inquiry.* Philadelphia: Westminster, 1974.

Kucharek, Casimir A. *The Sacramental Mysteries. A Byzantine Approach.* Allendale, NJ: Alleluia, 1976.

Küng, Hans, ed. *The Sacraments. An Ecumenical Dilemma.* Conc(USA) 24. New York: Paulist, 1967.

Marty, Martin E. *Baptism.* Philadelphia: Fortress, (1962) 1977.

————. *The Lord's Supper*. Philadelphia: Fortress, 1980.

Piolanti, Antonio. *The Holy Eucharist*. Translated by L. Penzo. New York: Desclee, 1961.

Rahner, Karl. *The Church and the Sacraments*. Translated by W. J. O'Hara. Edinburgh: Nelson, 1963.

Schillebeeckx, Edward. *The Eucharist*. Translated by N. D. Smith. New York: Sheed and Ward, 1968.

————, ed. *Sacramental Reconciliation*. Conc(USA) 61. New York: Herder and Herder, 1971.

Schlink, Edmund. *The Doctrine of Baptism*. Translated by H. J. A. Bouman. St. Louis, MO: Concordia, 1972.

Wainwright, Geoffrey. *Eucharist and Eschatology*. 3rd ed. London: Epworth, 1978.

Confession, Penance, and Penitence:

Anciaux, Paul *The Sacrament of Penance*. New York: Sheed and Ward, 1962.

Bowman, George W., III. *The Dynamics of Confession*. Richmond: John Knox, 1969.

Poschmann, Bernhard. *Penance and the Anointing of the Sick*. Translated and revised by F. Courtney. London: Brill and Oates, 1964.

Saint-Cyr, Carra de Vaux; Remy, Pierre; Duquoc, Christian; de Regis, Phillippe, Gerest, Regis-Claude; Liege, P. A.; and Bourgin, Claude. *The Sacrament of Penance*. Translated by R. L. Sullivant, A. Cunningham, and M. Renelle. Glen Rock, NJ: Deus Books, 1966.

Law and Gospel:

Althaus, Paul. *The Divine Command*. A New Perspective on Law and Gospel. Social Ethics Series, no. 9. Translated by W. H. Lazareth. Philadelphia: Fortress, Facet Books, 1966.

Böckle, Franz. *Law and Conscience*. Translated by M. J. Donnelly. New York: Sheed and Ward, 1966.

Elert, Werner. *Law and Gospel*. Social Ethics Series no. 16. Translated by E. H. Schroeder. Philadelphia: Fortress, Facet Books, 1967.

Forde, Gerhard. *The Law-Gospel Debate. An Interpretation of Its Historical Development*. Minneapolis: Augsburg, 1969.

Knight, George A. F. *Law and Grace. Must a Christian Keep the Law of Moses?*. London: SCM, 1962.

Myers, Jacob M. *Grace and Torah*. Philadelphia: Fortress, 1975.

Wingren, Gustaf. *Creation and Gospel. The New Situation in European Theology*. Introduction and bibliography by Henry Vander Goot. New York: Mellen, 1979.

Renewal of Liturgy:

Bouyer, Louis. *The Liturgy Revived. A Doctrinal Commentary of the Conciliar Constitution of the Liturgy*. Notre Dame, IN: University of Notre Dame, 1964.

Jasper, Ronald C. D. *The Renewal of Worship*. London: Oxford University, 1965.

Mitchell, Leonel. *Liturgical Change. How Much Do We Need?* New York: Seabury, 1975.

Robinson, John A. T. *Liturgy Coming to Life*. London: Mowbray, 1960.

Shands, Alfred R. *The Liturgical Movement and the Local Church*. 2nd ed. New York: Morehouse-Barlow, 1965.

Shepherd, Massey H., Jr., ed. *The Liturgical Renewal of the Church*. New York: Oxford University, 1960.

Wainwright, Geoffrey. *Doxology. The Praise of God in Worship, Doctrine of Life*. New York: Oxford University, 1980.

White, James F. *Christian Worship in Transition*. Nashville: Abingdon, 1976.
————. *New Forms of Worship*. Nashville: Abingdon, 1971.

E. The Church in Mission
*Church Renewal*s
Aubert, Roger, ed. *Historical Problems of Church Renewal*. Conc(USA) 7. New York: Paulist, 1965.
Bieler, Andre. *The Politics of Hope*. Foreword by Dom Helder Camara. Translated by D. Pardee. Grand Rapids: Eerdmans, 1974.
Jones, James W. *Filled with New Wine. The Charismatic Renewal of the Church*. New York: Harper, 1974.
Küng, Hans. *Truthfulness. The Future of the Church*. Translated by E. Quinn. New York: Sheed and Ward, 1968.
Lundin, Jack W. *A Church for an Open Future. Biblical Roots and Parish Renewal*. Foreword by Martin Marty. Philadelphia: Fortress, 1977.
McBrien, Richard P. *The Remaking of the Church*. New York: Harper, 1973.
Muller, Alois, and Greinacher, Norbert, eds. *Ongoing Reform of the Church*. Conc-(USA) 73. New York: Herder and Herder, 1972.
O'Dea, Thomas F. *The Catholic Crisis*. Boston: Beacon, 1968.
Reumann, John, ed. *The Church Emerging. A U.S. Lutheran Case Study*. Philadelphia: Fortress, 1977.
Shook, L. K., ed. *Congress on the Theology of the Renewal of the Church*. 2 vols. New York: Herder, 1968.
Tracy, David; Küng, Hans; and Metz, Johann-Baptist. *Toward Vatican III. The Work That Needs to Be Done*. New York: Seabury, 1978.

Church and Home Mission:
Demerath, Nicholas J. *Social Class in American Protestantism*. Chicago: Rand McNally, 1965.
Ellison, Craig W., ed. *The Urban Mission*. Grand Rapids: Eerdmans, 1974.
Fevold, Eugene L. *The Story of Home Missions in the Evangelical Lutheran Church 1917-1960*. n.p., 1962.
Frost, Naomi. *Toward Interdependence. Mission U.S.A.* New York: Lutheran Council in the U.S.A., 1975.
Gardner, E. Clinton. *The Church as a Prophetic Community*. Philadelphia: Westminster, 1967.
Webber, George W. *The Congregation in Mission. Emerging Structures for the Church in an Urban Society*. New York: Abingdon, 1964.
Winter, Gibson. *The Suburban Captivity of the Churches. An Analysis of Protestant Responsibility in the Expanding Metropolis*. Garden City, NY: Doubleday, 1961.

Church and Foreign Mission:
Beyerhaus, Peter. *Missions. Which Way? Humanization or Redemption?* Preface by H. Lindsell. Foreword by D. McGavran. Translated by M. Clarkson. Grand Rapids: Zondervan, 1971.
Blauw, Johannes. *The Missionary Nature of the Church. A Survey of the Biblical Theology of Mission*. New York: McGraw-Hill, 1962.
Braaten, Carl E. *The Flaming Center. A Theology of the Christian Mission*. Philadelphia: Fortress, 1977.
Costas, Orlando E. *Theology of the Crossroads in Contemporary Latin America. Missiology in Mainline Protestantism 1969-1974*. Amsterdam: Rodopi, 1976.

Cotter, James P. *The Word in the Third World*. Washington, DC: Corpus, 1968.

Hillman, Eugene. *The Church as Mission*. New York: Herder, 1965.

Newbigin, James E. L. *The Open Secret. Sketches for a Missionary Theology*. Grand Rapids: Eerdmans, 1978.

Reilly, Michael C. *Spirituality for Mission. Historical, Theological, and Cultural Factors for a Present-Day Missionary Spirituality*. Maryknoll, NY: Orbis, 1978.

Recent Ecclesiologies:

Dulles, Avery. *Models of the Church*. Garden City, NY: Doubleday, 1974.

Fries, Heinrich. *Aspects of the Church*. Translated by T. O'Meara. Dublin: Gill, 1965.

Küng, Hans. *The Church*. Translated by R. and R. Ockenden. London: Burns and Oates, 1967.

Moltmann, Jürgen. *The Church in the Power of the Spirit. A Contribution to a Messianic Ecclesiology*. Translated by M. Kohl. New York: Harper, 1977.

Pittenger, Norman. *The Christian Church as Social Process*. London: Epworth, 1971.

Rahner, Karl. *The Shape of the Church to Come*. Translated and introduced by E. Quinn. New York: Seabury, 1974.

Watson, David. *I Believe in the Church*. Grand Rapids: Eerdmans, 1978.

INDEX OF NAMES

INDEX OF SUBJECTS

373

INDEX OF BIBLICAL REFERENCES

[handwritten notes:] Is the work persevered for it's sake or for its own sake - 31?

God hates visionary dreaming. 326-7.

INDEX OF APOSTOLIC FATHERS

(Authors to ca. 400, when cited; see also Index of Names)